SO-DSR-095

PROJECT MANAGEMENT IN PRACTICE

Fifth Edition

Jack R. Meredith
Wake Forest University

Scott M. Shafer
Wake Forest University

Samuel J. Mantel, Jr.
University of Cincinnati

Margaret M. Sutton
Sutton Associates

ch.1 1 ~27
ch.3 76 ~97
ch.4 112 ~134
ch.5 152 ~188
Appendix
        301 ~ 309
ch.6
    20. ~227

WILEY

VICE PRESIDENT AND EXECUTIVE PUBLISHER	George Hoffman
EXECUTIVE EDITOR	Lise Johnson
PROJECT EDITOR	Brian Baker
SENIOR CONTENT MANAGER	Lucille Buonocore
SENIOR PRODUCTION EDITOR	Anna Melhorn
DESIGN DIRECTOR	Harry Nolan
SENIOR DESIGNER	Madelyn Lesure
SENIOR MARKETING MANAGER	Kelly Simmons
COVER PHOTO CREDIT	© Murat Taner/ Corbis

This book was set in Goudy Oldstyle by codeMantra and printed and bound by Quad Graphics Versailles. This book is printed on acid-free paper. ∞

Founded in 1807, John Wiley & Sons, Inc. has been a valued source of knowledge and understanding for more than 200 years, helping people around the world meet their needs and fulfill their aspirations. Our company is built on a foundation of principles that include responsibility to the communities we serve and where we live and work. In 2008, we launched a Corporate Citizenship Initiative, a global effort to address the environmental, social, economic, and ethical challenges we face in our business. Among the issues we are addressing are carbon impact, paper specifications and procurement, ethical conduct within our business and among our vendors, and community and charitable support. For more information, please visit our website: *www.wiley.com/go/citizenship*.

Copyright © 2014, 2011, 2009 John Wiley & Sons, Inc.. All rights reserved.

No part of this publication may be reproduced, stored in a retrieval system or transmitted in any form or by any means, electronic, mechanical, photocopying, recording, scanning or otherwise, except as permitted under Sections 107 or 108 of the 1976 United States Copyright Act, without either the prior written permission of the Publisher, or authorization through payment of the appropriate per-copy fee to the Copyright Clearance Center, Inc., 222 Rosewood Drive, Danvers, MA 01923, website *www.copyright.com*. Requests to the Publisher for permission should be addressed to the Permissions Department, John Wiley & Sons, Inc., 111 River Street, Hoboken, NJ 07030-5774, (201) 748-6011, fax (201) 748-6008, website *www.wiley.com/go/permissions*.

Evaluation copies are provided to qualified academics and professionals for review purposes only, for use in their courses during the next academic year. These copies are licensed and may not be sold or transferred to a third party. Upon completion of the review period, please return the evaluation copy to Wiley. Return instructions and a free-of-charge return shipping label are available at *www.wiley.com/go/returnlabel*. If you have chosen to adopt this textbook for use in your course, please accept this book as your complimentary desk copy. Outside of the United States, please contact your local representative.

978-1-118-67466-6 (Main Book ISBN)

Printed in the United States of America

10 9 8 7 6 5 4 3 2

To Kiersten, Brandon, and Jeremy, my most successful projects.

J. R. M.

To Brianna and Sammy and Kacy, my most important
and rewarding projects.

S. M. S.

To Maggie, beloved daugther, valued colleague,
and treasured friend.

S. J. M. Jr.

To Dad: my teacher, my hero, . . . my friend.

M. M. S.

CONTENTS

3 PROJECT ACTIVITY AND RISK PLANNING 76

6 ALLOCATING RESOURCES TO THE PROJECT   200

7   MONITORING AND CONTROLLING THE PROJECT 244

8   EVALUATING AND TERMINATING THE PROJECT   280

PREFACE

THE APPROACH

Over the past several decades, more and more work has been accomplished through the use of projects and project management. The use of projects has been growing at an accelerated rate, and not just in engineering and information technology, but also in all the business disciplines: marketing, finance, human resources, accounting, operations, legal, and, of course, management. One of the most interesting areas of growth, however, has been in the use of projects to achieve the strategic goals of organizations. The exponential growth of membership in the Project Management Institute (PMI) is further convincing evidence, as are the sales of computer software devoted to project management. Several societal forces are driving this growth, and many economic factors are reinforcing it. We describe these in Chapter 1 of this book.

A secondary effect has also been a major contributor to the use of project activity. As the use of projects has grown, its very success as a way of getting complex activities carried out successfully has become well established. The result has been a striking increase in the use of projects to accomplish jobs that in the past would simply have been turned over to someone with the comment, "Take care of it."

What happened then was that some individual undertook to carry out the job with little or no planning, little or no assistance, few resources, and often with only a vague notion of what was really wanted. The simple application of routine project management techniques significantly improved the consistency with which the outcomes resembled what the organization had in mind when the chore was assigned. Later, this sort of activity came to be known as "enterprise project management," "management by projects," and several other names, all of which are described as the project-oriented organization.

Some of these projects were large, but most were quite small. Some were complex, but most were relatively straightforward. Some required the full panoply of project management techniques, but most did not. All of them, however, had to be managed and thus required a great many people to take on the role of project manager in spite of little or no education in the science or arcane art of project management.

One result was rising demand for education in project management. The number of college courses grew apace, as did the number of consulting firms offering seminars and workshops. Perhaps most striking was the growth in educational opportunities through post-secondary schools offering "short courses"—schools such as DeVry Institute, and ITT. In addition, short courses were offered by colleges and community colleges concentrating on both part-time and full-time education for individuals already in the work force. An exemplar of this approach is the University of Phoenix.

Communications from some instructors in these institutions told us that they would like a textbook that was shorter and focused more directly on the "technical" aspects of project management than those currently available. They were willing to forego most of the theoretical aspects of management, particularly if such were not directly tied to practice. Their students, who were not apt to take advanced course work in project management, had little use for understanding the historical development of the field. For example, they felt no need to read about the latest academic research on the management of knowledge-based projects in a manufacturing environment. Finally, instructors asked for increased use of project management application software, though they added that they did not want a replacement for the many excellent "step-by-step" and "computing-for-dummies" types of books that were readily available. They wanted the emphasis to be on managing projects, and not on managing project management software.

These requests sounded sensible to us, and we have tried to write such a book.

ORGANIZATION AND CONTENT

With few exceptions, both readers and instructors are most comfortable with project management texts that are organized around the project life cycle, and this book is so organized. In Chapter 1 we start by defining a project and differentiating project management from general management. After discussing the project life cycle, we briefly cover project selection. We feel strongly that project managers who understand why a project was selected by senior management also understand the firm's objectives for the project. Understanding those things, we know, will be of value in making the inevitable trade-offs between time, budget, and the specified output of the project.

Chapter 2 is devoted to the various roles the project manager must play and to the skills required to play them effectively. In addition, we cover the various ways in which projects can be organized. The nature of project teams, including multidisciplinary teams, and the behavioral aspects of projects are also discussed.

Project and risk planning, budgeting, and scheduling are covered in Chapters 3 to 5. Planning the project initiates our discussion in Chapter 3, where we introduce the work breakdown structure and other planning aids such as the RACI matrix, and end with a thorough discussion and illustration of risk management planning. Project budgeting is then described in Chapter 4 where we introduce the use of simulation through software such as Crystal Ball® to analyze financial risk. Risk analysis using Oracle's Crystal Ball® 11.1 (CB) simulations is demonstrated in several chapters with detailed instructions on building and solving simulation models. Software is used throughout the book, where relevant, to illustrate the use and power of such software to aid in managing projects. Chapter 4 also includes a helpful mathematical model for improving cost estimates, or any other numerical estimates used in planning projects. Chapter 5 initially uses standard manual methods for building project schedules, and Microsoft Project® 2010 (MSP) is then demonstrated for doing the same thing.

Chapter 6 deals with resource allocation problems in a multiproject setting. A major section of this chapter is devoted to the insights of E. Goldratt in his book *Critical Chain*.[*] Chapter 7 concerns monitoring and controlling the project, especially through the use of earned value analysis, which is covered in detail. The final chapter deals with auditing, evaluating, and terminating projects.

Interest in risk management has grown rapidly in recent years, but the subject gets only minimal attention in most introductory level project management textbooks. We deal with risk throughout this book, introducing methods of risk management and analysis where relevant to the subject at hand. For example, simulation is used in Chapter 4 for solving a project budgeting problem, in Chapter 5 on a scheduling problem, and in Chapter 6 for examining the impact of a generally accepted assumption about probabilistic project schedules that is usually false, and also to test the usually false assumption that multitasking is an efficient way to improve productivity.

We are certainly aware that no text on project management could be structured to reflect the chaos that seems to surround some projects throughout their lives, and a

---

[*]Goldratt, E. M. *Critical Chain*. Great Barrington, MA: North River, 1997.

into the chapters where it is used, which we have done. In this edition we have also tried to improve the flow of material and have moved some topics around a bit to achieve this. First, we moved the extensive Crystal Ball® simulation description out of the introductory Chapter 1 and into the budgeting Chapter 4 to illustrate how to simulate costs to evaluate budget risks. And we moved the discussion of risk management earlier, from Chapter 4 to the project planning Chapter 3, since risk pervades all the aspects of project planning, and especially scope, time, and cost. To make room for the risk discussion in Chapter 3, we moved the discussion of multidisciplinary teams to Chapter 2, which seems to be a better fit for the topic also.

Reviewers also asked us to comment about how budgets and activity expediting are actually handled in practice, so we checked many practice-oriented magazines and journals and then queried some project managers we knew. The result is a few paragraphs in Chapters 4 on budgeting and Chapter 6 on resource allocation describing the vagaries and real-world dynamics project managers commonly face in these areas.

Trade-Offs

Risk

Best Practice

PMBOK Guide

To further improve the student's perspective of project management from the view of project managers in actual practice, we describe their situation throughout the text as one of constantly making trade-offs between not only the three main goals of scope, time, and cost but also risk and other implied ancillary goals such as organizational improvement, strategic goals, and future opportunities. To highlight these areas where we talk about trade-offs and risk, we have added new icons to the book margins where important discussion on these topics appears. We have also added a new icon to indicate areas of discussion that we believe exemplify "best practice" in the project management field. And we have expanded our references to locations in PMBOK® that discuss the topic at hand for those who are also studying for the Project Management Professional® (PMP) or other certification exams offered by the Project Management Institute.

Last, we added a large number of additional problems and mini-cases to the appropriate chapters where reviewers asked for them. We also added another simulation example in Chapter 5 to illustrate costs in a network. We also reduced our discussion on some topics that reviewers suggested, such as the design structure matrix.

SUPPLEMENTS

The *Instructor's Manual* will provide assistance to the project management instructor in the form of answers/solutions to the questions, problems, incidents for discussion, and end-of-chapter cases. This guide will also reference relevant Harvard Business School type cases and readings, teaching tips, and other pedagogically helpful material. Wiley maintains a web site for this and other books. The address is *www.wiley.com/college/mantel*. The site contains an electronic version of the *Instructor's Manual*, an extensive set of PowerPoint slides, sample course outlines, and test questions to test student understanding.

ACKNOWLEDGMENTS

There is no possible way to repay the scores of project ma⋯⋯rs and students who have contributed to this book, often unknowingly. The profess⋯ have given us ide⋯ about how to manage projects, and students have taught us ho⋯ ⋯h project⋯ agement. We are grateful beyond our ability to express it.

We are also grateful to a small group of individuals, both ⋯e fn⋯ acquaintances, who have graciously shared their time and knowledge ⋯

James Cochran, *Louisiana Tech University*; James Evans, *University of Cincinnati*; Karen Garrison, *Lucidity Consulting Group*; Timothy Kloppenborg, *Xavier University, Ohio*; Samuel J. Mantel, III, *RadioShack, Inc.*; Jim McCarthy, *McCarthy Technologies, Inc.*; the late Gerhard Rosegger, (2008), *Case Western Reserve University*; and Stephen Wearne, *University of Manchester, Institute of Science and Technology*.

For this edition we thank the following reviewers: Jesus Jimenez, *Texas State University*; Steve MacQueen, *Midlands Technical College*; Al Morelli, *University of Southern California*; Dee Piziak, *Concordia University, Wisconsin*; James Szot, *The University of Texas at Dallas*; Marlee Walton, *Iowa State University*; and Richard Wendell, *University of Pittsburgh*.

Above all, we thank Suzanne Ingrao, *Ingrao Associates*, without whom this book would have been unreadable. Our gratitude is also extended to Wiley Editors Lisé Johnson and Brian Baker who did their best to keep us on track, on time, and of composed mind.

Finally, we owe a massive debt to those colleagues who reviewed the original manuscript of this book and/or its subsequent editions: Kwasi Amoako-Gyampah, *University of North Carolina at Greensboro*; James M. Buckingham, *United States Military Academy, West Point*; Michael J. Casey, *George Mason University*; Larry Crowley, *Auburn University*; Catherine Crummett, *James Madison University*; George R. Dean, *DeVry Institute of Technology, DuPage*; Geraldo Ferrer, *University of North Carolina at Chapel Hill*; Linda Fried, *University of Colorado, Denver*; William C. Giauque, *Brigham Young University*; Bertie Greer, *Northern Kentucky University*; David Harris, *University of New Mexico*; H. Khamooshi, *George Washington University*; Bill Leban, *Keller Graduate School of Management*; Leonardo Legorreta, *California State University, Sacramento*; William E. Matthews, *William Patterson University*; Sara McComb, *University of Massachusetts Amherst*; J. Wayne Patterson, *Clemson University*; Ann Paulson, *Edmonds Community College*; Patrick Philipoom, *University of South Carolina*; Arthur C. Rogers, *City University*; Dean T. Scott, *DeVry Institute of Technology, Pomona*; Richard V. Sheng, *DeVry Institute of Technology, Long Beach*; William A. Sherrard, *San Diego State University*; Kimberlee Snyder, *Winona University*; Louis C. Terminello, *Stevens Institute of Technology*; and Jeffrey L. Williams, *University of Phoenix*. We owe a special thanks to Byron Finch, *Miami University*, for a number of particularly thoughtful suggestions for improvement. While we give these reviewers our thanks, we absolve each and all of blame for our errors, omissions, and wrong-headed notions.

Jack R. Meredith
Broyhill Distinguished Scholar and Chair of Operations
School of Business
Wake Forest University
Winston Salem, NC 27109
meredijr@wfu.edu
(336) 758-4467
http://business.wfu.edu/apps/facprofiles.cfm?id=jack.meredith

Samuel J. Mantel, Jr.
Joseph S. Stern Professor Emeritus of Operations Management
College of Business Administration
University of Cincinnati
608 Flagstaff Drive
Cincinnati, OH 45215
mantelsj@earthlink.net
(513) 931-2465

Scott M. Shafer
Professor of Management and Associate Dean of Full-Time
MBA Program
School of Business
Wake Forest University
Box 7659
Salem, NC 27109
fu.edu
587
s.wfu.edu/apps/facprofiles.cfm?id=scott.shafer

Margaret M. Sutton
Sutton Associates
46 North Lake Avenue
Cincinnati, OH 45246
mmsutton@cinci.rr.com
(513) 543-2806

1

The World of Project Management

Once upon a time there was a heroine project manager. Her projects were never late. They never ran over budget. They always met contract specifications and invariably satisfied the expectations of her clients. And you know as well as we do, anything that begins with "Once upon a time . . ." is just a fairy tale.

This book is not about fairy tales. Throughout these pages we will be as realistic as we know how to be. We will explain project management practices that we know will work. We will describe project management tools that we know can help the project manager come as close as Mother Nature and Lady Luck will allow to meeting the expectations of all who have a stake in the outcome of the project.

1.1 WHAT IS A PROJECT?

Why this emphasis on project management? The answer is simple: Daily, organizations are asked to accomplish work activities that do not fit neatly into business-as-usual. A software group may be asked to develop an application program that will access U.S. government data on certain commodity prices and generate records on the value of commodity inventories held by a firm; the software must be available for use on April 1. The Illinois State Bureau for Children's Services may require an annually updated census of all Illinois resident children, aged 17 years or younger, living with an illiterate single parent; the census must begin in 18 months. A manufacturer initiates a process improvement project to offset higher energy costs.

Note that each work activity is *unique* with a specific *deliverable* aimed at meeting a *specific need or purpose*. These are *projects*. The routine issuance of reports on the value of commodity inventories, the routine counseling of single parents on nurturing their offspring, the day-to-day activities associated with running a machine in a factory—these are not projects. The difference between a project

PMBOK Guide

and a *nonproject* is not always crystal clear. For almost any precise definition, we can point to exceptions. At base, however, projects are unique, have a specific deliverable, and have a specific due date. Note that our examples have all those characteristics. The Project Management Institute (PMI) defines in its *Project Management Body of Knowledge (PMBOK Guide)*, 5th edition, a project as "A temporary endeavor undertaken to create a unique product, service, or result" (Project Management Institute, 2013).

Projects vary widely in size and type. The writing of this book is a project. The reorganization of Procter & Gamble (P&G) into a global enterprise is a project, or more accurately a program, a large integrated set of projects. The construction of a fly-in fishing lodge in Manitoba, Canada, is a project. The organization of "Cat-in-the-Hat Day" so that Mrs. Payne's third grade class can celebrate Dr. Suess's birthday is also a project.

Both the hypothetical projects we mentioned earlier and the real-world projects listed just above have the same characteristics. They are unique, specific, and have desired completion dates. They all qualify as projects under the PMI's definition. They have an additional characteristic in common—they are multidisciplinary. They require input from people with different kinds of knowledge and expertise. This multidisciplinary nature of projects means that they tend to be complex, that is, composed of many interconnected elements and requiring input from groups outside the project. The various areas of knowledge required for the construction of the fly-in fishing lodge are not difficult to imagine. The knowledge needed for globalization of a large conglomerate like P&G is quite beyond the imagination of any one individual and requires input from a diversified group of specialists. Working as a team, the specialists investigate the problem to discover what information, skills, and knowledge are needed to accomplish the overall task. It may take weeks, months, or even years to find the correct inputs and understand how they fit together.

A secondary effect of using multidisciplinary teams to deal with complex problems is conflict. Projects are characterized by conflict. As we will see in later chapters, the project schedule, budget, and specifications conflict with each other. The needs and desires of the client conflict with those of the project team, the senior management of the organization conducting the project and others who may have a less direct stake in the project. Some of the most intense conflicts are those between members of the project team. Much more will be said about this in later chapters. For the moment, it is sufficient to recognize that projects and conflict are often inseparable companions, an environment that is unsuitable and uncomfortable for conflict avoiders.

It is also important to note that projects do not exist in isolation. They are often parts of a larger entity or program, just as projects to develop a new engine and an improved suspension system are parts of the program to develop a new automobile. The overall activity is called a program. Projects are subdivisions of programs. Likewise, projects are composed of *tasks*, which can be further divided into *subtasks* that can be broken down further still. The purpose of these subdivisions is to allow the project to be viewed at various levels of detail. The fact that projects are typically parts of larger organizational programs is important for another reason, as is explained in Section 1.5.

Finally, it is appropriate to ask, "Why projects?" The reason is simple. We form projects in order to fix the responsibility and authority for the achievement of an organizational goal on an individual or small group when the job does not clearly fall within the definition of routine work.

Trends in Project Management

Many recent developments in project management are being driven by quickly changing global markets, technology, and education. Global competition is putting pressure on prices, response times, and product/service innovation. Computer and telecommunication technology, along with rapidly expanding higher education across the world allows the use of project management for types of projects and in regions where these sophisticated tools had never been considered before. The most important of these recent developments are covered in this book.

Achieving Strategic Goals   There has been a growing use of projects to achieve an organization's strategic goals, and existing major projects are screened to make sure that their objectives support the organization's strategy and mission. Projects that do not have clear ties to the strategy and mission are not approved. A discussion of this is given in Section 1.6, where the Project Portfolio Process is described.

Achieving Routine Goals   On the other hand, there has also been a growing use of project management to accomplish routine departmental tasks, normally handled as the usual work of functional departments; e.g., routine machine maintenance. Middle management has become aware that projects are organized to accomplish their performance objectives within their budgets and deadlines. As a result, artificial deadlines and budgets are created to accomplish specific, though routine, departmental tasks—a process called "projectizing."

Best Practice

Improving Project Effectiveness   A variety of efforts are being pursued to improve the process and results of project management, whether strategic or routine. One well-known effort is the creation of a formal Project Management Office (PMO, see Section 2.5) in many organizations that takes responsibility for many of the administrative and specialized tasks of project management. Another effort is the evaluation of an organization's project management "maturity," or skill and experience in managing projects (discussed in Section 7.5). This is often one of the responsibilities of the PMO. Another responsibility of the PMO is to educate project managers about the *ancillary goals* of the organization (Section 8.1), which automatically become a part of the goals of every project whether the project manager knows it or not. Achieving better control over each project through the use of phase gates (Sections 7.1 and 7.4), earned value (Section 7.3), critical ratios (Section 7.4), and other such techniques is also a current trend.

Best Practice

Virtual Projects   With the rapid increase in globalization of industry, many projects now involve global teams whose members operate in different countries and different time zones, each bringing a unique set of talents to the project. These are known as virtual projects because the team members may never physically meet before the team is disbanded and another team reconstituted. Advanced telecommunications and computer technology allow such virtual projects to be created, do their work, and complete their project successfully (see Section 2.1).

Quasi-Projects   Led by the demands of the information technology/systems departments, project management is now being extended into areas where the project's objectives are not well understood, time deadlines unknown, and/or budgets undetermined. This ill-defined type of project is extremely difficult to conduct and to date has often resulted in setting an artificial due date and budget, and then specifying project objectives to meet those limits. However, new tools for these quasi-projects are now being developed—prototyping, phase-gating, and others—to help these projects achieve results that satisfy the customer in spite of the unknowns.

Best Practice

> A project, then, is a temporary endeavor undertaken to create a unique product or service. It is specific, timely, usually multidisciplinary, and typically conflict ridden. Projects are parts of overall programs and may be broken down into tasks, subtasks, and further if desired. Current trends in project management include achieving strategic goals, achieving routine goals, improving project effectiveness, virtual projects, and quasi-projects.

1.2 PROJECT MANAGEMENT VS. GENERAL MANAGEMENT

As is shown in Table 1-1, project management differs from general management largely because projects differ from what we have referred to as "nonprojects." The naturally high level of conflict present in projects means that the project manager (PM) must have special skills in conflict resolution. The fact that projects are unique means that the PM must be creative and flexible, and have the ability to adjust rapidly to changes. When managing nonprojects, the general manager tries to "manage by exception." In other words, for nonprojects almost everything is routine and is handled routinely by subordinates. The manager deals only with the exceptions. For the PM, almost everything is an exception.

Major Differences

Certainly, general management's success is dependent on good planning. For projects, however, planning is much more carefully detailed and project success is absolutely dependent on such planning. The project plan is the result of integrating all information about a project's deliverables, generally referred to as the "scope" of the project, and its targeted date of completion. "Scope" has two meanings. One is "product scope," which defines the performance requirements of a project, and "project scope," which details the work required to deliver the product scope (see Chapter 5, p. 105 of PMBOK, 2013). To avoid confusion, we will use the term scope to mean "product scope" and will allow the work, resources, and time needed by the project to deliver the product scope to the customer to be defined by the project's plan (discussed in detail in Chapter 3). Therefore, the scope and due date of the project determine its plan, that is, its budget, schedule, control, and evaluation. Detailed planning is critically important. One should not, of course, take so much time planning that nothing ever gets done, but careful planning is a major contributor to project success. Project planning is discussed in Chapter 3 and is amplified throughout the rest of this book.

PMBOK Guide

Table 1-1 Comparison of Project Management and General Management

Dimension	Project Management	General Management
Type of Work Activity	Unique	Routine
Management Approach	Ability to adapt to change	Manage by exception
Planning	Critical	Important
Budgeting	Start from scratch, multiple budget periods	Modify budget from previous budget period
Sequence of Activities	Must be determined	Often predetermined
Location of Work	Crosses organizational units	Within an organizational unit
Managerial Hierarchy	Informal	Well defined

Project budgeting differs from standard budgeting, not in accounting techniques, but in the way budgets are constructed. Budgets for nonprojects are primarily modifications of budgets for the same activity in the previous period. Project budgets are newly created for each project and often cover several "budget periods" in the future. The project budget is derived directly from the project plan that calls for specific activities. These activities require resources, and such resources are the heart of the project budget. Similarly, the project schedule is also derived from the project plan.

In a nonproject manufacturing line, the sequence in which various things are done is set when the production line is designed. The sequence of activities often is not altered when new models are produced. On the other hand, each project has a schedule of its own. Previous projects with deliverables similar to the one at hand may provide a rough template for the current project, but its specific schedule will be determined by the time required for a specific set of resources to do the specific work that must be done to achieve each project's specific scope by the specific date on which the project is due for delivery to the client. As we will see in later chapters, the special requirements associated with projects have led to the creation of special managerial tools for budgeting and scheduling.

The routine work of most organizations takes place within a well-defined structure of divisions, departments, sections, and similar subdivisions of the total unit. The typical project cannot thrive under such restrictions. The need for technical knowledge, information, and special skills almost always requires that departmental lines be crossed. This is simply another way of describing the multidisciplinary character of projects. When projects are conducted side-by-side with routine activities, chaos tends to result—the nonprojects rarely crossing organizational boundaries and the projects crossing them freely. These problems and recommended actions are discussed at greater length in Chapter 2.

Even when large firms establish manufacturing plants or distribution centers in different countries, a management team is established on site. For projects, "globalization" has a different meaning. Individual members of project teams may be spread across countries, continents, and oceans, and speak several different languages. Some project team members may never even have a face-to-face meeting with the project manager, though transcontinental and intercontinental video meetings combining telephone and computer are common.

The discussion of structure leads to consideration of another difference between project and general management. In general management, there is a reasonably well defined managerial hierarchy. Superior-subordinate relationships are known, and lines of authority are clear. In project management this is rarely true. The PM may be relatively low in the hierarchical chain of command. This does not, however, reduce his or her responsibility of completing a project successfully. Responsibility without the authority of rank or position is so common in project management as to be the rule, not the exception.

Negotiation

With little legitimate authority, the PM depends on negotiation skills to gain the cooperation of the many departments in the organization that may be asked to supply technology, information, resources, and personnel to the project. The parent organization's standard departments have their own objectives, priorities, and personnel. The project is not their responsibility, and the project tends to get the leftovers, if any, after the departments have satisfied their own need for resources. Without any real command authority, the PM must negotiate for almost everything the project needs.

It is important to note that there are three different types of negotiation, *win-win* negotiation, *win-lose* negotiation, and *lose-lose* negotiation. When you negotiate the purchase of a car or a home, you are usually engaging in win-lose negotiation. The less you pay for a home or car, the less profit the seller makes. Your savings are the other party's losses—win-lose negotiation. This type of negotiation is never appropriate when dealing with other members of your organization. If you manage to "defeat" a department head and get resources or commitments that the department head did not wish to give you, imagine what will happen the next time you need something from this individual. The PM simply cannot risk win-lose situations when negotiating with other members of the organization.

Lose-lose negotiation occurs when one party is unwilling to assert his or her position aggressively while at the same time resists cooperating with the other party. This often occurs in situations where one or both of the parties are conflict avoiders. When one party is not willing to help the other party achieve his or her objective and at the same time is unwilling to pursue his or her own objectives, the end result is that both parties lose.

Within the organization, win-win negotiation is mandatory. In essence, in win-win negotiation both parties must try to understand what the other party needs. The problem you face as a negotiator is how to help other parties meet their needs in return for their help in meeting the needs of your project. When negotiation takes place repeatedly between the same individuals, win-win negotiation is the only sensible procedure. PMs spend a great deal of their time negotiating. General managers spend relatively little. Skill at win-win negotiating is a requirement for successful project managing (see Fisher and Ury, 1983; Jandt, 1987; and Raiffa, 1982).

One final point about negotiating: Successful win-win negotiation often involves taking a synergistic approach by searching for the "third alternative." For example, consider a product development project focusing on the development of a new printer. A design engineer working on the project suggests adding more memory to the printer. The PM initially opposes this suggestion, feeling that the added memory will make the printer too costly. Rather than rejecting the suggestion, however, the PM tries to gain a better understanding of the design engineer's concern.

Based on their discussion, the PM learns that the engineer's purpose in requesting additional memory is to increase the printer's speed. After benchmarking the competition, the design engineer feels the printer will not be competitive as it is currently configured. The PM explains his fear that adding the extra memory will increase the cost of the printer to the point that it also will no longer be cost competitive. Based on this discussion the design engineer and PM agree that they need to search for another (third) alternative that will increase the printer's speed without increasing its costs. A couple of days later, the design engineer identifies a new ink that can simultaneously increase the printer's speed and actually lower its total and operating costs.

Project management differs greatly from general management. Every project is planned, budgeted, scheduled, and controlled as a unique task. Unlike nonprojects, projects are often multidisciplinary and usually have considerable need to cross departmental boundaries for technology, information, resources, and personnel. Crossing these boundaries tends to lead to intergroup conflict. The development of a detailed project plan based on the scope and due date of the project is critical to the project's success.

Unlike their general management counterparts, project managers have responsibility for accomplishing a project, but little or no legitimate authority to command the required resources from the functional departments. The PM must be skilled at win-win negotiation to obtain these resources.

1.3   WHAT IS MANAGED? THE THREE GOALS OF A PROJECT

The performance of a project is measured by three criteria. Is the project on time or early? Is the project on or under budget? Does the project deliver the agreed-upon specification to the satisfaction of the customer? Figure 1-1 shows the three goals of a project. The performance of the project and the PM is measured by the degree to which these goals are achieved.

One of these goals, the project's specifications or "scope," is set primarily by the client (although the client agrees to all three when contracting for the project). It is the client who must decide what capabilities are required of the project's deliverables—and this is what makes the project unique. Some writers insist that "quality" is a separate and distinct goal of the project along with time, cost, and scope. We do not agree because we consider quality an inherent part of the project specifications.

If we did not live in an uncertain world in which best made plans often go awry, managing projects would be relatively simple, requiring only careful planning. Unfortunately, we do not live in a predictable (*deterministic*) world, but one characterized by chance events (*uncertainty*). This ensures that projects travel a rough road. Murphy's law seems as universal as death and taxes, and the result is that the most skilled planning is upset by uncertainty. Thus, the PM spends a great deal of time adapting to unpredicted change. The primary method of adapting is to trade-off one objective for another. If a construction project falls behind schedule because of bad weather, it may be possible to get back on schedule by adding resources—in this case, probably labor using overtime and perhaps some additional equipment. If the budget cannot be raised to cover the additional resources, the PM may have to negotiate with the client for a later delivery date of the building. If neither cost nor schedule can be negotiated, the client may be willing to cut back on some of the features in the building in order to allow the project to finish on time and budget (e.g., substituting carpet for tile in some of the spaces). As a final alternative, the contractor may have to "swallow" the added costs (or pay a penalty for late delivery) and accept lower profits.

Trade-Offs

This example illustrates a fundamental point. Namely, managing the trade-offs among the three project goals is in fact the primary role of the project manager. Furthermore, managing these trade-offs in the most effective manner requires that the

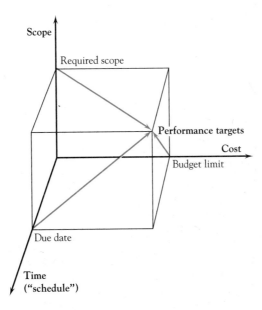

Figure 1-1   Scope, cost, and time project performance targets.

project manager have a clear understanding of how the project supports broader organizational goals. Thus, the organization's overall strategy is the most important consideration for managing the trade-offs that will be required among the three project goals.

All projects are always carried out under conditions of uncertainty. Well-tested software routines may not perform properly when integrated with other well-tested routines. A chemical compound may destroy cancer cells in a test tube—and even in the bodies of test animals—but may kill the host as well as the cancer. Where one cannot find an acceptable way to deal with a problem, the only alternative may be to stop the project and start afresh to achieve the desired deliverables.

As we note throughout this book, projects are all about uncertainty. Therefore, in addition to effectively managing trade-offs, effective project management requires an ability to deal with uncertainty. The time required to complete a project, the availability and costs of key resources, the timing of solutions to technological problems, a wide variety of macroeconomic variables, the whims of a client, the actions taken by competitors, even the likelihood that the output of a project will perform as expected, all these exemplify the uncertainties encountered when managing projects. While there are actions that may be taken to reduce the uncertainty, no actions of a PM can ever eliminate it.

As Hatfield (2008) points out, projects are complex and include interfaces, interdependencies, and many assumptions, any or all of which may turn out to be wrong. Also, projects are managed by people, which adds to the uncertainty. Gale (2008a) reminds us that the uncertainties include everything from legislation that can change how we do business, to earthquakes and other "acts of God." Therefore, in today's turbulent business environment, effective decision making is predicated on an ability to manage the ambiguity that arises while we operate in a world characterized by uncertain information. (Risk management is discussed in Chapter 11 of the PMBOK, 5th ed., 2013.)

PMBOK Guide

The first step in managing risk is to identify these potentially uncertain events and the likelihood that any or all may occur. This is called *risk analysis*. Different managers and organizations approach this problem in different ways. Gale advises expecting the unexpected; some managers suggest considering those things that keep one awake at night. Many organizations keep formal lists, a "risk register," and use their Project Management Office (PMO, discussed in Chapter 2) to maintain and update the list of risks and approaches that have been successful in the past in dealing with specific risks. This information is then incorporated into the firm's business-continuity and disaster-recovery plans. Every organization should have a well-defined process for dealing with risk, and we will discuss this issue at greater length in Chapter 3, Section 3.5. At this point we simply overview risk analysis.

Risk

Best Practice

The essence of risk analysis is to make estimates or assumptions about the probability distributions associated with key parameters and variables and to use analytic decision models or Monte Carlo simulation models based on these distributions to evaluate the desirability of certain managerial decisions. Real-world problems are usually large enough that the use of analytic models is very difficult and time consuming. With modern computer software, simulation is not difficult.

A mathematical model of the situation is constructed, and a simulation is run to determine the model's outcomes under various scenarios. The model is run (or replicated) repeatedly, starting from a different point each time based on random choices of values from the probability distributions of the input variables. Outputs of the model are used to construct statistical distributions of items of interest to decision makers, such as costs, profits, completion dates, or return on investment. These distributions are the *risk profiles* of the outcomes associated with a decision. Risk profiles can be analyzed by the manager when considering a decision, along with many other factors such as strategic concerns, behavioral issues, fit with the organization, cost and scheduling issues, and so on.

Risk

Thus we observe that in addition to managing trade-offs, another critical aspect of project management is managing uncertainty or risk. In fact, managing risk is actually tightly coupled with managing the three traditional goals of project management. For example, the more uncertainty the project manager faces, the greater the risk that the project will go over budget, finish late, and/or not meet its original scope. However, beyond these rather obvious relationships, there is also a more subtle connection. In particular, project risk represents a fourth trade-off opportunity at the project manager's disposal. For example, the project's budget can be increased in order to collect additional data that in turn will reduce the uncertainty related to how long it will take to complete the project. Likewise, the project's deadline can be reduced, but this will increase the uncertainty about whether it will be completed on time.

As a result of the relationship between uncertainty and the three traditional project goals, we adopt the view in this book that managing uncertainty is a fourth goal of project management. Thus, the primary role of the project manager is to effectively manage the trade-offs between cost, time, scope, and risk.

Trade-Offs

In the past, it was popular to label technical uncertainties as "technological risk." This is not very helpful, however, because it is not the technology that is uncertain. We can, in fact, do almost anything we wish, excepting perhaps faster-than-light travel and perpetual motion. What is uncertain is not technological success, but rather how much it will cost and how long it will take to reach success.

Trade-Offs

Most of the trade-offs PMs make are reasonably straightforward if the organization's strategy is well understood and trade-offs are discussed during the planning, budgeting, and scheduling phases of the project. Usually they involve trading time and cost, but if we cannot alter either the schedule or the budget, the specifications of the project may be altered or additional risk accepted. Frills on the finished product may be foregone, capabilities not badly needed may be compromised. From the early stages of the project, it is the PM's duty to know which elements of project performance are sacrosanct.

One final comment on this subject: Projects must have some flexibility. Again, this is because we do not live in a deterministic world. Occasionally, a senior manager (who does not have to manage the project) presents the PM with a document precisely listing a set of deliverables, a fixed budget, and a firm schedule. This is failure in the making for the PM. Unless the budget is overly generous, the schedule overlong, and the deliverables easily accomplished, the system is, as mathematicians say, "overdetermined." If Mother Nature so much as burps, the project will fail to meet its rigid parameters. A PM cannot be successful without flexibility to manage the trade-offs.

Projects have four interrelated objectives: to (1) meet the budget, (2) finish on schedule, (3) generate deliverables that satisfy the client, and (4) to minimize risks. Because we live in an uncertain world, as work on the project proceeds, unexpected problems are bound to arise. These chance events will threaten the project's schedule or budget or scope. The PM must now decide how to trade off one project goal against another (e.g., to stay on schedule by assigning extra resources to the project may mean it will run over the predetermined budget). If the schedule, budget, and scope are rigidly predetermined, the project is probably doomed to failure unless the preset schedule and budget are overly generous or the difficulty in meeting the specifications has been seriously overestimated.

1.4   THE LIFE CYCLES OF PROJECTS

PMBOK Guide

Trade-Offs

All organisms have a *life cycle*. They are born, grow, wane, and die. This is true for all living things, for stars and planets, for the products we buy and sell, for our organizations, and for our projects as well. A project's life cycle measures project completion as a function of either time (schedule) or resources (budget). The subject of project life cycles is discussed in PMBOK's Chapter 2 on Organizational Influences and Project Life Cycle. This life cycle must be understood because the PM's managerial focus subtly shifts at different stages of the cycle (Adams and Barndt, 1983; Kloppenborg and Mantel, 1990). During the early stages, the PM must make sure that the project plan really reflects the wishes of the client as well as the abilities of the project team and is designed to be consistent with the goals and objectives of the parent organization.

As the project goes into the implementation stage of its life cycle, the PM's attention turns to the job of keeping the project on budget and schedule—or, when chance interferes with progress, to negotiating the appropriate trade-offs to correct or minimize the damage. At the end of the project, the PM turns into a "fuss-budget" to assure that the specifications of the project are truly met, handling all the details of closing out the books on the project, making sure there are no loose ends, and that every "i" is dotted and "t" crossed.

Many projects are like building a house. A house-building project starts slowly with a lot of discussion and planning. Then construction begins, and progress is rapid. When the house is built, but not finished inside, progress appears to slow down and it seemingly takes forever to paint everything, to finish all the trim, and to assemble and install the built-in appliances. Progress is slow-fast-slow, as shown in Figure 1-2.

It used to be thought that the S-shaped curve of Figure 1-2 represented the life cycle for all projects. While this is true of many projects, there are important exceptions. Anyone who has baked a cake has dealt with a project that approaches completion by a very different route than the traditional S-curve, as shown in Figure 1-3.

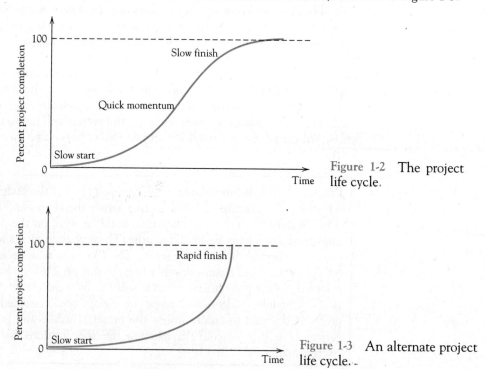

Figure 1-2   The project life cycle.

Figure 1-3   An alternate project life cycle.

The process of baking a cake is straightforward. The ingredients are mixed while the oven is preheated, usually to 350°F. The mixture (technically called "goop") is placed in a greased pan, inserted in the oven, and the baking process begins. Assume that the entire process from assembling the ingredients to finished cake requires about 45 minutes—15 minutes for assembling the materials and mixing, and 30 minutes for baking. At the end of 15 minutes we have goop. Even after 40 minutes, having baked for 25 minutes, it may look like cake but, as any baker knows, it is still partly goop inside. If a toothpick (our grandmothers used a broom straw) is inserted into the middle of the "cake" and then removed, it does not come out clean. In the last few minutes of the process, the goop in the middle becomes cake. If left a few minutes too long in the oven, the cake will begin to burn on the bottom. Project Cake follows a J-shaped path to completion much like Figure 1-3.

There are many projects that are similar to cake—the development of computer software, and many chemical engineering projects, for instance. In these cases the PM's job begins with great attention to having all the correct project resources at hand or guaranteed to be available when needed. Once the "baking" process is underway—the integration of various sets of code or chemicals—one can usually not add missing ingredients. As the process continues, the PM must concentrate on determining when the project is complete—"done" in the case of cake, or a fully debugged program in the case of software.

In later chapters, we will also see the importance of the shape of the project's life cycle on how management allocates resources or reacts to potential delays in a project. Management does not need to know the precise shape of the life cycle, but merely whether its completion phase is concave (Figure 1-2) or convex (Figure 1-3) to the baseline.

> There are two different paths (life cycles) along which projects progress from start to completion. One is S-shaped, and the other is J-shaped. It is an important distinction because identifying the different life cycles helps the PM to focus attention on appropriate matters to ensure successful project completion.

1.5   SELECTING PROJECTS TO MEET ORGANIZATIONAL OBJECTIVES

The accomplishment of important tasks and goals in organizations today is being achieved increasingly through the use of projects. A new kind of organization has emerged recently to deal with the accelerating growth in the number of multiple, simultaneously ongoing, and often interrelated projects in organizations. This project-oriented organization, often called "enterprise project management" (Levine, 1998), "management by projects" (Boznak, 1996), and similar names, was created to tie projects more closely to the organization's goals and strategy and to integrate and centralize management methods for the growing number of ongoing projects. Given that the organization has an appropriate mission statement and strategy, selected projects should be consistent with the strategic goals of the organization. In what follows, we first discuss a variety of common project selection methods. We then describe the process of strategically selecting the best set of projects for implementation, called the Project Portfolio Process.

Project selection is the process of evaluating individual projects or groups of projects and then choosing to implement a set of them so that the objectives of the parent organization are achieved. Before a project begins its life cycle, it must have been *selected* for funding by the parent organization. Whether the project was proposed by someone within the organization or an outside client, it is subject to approval by a more or less formal selection process. Often conducted by a committee of senior managers, the major function of the selection process is to ensure that several conditions are considered before a commitment is made to undertake any project. These conditions vary widely from firm to firm, but several are quite common: (1) Is the project potentially profitable? Does it have a chance of meeting our return-on-investment hurdle rate? (2) Is the project required by law or the rules of an industrial association; i.e., a "mandate?" (3) Does the firm have, or can it easily acquire, the knowledge and skills to carry out the project successfully? (4) Does the project involve building competencies that are considered consistent with our firm's strategic plan? (5) Does the organization currently have the capacity to carry out the project on its proposed schedule? (6) In the case of R&D projects, if the project is technically successful, does it meet all requirements to make it economically successful? This list could be greatly extended.

The selection process is often complete before a PM is appointed to the project. Why, then, should the PM be concerned? Quite simply, the PM should know exactly why the organization selected the specific project because this sheds considerable light on what the project (and hence the PM) is expected to accomplish, from senior management's point of view, with the project. The project may have been selected because it appeared to be profitable, or was a way of entering a new area of business, or a way of building a reputation of competency with a new client or in a new market. This knowledge can be very helpful to the PM by indicating senior management's goals for the project, which will point to the desirability of some trade-offs and the undesirability of others.

Trade-Offs

There are many different methods for selecting projects, but they may be grouped into two fundamental types, nonnumeric and numeric. The former does not use numbers for evaluation; the latter does. At this point it is important to note that many firms select projects before a detailed project plan has been developed. Clearly, if the potential project's scope, budget, and due dates have not been determined, it will be quite impossible to derive a reasonably accurate estimate of the project's success. Rough estimations may have to suffice in such cases, but specific plans should be developed prior to final project selection. Obviously, mandated projects are an exception. For mandates, budget estimates do not matter but scope and due dates are still important. Mandates must be selected. We will deal further with the selection problem when we consider the Project Management Office in Chapter 2.

Nonnumeric Selection Methods

The Sacred Cow   At times, the organization's Chief Executive Officer (CEO) or other senior executive either formally or casually suggests a potential product or service that the organization might offer to its customers. The suggestion often starts, "You know, I was thinking that we might . . . " and concludes with ". . . Take a look at it and see if it looks sensible. If not, we'll drop the whole thing."

Whatever the selection process, the aforementioned project will be approved. It becomes a "Sacred Cow" and will be shown to be technically, if not economically, feasible. This may seem irrational to new students of project management, but such a judgment ignores senior management's intelligence and valuable years of experience—as well as the subordinate's desire for long-run employment. It also overlooks the value of support from the top of the organization, a condition that is necessary for project success (Green, 1995).

The Operating/Competitive Necessity This method selects any project that is necessary for continued operation of a group, facility, or the firm itself. A "mandated" project obviously must be selected. If the answer to the "Is it necessary . . . ?" question is "yes," and if we wish to continue using the facility or system to stay in business, the project is selected. The Investment Committee of a large manufacturing company started to debate the advisability of purchasing and installing pumps to remove 18 inches of flood water from the floor of a small, but critical production facility. The debate stopped immediately when one officer pointed out that without the pumps the firm was out of business.

The same questions can be directed toward the maintenance of a competitive position. Some years ago, General Electric almost decided to sell a facility that manufactured the large mercury vapor light bulbs used for streetlights and lighting large parking lots. The lighting industry had considerable excess capacity for this type of bulb and the resulting depressed prices meant they could not be sold profitably. GE, however, felt that if they dropped these bulbs from their line of lighting products, they might lose a significant portion of all light bulb sales to municipalities. The profits from such sales were far in excess of the losses on the mercury vapor bulbs.

Comparative Benefits Many organizations have to select from a list of projects that are complex, difficult to assess, and often noncomparable, e.g., United Way organizations and R&D organizations. Such institutions often appoint a selection committee made up of knowledgeable individuals. Each person is asked to arrange a set of potential projects into a rank-ordered set. Typically, each individual judge may use whatever criteria he or she wishes to evaluate projects. Some may use carefully determined technical criteria, but others may try to estimate the project's probable impact on the ability of the organization to meet its goals. While the use of various criteria by different judges may trouble some, it results from a purposeful attempt to get as broad a set of evaluations as possible.

Rank-ordering a small number of projects is not inherently difficult, but when the number of projects exceeds 15 or 20, the difficulty of ordering the group rises rapidly. A Q-sort* is a convenient way to handle the task. First, separate the projects into three subsets, "good," "fair," and "poor," using whatever criteria you have chosen—or been instructed to use. If there are more than seven or eight members in any one classification, divide the group into two subsets, for instance, "good-plus" and "good-minus." Continue subdividing until no set has more than seven or eight members (see Figure 1-4). Now, rank-order the items in each subset. Arrange the subsets in order of rank, and the entire list will be in order.

The committee can make a composite ranking from the individual lists any way it chooses. One way would be to number the items on each individual list in order of rank, and then add the ranks given to each project by each of the judges. Projects may then be approved in the order of their composite ranks, at least until the organization runs out of available funds.

Numeric Selection Methods

Financial Assessment Methods Most firms select projects on the basis of their expected economic value to the firm. Although there are many economic assessment

---

* The Q-sort is a handy, useful, and easy-to-use technique. See Helin and Souder, 1974.

Steps	Results at Each Step

1. For each participant in the exercise, assemble a deck of cards, with the name and description of one project on each card.
2. Instruct each participant to divide the deck into two piles, one representing a high priority, the other a low-priority level. (The piles need not be equal.)
3. Instruct each participant to select cards from each pile to form a third pile representing the medium-priority level.
4. Instruct each participant to select cards from the high-level pile to yield another pile representing the very high level of priority; select cards from the low-level pile representing the very low level of priority.
5. Finally, instruct each participant to survey the selections and shift any cards that seem out of place until the classifications are satisfactory.

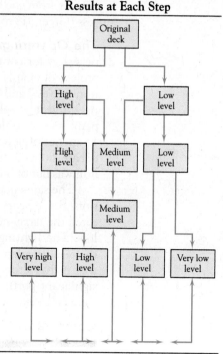

Figure 1-4   The Q-sort method.

Risk

methods available—payback period, average annual rate of return, internal rate of return, and so on—we will describe here two of the most widely used methods: *payback period* and *discounted cash flow.**

The payback period for a project is the initial fixed investment in the project divided by the estimated annual net cash inflows from the project (which include the cash inflows from depreciation of the investment). The ratio of these quantities is the number of years required for the project to return its initial investment. Because of this perspective, the payback period is often considered a surrogate measure of risk to the firm: the longer the payback period, the greater the risk. To illustrate, if a project requires an investment of $100,000 and is expected to return a net cash inflow of $25,000 each year, then the payback period is simply 100,000/25,000 = 4 years, assuming the $25,000 annual inflow continues at least 4 years. Although this is a popular financial assessment method, it ignores the time value of money as well as any returns beyond the payback period. For these reasons, it is not recommended as a project selection method, though it is valuable for cash budgeting. Of the financial assessment methods, the discounted cash flow method discussed next is recommended instead.

The discounted cash flow method considers the time value of money, the inflation rate, and the firm's return-on-investment (ROI) hurdle rate for projects. The annual cash inflows and outflows are collected and discounted to their *net present value* (NPV) using the organization's *required rate of return* (a.k.a. the *hurdle rate* or *cutoff rate*).

_____

* Explanations of the theory and methods of calculating the net present value of cash inflows are beyond the scope of this book. We recommend that the reader who could benefit from an explanation turn to any standard college textbook on finance (Moyer, McGuigan, and Kretlow, 2008, for instance).

$$\text{NPV(project)} = I_0 + \sum_{t=1}^{n} F_t / (1+k)^t$$

where

I_0 = the initial investment, which will be negative because it is an outflow

F_t = the net cash flow in period t

k = the required rate of return or hurdle rate

n = number of periods in life of project

If one wishes to include the potential effects of inflation or deflation in the calculation, it is quite easily done. The discounting term, $(1 + k)^t$, simply becomes $(1 + k + p_t)^t$, where p_t is the estimated rate of inflation or deflation for period t. If the required rate of return is 10 percent and we expect the rate of inflation will be 3 percent, then the discount factor becomes $(1 + .10 + .03)^t = (1.13)^t$ for that period.

In the early years of a project when outflows usually exceed inflows, the NPV of the project for those years will be negative. If the project becomes profitable, inflows become larger than outflows and the NPV for those later years will be positive. If we calculate the present value of the net cash flows for all years, we have the NPV of the project. If this sum is positive, the project may be accepted because it earns more than the required rate of return. The following boxed example illustrates these calculations. Although the example employs a spreadsheet for clarity and convenience in the analysis, we have chosen to illustrate the calculations using the NPV formula directly rather than using a spreadsheet function such as NPV (in Excel®) so the reader can better see what is happening. Once the reader understands how this works, we suggest using the simpler spreadsheet functions to speed up the process.

PsychoCeramic Sciences, Inc.*

PsychoCeramic Sciences, Inc. (PSI) is a large producer of cracked pots and other cracked items. The firm is considering the installation of a new manufacturing line that will, it is hoped, allow more precise quality control on the size, shape, and location of the cracks in its pots as well as in vases designed to hold artificial flowers.

    The plant engineering department has submitted a project proposal that estimates the following investment requirements: an initial investment of $125,000 to be paid up-front to the Pocketa-Pocketa Machine Corporation, an additional investment of $100,000 to install the machines, and another $90,000 to add new material handling systems and integrate the new equipment into the overall production system. Delivery and installation is estimated to take 1 year, and integrating the entire system should require an additional year. Thereafter, the engineers predict that scheduled machine overhauls will require further expenditures of about $15,000 every second year, beginning in the fourth year. They will not, however, overhaul the machinery in the last year of its life.

---

* The authors thank John Wiley & Sons for permission to adapt material from Meredith, J. R. and Mantel, S. J., Project Management: A Managerial Approach, 8th ed. New York, John Wiley & Sons, 2012 for use in this section and in Section 1.6.

The project schedule calls for the line to begin production in the third year, and to be up-to-speed by the end of that year. Projected manufacturing cost savings and added profits resulting from higher quality are estimated to be $50,000 in the first year of operation and are expected to peak at $120,000 in the second year of operation, and then to follow the gradually declining pattern shown in Table A.

Project life is expected to be 10 years from project inception, at which time the proposed system will be obsolete and will have to be replaced. It is estimated that the machinery will have a salvage value of $35,000. PSI has a 13 percent hurdle rate for capital investments and expects the rate of inflation to be about 2 percent per year over the life of the project. Assuming that the initial expenditure occurs at the beginning of the year and that all other receipts and expenditures occur as lump sums at the end of the year, we can prepare the Net Present Value analysis for the project as shown in Table A.

Because the first cash flow of − $125,000 occurs at the beginning of the first period, there is no need to discount it as it is already in present value terms. The remaining cash flows are assumed to occur at the end of their respective periods. For example, the $115,000 cash flow associated with 2017 is assumed to occur at the end of the fifth period. According to the results, the Net Present Value of the project is positive and, thus, the project can be accepted. (The project would have been rejected if the hurdle rate had been 15 percent or if the inflation rate was 4 percent, either one resulting in a discount rate of 17 percent.)

Risk

Perhaps the most difficult aspect related to the proper use of discounted cash flow is determining the appropriate discount rate to use. While this determination is made by senior management, it has a major impact on project selection, and therefore, on the life of the PM. For most projects the hurdle rate selected is the organization's cost of capital, though it is often arbitrarily set too high as a general allowance for risk. In the case of particularly risky projects, a higher hurdle rate may be justified, but it is not a good general practice. If a project is competing for funds with alternative investments, the hurdle rate may be the *opportunity cost of capital*, that is, the rate of return the firm must forego if it invests in the project instead of making an alternative investment. Another common, but misguided practice is to set the hurdle rate high as an allowance for resource cost increases. Neither risk nor inflation should be treated so casually. Specific corrections for each should be made if the firm's management feels it is required. We recommend strongly a careful risk analysis, which we will discuss in further detail throughout this book.

Because the present value of future returns decreases as the discount rate rises, a high hurdle rate biases the analysis strongly in favor of short-run projects. For example, given a rate of 20 percent, a dollar 10 years from now has a present value of only $.16, $(1/1.20)^{10} = 0.16$. The critical feature of long-run projects is that costs associated with them are spent early in the project and have high present values while revenues are delayed for several years and have low present values.

This effect may have far-reaching implications. The high interest rates during the 1970s and 1980s, and again in the 2000s, forced many firms to focus on short-run projects. The resulting disregard for long-term technological advancement led to a

Table A

	A	B	C	D	E	F	G
1					Discount	Net Present	
2	Year	Inflow	Outflow	Net Flow	Factor	Value	
3	A	B	C	(B − C)	$1/(1 + k + p)^t$	D × E	
4	2013*	$0.00	$125,000.00	−$125,000.00	1.00	−$125,000.00	
5	2013	0.00	100,000.00	−100,000.00	0.87	−86,957.00	
6	2014	0.00	90,000.00	−90,000.00	0.76	−68,053.00	
7	2015	50,000.00	0.00	50,000.00	0.66	32,876.00	
8	2016	120,000.00	15,000.00	105,000.00	0.57	60,034.00	
9	2017	115,000.00	0.00	115,000.00	0.50	57,175.00	
10	2018	105,000.00	15,000.00	90,000.00	0.43	38,909.00	
11	2019	97,000.00	0.00	97,000.00	0.38	36,466.00	
12	2020	90,000.00	15,000.00	75,000.00	0.33	24,518.00	
13	2021	82,000.00	0.00	82,000.00	0.28	23,310.00	
14	2022	65,000.00	0.00	65,000.00	0.25	16,067.00	
15	2022	35,000.00		35,000.00	0.25	8,651.00	
16							
17	Total	$759,000.00	$360,000.00	$399,000.00		$17,997.00	
18							
19		*t = 0 at the beginning of 2013					
20							
21	Formulae						
22	Cell D4		= (B4−C4) copy to D5:D15				
23	Cell E4		= 1/(1 + 0.13 + 0.02)^0				
24	Cell E5		= 1/(1 + 0.13 + 0.02)^1				
25	Cell E6		= 1/(1 + 0.13 + 0.02)^(A6−2012) copy to E7:E15				
26	Cell F4		= D4*E4 copy to F5:F15				
27	Cell B17		Sum(B4:B15) copy to C17, D17, F17				
28							

deterioration in the ability of some United States firms to compete in world markets (Hayes and Abernathy, 1980).

The discounted cash flow methods of calculation are simple and straightforward. Like the other financial assessment methods, it has a serious defect. First, it ignores all nonmonetary factors except risk. Second, because of the nature of discounting, all the discounted methods bias the selection system by favoring short-run projects. Let us now examine a selection method that goes beyond assessing only financial profitability.

Financial Options and Opportunity Costs A more recent approach to project selection employs financial analysis that recognizes the value of positioning the organization to capitalize on future opportunities. It is based on the financial options approach to valuing prospective capital investment opportunities. Through a financial option an organization or individual acquires the right to do something but is not required to exercise that right. For example, you may be familiar with stock options. When a person or organization purchases a stock option, they acquire the right to purchase a specific number of shares of a particular stock at a specified price within a specified time frame. If the market price of the stock moves above the specified option price within the specified time frame, the entity holding the option can exercise its right and thereby purchase the stock below the fair market price. If the market price of the stock remains below the specified option price, the entity can choose not to exercise its right to buy the stock.

To illustrate the analogy of financial options to project selection, consider a young biotech firm that is ready to begin clinical trials to test a new pharmaceutical product in humans. A key issue the company has to address is how to produce the drug both now in the low volumes needed for the clinical trials and in the mass quantities that will be needed in the future should the new drug succeed in the clinical trial phase. Its options for producing the drug in low volumes for the clinical trials are to invest in an in-house pilot plant or to immediately license the drug to another company. If it invests in an in-house pilot plan, it then has two future options for mass producing the drug: (1) invest in a commercial scale plant or (2) license the manufacturing rights. In effect then, investing now in the pilot plant provides the pharmaceutical company with the option of building a commercial scale plant in the future, an option it would not have if it chooses to license the drug right from the start. Thus by building the in-house pilot plant the pharmaceutical company is in a sense acquiring the right to build a commercial plant in the future. While beyond the scope of this book, we point out to the reader that in addition to the traditional approaches to project selection, the decision to build the pilot plant can also be analyzed using valuation techniques from financial options theory. In this case the value of having the option to build a commercial plant can be estimated.

In addition to considering the value of future opportunities a project may provide, the cost of not doing a project should also be considered. This approach to project selection is based on the well-known economic concept of "opportunity cost." Consider the problem of making an investment in one of only two projects. An investment in Project A will force us to forgo investing in Project B, and *vice versa*. If the return on A is 12 percent, making an investment in B will have an opportunity cost of 12 percent, the cost of the opportunity forgone. If the return on B is greater than 12 percent, it may be preferred over selecting Project A.

The same selection principle can be applied to timing the investment in a given project. R&D projects or projects involving the adoption of new technologies, for example, have values that may vary considerably with time. It is common for the passage of time to reduce uncertainties involved in both technological and commercial projects. The value of investing now may be higher (or lower) than investing later. If a project is delayed, the values of its costs and revenues at a later period should be discounted to their present value when compared to an investment not delayed.

Occasionally, organizations will approve projects that are forecast to lose money when fully costed and sometimes even when only direct costed. Such decisions by upper management are not necessarily foolish because there may be other, more important reasons for proceeding with a project, such as to:

• Acquire knowledge concerning a specific or new technology
• Get the organization's "foot in the door"

- Obtain the parts, service, or maintenance portion of the work
- Allow them to bid on a lucrative, follow-on contract
- Improve their competitive position
- Broaden a product line or line of business

PMBOK Guide

Of course, such decisions are expected to lose money in the short term only. Over the longer term they are expected to bring extra profits to the organization. It should be understood that "lowball" or "buy-in" bids (bidding low with the intent of cutting corners on work and material, or forcing subsequent contract changes) are unethical practices, violate the PMI Code of Ethics for Project Managers (see PMBOK, p. 2, 2013), and are clearly dishonest.

Scoring Methods   Scoring methods were developed to overcome some of the disadvantages of the simple financial profitability methods, especially their focus on a single criterion. The simplest scoring approach, the *unweighted 0–1 factor method*, lists multiple criteria of significant interest to management. Given a list of the organization's goals, a selection committee, usually senior managers familiar with both the organization's criteria and potential project portfolio, check off, for each project, which of the criteria would be satisfied; for example, see Figure 1-5. Those projects that exceed a certain number of check-marks may be selected for funding.

Project _____

Rater _____ Date _____

	Qualifies	Does Not Qualify
No increase in energy requirements	x	
Potential market size, dollars	x	
Potential market share, percent	x	
No new facility required	x	
No new technical expertise required		x
No decrease in quality of final product	x	
Ability to manage project with current personnel		x
No requirement for reorganization	x	
Impact on work force safety	x	
Impact on environmental standards	x	
Profitability		
Rate of return more than 15% after tax	x	
Estimated annual profits more than $250,000	x	
Time to break-even less than 3 years	x	
No need for external consultants		x
Consistency with current line of business		x
Impact on company image		
With customers	x	
With our industry		x
Totals	12	5

Figure 1-5   A sample project selection form, an unweighted 0–1 scoring model.

Best Practice

All the criteria, however, may not be equally important and the various projects may satisfy each criterion to different degrees. To correct for these drawbacks, the *weighted factor scoring method* was developed. In this method, a number of criteria, *n*, are considered for evaluating each project, and their relative importance weights, w_j, are estimated. The sum of the weights over all the *j* criteria is usually set arbitrarily at 1.00, though this is not mandatory. It is helpful to limit the criteria to just the major factors and not include criteria that are only marginal to the decision, such as representing only 2 or 3 percent importance. A rule of thumb might be to keep *n* less than eight factors because the higher weights, say 20 percent or more, tend to force the smaller weights to be insignificant. The importance weights, w_j, can be determined in any of a number of ways: a particular individual's subjective belief, available objective factors such as surveys or reports, group composite beliefs such as simple averaging among the group members, and so on.

In addition, a score, s_{ij}, must be determined for how well each project *i* satisfies each criterion *j*. Each score is multiplied by its category weight, and the set of scores is summed to give the total weighted score, $S_i = \Sigma_j s_{ij} w_j$ for each project, *i*, from which the best project is then selected. Typically, a 5-point scale is used to ascertain these scores, though 3-, 7-, and even 9-point scales are sometimes used. The top score, such as 5, is reserved for excellent performance on that criterion such as a return on investment (ROI) of 50 percent or more, or a reliability rating of "superior." The bottom score of 1 is for "poor performance," such as an ROI of 5 percent or less, or a reliability rating of "poor." The middle score of 3 is usually for average or nominal performance (e.g., 15–20% ROI), and 4 is "above average" (21–49% ROI) while 2 is "below average" (6–14% ROI). Notice that the bottom score, 1, on one category may be offset by very high scores on other categories. Any condition that is so bad that it makes a project unacceptable, irrespective of how good it may be on other criteria, is a *constraint*. If a project violates a constraint, it is removed from the set and not scored.

Note two characteristics in these descriptions. First, the categories for each scale need not be in equal intervals—though they should correspond to the subjective beliefs about what constitutes excellent, below average, and so on. Second, the five-point scales can be based on either quantitative or qualitative data, thus allowing the inclusion of financial and other "hard" data (cash flows, net present value, market share growth, costs) as well as "soft" subjective data (fit with the organization's goals, personal preferences, attractiveness, comfort). And again, the soft data also need not be of equal intervals. For example, "superior" may rate a 5 but "OK" may rate only a 2.

The general mathematical form of the weighted factor scoring method is

$$S_i = \sum_{j=1}^{n} s_{ij} w_j$$

where

S_i = the total score of the *i*th project

s_{ij} = the score of the *i*th project on the *j*th criterion

w_j = the weight or importance of the *j*th criterion

Using a Weighted Scoring Model to Select

As a college student, you now find that you need to purch_
to get to your new part-time job and around town more quick.
going to be your "forever" car, and your income is limited; basicali,
reliable wheels. You have two primary criteria of equal importance, c
reliability. You have a limited budget and would like to spend no more .
$4,200 on the car. In terms of reliability, you can't afford to have the car breꞈ
down on your way to work, or for that matter, cost a lot to repair. Beyond these
two major criteria, you consider everything else a "nicety" such as comfort,
heat and air, appearance, handling, and so on. Such niceties you consider only
half as important as either cost or reliability. Table B shows a set of scales you
created for your three criteria, converted into quantitative scores.

Table B: Criteria Scales and Equivalent Scores

	Scores				
Criterion	**1**	**2**	**3**	**4**	**5**
Cost	>$5,000	$4,000–5,000	$3,000–4,000	2,000–3,000	<$2,000
Reliability	poor	mediocre	ok	good	great
Niceties	none	few	some	many	lots

You have identified three possible cars to purchase. Your sorority sister is
graduating this semester and is looking to replace "Betsy," her nice subcom-
pact. She was going to trade it in but would let you have it for $3,400, a fair
deal, except the auto magazines rate its reliability as below average. You have
also seen an ad in the paper for a more reliable Minicar for $4,100 but the ad
indicates it needs some body work. Last, you tore off a phone number from a
campus poster for an old Japanese Import for only $2,900.

In Table C, you have scored each of the cars on each of the criteria, calculated their weighted scores, and summed them to get a total. The weights
for the criteria were obtained from the following logic: If Y is the importance
weight for Cost, then Y is also the importance for Reliability and ½Y is the
importance for Niceties. This results in the formula

$$Y + Y + \tfrac{1}{2}Y = 1.00 \text{ or } Y = 0.4$$

Thus, Cost has 0.4 importance weight, as does Reliability, and Niceties has
0.2 importance.

Table C: Weighted Total Scores for Each Car

	Criteria (and Weights)			
Alternative Car	**Cost (0.4)**	**Reliability (0.4)**	**Niceties (0.2)**	**Total**
Betsy	3 × 0.4 = 1.2	2 × 0.4 = 0.8	4 × 0.2 = 0.8	2.8
Minicar	2 × 0.4 = 0.8	4 × 0.4 = 1.6	1 × 0.2 = 0.2	2.6
Import	4 × 0.4 = 1.6	3 × 0.4 = 1.2	1 × 0.2 = 0.2	3.0

Based on this assessment, it appears that the Import with a total weighted score of 3.0 may best satisfy your need for basic transportation. As shown in Table D, spreadsheets are a particularly useful tool for comparing options using a weighted scoring model.

Table D: Creating a Weighted Scoring Model in a Spreadsheet

	A	B	C	D	E
1	Criteria	Cost	Reliability	Niceties	
2	Weights	0.4	0.4	0.2	
3					
4	Alternative Car	Cost	Reliability	Niceties	Total
5	Betsy	3	2	4	2.8
6	Minicar	2	4	1	2.6
7	Import	4	3	1	3.0
8					
9	Formula				
10	Cell E5	= SUMPRODUCT(B$2:D$2,B5:D5)			
11		(copy to cells E6:E7)			

Project selection is an inherently risky process. Throughout this section we have treated risk by "making allowance" for it. Managing and analyzing risk can be handled in a more straightforward manner. By estimating the highest, lowest, and most likely values that costs, revenues, and other relevant variables may have, and by making some other assumptions about the world, we can estimate outcomes for the projects among which we are trying to make selections. This is accomplished by simulating project outcomes. In Chapter 4, Section 4.5, we will demonstrate how to do this using Crystal Ball® (CB) on a sample selection problem.

> The PM should understand why a project is selected for funding so that the project can be managed to optimize its advantages and achieve its objectives. There are two types of project selection methods: numeric and nonnumeric. Both have their advantages. Of the numeric methods, there are two subtypes—methods that assess the profits associated with a project and more general methods that measure nonmonetary advantages in addition to the monetary pluses. Of the financial methods, the discounted cash flow is best. In our judgment, however, the weighted scoring method is the most useful.

1.6 THE PROJECT PORTFOLIO PROCESS

The Project Portfolio Process (PPP) attempts to link the organization's projects directly to the goals and strategy of the organization. This occurs not only in the project's initiation and planning phases, but also throughout the life cycle of the projects as they are managed and eventually brought to completion. This topic is compared to project and program management in PMBOK's Chapter 1: Introduction. Thus, the PPP is also

PMBOK Guide

Risk

a means for monitoring and controlling the organization's strategic projects, as will be reiterated in Chapter 7: Monitoring and Controlling the Project. On occasion this will mean shutting down projects prior to their completion because their risks have become excessive, their costs have escalated beyond their expected benefits, another (or a new) project does a better job of supporting the goals, or any of a variety of similar reasons. The steps in this process generally follow those described in Longman, Sandahl, and Speir (1999) and Englund and Graham (1999).

Step 1: Establish a Project Council

The main purpose of the Project Council is to establish and articulate a strategic direction for projects. The Council will also be responsible for allocating funds to those projects that support the organization's goals and controlling the allocation of resources and skills to the projects. In addition to senior management, other appropriate members of the Project Council include: project managers of major projects; the head of the Project Management Office (if one exists, and the Council can also be housed in the PMO); particularly relevant general managers, that is, those who can identify key opportunities and risks facing the organization; and finally, those who can derail the progress of the PPP later in the process.

Step 2: Identify Project Categories and Criteria

In this step, various project categories are identified so the mix of projects funded by the organization will be spread appropriately across those areas making major contributions to the organization's goals. In addition, within each category criteria are established to discriminate between very good and even better projects using the weighted scoring model previously discussed. The criteria are also weighted to reflect their relative importance.

The first task in this step is to list the goals of each existing and proposed project— that is, the mission, or purpose, of each project. Relating these to the organization's goals and strategies should allow the Council to identify a variety of categories that are important to achieving the organization's goals. One way to position many of the projects (particularly product/service development projects) is in terms of the extent of product and process changes. Wheelwright and Clark (1992) have developed a matrix called the *aggregate project plan* illustrating these changes, as shown in Figure 1-6. Based on the extent of product change and process change, they identified four separate categories of projects:

Best Practice

1. *Derivative projects* These are projects with objectives or deliverables that are only incrementally different in both product and process from existing offerings. They are often meant to replace current offerings or add an extension to current offerings (lower priced version, upscale version).

2. *Platform projects* The planned outputs of these projects represent major departures from existing offerings in terms of either the product/service itself or the process used to make and deliver it, or both. As such, they become "platforms" for the next generation of organizational offerings, such as a new model of automobile or a new type of insurance plan. They form the basis for follow-on derivative projects that attempt to extend the platform in various dimensions.

3. *Breakthrough projects* Breakthrough projects typically involve a newer technology than platform projects. It may be a "disruptive" technology that is known to the

Figure 1-6 An example aggregate project plan.

industry or something proprietary that the organization has been developing over time. Examples here include the use of fiber-optic cables for data transmission, cash-balance pension plans, and hybrid gasoline-electric automobiles.

4. ***R&D projects*** These projects are "blue-sky," visionary endeavors, oriented toward using newly developed technologies, or existing technologies in a new manner. They may also be for acquiring new knowledge, or developing new technologies themselves.

The size of the projects plotted on the array indicates the size/resource needs of the project, and the shape may indicate another aspect of the project (for example, internal/external, long/medium/short term, or whatever aspect needs to be shown). The numbers indicate the order, or time frame, in which the projects are to be (or were) implemented, separated by category, if desired.

The aggregate project plan can be used to:

- View the mix of projects within each illustrated aspect (shape)

- Analyze and adjust the mix of projects within each category or aspect

- Assess the resource demands on the organization, indicated by the size, timing, and number of projects shown

- Identify and adjust the gaps in the categories, aspects, sizes, and timing of the projects

- Identify potential career paths for developing project managers, such as team members of a derivative project, then team member of a platform project, manager of a derivative project, member of a breakthrough project, and so on

Step 3: Collect Project Data

For each existing and proposed project, assemble the data appropriate to that category's criteria. Include the timing, both date and duration, for expected benefits and resource needs. Use the project plan, a schedule of project activities, past experience, expert opinion, whatever is available to get a good estimate of these data. If the project is new, you may want to fund only enough work on the project to verify the assumptions.

Next, use the criteria score limits, or constraints as described in our discussions of scoring models, to screen out the weaker projects. For example, have costs on existing projects escalated beyond the project's expected benefits? Has the benefit of a project lessened because the organization's goals have changed? Also, screen *in* any projects that do not require deliberation, such as projects mandated by regulations or laws, projects that are competitive or operating necessities (described above), projects required for environmental or personnel reasons, and so on. The fewer projects that need to be compared and analyzed, the easier the work of the Council.

When we discussed financial models and scoring models, we urged the use of multiple criteria when selecting projects. ROI on a project may be lower than the firm's cut-off rate, or even negative, but the project may be a platform for follow-on projects that have very high benefits for the firm. Wheatly (2009) also warns against the use of a single criterion, commonly the return on investment (ROI), to evaluate projects. A project aimed at boosting employee satisfaction will often yield improvements in output, quality, costs, and other such factors. For example, Mindtree, of Bangalore, India, measures benefits on five dimensions; revenue, profit, customer satisfaction, employee satisfaction, and intellectual capital created—in sum, "Have we become a better company?"

Step 4: Assess Resource Availability

Next, assess the availability of both internal and external resources, by type, department, and timing. Note that labor availability should be estimated conservatively. Timing is particularly important, since project resource needs by type typically vary up to 100 percent over the life cycle of projects. Needing a normally plentiful resource at the same moment it is fully utilized elsewhere may doom an otherwise promising project. Eventually, the Council will be trying to balance aggregate project resource needs over future periods with resource availabilities, so timing is as important as the amount of maximum demand and availability. Many managers insist on trying to schedule resource usage as closely as possible to system capacity. This is almost certain to produce a catastrophe (see Chapter 6, Section 6.3, subsection on Resource Loading/Leveling and Uncertainty).

Step 5: Reduce the Project and Criteria Set

In this step, multiple screens are employed to reduce the number of competing projects. As noted earlier, the first screen is each project's support of the organization's goals. Other possible screens might be criteria such as:

- Whether the required competence exists in the organization
- Whether there is a market for the offering
- The likely profitability of the offering
- How risky the project is

- If there is a potential partner to help with the project
- If the right resources are available at the right times
- If the project is a good technological/knowledge fit with the organization
- If the project uses the organization's strengths, or depends on its weaknesses
- If the project is synergistic with other important projects
- If the project is dominated by another existing or proposed project
- If the project has slipped in its desirability since the last evaluation

Step 6: Prioritize the Projects within Categories

Apply the scores and criterion weights to rank the projects within each category. It is acceptable to hold some hard-to-measure criteria out for subjective evaluation, such as riskiness, or development of new knowledge. Subjective evaluations can be translated from verbal to numeric terms easily by the Delphi* Method, pairwise comparisons, or other methods.

It is also possible at this time for the Council to summarize the "returns" from the projects to the organization. This, however, should be done by category, not for each project individually, since different projects are offering different packages of benefits that are not comparable. For example, R&D projects will not have the expected monetary return of derivative projects; yet it would be foolish to eliminate them simply because they do not measure up on this (irrelevant, for this category) criterion.

Step 7: Select the Projects to Be Funded and Held in Reserve

The first task in this step is to determine the mix of projects across the various categories (and aspects, if used) and time periods. Next, be sure to leave some percent (the common 10–15% is often insufficient) of the organization's resource capacity free for new opportunities, crises in existing projects, errors in estimates, and so on. Then allocate the categorized projects in rank order to the categories according to the mix desired. It is usually good practice to include some speculative projects in each category to allow future options, knowledge improvement, additional experience in new areas, and so on. The focus should be on committing to fewer projects but with sufficient funding to allow project completion. Document why late projects were delayed and why any were defended.

Step 8: Implement the Process

The first task in this final step is to make the results of the PPP widely known, including the documented reasons for project cancellations, deferrals, and nonselection as was mentioned earlier. Top management must now make their commitment to this project portfolio process totally clear by supporting the process and its results. This may require a PPP champion near the top of the organization. As project proposers come to understand and appreciate the workings and importance of the PPP, their proposals will more closely fit the profile of the kinds of projects the organization wishes to fund. As this

---

* The Delphi Method, developed more than 40 years ago, is still unequaled as a method for transforming the diverse subjective opinions of a group into a numeric scale. See Dalkey, 1969.

happens, it is important to note that the Council will have to concern itself with the reliability and accuracy of proposals competing for limited funds. Senior management must fully fund the selected projects. It is unethical and inappropriate for senior management to undermine PPP and the Council as well as strategically important projects by playing a game of arbitrarily cutting X percent from project budgets. It is equally unethical and inappropriate to pad potential project budgets on the expectation that they will be arbitrarily cut.

Finally, the process must be repeated on a regular basis. The Council should determine the frequency, which to some extent will depend on the speed of change within the organization's industry. For some industries, quarterly analysis may be best, while in slow-moving industries yearly may be fine.

In an article on competitive intelligence, Gale (2008b) reports that Cisco Systems Inc. constantly tracks industry trends, competitors, the stock market, and end users to stay ahead of their competition and to know which potential projects to fund. Pharmaceutical companies are equally interested in knowing which projects to drop if competitors are too far ahead of them, thereby saving millions of dollars in development and testing costs.

Hildebrand (2008) suggests giving another task to the Project Council (or the PMO): formulating a change-response strategy so the company can modify the project portfolio quickly when unexpected events occur. Although significant events seem to occur without warning, most, but not all, significant events follow a stream of lesser events or cues that might have been identified through standard risk identification techniques. Advanced preparation to define the types of data, control, and execution resources needed to make wise decisions in the midst of a crisis will pay substantial dividends. Practice exercises or simulations can enhance the firm's ability for effective crisis response. If project staffs understand how the portfolio was originally built and why specific projects were selected or dropped, they will be more likely to understand what a crisis implies for the portfolio and to support crisis-related decisions.

> Projects are often subdivisions of major programs. Long-run success is determined by the organization's portfolio of projects. Classified by the extent of innovation in product and process, there are four types of projects: derivative, breakthrough, platform, and R & D projects. The actual mix of projects is a direct expression of the organization's competitive strategy. A proper mix of project categories can help ensure its long-run competitive position. It is important for the Project Council or PMO to preplan project portfolio adjustments to respond to significant changes in the state of competition and other industrial crises.

1.7 THE MATERIALS IN THIS TEXT

When reading a text, it is helpful to understand how the book is organized and where it will take the reader. Following this introductory chapter, our attention goes to the various roles the PM must play and the ways projects are organized. Chapter 2 focuses on the behavioral and structural aspects of projects and their management. It describes the PM's roles as communicator, negotiator, and manager. It also includes a discussion of project management as a profession and reports briefly on the Project Management Institute (PMI), the PM's professional organization. Then attention turns to the ways in which projects can be organized within the parent establishment. *Matrix organization* is discussed at length as are the conflicts and managerial problems that matrix organizations tend to foster. Finally, the chapter moves to the *project team*: its purposes and the widespread use of transdisciplinary teams. Using transdisciplinary teams to plan and carry out the project is a source of both creativity and conflict. The process of building effective teams is briefly covered.

The remainder of the book is designed to conform to the life cycle of any project, whatever the shape of the life cycle curve. Chapter 3 covers the process of *planning and launching the project*, construction of the *work breakdown structure* (WBS), and *responsibility charts*. These activities require the project team to estimate resource and time requirements for accomplishing what the project plan has described. Chapter 4 not only discusses the construction of a *project budget*, it also presents a method of improving one's estimating skills. Because any estimate is a forecast, the allied subject of risk management is introduced.

Chapter 5 covers scheduling, the Program Evaluation Review Technique (PERT), the Critical Path Method (CPM), and Gantt charts, the most common ways of illustrating the *project schedule*. Schedules will be calculated under conditions of uncertainty in two ways: (1) using standard probability theory, and (2) using simulation. In Chapter 6 *resource allocation* is discussed. To begin, we consider the problem of *crashing* a project, i.e., using additional resources in order to shorten project duration. Then we deal with two fundamental problems of resource management. First, a schedule of resource usage must be prepared (a.k.a., *resource loading*). Second, we adjust the resource loads to avoid gluts and shortages of valuable resources, (a.k.a., *resource leveling*). The problems of resource usage when there are multiple projects competing for a limited resource pool are then covered, as are ways of dealing with these problems. The chapter ends with a discussion of Goldratt's *Critical Chain* (1997).

The subjects of Chapter 7 are monitoring and controlling projects. The nature of project data collection is explained, and various types of project reports, including *earned value reports*, are illustrated and discussed. Following this, we cover the general purposes and mechanisms for project control. The chapter ends with a section devoted to the *control of change* on a project. It is here that we discuss "*scope creep*" and how to control it.

Chapter 8 deals with *evaluating*, *auditing*, and *terminating* projects. The project team often fears evaluation and auditing. Team members usually equate these activities with fault finding, but when correctly used they are valuable aids for the PM and team. Project termination is usually ignored or treated as a trivial problem in practice—and in most works on project management. We feel it is an important and complex process that may cause serious problems if not handled properly.

Throughout this book there are illustrations of the tools and reports used by project managers. Many of these were produced using Microsoft Project® (MSP), Crystal Ball® (CB), and Excel®. (All illustrations and applications generated by MSP, CB, and Excel®, or any other application software will be clearly identified.) There is a large number of spreadsheets and literally hundreds of project management software packages on the market. Most of them perform with reasonable competence in the tasks for which they were designed. Of the packages intended for overall project management, MSP is by far the favorite, with roughly half the total market. There is also a large number of specialized software packages, for example, report generators, and special risk management packages. Most are compatible with MSP or Excel®, often seamlessly so, and we mention some of them when relevant. In the past decade or two, spreadsheet software has become highly sophisticated. Excel®, for example, can perform simulations and statistical analysis as well as handle the usual arithmetic, accounting, and financial calculations.

Risk

When one reads the literature of project management, one sees much about *risk management*. Too often, it may seem to the reader that risk management is a highly specific task. It isn't. Risk management is a reference to a class of ideas, methods, and techniques that aids the management of projects being carried out in an uncertain world. Outside factors can affect projects in a wide variety of ways, and so our discussions of risk management cannot be restricted to a chapter on the subject. They appear throughout the book. Tools and techniques are introduced as they are needed to deal with specific problems. The reader should note that these tools have wide application beyond project management and most are valuable for the general manager as well as the PM.

With this introduction, let us begin our study of project management.

REVIEW QUESTIONS

1. What is the primary role of a project manager?

2. Contrast a project from a nonproject.

3. Contrast win-lose negotiation, lose-lose negotiation, and win-win negotiation and explain why the latter is so important in project management.

4. Identify the three goals of a project and describe how the project manager achieves them. What does it mean for a project to be "overdetermined?"

5. Contrast the two types of project life cycles and discuss why it is important to know which type the current project is following.

6. How does the weighted scoring approach avoid the drawbacks of the NPV approach? Can the two approaches be combined? How? What weights would be appropriate if they were combined?

7. What advantages are lost if the sum of the weights in a weighted scoring approach does not add to 1.0? Why is it suggested that factors with less than 2 percent or 3 percent impact not be considered in this approach?

8. Draw a distinction between a project and a program. Why is the distinction important?

9. Why is it important for a project to have "flexibility"?

10. Why are R&D projects in a company's Aggregate Project Plan significantly different in type from the firm's Derivative, Breakthrough, and Platform projects?

DISCUSSION QUESTIONS

11. Contrast the three types of nonnumeric project selection methods. Could any specific case combine two of them, such as the sacred cow and the operating necessity, or the comparative benefits and the competitive necessity?

12. What errors in a firm's project portfolio might the Wheelwright and Clark aggregate project plan graphically identify?

13. You are the project manager of a team of software specialists working on a project to produce a piece of application software in the field of project management. Give some examples of things that might go wrong on such a project and the sorts of trade-offs you might have to make.

14. In Figure 1-6, what distribution of large and small circles and squares across the four boxes would characterize a strong, well-positioned product development business? A weak business?

15. Give several examples of projects found in your city, region, or country—avoiding those used as examples in the chapter.

16. For each of the projects identified in the answer to Question 15, is the life cycle for the project S-shaped or J-shaped?

17. Construct a list of factors, conditions, and circumstances you think might be important for a manufacturing firm to evaluate during the project selection process. Do the same for a computer repair shop.

18. How might you use project management for doing a major school work assignment?

PROBLEMS

19. A 4-year financial project is forecast to have net cash inflows of $20,000; $25,000; $30,000; and $50,000 in the next 4 years. It will cost $75,000 to implement the project, payable at the beginning of the project. If the required rate of return is 0.2, conduct a discounted cash flow calculation to determine the NPV.

20. A company has established a project team to identify a location for a new manufacturing facility. Use a weighted scoring model to analyze three candidate locations (A, B, C) for setting up the new factory. The relative weights for each criterion are shown in the following table. A score of 1 represents unfavorable, 2 satisfactory, and 3 favorable.

		Location		
Category	Weight	A	B	C
Labor costs	20	1	2	3
Labor productivity	20	2	3	1
Labor supply	10	2	1	3
Union relations	10	3	3	2
Material supply	10	2	1	1
Transport costs	25	1	2	3
Infrastructure	5	2	2	2

21. (a) Compare your answer in Problem 20 to the answer you would have found if you had used an unweighted, 0-1 scoring model. Assume that a score of 1 means does not qualify and a 2 or 3 means it does qualify.

(b) Next, revise the unweighted model by deleting all categories that, as recommended, have a weight of less than 20 percent. Compare to your answer to (a) above and also Problem 20. Which method seems best?

22. Using a spreadsheet for Problem 20, find the following:

(a) What would be your recommendation if the weight for the transportation cost went down to 10 and the weight for union relations went up to 25?

(b) Suppose location A received a score of 3 for transport cost and location C received a score of 2 for transport cost. Would your recommendation change under these circumstances?

(c) The VP of Finance has looked at your scoring model and feels that tax considerations should be included in the model with a weight of 15. In addition, the VP has scored the locations on tax considerations as follows: A-3, B-2, and C-1. How does this affect your recommendation?

23. Nina has been asked to lead a team that has been tasked with finding a new location for a boutique concept her company would like to test. The team has identified four candidate shopping centers to locate the new boutique in. Some cater to a higher class of clientele than others, some are in an indoor mall, some have a much greater volume than others, and, of course, rent varies considerably. Because of the nature of the boutique, the team has decided that the class of clientele is the most important consideration. Following this, the team considered expenses and rent as the next most important criterion—probably 90 percent as important as clientele. An indoor, temperature-controlled mall is a big help for stores such as the concept being considered where 70 percent of sales are from passersby slowly strolling and window shopping. Thus, the team rates this as about 95 percent as important as rent. Last, a higher volume of shoppers means more potential sales; thus the team rates this factor as 80 percent as important as rent.

As an aid in visualizing her location alternatives, the team has constructed the following table. A "good" is scored as 3, "fair" as 2, and "poor" as 1. Use a weighted score model to help Nina and her team come to a decision.

	Location			
	1	2	3	4
Class of clientele	fair	good	poor	good
Rent	good	fair	poor	good
Indoor mall	good	poor	good	poor
Volume	good	fair	good	poor

24. Using a spreadsheet for Problem 23, determine how Nina's ability to negotiate a lower rent at location 3, thereby raising its ranking to "good," will affect the overall rankings of the four locations.

INCIDENT FOR DISCUSSION

Broken Welds

A manufacturer of mountain bicycles designed an automated system for welding bike frames. For 3 years, the system worked nicely, handling about 1000 frames per shift. Production was scheduled for two shifts per day. The system was designed to weld the frame and then to check the quality of each weld. The welded frames were then transported to another plant for assembly.

Recently, a few of the frames had failed. Careful testing showed that a foreign substance in the welding rod purchased from an outside vendor possibly contributed to the failure. When checked, however, the rods conformed to the specifications given to the Purchasing Department and guaranteed by the vendor. The Chief Engineer ordered the Production Department's Project Leader, Alison Passette, to create a project immediately to find out precisely what was causing the failures and to find a way to solve the problem. This project was to take priority over all other projects in the department.

Alison was familiar with the Chief Engineer's tendency to overreact to any glitches in the production process, so she decided to determine the impact of the proposed project on all the other projects in the department. She also discussed the problem with Ken Kelsey, one of her welding experts, who felt sure he could solve the welding problems by determining what foreign substance, if any, caused the problem. He could then set up a system to detect the presence of the substance and reweld the affected frames. Of course, he added, they would also have to change their specifications for the welding rod to eliminate the chemical responsible for the failures.

Questions: What information does Alison need to determine the probable impact of Kelsey's proposed project on the other projects in the department? Should her findings affect her decision about Kelsey's project? How?

C A S E

United Screen Printers

United Screen Printers (USP) produces a wide range of decals for displaying promotional messages on fleet vehicles (including delivery vans, eighteen-wheelers, and aircraft). Its decals range from flat-color designs to full-color photographic reproductions.

Although it is one of the oldest forms of printing, screen printing is superior to most of the more modern approaches because it permits making heavier deposits of ink onto a surface, resulting in more vibrant and longer lasting finishes. Screen printing works by blocking out areas on a silk screen so that ink passes through only the unblocked areas to make an impression on the vinyl decal.

Many in the industry believe that the economics of fleet graphics makes them an extremely attractive form of advertising and should lead to their continued penetration of a largely untapped market. One industry source estimated that the cost of fleet graphics works out to be $2.84 per 1,000,000 visual impressions. Given the highly cost effective nature of using fleet graphics as a form of advertising, it is speculated that organizations will increasingly exploit this form of advertising. In addition, as organizations become better aware of this advertising medium, it is likely they will want to change their message more frequently. According to managers at USP, this may be one of the major factors that is apparently driving the competition to focus more on short lead-times and prices, and less on decal durability.

USP is about to begin its annual evaluation of proposed projects. Six projects have been proposed as described below.

1. *Purchase new large press*. There is currently a 3½- to 4-week backlog in the screen printing department. The result of this is that USP's total lead-time is 4 to 6 weeks in comparison to an industry average lead-time of 3.5 to 4 weeks. In a typical month, USP ships 13 percent of its orders early, 38 percent on-time, and 49 percent late. It has been estimated that 75 percent of the backlog is waiting for press 6, the largest press in the shop. Furthermore, press 6 is in dire need of replacement parts but USP has been unable thus far to locate a source for these parts. Given the problem of finding replacement parts and the fact that the press is somewhat outdated, this proposal calls for purchasing a new large press for $160,000. Based on estimates that a new large press could process jobs 50 percent to 100 percent faster than press 6, it is calculated that the payback period for a new large press would be 1 year.

2. *Build new headquarters*. USP's CEO fervently believes that the company needs to have a strong corporate identity. He therefore purchased land and had plans drawn up for the construction of a new

corporate headquarters. Analysis of the new head-quarters indicated that although it would improve operating efficiencies, the savings generated would not pay for the new building (estimated to cost $4 million). Many of the board members viewed the project as too risky since it would increase the company's debt as a percent of capital from almost zero to 50 percent.

3. *Pursue ISO 9000 certification.* This proposal also comes from USP's CEO. ISO 9000 is a set of standards that provides customers with some assurance that a supplier follows accepted business practices. In some industries, obtaining ISO 9000 certification is essential, such as in industries that export to Europe and the domestic automobile industry. It was less clear what competitive advantage pursuing ISO 9000 would provide USP at this time. On the other hand, the process alone would help it document and perhaps improve its processes. The cost of this initiative was estimated to be $250,000 to $300,000 and would take 1 year to complete.

4. *Develop formal procedure for mixing inks.* This proposal comes from USP's plant manager. At present, mixing inks is a highly specialized skill that consumes 2 to 3 hours of the team leader's time each day. This project would focus on developing ink formulas to make the task of mixing inks more routine, and less specialized and subjective. The team leader is paid

$25,000 annually. The cost of pursuing this project is estimated to be $10,000.

5. *Purchase and install equipment to produce four-color positives in-house.* The lead-time to have positives made by an outside supplier is typically one week and costs $1,500 to $6,000. According to this proposal, the cost of purchasing the equipment to produce four-color positives in-house would be approximately $150,000 plus $25,000 for installation and training. The variable costs of producing positives in house are estimated to be $375 per job. If produced in-house, the lead-time for the four-color positives would be approximately an hour-and-a-half.

6. *Purchase inkjet printers.* An alternative to purchasing a new screen printing press is to add capacity based on newer technology. Given the inkjet's production rate, six inkjet printers at a cost of $140,000 would be needed to provide the equivalent capacity of a new large screen printing press. The major disadvantage of the inkjet printers is that compared to the screen printing process, the outdoor durability is more limited. In general, inkjet printers are more economical for small orders, while screen printing presses are more economical for large orders.

USP currently has annual sales of approximately $7 million. It typically allocates up to 10 percent of sales to these types of projects.

QUESTIONS

1. Construct an aggregate project plan for USP.
2. What criteria would you recommend USP use in selecting its projects this year?
3. Based on your recommended criteria and the aggregate project plan, what projects would you recommend

USP fund this year? Are there any types of projects you would recommend USP pursue that were not proposed?
4. What, if any, additional information would you want in making your recommendations? How would you go about obtaining this information?

C A S E

Handstar Inc.

Handstar Inc. was created a little over 4 years ago by two college roommates to develop apps for smartphones. It has since grown to ten employees with annual sales approaching $1.5 million. Handstar's original product was an expense report app that allowed users to record expenses on their smartphone and then export

their expenses into a spreadsheet that then created an expense report in one of five standard formats. Based on the success of its first product, Handstar subsequently developed three additional apps: an app for tracking and measuring the performance of investment portfolios, a calendar app, and an email app.

The two founders of Handstar have recently become concerned about the competitiveness of the firm's offerings, particularly since none of them has been updated since their initial launch. Therefore, they asked the directors of product development and marketing to work together and prepare a list of potential projects for updating Handstar's current offerings as well as to develop ideas for additional apps. The directors were also asked to estimate the development costs of the various projects, product revenues, and the likelihood that Handstar could retain or obtain a leadership position for the given app. Also, with the increasing popularity of mobile computing, the founders asked the directors to evaluate the extent to which the products made use of the Web.

The product development and marketing directors identified three projects related to updating Handstar's existing products. The first project would integrate Handstar's current calendar app with its email app. Integrating these two apps into a single app would provide a number of benefits to users such as allowing them to automatically enter the dates of meetings into the calendar based on the content of an email message. The directors estimated that this project would require 1250 hours of software development time. Revenues in the first year of the product's launch were estimated to be $750,000. However, because the directors expected that a large percentage of the users would likely upgrade to this new product soon after its introduction, they projected that annual sales would decline by 10 percent annually in subsequent years. The directors speculated that Handstar was moderately likely to obtain a leadership position in email/calendar apps if this project were undertaken and felt this app made moderate use of the Web.

The second project related to updating the expense report app. The directors estimated that this project would require 400 hours of development time. Sales were estimated to be $250,000 in the first year and to increase 5 percent annually in subsequent years. The directors speculated that completing this project would almost certainly maintain Handstar's leadership position in the expense report category, although it made little use of the Web.

The last product enhancement project related to enhancing the existing portfolio tracking app. This project would require 750 hours of development time and would generate first-year sales of $500,000. Sales were projected to increase 5 percent annually in subsequent years. The directors felt this project would have a high probability of maintaining Handstar's leadership position in this category and the product would make moderate use of the Web.

The directors also identified three opportunities for new products. One project was the development of a spreadsheet app that could share files with spreadsheet programs written for PCs. Developing this app would require 2500 hours of development time. First-year sales were estimated to be $1,000,000 with an annual growth rate of 10 percent. While this app did not make use of the Web, the directors felt that Handstar had a moderate chance of obtaining a leadership position in this product category.

The second new product opportunity identified was an app for browsing the Web. Developing this app would require 1875 development hours. First-year sales were estimated to be $2,500,000 with an annual growth rate of 15 percent. Although this app made extensive use of the Web, the directors felt that there was a very low probability that Handstar could obtain a leadership position in this product category.

The final product opportunity identified was a trip planner app. This product would require 6250 hours of development time. First-year sales were projected to be $1,300,000 with an annual growth rate of 5 percent. Like the Web browser app, the directors felt that there was a low probability that Handstar could obtain a leadership position in this category, although the program would make extensive use of the Web.

In evaluating the projects, the founders believed it was reasonable to assume each product had a 3-year life. They also felt that a discount rate of 12 percent fairly reflected the company's cost of capital. An analysis of payroll records indicated that the cost of software developers is $52 per hour including salary and fringe benefits. Currently there are four software developers on staff, and each works 2500 hours per year.

QUESTIONS

1. Which projects would you recommend Handstar pursue based on the NPV approach?

2. Assume the founders weigh a project's NPV twice as much as both obtaining/retaining a leadership position and making use of the Web. Use the weighted factor scoring method to rank these projects. Which projects would you recommend Handstar pursue?

3. In your opinion is hiring an additional software development engineer justified?

BIBLIOGRAPHY

ADAMS, J. R., and S. E. BARNDT. "Behavioral Implications of the Project Life Cycle." In D. I. Cleland, and W. R. King, eds., *Project Management Handbook*. New York: Van Nostrand Reinhold, 1983.

BOZNAK, R. G. "Management of Projects: A Giant Step Beyond Project Management." *PM Network*, January 1996.

DALKEY, N.C. *The Delphi Method: An Experimental Study of Group Opinion* (RM-5888-PR) Santa Monica, CA: The Rand Corporation, June 1969.

ENGLUND, R. L., and R. J. GRAHAM. "From Experience: Linking Projects to Strategy." *Journal of Product Innovation Management*, Vol. 16, No. 1, 1999.

FISHER, R., and W. URY. *Getting to Yes*. Harmondsworth, Middlesex, G. B.: Penguin Books, 1983. (This is a classic book on win-win negotiations, in addition to being good reading.)

GALE, S. F. "The Great Unknown." *PM Network*, May 2008a.

GALE, S. F. "In the Know." *PM Network*, July 2008b.

GOLDRATT, E. M. *Critical Chain*. Great Barrington, MA: North River, 1997.

GREEN, S. G. "Top Management Support of R&D Projects: A Strategic Leadership Perspective." *IEEE Transactions on Engineering Management*, August 1995. (What Prof. Green has to say about the role of a project champion in support of R&D projects applies equally well to all sorts of projects.)

HATFIELD, M. "Danger Ahead." *PM Network*, March, 2008.

HAYES, R., and W. J. ABERNATHY. "Managing Our Way to Economic Decline." *Harvard Business Review*, July–August 1980. (An excellent, persuasive, and timeless blast at those who focus their business decisions solely on short-run profits.)

HELIN, A. F., and W. E. SOUDER. "Experimental Test of a Q-Sort Procedure for Prioritizing R&D Projects." *IEEE Transactions on Engineering Management*, November 1974.

HILDEBRAND, C. "In Flux." *PM Network*, December 2008.

JANDT, F. E. *Win-Win Negotiating*. New York: John Wiley, 1987.

KAPLAN, R. S. "Must CIM Be Justified by Faith Alone?" *Harvard Business Review*, March–April 1986.

KLOPPENBORG, T. J., and S. J. MANTEL, Jr. "Trade-offs on Projects: They May Not Be What You Think." *Project Management Journal*, March 1990.

LEVINE, H. A. "Enterprise Project Management: What Do Users Need? What Can They Have?" *PM Network*, July 1998. ·

LONGMAN, A., D. SANDAHL, and W. SPEIR. "Preventing Project Proliferation." *PM Network*, July 1999.

MEREDITH, J. R., and S. J. MANTEL, Jr. *Project Management: A Managerial Approach*, 8th ed., New York: John Wiley, 2012.

MOYER, R. C., J. R. McGUIGAN, and W. J. KRETLOW. *Contemporary Financial Management*, 10th ed., Cincinnati: South-Western, 2008.

PENNYPACKER, J. S., and K. P. GRANT. "Project Management Maturity: An Industry Benchmark." *Project Management Journal*, March 2003. (This article, based on a survey of 123 firms, utilizes a two-dimensional framework to assess organizational project delivery capability. Organizations can use the results of the study to benchmark their level of project management maturity.)

Project Management Institute Standards Committee. A. *Guide to the Project Management Body of Knowledge PMBOK® Guide*, 5th ed., Newtown Square, PA: Project Management Institute, 2013. (A must own, and read, by every project manager.)

RAIFFA, H. *The Art and Science of Negotiation*. Cambridge: Belknap/Harvard Press, 1982. [Like Fisher and Ury (1983), this is a classic on the subject of win-win negotiation. Probably the most influential book in its field, and justly so.]

SHARPE, P., and T. KEELIN. "How SmithKline Beecham Makes Better Resource-Allocation Decisions." *Harvard Business Review*, March–April 1998. (An excellent process for selecting projects as well as for constructing a project portfolio. The ability to implement the process depends on a fairly sophisticated senior management team.)

SHEFFI, Y. *The Resilient Enterprise*, Cambridge, MA: The MIT Press, 2005.

WHEATLY, M. "Beyond the Numbers." *PM Network*, August 2009.

WHEELWRIGHT, S. C., and K. B. CLARK. "Creating Project Plans to Focus Product Development." *Harvard Business Review*, March–April 1992.

2

The Manager, the Organization, and the Team

Once a project has been selected, the next step is for senior management to choose a project manager (PM). It is the PM's job to make sure that the project is properly planned, implemented, and completed—and these activities will be the subjects of the chapters that follow this one.

While PMs are sometimes chosen prior to a project's selection, the more typical case is that the selection is announced following a meeting between senior management and the prospective PM. This appointment sometimes comes as a complete surprise to the candidate whose only obvious qualification for the job is not being otherwise fully occupied on a task more important than the project (Patterson, 1991). At this meeting, the senior manager describes the project and emphasizes its importance to the parent organization, and also to the future career of the prospective PM. (In the language of the Mafia, "It's an offer you can't refuse.") Occasionally, the senior manager will add further information about the project including a fixed budget, due date, and scope. This is an offer you must refuse, as politely as possible, because, as we noted in Chapter 1, some flexibility is required and there is little chance that you can be successful in meeting all the overdetermined targets.

After a brief consideration of the project, the PM comes to a tentative decision about what talents and knowledge are apt to be required. The PM and/or a senior manager then calls a meeting of people who have the requisite talent and knowledge, and the planning begins. This is the *launch meeting,* and we will delay further consideration of it until Chapter 3 in which we take up the planning process in detail. First, we must examine the skills required by the person who will lead a team of individuals to carry out a carefully coordinated set of activities in an organizational setting seemingly designed expressly to prevent cooperation. It is helpful if we make a few mild assumptions to ease the following discussions. First, assume that the project's parent organization is medium-to large-size, and is functionally organized (i.e., organized into functions such as marketing, manufacturing, R&D, human resources, and the like). Further assume that the project has some well-defined components or technologies and that the project's output is being delivered to an arm's-length client. These assumptions are not critical. They merely give a context to our discussions.

Before we proceed, an experienced project manager has suggested that we share with the reader one of her reactions to the materials in this book. To the student or the inexperienced PM, it is the project budgets, the schedules with Gantt charts and PERT/CPM networks, the reports and project management software, and the mysteries of resource allocation to multiple projects that appear to be the meat of the PM's job. But these things are not hard to learn, and once understood, can, for the most part, be managed by making appropriate inputs to project management software. The hard part of project management is playing the many roles of the PM. The hard part is negotiating with stubborn functional managers and clients who have their own legitimate axes to grind. The hard part is keeping the peace among project team members, each of whom knows, and is quick to tell, the proper ways to do things. The hard part is dealing with senior managers who allow their wild guesses about budget and scope made in the early consideration of the project during the selection process to become fixed in concrete. The hard part is being surrounded by the chaos of trying to run a project in the midst of a confused mass of activity representing the normal business of the organization. These are the things we discuss in this chapter, because *these are the hard parts*. PMBOK covers the material in this chapter primarily in Chapter 9 on Human Resources.

PMBOK Guide

2.1   THE PM'S ROLES

Trade-Offs

In the previous chapter it was noted that the primary role of the PM was to manage trade-offs. In addition to managing trade-offs, the PM also has several other important roles including serving as a facilitator, communicator, virtual project manager, and convener and chair of meetings.

Facilitator

First, to understand the PM'S roles, it is useful to compare the PM with a functional manager. The head of a function such as manufacturing or marketing directs the activities of a well-established unit or department of the firm. Presumably trained or raised from the ranks, the functional manager has expertise in the technology being managed. He is an accountant, or an industrial engineer, or a marketing researcher, or a shop foreman, or a . . . . The functional manager's role, therefore, is mainly that of supervisor (literally "overseer"). Because the project's place in the parent organization is often not well defined and does not seem to fit neatly in any one functional division, neither is the PM's place neatly defined. Because projects are often multidisciplinary, the PM rarely has technical competence in more than one or two of the several technologies involved in the project. As a result, the PM is not a competent overseer and thus has a different role. The PM is a *facilitator*.

Facilitator vs. Supervisor The PM must ensure that those who work on the project have the appropriate knowledge and resources, including that most precious resource, time, to accomplish their assigned responsibilities. The work of a facilitator does not stop with these tasks. For reasons that will be apparent later in this chapter, the project is often beset with conflict—conflict between members of the project team, conflict between the team and senior managers (particularly managers of the functional divisions), conflict with the client and other outsiders. The PM must manage these conflicts by negotiating resolution of them.

Actually, the once sharp distinction between the manager-as-facilitator and the manager-as-supervisor has been softened in recent years. With the slow but steady adoption of the participative management philosophy, the general manager has become more and more like the project manager. In particular, responsibility for the planning and organization of specific tasks is given to the individuals or groups that must perform them, always constrained, of course, by company policy, legality, and conformity to high ethical standards. The manager's responsibility is to make sure that the required resources are available and that the task is properly concluded. The transition from traditional authoritarian management to facilitation continues because facilitation is more effective as a managerial style.

A second important distinction between the PM and the traditional manager is that the former uses the *systems approach* and the latter adopts the *analytical approach* to understanding and solving problems. The analytical approach centers on understanding the bits and pieces in a system. It prompts study of the molecules, then atoms, then electrons, and so forth. The systems approach includes study of the bits and pieces, but also an understanding of how they fit together, how they interact, and how they affect and are affected by their environment. The traditionalist manages his or her group (a *subsystem* of the organization) with a desire to optimize the group's performance. The systems approach manager conducts the group so that it contributes to total system optimization. It has been well demonstrated that if all subsystems are optimized, a condition known as *suboptimization*, the total system is not even close to optimum performance. (Perhaps the ultimate example of suboptimization is "The operation was a success, but the patient died.") We take this opportunity to recommend to you an outstanding book on business, *The Goal*, by Goldratt and Cox (1992). It is an easy-to-read novel and a forceful statement on the power of the systems approach as well as the dangers of suboptimization.

Systems Approach   To be successful, the PM must adopt the systems approach. Consider that the project is a system composed of tasks (subsystems) which are, in turn, composed of subtasks, and so on. The system, a project, exists as a subsystem of the larger system, a program, that is a subsystem in the larger system, a firm, which is . . . and so on. Just as the project's objectives influence the nature of the tasks and the tasks influence the nature of the subtasks, so does the program and, above it, the organization influence the nature of the project. To be effective, the PM must understand these influences and their impacts on the project and its deliverables.*

Think for a moment about designing a new airplane—a massive product development project—without knowing a great deal about its power plant, its instrumentation, its electronics, its fuel subsystems—or about the plane's desired mission, the intended takeoff and landing facilities, the intended carrying capacity, and intended range. One cannot even start the design process without a clear understanding of the subsystems that might be a part of the plane and the larger systems of which it will be a part as well as those that comprise its environment.

Given a project and a deliverable with specifications that result from its intended use in a larger system within a known or assumed environment, the PM's job is straightforward. Find out what tasks must be accomplished to produce the deliverable. Find out what resources are required and how those resources may be obtained. Find out what personnel are needed to carry out production and where they may be obtained.

---

*For those not familiar with general systems thinking, we strongly recommend C. West Churchman's highly readable softback (1979) or an excellent text by Schoderbek, Schoderbek, and Kefalas (1990). Both are out of print but are widely available in university libraries and from Amazon.com.

Find out when the deliverable must be completed. In other words, the PM is responsible for planning, organizing, staffing, budgeting, directing, and controlling the project; the PM "manages" it. But others, the functional managers for example, will staff the project by selecting the people who will be assigned to work on the project. The functional managers also may develop the technical aspects of the project's design and dictate the technology used to produce it. The logic and illogic of this arrangement will be revisited later in this chapter.

Micromanagement   At times, the PM may work for a program manager who closely supervises and second-guesses every decision the PM makes. Such bosses are also quite willing to help by instructing the PM exactly what to do. This unfortunate condition is known as *micromanagement* and is one of the deadly managerial sins. The PM's boss rationalizes this overcontrol with such statements as "Don't forget, I'm responsible for this project," "This project is very important to the firm," or "I have to keep my eye on everything that goes on around here." Such statements deny the value of delegation and assume that everyone except the boss is incompetent. This overweening self-importance practically ensures mediocre performance, if not outright project failure. Any project successes will be claimed by the boss. Failures will be blamed on the subordinate PM.

There is little a PM can do about the "My way or the highway" boss except to polish the résumé or request a transfer. (It is a poor career choice to work for a boss who will not allow you to succeed.) As we will see later in this chapter, the most successful project teams tend to adopt a *collegial style*. Intrateam conflict is minimized or used to enhance team creativity, cooperation is the norm, and the likelihood of success is high.

Communicator

The PM must be a person who can handle responsibility. The PM is responsible to the project team, to senior management, to the client, and to anyone else who may have a stake in the project's performance or outcomes. Consider, if you will, the Central Arizona Project (CAP). This public utility moves water from the Colorado River to Phoenix, several other Arizona municipalities, and to some American Indian reservations. The water is transported by a system of aqueducts, reservoirs, pipes, and pumping stations. Besides the routine delivery of water, almost everything done at CAP is a project. Most of the projects are devoted to the construction, repair, and maintenance of their system. Now consider a PM's responsibilities. A maintenance team, for instance, needs resources in a timely fashion so that maintenance can be carried out according to a precise schedule. The PM's clients are municipalities. The drinking public (water, of course) is a highly interested stakeholder. The system is even subject to partisan political turmoil because CAP-supplied water is used as a political football in Tucson.

The PM is in the middle of this muddle of responsibility and must manage the project in the face of all these often-conflicting interests. CAP administration, the project teams, the municipalities (and their Native American counterparts), and the public all communicate with each other—often contentiously. In general, we often call this the "context" of the project. More accurately, given the systems approach we have adopted, this is the *environment* of the project.

Figure 2-1 shows the PM's position and highlights the communication problem involved in any project. The solid lines denote the PM's communication channels. The dotted lines denote communication paths for the other parties-at-interest in the project. Problems arise when some of these parties propagate communications that may mislead other parties, or directly conflict with other messages in the system. It is the PM's responsibility to introduce some order into this communication mess.

Figure 2-1 Communication paths between a project's parties-at-interest.

For example, assume that senior management calls for tighter cost control or even for a cost reduction. The project team may react emotionally with a complaint that "They want us to cut back on project quality!" The PM must intervene to calm ruffled team feathers and, perhaps, ask a senior manager to reassure the project team that high quality is an organizational objective though not every gear, cog, and cam needs to be gold-plated.

Trade-Offs

Similarly, the client may drop in to check on a project and blithely ask a team member, "Would it be possible to alter the specs to include such-and-such?" The team member may think for a moment about the technical problems involved and then answer quite honestly, "Yeah, that could be done." Again, the PM must intervene— if and when the question and answer come to light—to determine the cost of making such a change, as well as the added time that would be required. The PM must then ask whether the client wishes to alter the project scope given the added cost and delayed delivery. This scenario is so common it has a name, *scope creep*. It is the PM's nightmare.

Virtual Project Manager

More and more often, project teams are geographically dispersed. Many projects are international, and team members may be on different continents, for example, aircraft engine design and engine construction. Many are carried out by different organizations in different locations. For example, Boeing created global supplier/strategic partner teams for their new 787 Dreamliner aircraft to co-design and produce various portions of the new plane: the vertical fin in Seattle, WA, the cockpit in Wichita, KS, the wings in Japan, and the center fuselage in Italy. Similarly, many projects involve different divisions of one firm where the divisions are in different cities. These geographically dispersed projects are often referred to as "virtual projects, possibly because so much of the intra-project communication is conducted via email, through websites, by telephone or video conferencing, and other high-technology methods. In recent decades, the international dispersion of industry, "globalization," has dramatically increased the communication problems, adding the need for translators to the virtual communication networks. An interesting view of "virtual" people who work in one country but live in another (often on another continent) is given in a *Wall Street Journal* article (Flynn, 1999).

Long-distance communication is commonplace and no longer prohibitively expensive. It may, however, be beset with special problems. In the case of written and voice-only communication (and even in video conferencing when the camera is not correctly aimed), the communicators cannot see one another. In such cases we realize how much we depend on feedback—the facial expression and body language that let us know if our messages are received and with what level of acceptance. Two-way, real-time communication is the most effective way to transmit information or instructions.

For virtual projects to succeed, communication between PM and project team must be frequent, open, and two-way.

The PM's responsibility for communication with senior management poses special problems for any PM without fairly high levels of self-confidence. Formal and routine progress reports aside (cf. Chapter 7), it is the PM's job to keep senior management up to date on the state of the project. It is particularly important that the PM keep management informed of any problems affecting the project—or any problem likely to affect the project in the future. A golden rule for anyone is **"Never let the boss be surprised!"** Violations of this rule will cost the PM credibility, trust, and possibly his or her job. Where there is no trust, effective communication ceases. Senior management must be informed about a problem in order to assist in its solution. The timing of this information should be at the earliest point a problem seems likely to occur. Any later is too late. This builds trust between the PM and senior managers. The PM who is trusted by the *project champion* and can count on assistance when organizational clout is needed is twice blessed.

The PM is also responsible to the client. Clients are motivated to stay in close touch with a project they have commissioned. Because they support the project, they feel they have a right to intercede with suggestions (requests, alterations, demands). Cost, schedule, and scope changes are the most common outcome of client intercession, and the costs of these changes often exceed the client's expectations. Note that it is not the PM's job to dissuade the client from changes in the project's scope, but the PM must be certain that the client understands the impact of the changes on the project's goals of delivery time, cost, and scope.

The PM is responsible to the project team just as team members are responsible to the PM. As we will see shortly, it is very common for project team members to be assigned to work on the project, but to report to a superior who is not connected with the project. Thus, the PM will have people working on the project who are not "direct reports." Nonetheless, the relationship between the team and the PM may be closer to boss-subordinate than one might suspect. The reason for this is that both PM and team members often develop a mutual commitment to the project and to its successful conclusion. The PM facilitates the work of the team, and helps them succeed. As we will see in the final chapter, the PM may also take an active interest in fostering team members' future careers. Like any good boss, the PM may serve as advisor, counselor, confessor, and interested friend.

Meetings, Convener and Chair

The two areas in which the PM communicates most frequently are reports to senior management and instructions to the project team. We discuss management reports in Chapter 7 on monitoring and controlling the project. We also set out some rules for conducting successful meetings in Chapter 7. Communication with the project team typically takes place in the form of project team meetings. When humorist Dave Barry reached 50, he wrote a column listing 25 things he had learned in his first 50 years of living. Sixteenth on the list is "If you had to identify, in one word, the reason why the human race has not and never will achieve its full potential, that word would be 'meetings'."

Most of the causes of meeting-dread are associated with failure to adopt common sense about when to call meetings and how to run them. As we have said, one of the first things the PM must do is to call a "launch meeting" (see Chapter 3). Make sure that the meeting starts on time and has a prearranged stopping time. As convener of the meeting, the PM is responsible for taking minutes and keeping the meeting on track. The PM should also make sure that the invitation to the meeting includes a written agenda that clearly explains the purpose for the meeting and includes sufficient information on the project to allow the invitees to come prepared—and they are expected to do so. For some rules on conducting effective meetings that do not result in angry colleagues, see the subsection on meetings in Chapter 7.

> The PM is a facilitator, unlike the traditional manager who is a supervisor. The PM must adopt the systems approach to making decisions and managing projects. Trying to optimize each part of a project, suboptimization, does not produce an optimized project. Multiple communication paths exist in any project, and some paths bypass the PM, causing problems. Much project communication takes place in meetings that may be run effectively if some simple rules are followed. In virtual projects much communication is via high technology channels. Above all, the PM must keep senior management informed about the current state of the project.

2.2 THE PM'S RESPONSIBILITIES TO THE PROJECT

Trade-Offs

The PM has three overriding responsibilities to the project. First is the acquisition of resources and personnel. Second is dealing with the obstacles that arise during the course of the project. Third is exercising the leadership needed to bring the project to a successful conclusion and making the trade-offs necessary to do so.

Acquiring Resources

Acquiring resources and personnel is not difficult. Acquiring the necessary quality and quantity of resources and personnel is, however. Senior management typically suffers from a mental condition known as "irrational optimism." While the disease is rarely painful to anyone except PMs, the suffering among this group may be quite severe.

It has long been known that the farther one proceeds up the managerial ladder, the easier, faster, and cheaper a job appears to be compared to the opinion of the person who has to do the work (Gagnon and Mantel, 1987). The result is that the work plan developed by the project team may have its budget and schedule cut and then cut again as the project is checked and approved at successively higher levels of the organization. At times, an executive in the organization will have a strong interest in a pet project. In order to improve the chance that the pet project will be selected, the executive may deliberately (or subconsciously) understate the resource and personnel commitments required by the project. Whatever the cause, it is the PM's responsibility to ensure that the project has the appropriate level of resources. When the project team needs specific resources to succeed, there is no acceptable excuse for not getting them—though there may be temporary setbacks.

When a human resource is needed, the problem is further complicated. Most human resources come to the project on temporary assignment from the functional departments of the organization. The PM's wants are simple—the individual in the organization who is most competent on the specific task to be accomplished. Such individuals are, of course, precisely the people that the functional managers are least happy to release from their departmental jobs for work on the project, either full- or part-time. Those workers the functional manager is prone to offer positions are usually those whom the PM would least like to have.

Lack of functional manager enthusiasm for cooperation with the project has another source. In many organizations, projects are seen as glamorous, interesting, and high-visibility activities. The functional manager may be jealous or even suspicious of the PM who is perceived to have little or no interest in the routine work that is the bread and butter for the parent organization.

Fighting Fires and Obstacles

Still another key responsibility of the PM is to deal with obstacles. All projects have their crises—fires that must be quenched. The successful PM is also a talented and seasoned fire fighter. Early in the project's life cycle, fires are often linked to the need for resources. Budgets get cut, and the general cuts must be transformed into highly specific cuts in the quantities of highly specific resources. An X percent cut must be translated into Y units of this commodity or Z hours of that engineer's time. (An obvious reaction by the PM is to pad the next budget submitted. As we argue just below and in Chapters 4 and 6, this is unethical, a bad idea, and tends to cause more problems than it solves.)

As work on the project progresses, most fires are associated with technical problems, supplier problems, and client problems. Technical problems occur, for example, when some subsystem (e.g., a computer routine) is supposed to work but fails. Typical supplier problems occur when subcontracted parts are late or do not meet specifications. Client problems tend to be far more serious. Most often, they begin when the client asks "Would it be possible for this thing to . . . ?" Again, scope creep.

Most experienced PMs are good fire fighters. If they do not develop this skill, they do not last as PMs. People tend to enjoy doing what they are skilled at doing. Be warned: When you find a skilled fire fighter who fights a lot of fires and enjoys the activity, you may have found an arsonist. At one large, highly respected industrial firm we know, there is a wisecrack commonly made by PMs. "The way to get ahead around here is to get a project, screw it up, and then fix it. If it didn't get screwed up, it couldn't have been very hard or very important." We do not believe that anyone purposely botches projects (or knowingly allows them to be botched). We do, however, suspect that the attitude breeds carelessness because of the belief that they can fix any problem and be rewarded for it.

Leadership and Making Trade-Offs

Trade-Offs

In addition to being responsible for acquiring resources for the project and for fighting the project's fires, the PM is also responsible for making the trade-offs necessary to lead the project to a successful conclusion. As noted in the previous chapter, the primary role of the PM is managinge trade-offs and as such this issue is a key feature of the remainder of this book. In each of the following chapters and particularly in the chapters on budgeting, scheduling, resource allocation, and control, we will deal with many examples of trade-offs. They will be specific. At this point, however, we should establish some general principles.

The PM is the key figure in making trade-offs between project cost, schedule, scope, and risk. Which of these has higher priority than the others is dependent on many factors having to do with the project, the client, and the parent organization. If cost is more important than time for a given project, the PM will allow the project to be late rather than incur added costs. If a project has successfully completed most of its specifications, and if the client is willing, both time and cost may be saved by not pursuing some remaining specifications. It is the client's choice.

Of the three project goals, scope (specifications and client satisfaction) is usually the most important. Schedule is a close second, and cost is usually subordinate to the other two. Note the word "usually." There is anecdotal evidence that economic downturns result in an increased level of importance given to cost. There are many other exceptions, and this is another case where the political acuity of the PM is of primary importance. While deliverables are almost always paramount when dealing with an "arm's-length" client, it is not invariably so for an inside client. If the parent firm has inadequate profits, some specifications may be sacrificed for cost savings. Organizational policy may influence trade-offs. Grumman Aircraft (now a part of Northrop-Grumman) had a longstanding policy of on-time delivery. If a Grumman project for an outside client fell behind on its schedule, resources (costs) were added to ensure on-time delivery.

The global financial crisis is causing headaches for project managers around the world. Swanson (2009) reports that in Hong Kong there are now thousands of PMs from China suddenly available and willing to manage projects for substantially lower than prevailing wages. As a result, Hong Kong PMs are finding that they need to increase their value to business in order to compete with the new arrivals from China. Because the Hong Kong firms are now outsourcing many project tasks, the Hong Kong PMs are acquiring new skill sets to deal with people and organizations with whom they have not previously dealt. They are learning networking, communication, and leadership skills to augment their technical skills. They also focus on delivering "business" results such as increased revenues, improved profit margins, cost reductions, and they make sure that these appear in the organization's financial statements.

Another type of trade-off occurs between projects. At times, two or more projects may compete for access to the same resources. This is a major subject in Chapter 6, but the upshot is that added progress on one project may be traded off for less progress on another. If a single PM has two projects in the same part of the project life cycle and makes such a trade-off, it does not matter which project wins, the PM will lose. We strongly recommend that any PM managing two or more projects do everything possible to avoid this problem by making sure that the projects are in different phases of their life cycles. We urge this with the same fervor we would urge parents never to act so as to make it appear that one child is favored over another.

Negotiation, Conflict Resolution, and Persuasion

It is not possible for the PM to meet these responsibilities without being a skilled negotiator and resolver of conflict. The acquisition of resources requires negotiation. Dealing with problems, conflict, and fires requires negotiation and conflict resolution. The same skills are needed when the PM is asked to lead the project to a successful conclusion—and to make the trade-offs required along the way.

In Chapter 1 we emphasized the presence of conflict in all projects and the resultant need for win-win negotiation and conflict resolution. A PM without these skills cannot be successful. There is no stage of the project life cycle that is not characterized by specific types of conflict. If these are not resolved, the project will suffer and possibly die. For new PMs, training in win-win negotiation is just as important as training in PERT/CPM, budgeting, project management software, and project reporting. Such training is not merely useful, it is a necessary requirement for success. While an individual who is not (yet) skilled in negotiation may be chosen as PM for a project, the training should start immediately. A precondition is the ability to handle stress. Much has been written about negotiation and conflict resolution; there is no need to repeat it here. We refer you again to the bibliography for Chapter 1.

Trade-Offs

Projects must be selected for funding, and they begin when senior management has been persuaded that they are worthwhile. Projects almost never proceed through their life cycles without change. Changes in scope are common. Trade-offs may change what deliverable is made, how it is made, and when it is delivered. Success at any of these stages depends on the PM's skill at persuading others to accept the project as well as changes in its methods and scope once it has been accepted. Any suggested change will have supporters and opponents. If the PM suggests a change, others will need to be persuaded that the change is for the better. Senior management must be persuaded to support the change just as the client and the project team may need to be persuaded to accept change in the deliverables or in the project's methods or timing.

Persuasion is rarely accomplished by "my way or the highway" commands. Neither can it be achieved by locker-room motivational speeches. In an excellent article in the *Harvard Business Review*, Jay Conger (1998) describes the skill of persuasion as having four essential parts: (1) effective persuaders must be credible to those they are trying to persuade; (2) they must find goals held in common with those being persuaded; (3) they must use "vivid" language and compelling evidence; and (4) they must connect with the emotions of those they are trying to persuade. The article is complete with examples of each of the four essential parts.

Trade-Offs

> The PM is responsible for acquiring the human and material resources needed by the project. The PM is also responsible for exercising leadership, fire fighting, and dealing with obstacles that impede the project's progress. Finally, the PM is responsible for making the trade-offs between budget, schedule, and scope that are needed to ensure project success. To be successful at meeting these responsibilities, the PM must be skilled at negotiation, conflict resolution, and persuasion.

2.3   SELECTION OF A PROJECT MANAGER

A note to senior management: It is rarely a good idea to select a project manager from a list of engineers (or other technical specialists) who can be spared from their current jobs at the moment. Unfortunately, in many firms this appears to be the primary criterion for choice. We do not argue that current availability is not one among several appropriate criteria, but that it is only one of several—and never the most important. Neither does the list of criteria begin with "Can leap over tall buildings with a single bound."

The most important criterion, by far, is that the prospective PM, in the language of sales people, is a "closer." Find individuals who complete the tasks they are given. As any senior manager knows, hard workers are easy to find. What is rare is an individual who is driven to finish the job. Given a set of such people, select those who meet the following criteria at reasonably high levels.

Credibility

For the PM, credibility is critical. In essence, it means that the PM is believable. There are two areas in which the PM needs believability. The first is *technical credibility*, and the second is *administrative credibility*. The PM is not expected to have an expert's knowledge of each of the technologies that may be germane to the project. The PM should, however, have expertise in one or more areas of knowledge relevant to the project. In particular, the PM must know enough to explain the current state of the project, its progress, and its technical problems to senior management who may lack technical training. The PM should also be able to interpret the wishes of management and the client to the project team (Grant, Baumgardner, and Stone, 1997; Matson, 1998).

While quite different, administrative credibility is just as significant to the project. For management and the client to have faith in the viability of the project, reports, appraisals, audits, and evaluations must be timely and accurate. For the team, resources, personnel, and knowledge must be available when needed. For all parties, the PM must be able to make the difficult trade-offs that allow the project to meet its objectives as well as possible. This requires mature judgment and considerable courage.

Trade-Offs

Sensitivity

There is no need to belabor what should, by now, be obvious. The PM needs a finely tuned set of political antennae as well as an equally sensitive sensor of interpersonal conflict between team members, or between team members (including himself or herself) and other parties-at-interest to the project. As we will see, open and honest intrateam communication is critical to project success. Also needed are technical sensors that indicate when technical problems are being swept under the rug or when the project is about to fall behind its schedule.

Leadership, Style, Ethics

A leader is someone who indicates to other individuals or groups the direction in which they should proceed. When complex projects are decomposed into a set of tasks and subtasks, it is common for members of the project to focus on their individual tasks, thereby ignoring the project as a whole. This fosters the dreaded suboptimization that we mentioned early in this chapter. Only the PM is in a position to keep team members working toward completion of the whole project rather than its parts. In practice, leaders keep their people energized, enthusiastic, well organized, and well informed. This, in turn, will keep the team well motivated.

At the beginning of this chapter, we noted that the PM's role should be facilitative rather than authoritarian. Now let us consider the style with which that role is played. There has been much research on the best managerial style for general management, and it has been assumed that the findings apply to PMs as well. Recent work has raised some questions about this assumption. While there is little doubt that the most effective overall style is participative, Professor Shenhar of the Stevens Institute of Technology adds another dimension to style (1998). He found that as the level of technological uncertainty of a project went from "low tech" to "very high tech," the appropriate management style (while being fundamentally participative) went from "firm" to "highly flexible." In addition, he found that the complexity of the project, ranked from "simple" to "highly complex," called for styles varying from "informal" to "highly formal." To sum up, the more technically uncertain a project, the more flexible the style of management should be. The more complex a project, the more formal the style should be. In this context, flexibility applies primarily to the degree that new ideas and approaches are considered. Formality applies primarily to the degree to which the project operates in a structured environment.

Professor Shenhar's work has the feeling of good sense. When faced with technological uncertainty, the PM must be open to experimentation. In the same way, if a project is highly complex with many parts that must be combined with great care, the PM cannot allow a haphazard approach by the project team. In the end, the one reasonably sure conclusion about an effective management style for PMs is that it must be participative. Autocrats do not make good project managers.

Another aspect of leadership is for the PM to have—and to communicate—a strong sense of ethics. In recent years, the number and severity of unethical practices by business executives (and politicians) have increased dramatically. Because projects differ from one to another, there are few standard procedures that can be installed to ensure honest and ethical behavior from all parties-at-interest to the project. One has only to read a daily paper to find examples of kickbacks, bribery, covering up mistakes, use of substandard materials, theft, fraud, and outright lies on project status or performance. Dishonesty on anyone's part should not be permitted in projects.

Due, however, to the increasing number of multicultural projects, it is easy to make ethical missteps when managing a project in an unfamiliar country. Jones (2008) notes that what may be common practice in one country may be illegal in another—paying (bribing) a government agent to fast-track an approval, leaving out obvious information in a bid, inviting a client (or being invited) to dinner, and so on. Discovering another culture's ethical standards is difficult. One can engage local partners who have demonstrated knowledge of a local culture and are willing to share their information. Organizations should ensure that their employees are trained to recognize potential ethical issues and to communicate anything that seems amiss with their superiors. Insisting that employees follow the highest ethical standards, both domestic and foreign, may result in the firm having to abandon a project or a bid when it compromises those standards, but having a solid reputation for integrity will be a strong long-run benefit to the firm.

The Project Management Institute (PMI) has developed a Code of Ethics for the profession. The Code is the thoughtful result of an extended discussion and debate on ethical conduct in the project management profession. A new version of the Code, resulting from even more extended discussions, appeared in 2006. It is roughly eight times the length of the earlier version, including two Appendices. The new Code is available to anyone at the PMI website, *www.PMI.org*.

The new Code should be read carefully by anyone contemplating a career in project management. It accents behavior that will lead to high trust levels among team members, and between the team and the client and senior management as well as other stakeholders. The section titled "Honesty" should be reread . . . and reread . . . and reread. We will revisit the subjects of honesty and trust throughout this book.

Successful PMs have some common characteristics. They are "closers." They also have high administrative and technical credibility, show sensitivity to interpersonal conflict, and possess the political know-how to get help from senior management when needed. In addition, the PM should be a leader, and adopt a participatory management style that may have to be modified depending on the level of technological sophistication and uncertainty involved in the project. Another critical project management skill is the ability to direct the project in an ethical manner.

2.4 PROJECT MANAGEMENT AS A PROFESSION

It should be obvious to the reader that project management is a demanding job. Planning and controlling the complexities of a project's activities, schedule, and budget would be difficult even if the project had the highest claim on the parent organization's knowledge and resources, and if the PM had full authority to take any action required to keep the project on course for successful completion. Such is never the case, but all is not lost because there are tools available to bring some order to the chaos of life as a PM—to cope with the difficulties of planning and the uncertainties that affect budgets and schedules. Also, as we have indicated, it is possible to compensate for missing authority through negotiation. Mastering the use of project management tools requires specialized knowledge that is often acquired through academic preparation, which is to say that *project management is a profession.* The profession comes complete with career paths and an excellent professional organization.

The Project Management Institute (PMI) was founded in 1969. By 1990, the PMI had 7500 members. It grew to 17,000 by 1995, but 5 years later membership had exploded to more than 64,000. By 2012, the PMI had more than 380,000 members worldwide. The exponential growth of the PMI is the result of the exponential growth in the use of projects and PMs as a way of getting things done. For example, a senior vice president of an international chemical firm installed project management as a way of controlling the workloads on his technical specialists and on a few overloaded facilities—project management having tools to handle the allocation of scarce resources. In another instance, a new CEO of a large hospital mandated that all nonroutine, one-time operations be managed as projects so that she could have information on the nature and status of all such activities.

In Chapter 1 we mentioned the project-oriented organization. In these firms all nonroutine activities are organized as projects. In addition, the process of instituting change in routine operations is also commonly organized as a project. The motives behind this approach to handling change are the same as those motivating the chemical firm VP and the hospital CEO, the need to control and to have information about what is happening in the organization.

PMBOK Guide

To establish standards for project management and to foster professionalism in the field, the PMI has codified the areas of learning required to manage projects. This *Project Management Body of Knowledge,* 5th edition (PMBOK) has been compiled into a book published by the PMI, also available as a CD. It serves as a basis for practice and education in the field (PMI Standards Committee, 2013). PMBOK devotes Chapter 9 to human resource management, including organizational planning, staffing, and team development. The PMI also publishes two important periodicals: first, the *Project Management Journal,* oriented to project management theory, though its articles are almost uniformly related to the actual practice of project management; and second, the *PM Network* magazine, which is a trade journal aimed at practitioners. Both publications are valuable for the experienced PM as well as the neophyte or student. The PMI also offers certification testing programs for project managers. By 2013, almost 500,000 individuals had been certified by the PMI as Project Management Professionals (PMPs) or as Certified Associates in Project Management (CAPM).

The fantastic variety of projects being conducted today ranges from esoteric research on gene identification to specialized maintenance of machine tools. A quick glance at any daily paper will describe multiple projects such as cleaning up the image of downtown, improving air quality in various global cities, and reports of projects concerning natural disasters such as earthquakes.

Opportunities for careers in project management abound, but where can people who are competent to manage projects be found, or how can they be trained? A rapidly growing number of colleges, universities, and technical institutes have developed courses and degree programs in project management. In recent years, many local chapters of the PMI have also offered training programs of varying length and depth. Nonetheless, the demand for project managers far exceeds the supply. (*PMI Today*, a supplement to *PM Network*, is recommended for more information on training and employment opportunities.)

The career path for the PM usually starts with work on a small project, and then on some larger projects. If the individual survives life as a project worker, graduation to the next level comes in the form of duty as a "project engineer" or as a "deputy" PM for a project. Then comes duty as the manager of a small project, and then as PM of larger ones. All of this, of course, presumes a track record of success.

The highest visibility for a PM is to manage a "megaproject," either successfully or unsuccessfully. As Gale (2009) points out, success is defined as bringing the megaproject in on time and on budget. There is no room for error. The main difference between a "normal" project and a megaproject is that the technical issues tend to disappear on a megaproject. Instead, the PM's hardest tasks are those of communicating, managing vendors and contractors, dealing with stakeholders, running smooth task processes, guiding the project team, engaging the client, helping map the project to the business objectives, and handling the political and cultural issues.

PMBOK Guide

A professional organization, the Project Management Institute (PMI) has been devoted to project management. The growth in the field has been exponential. Among other reasons for this growth is the project-oriented organization. The PMI has published the *Project Management Body of Knowledge* (PMBOK). It also publishes two professional periodicals. Many courses and degree programs in project management are available. Project management has numerous career possibilities.

2.5 FITTING PROJECTS INTO THE PARENT ORGANIZATION

PMBOK Guide

Earlier in this chapter we referred several times to problems caused by the way projects are organized and fit in as a part of the parent organization. It is now time to deal with this subject. Project organization is also discussed in Chapter 2: Organizational Influences and Project Life Cycle of PMBOK. It would be most unusual for a PM to have any influence over the interface between the project and the parent organization. This arrangement is a matter of company policy and usually is decided by senior management. The nature of the interface, however, has a major impact on the PM's life, and it is necessary that the PM understand why senior managers make what appears to be the worst of all possible choices for the interface.

More on "Why Projects?"

Before examining the alternative ways in which a project can interface with the organization, it is useful to add to our understanding of just why organizations choose to conduct so much of their work as projects. We spoke previously of project-oriented firms. In addition to the managerial reasons that caused the rapid spread of such organizations, there were also strong economic reasons. First, devising product development programs by integrating product design, engineering, manufacturing, and marketing functions in one team not only improved the product, it also allowed significant cuts in the *time-to-market* for the product. For example, in the 1990s Chrysler Motors (now owned by Fiat) cut almost 18 months from the new product development time required for design-to-street and produced designs that were widely rated as outstanding. This brought new Chrysler models to market much faster than normal in the automotive industry. Quite apart from the value of good design, the economic value of the time saved is immense and derives from both reduced design labor and overhead, plus earlier sales and return on the investment—in this case amounting to hundreds of millions of dollars. The same methods were used to enable General Motors to redesign and reimage their Cadillac and Buick models in response to the sharp decline in demand during the steep business downturn of 2008. This same process also allows a firm to tailor special versions of standard products for individual clients. We will have more to say about this process at the end of this chapter.

Second, the product development/design process requires input from different areas of specialized knowledge. The exact mix of knowledge varies from product to product or service to service. Teams of specialists can be formed, do their work, and disband. The make-up of such teams can easily be augmented or changed.

Third, the explosive expansion of technical capabilities in almost every area of the organization tends to destabilize the structure of the enterprise. Almost all industries have experienced the earthquakes of changed technology, revamped software systems, altered communication systems; followed by mergers, downsizing, spin-offs, and other catastrophes—all of which require system-wide responsiveness. Dealing with the threat of climate change is going to require massive, worldwide changes in technology. It will undoubtedly involve the use of multifirm, multiindustry, and multinational projects to develop and implement the necessary technological changes. Traditional organizations have difficulty dealing with rapid, large-scale change, but project organizations can.

Fourth, like our hospital CEO, many upper-level managers we know lack confidence in their ability to cope with and respond to such large-scale, rapid change in their organizations. Organizing these changes as projects gives the managers some sense of accountability and control.

Finally, the rapid growth of globalized industry often involves the integration of activities carried out by different firms located in different countries, often on different continents. Organizing such activities into a project improves the firm's ability to ensure overall compliance with the laws and regulations of dissimilar governments as well as with the policies of widely assorted participating firms.

All these factors fostered the expanded use of projects, but traditional ways of organizing projects were too costly and too slow, largely because of how they linked to the parent firm. In the years following World War II, projects came into common use. Most of the early projects were created to solve large-scale government problems, many of which were related to national defense—the building of an intercontinental ballistic missile, the construction of an interstate highway system, the development and deployment of a missile defense system, and similar massive projects (Hughes, 1998). At the same time, private industry tentatively began to use projects to develop new medicinal drugs, larger and faster commercial airliners, large-scale computing machines, shopping malls, and apartment complexes with hundreds of units. All such projects had several things in common: They were large, complex, and often required the services of hundreds of people. The natural way to organize such projects came to be known as the *pure project organization*.

Pure Project Organization

Consider the construction of a football stadium or a shopping mall. Assume that the land has been acquired and the design approved. Having won a competitive bid, a contractor assigns a project manager and a team of construction specialists to the project. Each specialist, working from the architectural drawings, develops a set of plans to deal with his or her particular specialty area. One may design and plan the electrical systems, another the mechanicals, still another the parking and landscaping, and so forth. In the meantime, someone is arranging for the timely delivery of cranes, earth movers, excavation equipment, lumber, cement, brick, and other materials. And someone is hiring a suitable number of local construction workers with the appropriate skills. See Figure 2-2 for a typical pure project organization.

The supplies, equipment, and workers arrive just when they are needed (in a perfect world), do the work, complete the project, and disband. The PM is, in effect, the CEO of the project. When the project is completed, accepted by the client, equipment returned, and local workers paid off, then the PM and the specialists return to their parent firm and await the next job.

For large projects, the pure project organization is effective and efficient, but for small projects it is a very expensive way to operate. In the preceding example, we assumed that there was always work for each member of the labor force. On a very large project, that assumption is approximately true. On a small project, the normal ebb and flow of work is not evened out as it is on large projects with a large number of workers. On small projects, therefore, it is common to find personnel shortages one week and overages the next. Also, on small projects the human resources person or the accountant is rarely needed full-time. Often such staff persons may be needed one-quarter or one-half time; but humans do not come in fractions. They are always integers. Remember also that pure projects are often carried out at some distance from the home office, and a quarter-time accountant cannot go back to the home office when work on the project slacks off. Part-time workers are not satisfactory either. They never seem to be on site when they are needed.

There are other drawbacks to the pure project. While they have a broad range of specialists, they have limited technological depth. If the project's resident specialist in a given area of knowledge happens to be lacking in a specific subset of that area, the project must hire a consultant, add another specialist, or do without. If the parent organization

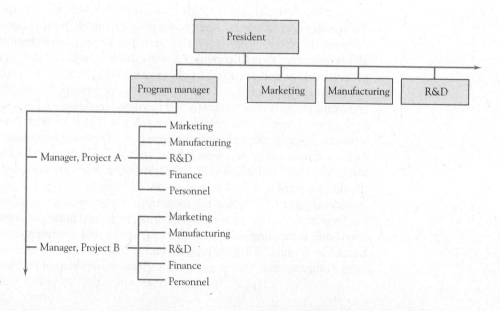

Figure 2-2 Pure project organization.

has several concurrent pure projects drawing on the same specialty areas, they develop fairly high levels of duplication in these specialties. This is expensive.

There are other problems, and one of the most serious is seen in R&D projects or in projects that have fairly long lives. People assigned to the project tend to form strong attachments to it. The project begins to take on a life of its own. A disease we call "projectitis" develops. One pronounced symptom is worry about "Is there life after the project?" Foot dragging as the project end draws near is common, as is the submission of proposals for follow-up projects in the same area of interest—and, of course, using the same project team.

Functional Project Organization

Some projects have a very different type of structure. Assume, for example, that a project is formed to install a new production machine in an operating production line. The project includes the removal of the old machine and the integration of the new machine into the production system. In such a case, we would probably organize the project as an appendage to the Manufacturing division where the production system is located. Figure 2-3 shows a typical example of functional project organization with the project in this case, attached to the manufacturing function.

Quite unlike pure projects that are generally separated from the day-to-day operations of the parent organization, functionally organized projects are embedded in the functional group where the project will be used. This immediately corrects some of the problems associated with pure projects. First, the functional project has immediate, direct, and complete contact with the most important technologies it may need, and it has in-depth access. Second, the fractional resource problem is minimized for anyone working in the project's home functional group. Functionally organized projects do not have the high personnel costs associated with pure projects because they can easily assign people to the project on a part-time basis. Finally, even projectitis will be minimal because the project is not removed from the parent organization and specialists are not divorced from their normal career tracks.

There are, however, two major problems with functionally organized projects. First, communications across functional department boundaries are rarely as simple as most firms think they are. When technological assistance is needed from another division, it may or may not be forthcoming on a timely basis. Technological depth is certainly present, but technological breadth is missing. The same problem exists with communication outside the function. In the pure project, communication lines are short and messages move rapidly. This is particularly important when the client is sending or receiving messages. In most functionally organized projects, the lines of communication to people or units outside the functional division are slow and tortuous. Traditionally,

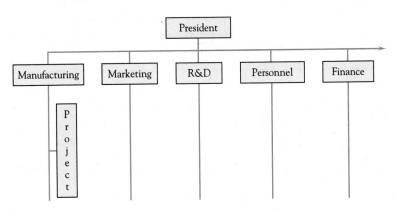

Figure 2-3 Functional project organization.

messages are not to be sent outside the division without clearing through the division's senior management. Insisting that project communications follow the organizational chain of command imposes impossible delays on most projects. It most certainly impedes frank and open communication between project team members and the project client.

Another major problem besets functionally organized projects. The project is rarely a high-priority item in the life of the division. The task of Manufacturing is to produce product. The job of Marketing is to sell. Manufacturing may have a sincere interest in a new machine or Marketing in a new product, but those projects do not make "here and now" contributions to the major objectives of the divisions. We have already noted the tendency of managers to focus on short-run goals. After all, managerial bonuses are usually linked to short-run performance. Given this bias, functionally organized projects often get short shrift from their sponsoring divisions.

Matrix Project Organization

In an attempt to capture the advantages of both the pure project and the functionally organized project as well as to avoid the problems associated with each type, a new type of project organization—more accurately, a combination of the two—was developed.

To form a matrix organized project, a pure project is superimposed on a functionally organized system as in Figure 2-4. The PM reports to a program manager or a vice-president of projects or some senior individual with a similar title whose job it is to coordinate the activities of several or all of the projects. These projects may or may not be related, but they all demand the parent's resources and the use of resources must be coordinated, if not the projects themselves. This method of organizing the interface between projects and the parent organization succeeds in capturing the major advantages of both pure and functional projects. It does, however, create some problems that are unique to this matrix form. To understand both the advantages and disadvantages, we will examine matrix management more closely.

As the figure illustrates, there are two distinct levels of responsibility in a matrix organization. First, there is the normal functional hierarchy that runs vertically in the figure and consists of the regular departments such as marketing, finance, manufacturing, human resources, and so on. (We could have illustrated a bank or university or an enterprise organized on some other principle. The departmental names would differ, but the structure of the system would be the same.) Second, there are horizontal structures, the projects that overlay the functional departments and, presumably, have some access to the functional department's competencies. Heading up these horizontal projects are the project managers.

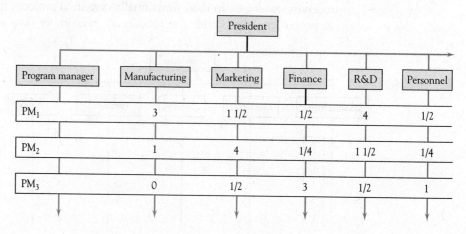

Program manager	Manufacturing	Marketing	Finance	R&D	Personnel
PM$_1$	3	1 1/2	1/2	4	1/2
PM$_2$	1	4	1/4	1 1/2	1/4
PM$_3$	0	1/2	3	1/2	1

Figure 2-4 Matrix project organization.

A close examination of Figure 2-4 shows some interesting details. Project 1 has assigned to it three people from the Manufacturing division, one and one-half from Marketing, a half-time person from Finance, four from R&D, and one-half from Personnel, plus an unknown number from other divisions not shown in the figure. Other projects have different make-ups of people assigned. This is typical of projects that have different objectives. Project 2, for example, appears to be aimed at the development of a new product with its concentration of Marketing representation, plus significant assistance from R&D, representation from Manufacturing, and staff assistance from Finance and Personnel. The PM controls what these people do and when they do it. The head of a functional group controls who from the group is assigned to the project and what technology is appropriate for use on the project.

Advantages   We can disregard the problems raised by the split authority for the moment and concentrate on the strong points of this arrangement. Because there are many possible combinations of the pure project and the functional project, the matrix project may have some characteristics of each organizational type. If the matrix project closely resembles the pure project with many individuals assigned full-time to the project, it is referred to as a "strong" matrix or a "project" matrix. If, on the other hand, functional departments assign resource capacity to the project rather than people, the matrix is referred to as a "weak" matrix or a "functional" matrix. The project might, of course, have some people and some capacity assigned to it, in which case it is sometimes referred to as a "balanced" matrix. (The *Random House Unabridged Dictionary* defines "balanced" as "being in harmonious or proper arrangement . . ." In no way does the balanced matrix qualify as "balanced.") None of the terms—strong, weak, balanced—is precise, and matrix projects may be anywhere along the continuum from strong to weak. It may even be stronger or weaker at various times during the project's life.

The primary reason for choosing a strong or weak matrix depends on the needs of both the project and the various functional groups. If the project is likely to require complex technical problem solving, it will probably have the appropriate technical specialists assigned to it. If the project's technology is less demanding, it will be a weaker matrix that is able to draw on a functional group's capacity when needed. A firm manufacturing household oven cleaners might borrow chemists from the R&D department to develop cleaning compounds that could dissolve baked-on grease. The project might also test whether such products were toxic to humans by using the capacity of the firm's Toxicity Laboratory rather than having individual toxicity testers assigned to the project team.

One of the most important strengths of the matrix form is this flexibility in the way it can interface with the parent organization. Because it is, or can be, connected to any or all of the parent organization's functional units, it has access to any or all of the parent organization's technology. The way it utilizes the services of the several technical units need not be the same for each unit. This allows the functional departments to optimize their contributions to any project. They can meet a project's needs in a way that is most efficient. Being able to share expertise with several projects during a limited time period makes the matrix arrangement far less expensive than the pure project with its duplication of competencies, and just as technologically "deep" as the functional project. The flexibility of the matrix is particularly useful for globalized projects that often require integrating knowledge and personnel coming from geographically dispersed independent business units, each of which may be organized quite differently than the others.

The matrix has a strong focus on the project itself, just as does the pure project. In this, it is clearly superior to the functional project that often is subordinate to the regular work of the functional group. In general, matrix organized projects have the advantages of both pure and functional projects. For the most part, they avoid the major disadvantages of each. Close contact with functional groups tends to mitigate projectitis. Individuals involved with matrix projects are never far from their home department and do not develop the detached feelings that sometimes strike those involved with pure projects.

Disadvantages With all their advantages, matrix projects have their own, unique problems. By far the most significant of these is the violation of an old dictum of the military and of management theory, the Unity of Command principle: For each subordinate, there shall be one, and only one, superior. In matrix projects, the individual specialist borrowed from a function has two bosses. As we noted above, the project manager may control which tasks the specialist undertakes, but the specialist reports to a functional manager who makes decisions about the specialist's performance evaluation, promotion, and salary. Thus, project workers are often faced with conflicting orders from the PM and the functional manager. The result is conflicting demands on their time and activities. The project manager is in charge of the project, but the functional manager is usually superior to the PM on the firm's organizational chart, and may have far more political clout in the parent organization. Life on a matrix project is rarely comfortable for anyone, PM or worker.

As we have said, in matrix organizations the PM controls administrative decisions and the functional heads control technological decisions. This distinction is simple enough when writing about project management, but for the operating PM the distinction, and partial division of authority and responsibility, is complex indeed. The ability of the PM to negotiate anything from resources to technical assistance to delivery dates is a key contributor to project success. As we have said before and will certainly say again, success is doubtful for a PM without strong negotiating skills.

While the ability to balance resources, schedules, and deliverables between several projects is an advantage of matrix organization, that ability has its dark side. The organization's full set of projects must be carefully monitored by the program manager, a tough job. Further, the movement of resources from project to project in order to satisfy the individual schedules of the multiple projects may foster political infighting among the several PMs. As usual, there are no winners in these battles. Naturally, each PM is more interested in ensuring success for his or her individual project than in maintaining general organization-wide goals. Not only is this suboptimization injurious to the parent organization, it also raises serious ethical issues. In Chapter 1 we discussed some of the issues involved in aggregate planning, and we will have much more to say on this matter in Chapter 6.

Intrateam conflict is a characteristic of all projects, but the conflicts seem to us to be particularly numerous and contentious in matrix projects. In addition to conflicts arising from the split authority and from the violation of Unity of Command, another major source of conflict appears to be inherent in the nature of the transdisciplinary teams in a matrix setting. Functional projects have such teams, but team members have a strong common interest, their common functional home. Pure projects have transdisciplinary teams, but the entire team is full-time and committed to the project. Matrix project teams are transdisciplinary, but team members are often not full-time, have different functional homes, and have other commitments than the project. They are often committed to their functional area or to their career specialty, rather than to the project. As we emphasize in the next section, high levels of trust between project team members is critical for optimum team performance. Conflicts do not necessarily lead to distrust on a project team, but unless matrix organized teams are focused on the project rather than on their individual contribution to it, distrust between team members is almost certain to affect project outcomes negatively.

Figure 2-5 Mixed project organization.

A young man of our acquaintance works one-quarter time on each of two projects and half-time in his functional group, the mechanical engineering group in an R&D division. He estimates that approximately three-quarters of the time he is expected to be in two or more places at the same time. He indicated that this is normal.

With all its problems, there is no real choice about project organization for most firms. Functional projects are too limited and too slow. Pure projects are far too expensive. Matrix projects are both effective and efficient. They are here to stay, conflict and all.

Mixed Organizational Systems

Functional, matrix, and pure projects exist side by side in some organizations (see Figure 2-5). In reality, they are never quite as neatly defined as they appear here. Matrix or functional projects may be organized, become very successful and expand into pure projects. It may not stop there, with the pure project growing into an operating division of the parent firm, perhaps becoming a subsidiary or even a stand-alone, venture firm. There are many such cases (e.g., Texas Instruments and the Speak and Spell toy developed by one of its employees).

The ability to organize projects to fit the needs of the parent firm has allowed projects to be used under conditions that might be quite difficult were project organization constrained to one or two specific forms. As the hybridization increases, though, the firm risks increasing the level of conflict in and between projects because of duplication, overlapping authority, and increased friction between project and functional management.

The Project Management Office and Project Maturity

Risk

There is another way of solving some of the problems of choosing one or another organizational form for projects. The parent organization can set up a project management office (PMO), more or less like a functional group. This group may act as staff to some or to all projects (Block, 1998; Bolles, 1998). The project office may handle some or all of the budgeting, scheduling, reporting, scope, compliance with corporate governance, and risk management activities while the functional units supply the technical work. The PMO often serves as a repository for project documents and histories. However, the PMO must never replace the project manager as officer in charge of and accountable for the project.

This approach is particularly useful when the system operates many small projects with short lives. For example, facility maintenance projects may be operated this way. Maintenance team leaders act as PMs, and the PMO keeps the records and makes reports. Because the teams are semi-permanent groups, they develop techniques for working together and often specialize in specific types of maintenance problems. Reports and records are standardized, and the system has few of the administrative problems of many maintenance systems.

At times the PMO is effective, and at times it is not. Based on limited observation, it appears to us that the system works well when the functional specialists have fairly routine projects. If this is not the case, the team must be involved in generating the project's budget, schedule, and scope, and must be kept well informed about the progress of the project measured against its goals. Some years ago, a large pharmaceutical firm used a similar arrangement on R&D projects, the purpose being to "protect" their scientists from having to deal with project schedules, budgets, and progress reports, all of which were handled by the PMO. The scientists were not even bothered with having to read the reports. The result was precisely what one might expect. All projects were late and over budget—very late and far over budget.

But in another case, the US Federal Transportation Security Administration had only 3 months and $20 million to build a 13,500 square foot coordination center, involving the coordination of up to 300 tradespeople working simultaneously on various aspects of the center (PMI, May 2004). A strong Project Management Office was crucial to making the effort a success. The PMO accelerated the procurement and approval process, cutting times in half in some cases. They engaged a team leader, a master scheduler, a master financial manager, a procurement specialist, a civil engineer, and other specialists to manage the multiple facets of the construction project, finishing the entire project in 97 days and on budget, receiving an award from the National Assn. of Industrial and Office Properties for the quality of its project management and overall facility.

In general, however, the role of the PMO is much broader than this example, and it is now not uncommon to find several different types of PMOs existing at different levels of large firms with different, but sometimes overlapping, areas of operation. They have titles such as CPMO for Corporate Project Management Office, or EPMO for Enterprise Project Management Office, and many other variants. It is also common to find an EPMO (or CPMO) followed by a PMO for each unit of the parent organization that actually carries out the projects and reports to the senior EPMO.

Involvement of senior management in EPMOs allows the EPMO to provide some important functions. The EPMO (or PMO if there is only one in the firm) is in a unique position to maintain oversight of the entire portfolio of projects carried out by the firm, acting as a project selection committee, making sure that the set of projects is consistent with the firm's strategies, generating and insuring compliance with matters of corporate governance, maintaining project histories as well as composite data on project costs, schedules, etc., setting project or program priorities across departments, helping projects to acquire resources, and similar issues. Project champions, senior managers who have a strong interest in a project or program and may use their political clout to help the project with priority issues or resource acquisition when such clout may be useful, are often appropriate members of the EPMOs. Again, care must be taken for the EPMO or its individual members to avoid usurping the PM as the accountable, officer-in-charge of the project.

While such activities are necessary and, indeed, helpful, EPMO actions sometimes may cause significant management problems. Because many senior managers have little or no training in project management, they tend to focus on assessment of project progress and evaluation by using planned cost versus actual cost as a primary measurement tool. (We will discuss the problems caused by this simplistic measure several times in the following chapters, and in some detail in Chapter 7 on Project Control.) As senior management has become aware of these and other problems, many EPMOs have taken on the task of assuring that the organization is following "best practices" for the management of its projects. The EPMO is expected to monitor and continuously improve the organization's project management skills. In the past few years, a number of different ways to measure this "project management maturity" (Pennypacker et al., 2003) have been suggested, such as basing the evaluation on PMI's *PMBOK Guide* (Lubianiker, 2000; see also www.pmi.org) or the ISO 9001 standards of the International Organization for Standardization.

Best Practice

PMBOK Guide

Quite a few consulting firms, as well as scholars, have devised formal maturity measures; one such, PM3, is described by R. Remy (1997). In this system, the final project management "maturity" of an organization is assessed as being at one of five levels: **ad-hoc** (disorganized, accidental successes and failures); **abbreviated** (some processes exist, inconsistent management, unpredictable results); **organized** (standardized processes, more predictable results); **managed** (controlled and measured processes, results more in line with plans); and **adaptive** (continuous improvement in processes, success is normal, performance keeps improving).

PMBOK Guide

Risk

Another maturity model was applied to 38 organizations in four industries (Ibbs and Kwak, 2000). The survey included 148 questions covering six processes/life cycle phases (initiating, planning, executing, controlling, closing, and project-driven organization environment) and ten PMBOK knowledge areas (integration, scope, time, cost, quality, human resources, communication, risk, procurement, and stakeholders). The model assesses project management maturity in terms of five stages called: ad hoc, planned, managed, integrated, and sustained.

Regardless of the model form, it appears that most organizations do not score very well in maturity tests. On one form, about three-quarters are no higher than level 2 (planned) and fewer than 6 percent are above level 3. Individual firms ranged from 1.8 to 4.6 on the five-point scale.

The rapid growth in the use of projects has made the traditional ways of creating an interface between projects and the parent organization inadequate in many cases. Pure project organizations, unless very large, are too costly and lack technological depth. Functionally organized projects lack technological breadth, are slow to act, and have other faults. Linking the two forms into matrix organized projects combines the strengths of the traditional forms and avoids most of their weaknesses. It has severe problems of its own, however, caused by split responsibility for the project with the PM controlling what must be done and when, and the functional manager controlling who will do things and how. It also violates the principle of Unity of Command. Some organizations operate all three types of projects simultaneously. Project management offices may be set up to achieve consistent project administration when the firm is operating a number of differently organized projects. Project maturity measurement models have been developed to measure the degree to which individual organizations have mastered state-of-the-art project management practices.

2.6 THE PROJECT TEAM

We have mentioned the project team several times in the foregoing sections. Effective team members have some characteristics in common. Only the first of these is usually taken into account.

1. They must be *technically competent*. This is so obvious that it is often the only criterion applied. While the functional departments will always remain the ultimate source of technological problem solving for the project, it requires a technically competent person to know exactly when additional technical knowledge may be required by the project.

2. Senior members of the project team must be *politically sensitive*. It is rarely possible to complete a project of reasonable size and complexity without incurring problems that require aid from the upper echelons of executive row; that is, from a *project champion* (Pinto and Slevin, 1989). Getting such aid depends on the PM's ability to proceed without threatening, insulting, or bullying important people in the functional groups. To ensure cooperation and assistance, there is a delicate balance of power that must be maintained between the project and the functional departments, and between one project and others.

3. Members of the project team need a strong *problem orientation*. This characteristic will be explained in more detail shortly. For now, take the phrase to mean that the team's members should be concerned about solving any problems posed by the project, not merely about those subproblems that concern their individual academic or technical training.

4. Team members need a strong *goal orientation*. Projects are uncomfortable environments for people with a 9-to-5 view of work. In particular, neither project teams nor PMs can succeed if their focus is on activity rather than results. On the other hand, the project will not be successful if the project team dies from overwork. One project team member of our acquaintance was bemoaning a series of 60+ hour weeks. "They told me that I would work about 50 hours in an average week. I've been on this project almost 18 months, and we haven't had an average week yet."

5. Project workers need *high self-esteem*. Project members who hide mistakes and failure are disasters waiting to happen. Team members must be sufficiently self-confident and have sufficient trust in their fellow team members (Lencioni, 2002) that they can immediately acknowledge their own errors and point out problems caused by the errors of others. PMs should note that "shooting the messenger" who brings bad news will instantly stop the flow of negative information. The result is that the golden rule we stated above, "Never let the boss be surprised," will be violated, too.

Gathering such a team is a nontrivial job. If it is done well, motivation of team members is rarely a problem. Remember that the functional managers control the pay and promotion of project workers in a matrix system. Fortunately, it has been shown that a sense of achievement, growth, learning, responsibility, and the work itself are strong motivators, and the project is a high-visibility source of these.*

In a large project, the PM will have a number of "assistant managers" on the project team—a senior engineer, field manager, contract administrator, support services manager, and several other individuals who can help the PM determine the project's needs for staff and resources. (In the next chapter we will see precisely how the staff and resource requirements are determined.) They can also help to manage the project's schedule, budget, and technical performance. For a large project, such assistance is necessary. For a small project the PM will probably play all these roles.

Matrix Team Problems

The smaller the project, the more likely it is to be organized as a weak (functional) matrix. In such projects the PM may have no direct reports. The PM contracts with functional managers for capacity, but often knows most of the individuals who are

---

*Herzberg (1968) is a classic article and still an outstanding discussion of motivation in the work place. It is one of the *Harvard Business Review*'s most widely reprinted articles. It is still available from the *HBR*.

doing the actual work. Thus, the PM can usually communicate directly with project workers, even in the weakest of matrices. In the case of small projects, this ability to communicate directly with members of the project team (even though they are not officially a team at all) is important. It is the only way the PM can keep the project a coordinated effort and on course. Again, the ability to communicate with and direct functional specialists working on project tasks is dependent on the PM's ability to negotiate with the functional manager. Actually, the negotiation is not too difficult because the PM is tacitly taking responsibility to direct the workers' performance. If the PM is getting good performance from the functional specialists, this relieves the functional manager of some responsibility and accountability.

For matrix projects, it is particularly important to maintain good morale for the few project workers that may be assigned to the team. A PMO (a.k.a. a project "war room") is helpful, serving as a control center, conference room for project meetings, a coffee shop, technical discussion center, and crisis center. Earlier in this chapter, we noted the use of a project staff office with a purpose of supplying the project with administrative assistance. The war room may also provide such a purpose, but its ability to serve as a focal point for project team activity and heighten the project's *esprit de corps* makes a significant contribution to matrix projects. The Walt Disney Co. sets up division-wide project war rooms and expects the PMs, the functional managers, and the division executive team to use the war room to stay abreast of project timelines and to identify areas of organizational impact on the project or vice versa.

A number of factors make matrix project teams unusually difficult to manage. Such teams are seen by their members to be temporary, so the tendency to develop team loyalty is limited. The technical specialists working on the teams are often perfectionists and have a strong desire to keep tinkering with a project deliverable that already meets the client's specifications and expectations. While project managers usually blame the client for scope creep, it is not uncommon for the project team to be the primary cause. The principal source of management problems for the PM, however, is the level of conflict in project teams.

Intrateam Conflict

Conflict is no stranger to any workplace, but matrix projects seem to have far more than their share. The causes are many, but more than three decades ago Thamhain and Wilemon (1975) published their outstanding research on conflict in projects and this work remains absolutely relevant today. They identified several different sources of conflict and noted that the sources seemed to differ when the project was in different stages of its life cycle. They also made some recommendations for dealing with the conflicts. These are shown in Table 2-1. Table 2-2 shows the relative frequency of the various sources of conflict, and Figure 2.6 illustrates them.

A reading of the recommendations Thamhain and Wilemon made for reducing or preventing these conflicts reveals four common threads: (1) many of the recommendations feature careful project planning; (2) many are based on the practice of participative management; (3) many require interaction and negotiation between the PM and the functional departments; and (4) there is great emphasis on communication between the PM and all parties-at-interest to the project. Our next chapter is devoted to careful project planning, and we have already discussed the need for negotiation and communication. Participative management is a requirement for proper project planning, and it will be covered in the project-planning chapter. We will continue to mention, if not belabor, these four themes throughout the rest of this book.

Table 2-1   Major Sources of Conflict during Various Stages of the Project Life Cycle*

Life Cycle Phase	Conflict Source	Major Conflict Source and Recommendations for Minimizing Dysfunctional Consequences	
		Recommendations	
Project formation	Priorities	Clearly defined plans. Joint decision making and/or consultation with affected parties. Stress importance of project to organization goals.	
	Procedures	Develop detailed administrative operating procedures to be followed in conduct of project.	
		Secure approval from key administrators.	
		Develop statement of understanding or charter.	
	Schedules	Develop schedule commitments in advance of actual project commencement.	
		Forecast other departmental priorities and possible impact on project.	
Buildup phase	Priorities	Provide effective feedback to support areas on forecasted project plans and needs via status review sessions.	
	Schedules	Schedule work breakdown packages (project subunits) in cooperation with functional groups.	
	Procedures	Contingency planning on key administrative issues.	
Main program	Schedules	Continually monitor work in progress.	
		Communicate results to affected parties.	
		Forecast problems and consider alternatives.	
		Identify potential trouble spots needing closer surveillance.	
	Technical	Early resolution of technical problems.	
		Communication of schedule and budget restraints to technical personnel.	
		Emphasize adequate, early technical testing.	
		Facilitate early agreement on final designs.	
	Labor	Forecast and communicate staffing requirements early.	
		Establish staffing requirements and priorities with functional and staff groups.	
Phaseout	Schedules	Close schedule monitoring in project life cycle.	
		Consider reallocation of available staff to critical project areas prone to schedule slippages.	
		Attain prompt resolution of technical issues which may affect schedules.	
	Personality and labor	Develop plans for reallocation of people upon project completion.	
		Maintain harmonious working relationships with project team and support groups. Try to loosen-up high-stress environment.	

*Source: Thamhain and Wilemon, 1975.

Table 2-2   Number of Conflicts During a Sample Project*

Sources of Conflict	Phase of Project				
	Start	**Early**	**Main**	**Late**	**Total**
Project priorities	27	35	24	16	102
Admin. procedures	26	27	15	9	77
Technical trade-offs	18	26	31	11	86
Staffing	21	25	25	17	88
Support cost estimates	20	13	15	11	59
Schedules	25	29	36	30	120
Personalities	16	19	15	17	67
Total	**153**	**174**	**161**	**111**	**111**

*Source: Thamhain and Wilemon, 1975.

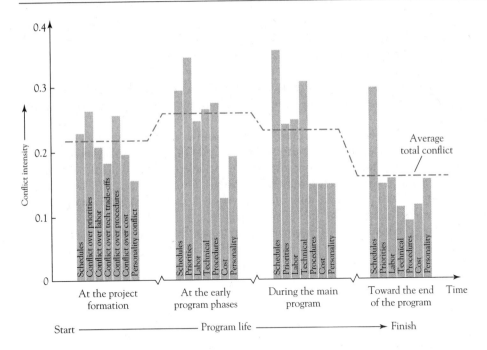

Figure 2-6 Conflict intensity over the project life cycle. *Source*: Thamhaun et al., 1975.

Certain aspects of the data in Table 2-2 seem significant. Schedules are a major source of conflict throughout the project's life. Priorities are a close second, particularly in the first two stages of the project's life. Because the distinction between the project's "start" and the "early" phase of its life is probably unclear, we can lump them together for the observation that a lion's share of the conflicts will come near the beginning of the project—and the PM must be prepared to deal with them.

One should not get the idea that conflict in the project team is all bad. Intrateam conflict often enhances team creativity. Out of arguments about competing good ideas come better ideas. For this to happen, however, parties to the conflict must be more interested in solving the problems at hand than they are about winning a victory for "their side." As we have already noted, some people are discipline oriented and others are problem oriented. Discipline-oriented individuals form what one writer calls a "NOT" (Name-Only Team), which he defines as a group of individuals working independently (Dewhurst, 1998). The intrateam conflict caused by such people is usually perceived to be "interpersonal" or "political." If such conflicts are the major force in project decisions, the project is apt to have problems. We strongly recommend Lencioni's *The Five Dysfunctions of a Team* (2002) to the reader's attention and we again emphasize our earlier advice to the PM to recruit problem-oriented team members whenever possible.

A great deal has been written about conflict resolution as well as about negotiation (see Afzalur, 1992, for example). Those two literatures have much in common. Both make it clear that the key to resolving conflict lies in the mediator's ability to transform win-lose situations into win-win solutions. This is also true when the mediator (usually the PM) is one of the parties to the conflict. One of the most important things a PM can do is develop sensitivity for conflict and then intervene early, before the conflict has hardened into hostility. Conflict avoidance, while it may appear to provide short-term comfort, is never a useful course of action for the PM.

Interpersonal conflict, unfortunately, never stays interpersonal. It impacts on the relationships between various groups and spills over to affect the ways in which these groups cooperate or fail to cooperate with each other. This, in turn, affects the ability of the PM to keep the project on course. The most difficult aspect of managing a project is the coordination and integration of its various elements so that they meet their joint goals of performance, schedule, and budget in such a way that the total project meets its goals.

When the project is complex, involving input and work from several departments or groups and possibly other contributions from several outside contractors, the intricate process of coordinating the work and timing of these inputs is difficult. When the groups are in conflict, the process is almost impossible. The task of bringing the work of all these groups together to make a harmonious whole is called *integration management*, (a.k.a. *systems engineering*). The job of managing this work across multiple groups is called *interface coordination* (a.k.a. *interface management*). Both integration management and interface management are carried out by multidisciplinary teams, as described next.

A PM should strive to acquire project team members who are technically competent, politically sensitive, problem- and goal oriented, and have high self-esteem. On small projects with a matrix organization, the project may be supplied with functional capacity, rather than full- or part-time people to do the work. It is important for the PM to establish good communication with the people doing the work. A project war room will help with coordination and morale. Intrateam conflict is common on matrix projects. Different sources of conflict occur at differing stages of the project's life cycle. Careful planning, participative management, win-win negotiation with functional groups, and open communication between all parties will help resolve conflict.

2.7 MULTIDISCIPLINARY TEAMS—BALANCING PLEASURE AND PAIN

Earlier we promised further discussion of multidisciplinary teams (MTs) on projects. We will now keep that promise. Using MTs (*or transdisciplinary teams* as they are sometimes called) raises serious problems for the PM. When used on sizable, complex projects that necessitate inputs from several different departments or groups, the process of managing the way these groups work together is called *interface coordination*. It is an arduous and complicated job. Coordinating the work of these groups and the timing of their interaction is called *integration management*. Integration management is also arduous and complicated. Above all, MTs are almost certain to operate in an environment of conflict. As we will see, however, conflict is not an unmitigated disaster.

A great deal has been written about the care and feeding of teams, and much of it has been encapsulated in a delightful short work by Patrick Lencioni (2002). He writes of the "Five Dysfunctions of a Team." They are "absence of trust," "fear of conflict," "lack of commitment," "avoidance of accountability," and "inattention to results." These dysfunctions transform a team into a collection of individuals in spite of the appearance of harmony (artificial) among the team members. We have emphasized that team members be honest in their dealings with one another, which is required for the development of intrateam trust. Also, it is imperative that all members understand that they are mutually dependent on each other for achievement of the team's goals.

Integration Management

The problems of integration management are easily understood if we consider the traditional way in which products and services were designed and brought to market. The different groups involved in a product design project, for example, did not work together. They worked independently and sequentially. First, the product design group developed a design that seemed to meet the marketing group's specifications. This design was submitted to top management for approval, and possible redesign if needed. When the design was accepted, a prototype was constructed. The project was then transferred to the engineering group who tested the prototype product for quality, reliability, manufacturability, and possibly altered the design to use less-expensive materials. There were certain to be changes, and all changes were submitted for management approval, at which time a new prototype was constructed and subjected to testing.

After qualifying on all tests, the project moved to the manufacturing group who proceeded to plan the actual steps required to manufacture the product in the most cost-effective way, given the machinery and equipment currently available. Again, changes were submitted for approval, often to speed up or improve the production process. If the project proceeded to the production stage, distribution channels had to be arranged, packaging designed and produced, marketing strategies developed, advertising campaigns developed, and the product shipped to the distribution centers for sale and delivery.

Conflicts between the various functional groups were legendary. Each group tried to optimize its contribution, which led to suboptimization for the system. This process worked reasonably well, if haltingly, in the past, but was extremely time consuming and expensive—conditions not tolerable in today's competitive environment.

To solve these problems, the entire project was changed from one that proceeded sequentially through each of the steps from design to sale, to one where the steps were carried out concurrently. Parallel tasking (a.k.a. concurrent engineering or *simultaneous engineering*) was invented as a response to the time and cost associated with the traditional method. (The word "engineering" is used here in a generic sense.) Many years before the General Motors example noted in Section 2.6, Chrysler used parallel tasking to make their PT Cruiser ready for sale in Japan 4 months after it was introduced in the United States. U.S. automobile manufacturers usually took about 3 years to modify a car or truck for the Japanese market (*Autoweek*, May 22, 2000, p. 9). Possibly, "PT" for parallel tasking was the source of PT for the Cruiser.

Parallel tasking has been widely used for a great diversity of projects. For example, PT was used in the design and marketing of services by a social agency; to design, manufacture, and distribute ladies' sportswear; to design, plan, and carry out a campaign for political office; to plan the maintenance schedule for a public utility; and to design and construct the space shuttle. Parallel tasking has been generally adopted as the proper way to tackle problems that are multidisciplinary in nature.

Monte Peterson, CEO of Thermos (now a subsidiary of Nippon Sanso, Inc.), formed a flexible interdisciplinary team with representatives from marketing, manufacturing, engineering, and finance to develop a new grill that would stand out in the market. The interdisciplinary approach was used primarily to reduce the time required to complete the project. For example, by including the manufacturing people in the design process from the beginning, the team avoided some costly mistakes later on. Initially, for instance, the designers opted for tapered legs on the grill. However, after manufacturing explained at an early meeting that tapered legs would have to be custom made, the design engineers changed the design to straight legs. Under the previous system, manufacturing would not have known about the problem with the tapered legs until the design was completed. The output of this project was a revolutionary electric grill that used a new technology to give food a barbecued taste. The grill won four design awards in its first year.

The word "engineering" is used in its broadest sense, that is, the art of making practical application of science. Precisely *which* sciences is not specified. If the team members are problem oriented, parallel tasking works very well. Some interesting research has shown that when problem-oriented people with different backgrounds enter conflicts about how to deal with a problem, they often produce very creative solutions— and without damage to project quality, cost, or schedule (Hauptman and Hirji, 1996, p. 161). The group itself typically resolves the conflicts arising in such cases when they recognize that they have solved the problem. For some highly effective teams, conflict becomes a favored style of problem solving (Lencioni, 2002).

When team members are both argumentative and oriented to their own discipline, parallel tasking appears to be no improvement on any other method of problem solving. The PM will have to use negotiation, persuasion, and conflict resolution skills, but there is no guarantee that these will be successful. Even when intragroup conflict is not a serious issue with discipline-oriented team members, they often adopt suboptimization as the preferred approach to problem solving. They argue that experts should be allowed to exercise their specialties without interference from those who lack expertise.

The use of MTs in product development and planning is not without its difficulties. Successfully involving transfunctional teams in project planning requires that some structure be imposed on the planning process. The most common structure is simply to define the group's responsibility as being the development of a plan to accomplish whatever is established as the project objective. There is considerable evidence, however, that this will not prevent conflict on complex projects.

Interface Coordination—Interface Management

One of the PM's more difficult problems when working with MTs is coordinating the work of different functional groups interacting as team members. The team members come from different functional areas and often are not used to dealing with one another directly. For the most part, they have no established dependencies on each other and being co-members of a team is not sufficient to cause them to associate— unless the team has a mission that makes it important for the members to develop relationships.

One approach to the problem of interface coordination is to expose the structure of the work assigned to the team (Bailetti, Callahan, and DiPietro, 1994). One can identify and map the interdependencies between various members of the project team. Clearly, the way in which team members interact will differ during different phases of the project's work, so each major phase must be mapped separately. Figure 2-7 shows the mapping for the design of a silicon chip.

The logic of this approach to structuring MTs is reasonable. The original project plans and charts are a good initial source of information on interfaces, but project plans change during the execution of a large, complex project. Further, project plans

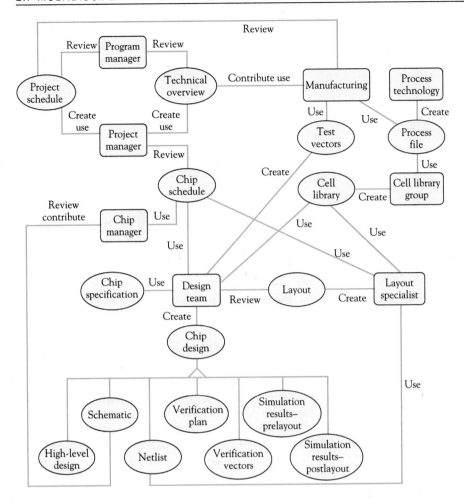

Figure 2-7 An interface mapping of a silicon chip design project (Bailetti, Callahan, and DiPietro, 1994).

assume, implicitly, that interfaces somehow change automatically during the different project phases—an assumption generally contrary to fact. This does not ignore the value of standard project planning and control tools of long-standing use; it simply uses interface maps to develop the coordination required to manage the interdependencies. The fundamental structure of this approach to interface management is shown in Figure 2-8.

No approach to interface coordination and management, taken alone, is sufficient. Mapping interfaces does not tell the PM what to do. The maps do, however, indicate which interfaces have a high potential for trouble. As usual, populating the project team with problem-oriented people will help. If a team member is strongly oriented toward making the project a success, rather than optimizing his or her individual contribution, it will be relatively easy for the PM to identify troublesome interfaces between members of the project team.

The Design Structure Matrix

One observation that can be made regarding integration management and parallel tasking is that both are fundamentally concerned with coordinating the flow of information. Furthermore, while the need to coordinate the flow of information is a challenge

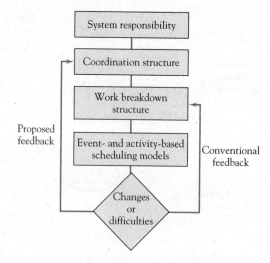

Figure 2-8   A coordination structure model for project management (Bailetti, Callahan, and DiPietro, 1994).

that confronts virtually all projects, the use of MTs tends to magnify this challenge. This is particularly true for new product development projects.

Compounding this problem is the fact that traditional project management planning tools such as Gantt charts and precedence diagrams (both discussed in Chapter 5) were developed primarily to coordinate the execution of tasks. This is because these tools were originally developed to help manage large but relatively well structured projects such as construction projects and ship building. However, in some cases such as new product development projects, the issue of information flows can be as important as the sequencing of tasks. In essence, traditional project management planning tools help identify which tasks have to be completed in order for other tasks to be started. Often, however, a more important issue is what information is needed from other tasks to complete a specific task?

To address the issue of information flows, Steven Eppinger (2001), a professor at MIT's Sloan School of Management, proposes the development and use of a *Design Structure Matrix (DSM)*. The first step in developing a DSM is to identify all the project's tasks and list them in the order in which they are typically carried out. This list of tasks makes up both the rows and columns of the DSM. Next, moving across one row at a time, all tasks that supply information to the task being evaluated are noted. When the DSM is completed, all the tasks that provide information that is needed to complete a given task can be determined by looking across that particular task's row. Likewise, moving down a particular task's column shows all the other tasks that depend on it for information. A key benefit of constructing a DSM is the ability to quickly identify and better understand how information is needed. It can also highlight potential information flow problems even before the project is started.

Comments on Empowerment and Work Teams

The use of a participatory management style has been, and will continue to be, emphasized in this book. In recent years several programs have been developed to institutionalize the participative style. Among these programs are Employee Involvement (EI), Six Sigma (SS), Quality Circles (QC), Total Quality Management (TQM), Self-Directed Work Teams (SDWT) [a.k.a. Self-Directed Teams (SDT) by dropping the word "work," which is what SDTs sometimes do], and Self-Managed Teams (SMT).

While these programs differ somewhat in structure and in the degree to which authority is delegated to the team, they are all intended to empower workers to use their knowledge and creativity to improve products, services, and production processes.

There is no doubt that some of these teams meet their goals, and there is also no doubt that many of them do not. Research on the effectiveness of these programs yields mixed results (Bailey, 1998). The research (and our experience supports this) leads to the tentative conclusion that the success or failure of empowerment teams probably has more to do with the way in which the team program is implemented than with the team itself. When empowerment team programs are implemented with a well-designed plan for involvement in solving actual problems, and when the teams have full access to all relevant information plus full support from senior management, the results seem to be quite good. When those conditions are not present, the results are mediocre at best.

Some of the more important advantages of empowerment are:

1. Teams generate high-quality solutions to appropriate problems.

2. Micromanagement is avoided.

3. The team is given accountability for some part of the project deliverable.

4. Synergistic solutions are frequent.

5. The PM has a tool for timely team evaluation and feedback.

All of these advantages are strong motivators for team members. If the team is self-directed, however, an additional element must be present for the team to have a reasonable chance at success. Senior management needs to spell out the project's goals and to be quite clear about the range of authority and responsibility of the team. "Self-directed" does not mean "without direction"—nor does it apply to the team's mission. Furthermore, taking an active role in the team's work is not "voluntary" for team members. There must be a well-publicized way of "deselecting" team members who do not actively participate and do not carry a fair share of the team's workload.

The rapid growth of virtual projects employing team members from different countries, industries, and cultures raises additional problems for empowering work teams. Customary worker/boss relationships and interactions vary widely across industrial and cultural boundaries. In such cases, the potential PM needs some training plus experience with the different cultures before taking full responsibility for empowering and leading globalized multidisciplinary teams.

For MTs and parallel tasking to be successful, whether or not the teams are self-directed, the proper infrastructure must be in place, proper guidance must be given to the teams, and a reward structure that recognizes high-quality performance should be in place.

All of the potential problems that MT and parallel tasking can suffer notwithstanding, teams are extraordinarily valuable during the process of planning a project. They are certainly worth the effort of managing and coordinating.

The task of managing the ways in which different groups interact during planning and implementation of projects is called "interface coordination." An important aid to interface coordination is mapping the interactions of the various groups. The task of integrating the work of these groups is called "integration management." Parallel tasking allows all groups involved in designing a project to work as a single group and join together to solve design

> problems simultaneously rather than separately and solving the problems sequentially. When information from some project activities is required to complete other activities, the Design Structure Matrix may be quite useful.

We hope that nothing in this chapter has made the PM's job seem simple. The best descriptor we can apply is "messy." The PM is surrounded by conflict and usually trapped in an irrational management structure, matrix management. It is most certainly a high-stress occupation.

Kent (2008) identifies six signs of excessive stress in the workplace; (1) inability to switch-off work issues, (2) disturbed sleep, (3) lack of pleasure in nonwork-related leisure activities, (4) difficulty concentrating or making decisions, (5) tendency to anger quickly, and (6) lack of energy. There are ways to deal with excessive stress. It is best if the organization is attuned to the problem and monitors their PMs and employees for work overload. Recall the chemical plant manager who installed project management as a method to control overloads. Also, the PM should be self-aware and spot the danger signals early. Kent suggests several ways to keep stress under control:

1. Keep a journal, taking time to reflect on the events of the day.

2. Prioritize all tasks facing you, eliminate tasks that do not really need to be done, transferring or delegating what you can, delaying low-priority items, and minimizing the scope of any sub-task that is not crucial to your overall task.

3. Give yourself time to unwind from high-stress meetings, perhaps by taking a short walk or doing 15 minutes of exercise or meditation. Avoid meditating on the high-stress meeting.

4. Engage in after-work physical activities that take your mind off the tasks.

5. Improve your physical surroundings so they are pleasant, enjoyable, and comfortable, helping you to relax.

6. Become aware of the control you do or do not have over events. One of the great laws of living is "Do not develop anxiety about things over which you have no control!"

One way PMs try to handle excess work is by "multitasking." As Hunsberger (2008) points out, this does not work. In fact, multitasking is a misnomer. What you are doing is switching back and forth between tasks. You lose time every time you do this. Her advice is to divide your task into small steps, prioritize them on a to-do list, be proactive by tackling and completing tasks as soon as possible, and then cross them off the list. If you can't finish in one sitting, leave notes that trigger your memory about where you were when you were interrupted. For further proof that multitasking does not work, see Chapter 6, Section 6.6.

Why on earth would any sane person select such a risky and demanding profession by choice? Perhaps because it is demanding, and because it is risky, and because when the PM has finished a job, has completed the project on time, on budget, and on scope, there is such a powerful sense of achievement. In many managerial jobs the only way that one knows one has done good work is when the boss says so—and bosses often forget to make such statements. PMs know when they have done good work. Managing a project is a high-visibility task, complete with high rewards, but it is no place for managerial wimps.

It is now time to consider planning.

REVIEW QUESTIONS

1. Explain why the systems approach is necessary to manage projects.

2. Can you think of any other desirable characteristics for team members than those listed in Section 2.6?

3. Explain the meaning and implications of "projectitis."

4. Review the chapter and make a list of all the advantages and disadvantages of matrix project organization you can find. Then add to the list any additional advantages or disadvantages that may have occurred to you.

5. What is meant by "micromanagement?" Why is it such a managerial sin?

6. List five reasons to organize a new product development project as a functionally organized project in the parent firm's Marketing department.

7. List five reasons to organize a new product development project as a transdisciplinary, matrix-organized project.

8. Exactly why were projects in the pharmaceutical company mentioned in Section 2.5 in the PMO subsection always late and over budget?

9. Why would the members of a "NOT" work independently if they were members of a designated team? What does "independently" mean in this context?

10. Why do so many "self-directed teams" perform poorly? What can be done to improve their performance?

11. What limitation associated with traditional project management techniques like Gantt charts and precedence diagrams does the Design Structure Matrix overcome?

DISCUSSION QUESTIONS

12. The chapter mentions that regular functional managers are moving from their classic authoritarian style to a facilitative, participatory style because it is more effective. Do you think it took managers 200 years to learn that, or is something else driving the change?

13. There is danger in letting the client "visit" the project operation too frequently, not the least of which is "scope creep" or informal change to the project's performance specifications. What other dangers might arise? How might the danger of scope creep be monitored and controlled?

14. How should a PM decide which problems (or potential problems) deserve being reported to management and which are not worth the trouble when attempting to "never surprise the boss?"

15. Discuss how you would go about getting competent staff from a functional department.

16. Another trade-off PMs have to make is between team process and progress—the purpose being to keep the peace, give the team an occasional rest, protect the larger organization or other projects, and so on. What might happen if the PM does not anticipate these trade-offs?

17. Usually projects involving high levels of technological uncertainty are quite complex. Yet Shenhar says to use a *flexible* management style with high-uncertainty projects, but a *formal* style with complex projects. Explain.

18. In many project-oriented organizations, even routine processes are treated as projects. Why do you think this happened? How is it accomplished?

19. A matrix organization is difficult to manage all by itself. What do you think the problems would be in managing mixed organizational systems?

20. Can you think of any circumstances where deferring conflict might be a wise course of action?

21. Give an example of a case in which project management could be important in your personal life. Explain why, as well as how and why you might organize such a project.

22. Explain the reasons for the growth and decay of each source of conflict in Figure 2-6, and for the Total as well.

23. What causes so much conflict on multidisciplinary teams? As a PM, what would you try to do to prevent or reduce such conflict?

24. Of what help is a "map of interdependencies" to a PM who is managing a transdisciplinary team?

25. What are the potential ramifications of not utilizing integration management techniques or parallel tasking while planning and implementing a project?

26. List the advantages of using an "empowered team" for planning. What conditions must be met for these advantages to accrue?

INCIDENTS FOR DISCUSSION

Samuel's Approach to Project Management

Joe Samuel was once again asked to be a project manager on a large project. This was the fourth time in the last 14 months, and he was glad to add this type of work experience to his résumé, but he dreaded the interpersonal relationship issues that always came up on projects. He felt like he was the project's babysitter, always checking on progress, making sure everyone on the team was happy and understood each other's roles, handing out assignments, and so on. Joe then remembered an article he had recently read about "tried and true project management practices." He thought "tried and true" had to be more managerially comfortable than his past experiences. He decided to accept the new project so that he could try out the new ideas.

The project Joe accepted was to make a decision on whether or not to close one of the company's distribution centers in order to improve responsiveness of their supply chain. Joe had been a manager of a supply chain service, so he felt very qualified to lead this effort. He defined the scope and deliverables of the project and detailed all of the major tasks of the project as well as most of the detail level steps in the project plan. At the first project team meeting, Joe felt very comfortable about the control and direction of the project, much more than any of the previous projects he had managed. He had specifically defined objectives and tasks for each member of the project team. He even determined completion dates for each task. He wrote individual "contracts" for each team member to sign as an indication of their commitment to completion of the designated tasks by the assigned schedule dates. The meeting went smoothly, with almost no comments or questions from the project team. Everyone picked up a copy of their "contract" and went off to work on the project. Joe felt great and was pleased with the success of his new approach to project management.

Questions: How do you think Joe will feel six weeks after the project is underway? Compare his new approach to project management with his previous approach.

HardTech, Inc.

HardTech Inc. is a 2-year-old electronics firm that was created by three friends who worked together as senior engineers at a *Fortune* 500 electronics firm; Jake Tyler, Caroline Ryan, and Mike Preston. The three developed a high-speed-processing chip that was designed for handheld scanning devices. Their startup became successful when they won a major contract from a large software company that wanted to integrate the chip into a handheld scanner for inventory management.

HardTech's three founders structured their firm as a traditional functional organizational structure, as that was the environment they came from. After 2 years, in addition to their production people, HardTech employed 17 development engineers including a manager, four designers with a design department manager, three people in the sales and marketing department, and two administrative personnel as support.

Tyler, Ryan, and Preston now felt ready to take their "show on the road." They wanted to launch three major initiatives: (1) to develop a chip that would work with grocery store scanners; (2) to get into the hospital point-of-care scanner market; and (3) to upgrade the chip they were using for their inventory management contract while maintaining their current commitments.

Tyler and Preston thought that the current organizational structure could handle the new initiatives. They wanted to assign each phase of the new development projects to a specific department. Ryan felt that the traditional approach would not support the need to be quick to market and that the current contract would always be the priority to each of the department managers. She wanted to set up project teams reporting directly to HardTech's three senior officers.

Questions: What organizational structure would you recommend HardTech use to complete the three initiatives outlined? Why?

C A S E

The Quantum Bank

Quantum Bank Inc. is a regional bank with branches throughout the southeast. In early 2011 the bank launched an app for mobile devices that provided its customers with the ability to check account balances, obtain information about the bank's various services, obtain contact information and email questions, and link to a variety of other useful sources of information. Given the app's tremendous success, competition from both traditional and nontraditional organizations, and the desire to expand its presence beyond its current geographical area, Quantum decided to significantly enhance its app. More specifically, Quantum would like to enhance its app to include a mobile bill payment service, allow customers to apply for credit cards and loans, open accounts, and manage their investment portfolios.

Vice-President of Information Systems, Stacey Thomas, has been charged with overseeing the project. One of her first tasks was to select the project manager. Because of the strategic importance of the project, she had a strong preference for staffing the project internally as opposed to employing the services of one of the many consulting firms available that specialize in these types of projects. After developing a list of ten or so possible candidates to serve as project manager, she was finally able to pare the list down to the two finalists described below.

Bill Fence Bill joined Quantum in 2005 after graduating from a well-respected small private school with a degree in computer science. His first assignment as a member of the bank's help desk provided him with exposure to a variety of areas in the bank. He quickly gained a reputation for being able to solve difficult technical problems. In addition, users of the bank's various computer systems were often heard commenting on how service oriented Bill was and on his ability to describe concepts in nontechnical terms.

Because of both his technical knowledge related to hardware and his ability to program, Bill was selected to develop the bank's first mobile app in 2010. Bill worked alone on this project and had frequent meetings with one of the bank's directors of Information Systems, who supervised the project. Initially, the director did most of the design work and Bill did the programming. Bill often proposed alternative ways for incorporating key features into the app, and the director would choose among the options Bill identified. Toward the end of the development project, Bill began to take a more active role in proposing features to include in the app.

The development project was largely completed on time and on budget considering the changes in the scope of the project that were made as the project progressed. Several suggestions that would have extended the app's functionality were tabled to be considered as updates after the app was officially launched.

In his current position as Webmaster, Bill is in charge of maintaining the bank's Web site. Although Bill's staff now includes a programmer and a hardware specialist, his approach is very much hands on, staying involved with all technical aspects of the site. Bill has developed an excellent rapport with his two direct reports, and they have emulated much of Bill's style, including working long hours and even competing to see who can accumulate the largest number of soft drink cans, empty candy wrappers, and computer printouts on one desk.

Andy Dover Andy Dover also joined the bank in 2005 after completing his MBA at a large public university. Andy entered graduate school immediately after graduating with a Civil Engineering undergraduate degree at the same university.

Andy spent his first year rotating between various departments in the bank's management training program. After completing this training, Andy requested permanent assignment to the operations group. His initial assignment was to oversee the check encoding operation. After implementing several process improvements, Andy was eventually promoted to senior operations analyst and worked on several large process improvement projects.

Performance evaluations of Andy suggested that one of his greatest strengths was his ability to step back from a problem and understand how the various issues were interrelated. His evaluations further recognized him as "a highly motivated self-starter with very good organizational skills." His organizational skills also helped him effectively present information, and he was often requested to make short presentations related to a particular project's status to senior management.

By almost all accounts, Andy was considered highly competent, completing assigned tasks in a timely fashion with little or no direct supervision. At the same time, Andy always made it a point to communicate regularly with other project team members to keep them abreast of his progress. He was often passionate about his ideas and was typically able to get buy-in from other team members for his ideas.

Andy is almost always seen carrying his planner. As an avid stock investor, he makes it a point to stay abreast of trends in technology. He has a basic understanding of how mobile computing works and knows all the important buzzwords. While he has fooled around and created a couple of apps, he knows very little about more sophisticated programming languages such as Java, and knows even less about computer hardware beyond its basic purpose.

QUESTIONS

1. Who would you recommend Stacey Thomas select to serve as project manager? Why?

2. How would you recommend this project be organized? Functional project? Pure project? Matrix? Why?

3. Do you agree with Ms. Thomas's decision that the project should be staffed internally? What are the major advantages of staffing the project with Quantum employees? Are there any advantages to utilizing the services of an outside consulting firm?

C A S E

Southern Care Hospital

Southern Care Hospital (SCH) is a large, nonprofit regional hospital located in the southeast. Several years ago it contracted with the healthcare division of a major medical equipment supplier to provide Six Sigma training to a group of its hospital employees. Since that time, numerous waves of Green Belts and Black Belts have been trained including people across all job ranks and representing most departments. Green Belt training entails two weeks of formal in-class training while Black Belt training entails the two weeks of Green Belt training plus an additional four weeks of training. Both Green Belt and Black Belt training require the completion of a Six Sigma project in addition to the in-class training.

One challenge currently facing SCH is significant levels of dissatisfaction from the medical staff regarding the three-day lead time it currently averages the nuclear medicine department to turn around the results of stress tests. In this case, "lead time" is defined as the elapsed time from when the stress test is ordered by a physician until the time when a radiologist from the nuclear medicine department signs off on the test results. Stress tests are used to determine the amount of stress the heart can endure before either an abnormal rhythm or insufficien flow of blood to the heart develops. Typically, the stress test is administered by increasing the level of difficulty as a patient walks on a treadmill or rides a stationary bike. During the stress test vital statistics are collected and monitored, including the patient's heart rate and blood pressure. Discussions with the medical staff indicate that they desire maximum lead times of a day and a half.

You have been selected to manage a Six Sigma project focusing on reducing the lead times associated with receiving the results of stress tests. Based on your past experience with similar projects, you have identified 20 major activities. SSH's steering committee has further granted you permission to select up to four team members from the available resource pool to staff the project.

Table 1 provides relevant background information on the 12 people currently available for assignment to a Six Sigma project. All resources are available to the project on a part-time basis and therefore support Six Sigma projects in addition to performing their normal job assignments. The table lists the employee name, job title, level of education, years of work experience, Six Sigma rank (i.e., Green Belt or Black Belt), the number of Six Sigma projects the employee has worked on, the average amount of savings that resulted from the Six Sigma projects the employee has worked on, the employee's hourly rate, and the percent of time the employee is available. The hourly rate represents what will be charged against your project's budget for work performed by a given employee. The percent available is based on a 40-hour work week. Therefore, the number of hours you can utilize a resource during a given week cannot exceed the available percentage times 40. To illustrate, Anna Frost can complete at most 8 hours (20% 40 hours/week) of project work per week.

To facilitate project planning, SSH uses an advanced Six Sigma database program to track the progress and performance of all ongoing projects. Furthermore, the HR department has developed a process to estimate the proficiency of employees completing various planned tasks in future Six Sigma projects based on the historical data contained in the database. The proficiency numbers can range between zero and 100, with a zero indicating no ability to perform the task and 100 implying extensive expertise and experience performing the task. Table 2 summarizes this information for the 12 employees listed in Table 1 for the 20 project tasks initially identified. Past experience with these estimates indicates they are fairly accurate over an entire project but that employee performance typically varies ±3 percentage points within a given week. Thus, an employee with an estimated proficiency of 90 on a particular task would be expected to perform in the 87–93 range on the task in any given week.

A final comment regarding the available resources is in order. Specifically, past experience with projects indicates that conflict occasionally arises when more than one Black Belt is assigned to the same task. When such conflict does arise, it tends to negatively impact both the time required to complete tasks that the Black Belts are jointly assigned to as well as the overall quality of the work performed.

QUESTIONS

1. Explain how you would execute your roles as project manager of this project.
2. As the project manager, how would you manage trade-offs?
3. How would you recommend this project be organized? Functional project? Pure project? Matrix? Why?
4. What criteria would you use in selecting resources to serve on your project team?
5. From the available resource pool, who would you select to be on your project team? Why?

Table 1   Background Information on Available Project Resources

First Name	Last Name	Job Title	Education	Years of Experience	SS Rank	SS Experience	# of SS Projects	Avg Proj Savings	Hourly Rate	Availability
Anna	Frost	Radiology Practice Administrator	MPH	11	GB	1	1	$50,000	$58	20%
Edward	Young	Radiology Office Administrator	B	7	GB	1	1	$62,000	$36	30%
Hazel	Vaughn	Radiology Supervisor	B	6	GB	2	1	$74,000	$40	30%
Howard	Payne	Radiology Supervisor	B	4	GB	1.5	1	$68,000	$30	35%
Joyce	Snyder	Radiology Info Sys Mgr	B	5	GB	3	3	$112,000	$35	50%
Ken	Inman	Radiology DB Mgr	B	3	GB	1.5	2	$95,000	$25	50%
Nick	Rogers	Adm of Special Projects	B	5	BB	3	6	$211,000	$33	50%
Peggy	Moss	Radiology Senior Bus Analyst	MBA	6	BB	3	6	$240,000	$40	50%
Peter	Foltz	Radiology Bus Analyst	B	3	GB	2	5	$187,000	$30	50%
Roberta	Jackson	Senior Nurse Manager	B	15	GB	1	1	$75,000	$42	20%
Susan	Osborne	Staff Nurse	B	8	GB	1	1	$35,000	$35	50%
Stephanie	Thomas	Staff Nurse	B	4	GB	1	1	$42,000	$30	50%

BIBLIOGRAPHY

AFZALUR, R. M. *Managing Conflict in Organizations*. Westport, CT: Praeger, 1992.

BLOCK, T. R. "The Project Office Phenomenon." *PM Network*, March 1998.

BOLLES, D. "The Project Support Office." *PM Network*, March 1998.

CHURCHMAN, C. W. *The Systems Approach*, rev. ed., New York: Delta, 1979.

CONGER, J. A. "The Necessary Art of Persuasion." *Harvard Business Review*, May–June 1998.

DEWHURST, H. D. "Project Teams: What Have We Learned?" *PM Network*, April 1998.

EPPINGER, S. F. "Innovation at the Speed of Information." *Harvard Business Review*, January 2001.

FLYNN, J. "E-Mail, Cellphones and Frequent-Flier Miles Let 'Virtual' Expats Work Abroad but Live at Home." *The Wall Street Journal*, New York: Dow Jones, October 25, 1999.

GAGNON, R. J., and S. J. Mantel, Jr. "Strategies and Performance Improvement for Computer-Assisted Design." *IEEE Transactions on Engineering Management*, November 1987.

GALE, S. F. "The Big Time." *PM Network*, February 2009.

GIFFIN, S. D. "A Taxonomy of Internet Applications for Project Management Communication." *Project Management Journal*, December 2002. (This article provides an interesting overview related to the ways that the Internet can be used to enhance project management communication.)

Table 2 Estimated Resource Proficiencies

						Resources							
Task	Anna Frost	Edward Young	Hazel Vaughn	Howard Payne	Joyce Snyder	Ken Inman	Nick Rogers	Peggy Moss	Peter Foltz	Roberta Jackson	Susan Osborne	Stephanie Thomas
Define Phase												
Establish Project Goals	98	91	86	83	90	83	92	95	91	85	82	78
Develop Project Charter	88	86	86	84	93	88	93	96	90	82	79	76
VOC Study	84	84	87	83	92	89	94	96	92	82	83	81
Develop CTQ Tree	75	75	85	80	88	94	94	97	95	78	78	78
Develop Process Map	78	78	85	80	90	88	92	94	96	75	76	74
Stakeholder Analysis	95	90	90	88	90	87	93	92	90	78	77	79
Measure Phase												
Collect Process Data	70	80	85	82	90	88	92	90	95	75	77	78
Develop Run Chart	75	80	84	82	86	88	92	94	90	76	75	77
Calculate DPMO	75	78	80	78	85	87	96	94	90	72	72	72
Revise Project Charter	93	90	92	91	92	88	93	95	90	85	82	80
Analyze Phase												
Cause and Effect Diagram	85	88	92	90	75	72	80	87	85	92	97	93
Summary Statistics and Test	65	65	68	65	70	72	85	88	80	64	63	65
Pareto Analysis	80	84	90	88	90	92	98	98	96	78	78	78
Regression Analysis	65	70	75	67	78	80	90	92	87	63	60	61
Improve Phase												
Develop Payoff Matrix	96	90	90	88	91	85	92	92	90	83	80	77
Identify Improvements	88	86	90	90	82	80	88	90	88	93	96	93
Develop Training Material	80	85	95	90	91	88	90	86	88	83	75	72
Control												
Develop Checklists	80	88	96	92	93	80	92	88	88	87	68	73
Develop SPC Charts	65	78	82	80	80	84	95	95	93	63	61	61
Develop Status Reports	90	95	92	93	87	80	88	89	86	86	76	72

GOLDRATT, E. M., and J. Cox. *The Goal*, 2nd rev. ed., Great Barrington, MA: North River Press, 1992. (One of the outstanding works in the entire literature of business. This novel is a powerful statement on the dangers of sub-optimization. Many companies assign it as required reading for their managers.)

GRANT, K. P., C. R. BAUMGARDNER, and G. S. STONE. "The Perceived Importance of Technical Competence to Project Managers in the Defense Acquisition Community." *IEEE Transactions on Engineering Management*, February 1997.

HERZBERG, F. H. "One More Time: How Do You Motivate Employees?" *Harvard Business Review*, January–February 1968.

HUGHES, T. P. *Rescuing Prometheus*. New York: Pantheon, 1998. (A wonderful book written by a historian. It is full of fascinating stories and valuable insights about the nature of complex projects and the management problems they raise.)

HUNSBERGER, K. "Juggling Act." *PM Network*, September 2008.

IBBS, C. W., and Y. H. KWAK. "Assessing Project Management Maturity." *Project Management Journal*. March 2000.

JONES, T. "Code of Conduct." *PM Network*, October 2008.

KENT, S. "Stretched Thin." *PM Network*, April 2008.

KOTHA, S., D. E. Oleson, R. Nolan, and P. M. Condit. "Boeing 787: The Dreamliner." Harvard Business School Publishing, Boston, MA, June 2005.

KOTTER, J. P. "What Effective General Managers Really Do." *Harvard Business Review*, November–December 1982. (An article that "tells it like it is." Most people who have never served as a manager do not believe it. Those who have managed general or project management know it is accurate.)

LENCIONI, P., *The Five Dysfunctions of a Team: A Leadership Fable*. San Francisco, Jossey-Bass, A Wiley Company, 2002. (Much like Goldratt's *The Goal*, this work is fictional and tells the story of a new senior manager who takes over a team of subordinates. It is a quick and easy read and well worth the brief time.)

LUBIANIKER, S. "Opening the Book on the Open Maturity Model." *PM Network*, March 2000.

MATSON, E. "Congratulations, You're Promoted" and "Project: You." *Fast Company*, as reprinted in *Engineering Management Review*, Winter 1998. (Two excellent articles that report hard fact with wry humor.)

MCCARTHY, J., and M. MCCARTHY. *Software for Your Head*, Boston: Addison-Wesley, 2002. (Subtitled "Core Protocols for Creating and Maintaining Shared Vision," this book is a unique approach to managing a project by team building. Also see "McCarthy" in the bibliography to Chapter 4.)

PATTERSON, N. "Selecting Project Managers: An Integrated List of Predictors." *Project Management Journal*, June 1991.

PENNYPACKER, J. S., and K. P. Grant. "Project Management Maturity: An Industry Benchmark." *Project Management Journal*, March 2003.

PINTO, J. K., and D. P. SLEVIN. "The Project Champion: Key to Implementation Success." *Project Management Journal*, December 1989. (See also Green, S. G., in the bibliography to Chapter 1.)

PINTO, J. K., and O. P. KHARBANDA. "Lessons for an Accidental Profession." *Business Horizons*, March–April 1995. (An absolutely wonderful article on project management, including "the vital dozen" rules for the project manager.)

PMI, "PMO Speeds Success for Transportation Facility," *PM Network*. May 2004.

PMI. "The Growing Gap Between Project Manager Supply and Demand." *PMI Today*, Newtown Square, PA Project Management Institute, June, 2009.

Project Management Institute Standards Committee. *A Guide to the Project Management Body of Knowledge*. 5th ed., Newtown Square, PA: Project Management Institute, 2013.

REMY, R. "Adding Focus to Improvement Efforts with PM^3." *PM Network*, July 1997.

SCHODERBEK, P. P., C. G. SCHODERBEK, and A. G. KEFALAS. *Management Systems: Conceptual Considerations*. 4th ed., Homewood, IL: Irwin, 1990.

SHENHAR, A. J. "From Theory to Practice: Toward a Typology of Project-Management Styles." *IEEE Transactions on Engineering Management*, February 1998.

SWANSON, S. A. "On the Map." *PM Network*, November 2009.

THAMHAIN, H. J., and D. L. WILEMON. "Conflict Management in Project Life Cycles." *Sloan Management Review*, Summer 1975.

3

Project Activity and Risk Planning

If problems arise during the life of a project, our first hunch would be that the project was not properly planned. Most of the time our hunch would be correct. Inadequate planning is more the case than the exception. We can only guess why. Perhaps the reason is that senior management and/or the PM and/or the project team are impatient. They want "to get on with it." Possibly some of the people who should be engaged in planning have heard Tom Peters, well-known searcher-for-excellence and management guru, comment that good planning almost never cuts implementation time and that "Ready, Fire, Aim" is the way good businesses do it.

As a matter of fact, Peters is wrong. There is a ton of research that concludes that careful planning is strongly associated with project success—and to the best of our knowledge there is no research that supports the opposite position. Clearly, planning can be overdone, a condition often called "paralysis by analysis." Somewhere in between the extremes is the happy medium that everyone would like to strike, but this chapter does not seek to define the golden mean between no planning and overplanning (Langley, 1995). We do, however, examine the nature of good planning, and we describe proven methods for generating plans that are adequate to the task of leading a project work force from the start of the project to its successful conclusion. We must start by deciding what things should be a part of a project plan.

3.1 THE BASIS OF A PROJECT PLAN—THE "PROJECT CHARTER"

Before considering how to plan, we should decide why we are planning and what information the plan should contain. The primary function of a project plan is to serve the PM as a map of the route from project start to finish. The plan should include the business case or the organization's expected financial benefits that will accrue as well as the strategic reasons for the project. The plan should contain sufficient information that, at any time, the PM knows what remains to be done, when, with what resources, by whom, when the task will be completed, and what deliverables the output should include. This information must be known at any level of detail from the most general overall level to the minutiae of the smallest subtask. As the project travels the route from start to finish, the PM needs also to know whether or not any changes in project plans are contemplated and whether or not any problems are likely to arise in the future. In other words, the PM needs to know the project's current state and its future expectations. Because PMs are sometimes appointed after the project has begun, the PM also needs to know the project's history to date.

PMBOK Guide

The PMBOK Project Plan (Chapter 4 and parts of the following chapter of PMBOK) is comprehensive and refers to the Project Charter and all the elements concerning the planning, execution, and control of the project. In practice, the charter is essentially an abridged version of what will later become the full project plan, thus containing summaries of the budget and schedule details. The major project stakeholders must sign off on the charter before initiation of the project. The list of signatories would include a person representing the project sponsor, the client/user, the Project Manager, and the Program Manager if the project is a part of an overall program. In some cases, representatives of other stakeholders may be asked to sign their approval. Clearly, this may require negotiation. Once agreed to, the charter cannot be altered by any signer without acceptance by the others.

A bias toward reality requires us to note that different stakeholders have different levels of clout. If senior management and the client both favor a change in the scope of the project, the project manager and his or her team would be well advised to accept the change in good grace unless there is some overriding reason why such a change would be infeasible. Occasionally, stakeholders not directly connected to the organization conducting the project or the client purchasing it can be so demanding that provision is made for them to sign off on specific changes. Consider, for example, People for the Ethical Treatment of Animals (PETA) and their battles with cosmetic firms over the use of animal testing for cosmetic products. Once completed, the Project Charter becomes the basis for the follow-on full project plan.

The multiple elements required in the Project Charter fall into one of the following eight categories.

1. **Purpose**. This section describes the *Business Case* for the project. The Business Case includes the strategic reasons for the project, its expected profitability and competitive effects, as well as the desired scope and any other technical results. The intent of the Business Case is to communicate to project team members (and others) the reasons why the organization is undertaking the project.

2. **Objectives**. This is a more detailed description of the project's scope, its deliverables and outcomes. Another approach to describing a project's objectives is the project *mission statement*. While somewhat similar to the Business Case, the focus of the mission statement is to communicate to project team members (and others) what will be done to achieve the project's overall objectives. To foster team understanding of the project as a whole, a representative group of team members and stakeholders are often included in the process of developing the statement of objectives.

3. **Overview**. This section contains a brief description of the project and its deliverables (the latter are the project scope), together with a list of the major milestones or significant events in the project schedule and any constraints on the project scope. It is intended for senior management. The technological and managerial approaches to the work are also described. An identification of the project as "derivative,"

"platform," or "breakthrough" might be included, as might the relationship between this project and others being undertaken or contemplated by the organization. Also noted are plans that go beyond the organization's standard management practices such as the use of consultants or subcontractors. This section should also describe the agreements made with the client or any third party such as reporting requirements; technical specifications of deliverables; delivery dates; any incentives or penalties; the procedures for making changes in the deliverables or project procedures; and similar agreements.

4. **Schedules**. Included in this section is a summary of schedules and milestones. The major tasks in the project are listed in a project Work Breakdown Schedule. (The WBS is discussed later in this chapter.) Listed with each task is the time required to perform it. The project plan's full schedule will then be constructed from these data.

5. **Resource requirements**. Estimates of project expenses, both capital and operating, are included here. The costs associated with each task are shown, and overhead and fixed charges are described. Appropriate account numbers to be charged are listed with the relevant cost items. This then becomes the *project budget*, though the PM may use a budget that deletes overhead and some fixed charges for day-to-day project management and control. (The details of budget preparation are covered in the next chapter.) In addition, cost monitoring and cost control procedures may be described here.

6. **Personnel and stakeholders**. This section describes the stakeholders, sponsor, project manager, and possibly some members of the project team. It notes any special skill requirements, necessary training, and special legal arrangements such as security clearances or nondisclosure agreements. Combined with the schedule, it may also note the time-phasing of personnel requirements. Sections 4, 5, and 6 may contain individual notations concerning managerial responsibility for control of each project area, detailing the managerial/informational accountability requirements for each person.

Risk

7. **Risk management**. "Learn from experience" is a widely ignored adage. This section is an attempt to remedy that condition. Planners should list the major and minor disasters that may strike projects similar to the one being undertaken—late subcontractor deliveries, bad weather, unreasonable deadlines, equipment failure, complex coordination problems, client changes in project scope, and similar dire happenings. The argument is often made that crises cannot be predicted but the only uncertainty is which crisis will occur and when. In any case, dealing with crises does not require a which-and-when prediction. Contingency plans to deal with the potential crises described here should be a standard part of the follow-on project plan and included in a permanent file in the PMO (or EPMO). It is well to remember that no amount of planning can prevent all crises—but developing contingency plans may prevent or soften the impact of some. Other methods for handling risks are covered later in this chapter.

8. **Evaluation methods**. Descriptions of all project evaluation procedures and quality standards are found in this section. Also included are procedures to ensure compliance with all corporate requirements for monitoring, collecting, and storing data on project performance, together with a description of the required project history.

It is hard to overstate the importance of a clear statement of the purpose of the project. It is not, repeat NOT, sufficient to state the project objectives without reference to its purpose. For example, to reach the Pudong International Airport from Shanghai's business center, China built a magnetic levitation (maglev) train that runs every 10 minutes (PMI, April 2004). Reaching speeds over 300 miles an hour, it whisks people to the airport 20 miles away in less than 8 minutes. However, according to the vice-director of the train company, "We are not lucky with ticket sales." The trains are virtually empty. The reason is simple. To meet the time deadline and budget, the train station was located 6 miles outside the city center, requiring lengthy public transportation to get there. The project met its technical, budgetary, and schedule objectives successfully. It failed, however, to meet the needs of the public. China is currently investigating extending the line to the downtown area, but that will be a much more expensive and time-consuming project.

The importance of a contract specifying the process of potential problem solving between the project's principals in addition to the content of project deliverables is made clear in the following example. $74 million of Philadelphia's $567 million Market Street Elevated train system reconstruction project went to PKF Mark III contractors for one portion of the system (PMI, Feb. 2005). The Philadelphia transportation authority (SEPTA), however, maintained that PKF is was far behind schedule, failed to meet the eight milestones of the contract, or complete any of the activities. PKF, in turn, maintained that SEPTA's failure to accept work performed in accordance with the contract constituted a change in project scope, and SEPTA's lack of timely action regarding submittals, requests for information and drawings, claims and change orders are what took the project off schedule. Both groups have gone into litigation to resolve the issue, but the delays of litigation threaten the loss of federal funding for the project. If mediation instead of litigation had been included in the initial contract, the problem might have been more quickly resolved.

One additional use for a careful, complete project plan is when the project may be small and routine, but it is also carried out frequently, as in some maintenance projects. The complete planning process may be conducted to form a template for such projects—with particular emphasis on evaluation methods. With this template, planning similar projects is simple—just fill in the blanks. If changes in the plan are contemplated, the prescribed evaluation methods can be employed. This allows a "continuous improvement" program, sometimes called "rolling wave" planning, to be implemented with ongoing evaluation of suggested changes.

> The project plan should contain eight elements: the project's purpose, a statement of objectives, a general overview, schedules of activities, a list of resource requirements or a project budget, a description of the stakeholders and personnel requirements, a description of potential risks, and the methods for evaluating the project. When all stakeholders have signed off on the plan, it becomes an operational Project Charter.

3.2 THE PLANNING PROCESS—OVERVIEW

A great deal has been written about planning. Some of the literature focuses on the strategic aspect of planning—(e.g., Webster, Reif, and Bracker, 1989) choosing and planning projects that contribute to the organization's goals (cf., the introduction to Section 1.5, in Chapter 1). Another body of writing is directed at the techniques of how to plan rather than what to plan (e.g., Pells, 1993; Prentis, 1989). These techniques, if we are to believe what we read, differ from industry to industry, from subject to subject. Architecture has a planning process; so does software development, as does construction, as well as pharmaceutical R&D projects, and campaigns for raising funds for charity.

As far as we can determine, the way that planning techniques vary in these different cases has more to do with nomenclature than substance. Consider, for example, the following planning process that has been divided into eight distinct steps.

1. Develop and evaluate the concept of the project. Describe what it is you wish to develop, including its basic performance characteristics, and decide if getting such a deliverable is worthwhile. If so, continue.

2. Carefully identify and spell out the actual capabilities that the project's deliverable must have to be successful. Design a system (product or service) that will have the requisite capabilities.

3. Create such a system (product or service), which is to say, build a prototype deliverable.

4. Test the prototype to see if it does, in fact, have the desired capabilities. If necessary, cycle back to step 3 to modify the prototype and retest it. Continue until the deliverable meets the preset requirements.

5. Integrate the deliverable into the system for which it was designed. In other words, install the deliverable in its required setting.

6. Validate the deliverable—which answers the question, "Now that we have installed the deliverable, does it still work properly?"

7. If the deliverable has been validated, let the client test it. Can the client operate the system? If not, instruct the client.

8. If the client can operate (and accepts) the deliverable, make sure that the client understands all standard operating and maintenance requirements. Then shake the client's hand, present the client with a written copy of maintenance and operating instructions, give the client the bill, and leave.

Risk

Reread the eight steps. Are they not an adequate description of the planning process for the design of a new pick-up truck, of a high-end hotel room, of a restaurant kitchen, of a machine tool, of a line of toys, etc.? They would need a bit of tweaking for some projects. An R&D project would need a more extensive risk analysis. If the project is a new pharmaceutical, for example, it would need toxicity and efficacy testing, and clearance from the FDA, but the general structure of the planning process is still adequate.

The eight steps above were originally written to describe the planning process for computer software (Aaron, Bratta, and Smith, 1993). There seem to be as many different planning sequences and steps as there are authors writing about planning. Almost all of them, regardless of the number of steps, meet the same criteria if they are meant to guide a project to a successful conclusion. The final plan must have the elements described in the previous section of this chapter.

> There are many techniques for developing a project plan and Project Charter. They are fundamentally similar. All of them use a systematic analysis to identify and list the things that must be undertaken in order to achieve the project's objectives, to test and validate the plan, and to deliver it to the user.

3.3 THE PLANNING PROCESS—NUTS AND BOLTS

This section deals with the problem of determining and listing the various tasks that must be accomplished in order to complete a project. The important matters of generating a project budget and developing a precise project schedule are left to succeeding chapters, though much of the raw material for doing those important things will come from the planning process described here.

The Launch Meeting—and Subsequent Meetings

Once senior management has decided to fund a major project, or a highly important small project, a *project launch meeting* should be called. Preparation for this meeting is required (Knutson, 1995; Martin and Tate, 1998).

When a PM is appointed to head a new project, the PM's first job is to review the project objectives (*project scope plus expected desirable outcomes that accrue to stakeholders from matters beyond the project's deliverables*) with the senior manager who has fundamental responsibility for the project. The purpose of this interview is threefold: (1) to make sure that the PM understands the expectations that the organization, the client, and other stakeholders have for the project; (2) to identify those among the senior managers (in addition to the manager who is party to this interview) who have a major interest in the project; and (3) to determine if anything about the project is atypical for projects of the same general kind (e.g., a product/service development project undertaken in order to extend the firm's market into a new area).

Armed with this background, the PM should briefly study the project with an eye to preparing an invitation list for the project launch meeting. At the top of the list should be at least one representative of senior management, a strong preference given to the individual with the strongest interest in the project, the probable project champion. (The champion is usually, but not necessarily, the senior manager with responsibility for the project.) Recall in Chapter 2 we noted that the project champion could lend the political clout that is occasionally needed to overcome obstacles to cooperation from functional managers—if such obstacles were not amenable to dissolution by the PM.

Next on the invitation list come the managers from the functional areas that will be called upon to contribute competencies or capacities to the project. If highly specialized technical experts will be needed, the PM can add individuals with the required expertise to the list, after clearing the invitation with their immediate bosses, of course.

The PM may chair the launch meeting, but the senior manager introduces the project to the group, and discusses its contributions to the parent organization. If known and relevant, the project's tentative priority may be announced, as should the tentative budget estimate used in the project selection process. If the due dates for deliverables have been contracted, this should also be made clear. The purpose of senior management's presence is to ensure that the group understands the firm's commitment to the project. It is particularly important for the functional managers to understand that management is making a real commitment, not merely paying lip service.

At this point, the PM can take over the meeting and begin a group discussion of the project. It is, however, important for the senior manager(s) to remain for this discussion. The continuing presence of these august persons more or less assures cooperation from the functional units. The purpose of the discussion is to develop a general understanding of what functional inputs the project will need.

Table 3-1   Program Launch Meeting Output, Human Resources Development

Goal of Program: Reduce employee turnover from 60 percent to 40 percent
Program Manager: Human Resources Director

Objective	Action Item
Improve employee morale	• Collect data from: • Exit interviews • Employee survey • Cultural audit • Interviewing "retained" employees • Seminars for all staff on personality types and working styles • Employee fitness center implemented • New employee luncheons with department heads • New hire "30-day" reunions • Complete pro forma for opening day care center • Overhaul of employee orientation program • Competitive salary analysis conducted and adjustments made
Broaden staff competencies	• Competencies for all positions completed and system established to maintain ongoing competencies
Attain stronger employee commitment to organizational standards for productivity, outcomes, and customer satisfaction	• Six-week series on management and leadership for managers • Leadership training for supervisors • Performance-based pay system developed • Job descriptions format redesigned around organizational effectiveness standards
Improve recruitment efforts	• Increase recruitment efforts, additional advertising, three job fairs • Hire recruiter • Implement defined contribution pension plan for new hires • Internet job hotline • Radio spots

Some launch meetings are restricted to brainstorming a problem. The output of such a meeting is shown in Table 3-1. In this case, the Director of Human Resources (HR) of a medium-size firm was asked by the Board of Directors to set up a program to improve employee retention. At the time, the firm had a turnover rate slightly above 60 percent per year among its technical employees. (A turnover rate of 50 percent was about average for the industry.) The HR Director held a launch meeting of all department heads, all senior corporate officers, and members of the Board. At this meeting, the group developed a list of "action items," each of which became a project.

When dealing with a single project, it is common for a preliminary plan to be generated at the launch meeting, but we question the advisability of this. For either functional managers or the PM to guess at budgets or schedules with no real study of the project's deliverables is not prudent. First, the transition from a "tentative, wild guesstimate" made by senior managers or the EPMO to "but you promised" is instantaneous in these cases. Second, there is no foundation for mutual discussion or negotiation about different positions taken publicly and based on so little knowledge or thought. It is sufficient, in our judgment, to get a firm commitment from functional managers to study the proposed project and return for another meeting with a technically (and politically) feasible plan for their group's input to the project.

It has been said, "If this means many planning meetings and extensive use of participatory decision making, then it is well worth the effort (Ford and McLaughlin, 1992, p. 316). If the emphasis is on "participative decision making," we agree. Actual planning at the launch meeting should not go beyond the most aggregated level unless the deliverables are well understood or the delivery date is cast in concrete and the organization has considerable experience with similar projects. Of course, if this is the case, a major launch meeting may not be required.

The results of the launch meeting should be that: (1) the project's scope is understood and temporarily fixed; (2) the various functional managers understand their responsibilities and have committed to develop an initial task and resource plan; and (3) any potential benefits to the organization outside the scope of the project are noted. In the meetings that follow, the project plan will become more and more detailed and firmer. When the group has developed what appears to be a workable plan with a schedule and budget that seem feasible, the plan moves through the appropriate management levels where it is approved, or altered and approved. If altered, it must be checked with those who did the planning. The planners may accept the alterations or a counterproposal may be made. The project plan may cycle up and down the managerial ladder several times before it receives final approval, at which time no further changes may be made without a formal *change order* (a procedure also described in the plan).

Irrespective of who alters (or suggests alterations to) the project plan during the process described above, it is imperative that everyone be kept fully informed. It is no more equitable for a senior manager to change a plan without consultation with the PM (and, hence, the project team) than it would be for the PM or the team to alter the plan without consultation and approval from senior management. If an arm's-length client is involved, the client's approval is required for any changes that will have an effect on the schedule, cost, or deliverable. Clearly, the PMO (or EPMO) can facilitate this process.

Open, honest, and frequent communication between the interested parties is critical for successful planning. What emerges from this process is sometimes called the project *baseline plan*. It contains all the nine elements noted in Section 3.1 and all amendments to the plan adopted as the project is carried out. As noted above, when senior management, the client, and other stakeholders have "signed-off" on the plan, it becomes a part of the *Project Charter*, a contract-like document affirming that all major parties-at-interest to the project are in agreement on the deliverables, the cost, and the schedule.

Sorting Out the Project—The Work Breakdown Structure (WBS)

PMBOK Guide

Inadequate up-front planning, especially failing to identify all important tasks, is a primary contributor to the failure of a project to achieve its cost and time objectives. Therefore, a primary purpose for developing a WBS is to ensure that any task required to produce a deliverable is not overlooked and thereby not accounted for and planned. PMBOK describes the construction of the WBS primarily in Chapter 5 on Scope, but it is also touched upon in Chapters 6 (Time), 7 (Cost), and 8 (Quality).

The previous subsection discussed the planning process as seen from the outside. The PM and the functional managers developed plans as if by magic. It is now time to be specific about how such plans may be generated. In order to develop a project plan that will take us from start to finish of a project, we need to know precisely what must be done, by whom, when, and with what resources. Every task, however small, that must be completed in order to complete the project should be listed together with any required material or human resources.

Making such a list is a nontrivial job. It requires a systematic procedure. While there are several systematic procedures that may be used, we advise a straightforward and conceptually simple way to attack the problem—the *hierarchical planning process*—which is how to build a Work Breakdown Structure (WBS) for the project.

To use this process, one must start with the project's objective(s). The planner, often the PM, makes a list of the major activities that must be completed to achieve the objective(s). The list may be as short as two or three activities, or as large as 20. Usually the number is between 5 and 15. We call these Level 1 activities. The planner now takes each Level 1 activity and delegates it to an individual or functional group. (The PM might delegate one or more Level 1 tasks to him- or herself.) The delegatee deals with the task as if it is itself a project and makes a plan to accomplish it; that is, he or she lists a specific set of Level 2 tasks required to complete each Level 1 task. Again, the breakdown typically runs between 5 and 15 tasks, but a few more or less does not matter. The process continues. For each Level 2 task, someone or some group is delegated responsibility to prepare an action plan of Level 3 subtasks. The procedure of successively decomposing larger tasks into their component parts continues until the lowest level subtasks are sufficiently understood so that there is no reason to continue. As a rule of thumb, the lowest level tasks in a typical project will have a duration of a few hours to a few days. If the team is quite familiar with the work, longer durations are acceptable for the lowest level tasks.

Another simple approach to creating the WBS begins by gathering the project team together and providing each member with a pad of sticky-notes. After defining the project's objectives, and Level 1 tasks, team members then write on the sticky-notes all the tasks they can think of that are required to complete the project. The sticky-notes can then be placed on the wall and arranged in various ways. One advantage of this approach is that it provides the entire team with a better understanding of the work needed to complete the project. The fact that it is a cooperative exercise also helps the project team to bond. Finally, this exercise can generate a WBS tree. Figure 3-1 illustrates the tree. A colleague called this a "Gozinto chart." (He said it was named after a famous Italian mathematician, Prof. Zepartzat Gozinto. The name has stuck.)

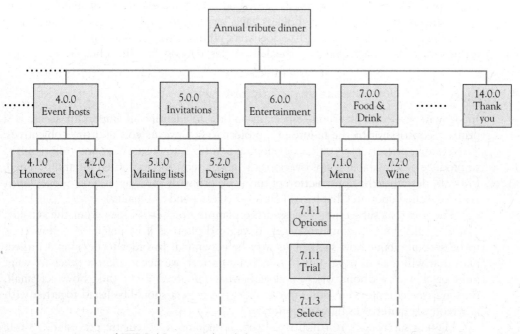

Figure 3-1　A partial WBS (Gozinto chart) for an Annual Tribute Dinner project.

Microsoft Project (MSP) will make a WBS list (but not a tree-chart) at the touch of a key. The task levels are appropriately identified; for example, the WBS number "7.5.4" refers to the "Level 3, task Number 4" that is needed for "Level 2, task 5" that is a part of "Level 1, task 7." (The PM has the option of using any other identification system desired, but must enter the identifiers manually.)

Task levels are appropriately organized on the MSP printout, with Level 1 tasks to the left and others indented by level. If one uses a tree diagram and each task is represented by a box with the WBS identifier number, one can add any information one wishes—given that it will fit in the box. Such an entry might be the proper account number to charge for work done on that task, or the name of the individual (or department) with task responsibility, or with a space for the responsible party's signature denoting that the person has accepted accountability by "signing-off." As we will see, additional information is often added by turning the "tree" into a list with columns for the additional data.

In doing hierarchical planning, only one rule appears to be mandatory. At any given level, the "generality" or "degree of detail" of the tasks should be roughly at the same level. One should not use highly detailed tasks for Level 1 plans, and one should not add very general tasks at Level 3 or more. This can best be done by finding all Level 2 subtasks for each Level 1 task before moving one's attention to the Level 3 subtasks. Similarly, break all Level 2 tasks into their respective Level 3 tasks before considering any Level 4 subtasks, if the breakdown proceeds that far. A friend of ours who was an internationally known artist and teacher of industrial design explained why. When producing a painting or drawing, an artist first sketches-in the main compositional lines in the scene. The artist then adds detail, bit by bit, over the whole drawing, continuing this process until the work is completed. If this is done, the finished work will have "unity." Unity is not achieved if individual areas of the picture are completed in detail before moving on to other areas. A young art student then made a pen-and-ink sketch of a fellow student, showing her progress at three different stages (see Figure 3-2).

We have said that the breakdown of Level 1 tasks should be delegated to someone who will carry out the Level 2 tasks. It is the same with Level 2 tasks being delegated to someone who will design and carry out the required Level 3 tasks. A relevant question is "Who are all these delegatees?" Let's assume that the project in question is of reasonable size, neither very large nor small. Assume further that the PM and the functional managers are reasonably experienced in dealing with similar projects. In such a case, the PM would probably start by working on Level 1. Based on her background, the PM might work on Level 2 of one or more of the Level 1 tasks. Where recent experience was missing, she would delegate to the proper functional manager the task of specifying the Level 2 tasks. In the same way, the latter would delegate Level 3 task specification to the people who have the appropriate knowledge.

In general, the job of planning should be delegated to the lowest competent level. At Level 1, this is usually the PM. At lower levels, functional managers and specialists are the best planners. In Chapter 2 (Section 2.1) we described that strange bugbear, the micromanager. It is common for micromanagers to preempt the planning function from subordinates or, as an alternative, to allow the subordinate to develop an initial plan that the micromanager will amend with potentially disastrous results. The latter is an event reported with some frequency (and accuracy) in *Dilbert*©.

Extensions of the Everyday WBS

The WBS can be reshaped and buttressed with some additional data often not included in the project's WBS. The WBS is generally oriented toward the project's deliverables. The additions increase its orientation toward the planning and administration of the

Figure 3-2 Three levels
of detail in hierarchical
planning.

work. It does this by using available material, while adopting a format that is not typically used by the WBS. Figure 3-3 illustrates a layout that helps to organize the required information. We refer to these layouts as "modified" WBSs. The additional data in the columns are: (1) estimates of the resources required for each task in the plan, (2) the estimated time required to accomplish each task, (3) information about who has responsibility for the task, and (4) data that will allow tasks to be sequenced so that the set may be completed in the shortest possible time. Once the project starting date is known, item 2 in the preceding list may be changed from the time required for a subtask completion to the date on which the subtask is scheduled for completion.

To understand the importance of item 4 in the list, consider a set of subtasks, all of which must be completed to accomplish a parent task on a higher level. It is common in such a set that one or more subtasks (A) must be completed before one or more other subtasks (B) may be started. The former tasks (A) are said to be *predecessors* of the *successor* tasks (B). For instance, if our project is to paint the walls of a room, we know that before we apply paint to a wall, we must do a number of predecessor tasks. These predecessors include: clear the floor area near the wall to be painted and cover with drop cloths; remove pictures from the wall; clean loose dirt, oil, grease, stains, and the like from the wall; fill and smooth any cracks or holes in the wall; lightly sand or score the wall if it has previously been painted with a high-gloss paint; wipe with a damp cloth or sponge to remove dust from the sanding; and mask any surrounding areas where this paint is not wanted. All these tasks are predecessors to the task "Paint the walls."

Modified WBS

Deliverables _____

_____

_____

Start date _____ Due date _____ Project duration _____

Key constraints and assumptions _____

_____

Tasks	Immediate Predecessor Tasks	Estimated Time Duration	Estimated Resources	Assigned To

Figure 3-3   A form to assist hierarchical planning.

The predecessor tasks for "paint the walls" have been listed in the order in which they might be done if only one person was working. If several people are available, several of these tasks might be done at the same time. Note that if three tasks can be done simultaneously, the total elapsed time required is the time needed for the longest of the three, not the sum of the three task times. This notion is critical for scheduling, so predecessors must be listed in the WBS. One convention is important. When listing predecessors, only the *immediate predecessors* are listed. If A precedes B and B precedes C, only B is a predecessor of C.

While Table 3-1 illustrates the output of a project launch meeting (more accurately a *program* launch meeting), Table 3-2 shows a WBS for one of the action items resulting from the launch meeting. With the exception of tasks 3 and 4, it is a Level 1 plan. Three

Table 3-2   A Modified WBS for Improving Staff Orientation

A Modified WBS for Improving Staff Orientation

Project Objective: *Enhance new employee orientation to improve retention and more effectively communicate organization's policies and procedures.*

Measurable Outcomes: *Increase in retention rate for new hires.*
New hires better understand mission, vision, and core values of organization.
Competency level of new hires increased.

Task	Duration	Predecessor	Resources	Assigned To
1. Orientation task force launched	2 weeks	—	Education Manager, Education Staff (3), two Department Managers, three Staff representatives, facilitator	HR Director
2. Compile orientation evaluations for areas of improvement	4 weeks	—		Education Secretary
3. Enhancement proposal prepared				
(a) Draft recommended changes	2 weeks	1, 2	Orientation Task Force	Education Manager
(b) Recommendation presented to execute team	1 week	3(a)	Education Manager	HR Director
(c) Review and finalize orientation enhancements	2 weeks	3(b)	Orientation Task Force	Education Manager
4. Orientation presentations enhanced				
(a) Work with speakers to review presentations	4 weeks	3(c)	Speakers, Education Staff	Education Staff
(b) Facilitate preparation of Power Point presentation	6 weeks	4(a)	IS trainer, Education Staff, Speaker	Education Staff
(c) Facilitate acquisition of videos on certain subjects	6 weeks	4(a)	Education Staff, Speaker	Education Staff
5. Review evaluation tool to measure outcomes	2 weeks	3	Education Manager	Education Manager
6. Facilitate physical changes necessary to orientation room	4 weeks	4	Education Staff, AV Staff, Facilities Staff	Education Manager
7. Implement revised orientation program	0 days	5, 6	Education Staff, Speakers, HR Staff	Education Manager
8. Evaluate feedback from first two orientation sessions	2 months	7	Education Staff	Education Manager
9. Present findings to executive team	1 week	8	Education Manager	HR Director
10. Evaluate feedback from first six orientation sessions	6 months	7	Education Manager	Education Manager
11. Develop continuous process improvement systems for feedback results	4 weeks	7	Education Staff	Education Manager

Level 2 items are shown for tasks 3 and 4. Because the HR Director is quite familiar with such projects, violating the one-level-only rule is forgivable. Note also that the HR Director has delegated some of the work to himself. Note also that instead of assumptions being shown at the beginning of the WBS, project evaluation measures were listed.

The WBS not only identifies the deliverable, but also may note the start date if it is known or other information one wishes to show. Once the subtasks and their predecessors have been listed along with the estimated subtask activity times, the probable duration for the set of subtasks, and thus the task due date, can be determined as we will see in Chapter 5. If the estimates for the durations and resource requirements for accomplishing the subtasks are subject to constraints (e.g., no overtime work is allowed) or assumptions (e.g., there will be no work stoppage at our subcontractor's plant), these should be noted in the WBS.

If one wishes, the information in the form shown in Figure 3-2 can be entered directly into Microsoft Project® (MSP). Alternatively, one can produce a WBS using MSP, directly, as shown in Figure 3-4. The project title can be entered in a header or footer to the form, as can other information such as a brief description of the deliverables, the name of the PM or the task manager, the project start and/or due dates, and the like.

Table 3-3 shows a WBS generated on MSP with task durations, and start and finish times for the Level 1 tasks in an infection control project. The project begins on September 12 and ends on November 30. As is customary, people work a five-day week so a three-week task has 15 work days and 21 calendar days (three weeks), *assuming that the individual or team is working full-time on the task.* As we will see in Chapter 5, one usually dares not make that assumption and should check carefully to determine whether or not it is a fact. If the one performing the task is working part-time, a task that requires 5 days of work, for example, may require several weeks of calendar time. We will revisit this problem in Chapter 5.

Project deliverables: Project manager:			**Project Title**		
ID	**Task Name**	**Duration**	**Predecessors**	**Resource Names**	**Assigned To**
1					
2					
3					
4					
5					
6					
7					
8					
9					
10					
Project start date: Project due date:					

Figure 3-4   A WBS as an output of MSP.

MSP makes the task of Level 1 planning of the broad project tasks quite straightforward. The same is true when the planners wish to generate a more detailed listing of all the steps involved in a project. The PM merely lists the overall tasks identified by the planning team as the activities required to produce the project deliverables—for example, the output of a brainstorming session. The PM and the planning team can then estimate task durations and use MSP to create a WBS. Table 3-4 shows a planning template used by a software company when they have their initial project brainstorming meetings about delivering on a customer request.

MSP has a planning wizard that guides the PM through the process of identifying all that is necessary to take an idea for a project activity and turn it into a useful WBS.

Table 3-5 is an example of a template developed by a computer systems support company. Company planners repeatedly performed the same steps when clients would ask for a local area network (LAN) installation. They treated each job as if it were a new project, because costs and resource assignments varied with each assignment. To improve efficiency, they developed a planning template using MSP. After meeting with a client, the project manager could add the agreed-upon project start date, and any constraints on the schedule required by the client. The steps to install the LAN remained the same. The start and finish dates, and the number of resources

Table 3-3   A WBS Showing Level 1 Tasks for an Infection Control Project (MSP)

Pulmonary Patient Infection Control Project
F. Nightingale, RN

ID	Task Name	Predecessors	Duration	Start	Finish	Resources
1	Form a task force to focus processes for pulmonary patients		2 wks	9/12	9/25	Infec. Control RN, Dr., Educator
2	Identify potential processes to decrease infection rate	1	3 wks	9/26	10/16	Team
3	Develop a treatment team process	1, 2	3 wks	9/26	10/16	Team
4	Education	3	1 wk	10/17	10/23	RNs, LPNs, CNAs
5	Implement processes on one unit as trial	4	3 wks	10/24	11/13	Unit staff
6	Evaluate	5	1 wk	11/14	11/20	Infec. Control RN
7	Make necessary adjustments	6	1 wk	11/21	11/27	Infec. Control RN
8	Implement hospital-wide	7	3 days	11/28	11/30	Unit staffs

Table 3-4   Template for a Brainstorming Planning Meeting

ID	Potential Steps	Objective	Success Measure	Barriers	Notes	Contact	E-mail Address
1	Idea 1						
2	Idea 2						
3	Idea 3						
4	Idea 4						
5	Idea 5						
6	Idea 6						

Table 3-5 An MSP Template for a LAN Installation Project

Template for LAN Installation Project

ID	Task Name	Duration	Start	Finish	Predecessors	Resource Names
1	Phase I—Planning and design of LAN	13 days				
2	Project start	0 days				
3	Technical specifications determined	10 days			2	Project Manager, System Analysts, Systems Consultant, Writers, Chief Editor, Senior Programmer, Vice President-Management Information Systems, Senior Writers, Administrative Assistant
4	Design plan developed	3 days			3	Project Manager, System Analysts, Chief Editor, Vice President–Management Information Systems
5	Phase II—Preparation for installation	22 days				
6	Equipment ordering	2 days			4	Administrative Assistant
7	System prototype	20 days			6	System Analysts, Systems Consultant, Programmers, Senior Programmer, Junior Programmers
8	Configuration	10 days			6	System Analysts, Programmers, Tester, Senior Testers
9	Testing	5 days			8	Tester, Senior Testers
10	Site analysis	5 days			6	System Analysts, Programmers, Tester, Junior Programmers
11	Phase III—Installation	13 days				
12	Site installation	3 days			7, 8, 10	Tester, Project Manager, System Analysts, Systems Consultant, Senior Testers
13	Documentation set-up	10 days			12	Writers, Chief Editor, Senior Writers
14	Phase IV—Installation follow-up	12 days				
15	Orientation for client	2 days			13	Project Manager, System Analysts, Systems Consultant, Programmers, Administrative Assistant
16	Support to client	5 days			12	
17	Post-installation review	3 days			16	Project Manager, System Analysts, Systems Consultant, Chief Editor, Vice President-Management Information Systems
18	System acceptance	0 days			17, 15	

needed to meet the schedule were adjusted for each individual client, but the adjustments were usually small. Once the schedule of a specific job was decided, the PM could determine the resources needed to meet that schedule and find the cost of the project.

Creating this kind of template is simple. The software can calculate the cost of each different project which is most helpful to the project manager if cost, prices, or schedules must be negotiated. If the client wants the project to be completed earlier than scheduled, the PM can add the additional resources needed and project management software can determine the costs associated with the change.

If the PM wishes to include other information in the project's modified WBS, there is no reason not to do so. Some include a column to list the status of resource or personnel availability. Others list task start dates.

> The project launch meeting sets the project scope, elicits cooperation of others in the organization, demonstrates managerial commitment to the project, and initiates the project plan. The plan itself is generated through a hierarchical planning process by which parts of the plan are sequentially broken down into finer levels of detail by the individuals or groups that will implement them. The result is a WBS that lists all the tasks required to carry out the plan together with task resource requirements, durations, predecessors, and identification of the people responsible for each task.

3.4 MORE ON THE WORK BREAKDOWN STRUCTURE AND OTHER AIDS

At times, PMs seem to forget that many of the conventional forms, charts, and tables that they must fill out are intended to serve as aids, not punishments. They also forget that the forms, charts, and tables are not cast in bronze, but, like Emeril's recipes, may be changed to fit the PM's taste. In addition to the matters just covered, there is more about the WBS and two other useful aids—the Responsible-Accountable-Consult-Informed Matrix (*RACI Matrix*), and *Mind Mapping*—that merits discussion.

The process of building a WBS is meaningful. The PM and individual team members may differ on the technical approach to working on the task, the type and quantity of resources needed, or the duration for each subtask. If so, negotiation is apt to accompany the planning process. As usual, participatory management and negotiation often lead to improved project performance and better ways of meeting the project's goals.

The RACI Matrix

PMBOK Guide

Like the WBS, the RACI Matrix comes in a variety of sizes and shapes. Typically, the RACI matrix is in the form of a table with the project tasks derived from the WBS listed in the rows and departments or individuals in the columns. PMBOK describes the RACI matrix in Chapter 9 on Human Resources. The value of the RACI Matrix is that it helps organize the project team by clarifying the responsibilities of the project team members. For an example of a simple RACI Matrix, see Figure 3-5.

WBS		Project Office					Field Operator	
Subproject	Task	Project Manager	Contract Administrator	Project Engineer	Industrial Engineer	Risk/Compliance Manager	Field Manager	
Determine need	A1	I		R	A			
	A2	C	I	A	R			
Solicit quotations	B1	I	C	A		C	R	
Write appropriate request	C1	C	A	I	R	I		
	C2		R	I	A			
	C3	R	C	A			C	
"	"							
"	"							
"	"							

Legend:

A = Accountable   C = Consult

R = Responsible   I = Inform

Figure 3-5   A RACI Matrix.

In Figure 3-5, letters are used to indicate the nature of the responsibility link between a person and a task. Note that there must be at least one A in every row, which means that someone must be accountable for completion of each task. For example, examine the row with the task "Solicit quotations." In this case the Project Engineer is accountable for the task being carried out while the Field Manager will be responsible for actually doing the work associated with soliciting quotations. The project's Contract Administrator and the Compliance Officer/Risk Manager must be consulted about the solicitation process. The PM must be informed before documents are sent to potential vendors. Note that a particular individual or department can be assigned multiple responsibility links. For example, it is common for a person to be both accountable and responsible for a particular task. Other common combinations include consult/inform and accountable/consult.

Standard RACI Matrix templates are available to facilitate their development. One can use symbols or numbers as opposed to letters to refer to different responsibility relationships, and the references may be to departments, job titles, or names. Only imagination and the needs of the project and PM bound the potential variety. Likewise, additional columns can be added to the RACI Matrix to capture the due dates of tasks, actual dates completed, the status of tasks, performance metrics, and so on.

A final observation is needed on this subject. When we speak to functional managers about project management, one comment we often hear is anger about changes in the project plan without notification to the people who are supposed to conduct the tasks or supply services to the project. One quote from the head of a statistics lab in a large consulting firm is typical. The head of the lab was speaking of the manager of a consulting project for a governmental agency when he said, "I pulled three of my best people off other work to reserve them for data analysis on the XYZ Project. They sat for days waiting for the data. That jerk [the PM] knew the data would be late and never bothered to let me know. Then the *%$#@% had the gall to come in here and ask me to speed up our analysis so he could make up lost time."

Make sure to use the Inform category, not simply to report progress, but also to report changes in due dates, resource requirements, and the like.

A Whole-Brain Approach to Project Planning

Best Practice

In today's fiercely competitive environment, project teams are facing increasing pressure to achieve project performance goals while at the same time completing their projects on time and on schedule. Typically project managers and project team members rely on the "left" side or the analytical part of the brain to address the challenges. Indeed, if you are a business or engineering student, the vast majority of techniques that you have been exposed to in your studies relies on the logical and analytical left side of your brain. On the other hand, art students and design students tend to be exposed to techniques that rely more on imagination and images which utilize the creative "right" side of the brain. Importantly, many activities associated with project management can be greatly facilitated through the use of a more balanced whole-brain approach (Brown and Hyer, 2002).

One whole-brain approach that is particularly applicable to project management in general, and project planning in particular, is mind mapping. Mind mapping is essentially a visual approach that closely mirrors how the human brain records and stores information. In addition to its visual nature, another key advantage associated with mind mapping is that it helps tap the creative potential of the entire project team, which, in turn, helps increase both the quantity and quality of ideas generated. Because project team members tend to find mind mapping entertaining, it also helps generate enthusiasm, helps get buy-in from team members, and often gets quieter team members more involved in the planning process.

To illustrate the creation of a mind map, consider a project launched at a graduate business school to improve its part-time evening MBA program for working professionals. The mind mapping exercise is initiated by taping a large sheet of paper (e.g., 6 ft × 3 ft) on a wall. (One good source of such paper is a roll of butcher's wrapping paper. Several sheets can be taped together to create a larger area if needed.) It is recommended that the paper be oriented in landscape mode to help stimulate the team's creativity as people are used to working in portrait mode. In addition, team members should stand during the mind mapping exercise.

The process begins by writing the project goal in the center of the page. As is illustrated in Figure 3-6, the part-time MBA project team defined the goal for the project as generating ideas for breakthrough performance in the part-time MBA program. In particular, notice the inspirational language used in defining the project goal which helps further motivate team members and stimulate their creativity.

Once the project goal is defined, team members can brainstorm to identify the major tasks that must be done to accomplish this goal. In developing the mind map for the project, the MBA team initially identified four major tasks: (1) define the role of working professional programs (WPPs), (2) generate ideas for improving current programs, (3) generate ideas for diversification, and (4) evaluate the ideas generated. As illustrated in Figure 3-7, these major tasks branch off from the project goal.

Developing the mind map proceeds in this fashion whereby components in the mind map are continuously broken down into more detailed tasks. For example, Figure 3-8

Figure 3-6 **Begin mind mapping with statement of project's objective.**

GENERATE IDEAS FOR BREAKTHROUGH PERFORMANCE IN PART-TIME PROGRAM

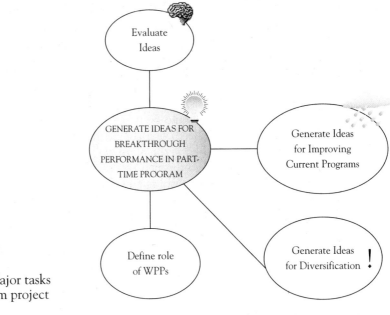

Figure 3-7 Major tasks branch off from project goal.

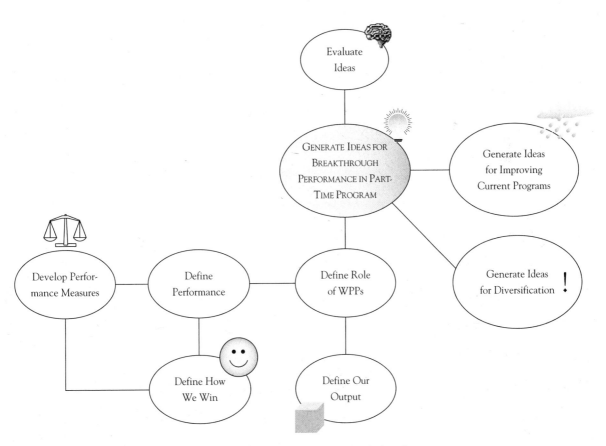

Figure 3-8 Major tasks are further broken down into more detailed tasks.

illustrates how the define role of the WPPs task was broken down into more detailed tasks. Figure 3-9 provides the final map for the MBA project.

A couple of comments regarding the process of mind mapping are in order. First, color, word size, word shape, and pictures should all be used to add emphasis. In fact, team members should be encouraged to use pictures and images in the mind map over using words. The brain processes and responds to symbols and pictures differently than it does to words. When using words, key words as opposed to full sentences should be used. Also, it should be noted that it is OK to be messy when developing the original mind map. Indeed, one should not expect the original mind map to resemble something as polished as the mind map shown in Figure 3-9. Rather, the mind map will typically need to go through several iterations of polishing and refining. It should also be noted that the polishing and refining can be greatly facilitated with the use of a computer graphics program.

In addition, multiple team members can and should contribute to the mind map simultaneously. In fact, one team member should be formally designated as the facilitator to ensure that all team members are contributing to keep team members focused on the project, and to ensure that team members are focusing on project tasks—not goals.

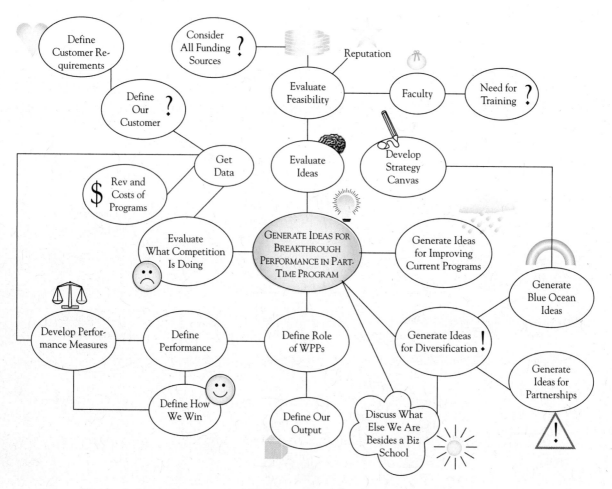

Figure 3-9   Final mind map for part-time MBA program project.

Finally, at the most detailed level, tasks should be expressed using a noun and a verb (e.g., develop measures, generate ideas, define output).

Unfortunately, it is all too common for projects to go over budget and/or be completed late. In many cases insufficient upfront planning is the major culprit. With inadequate upfront planning, important tasks are overlooked, which in turn results in underestimating the project budget and duration. Mind mapping is a fast and effective tool that can greatly facilitate project planning and help minimize problems that result from inadequate upfront planning.

Risk

A polished and refined mind map facilitates a number of other project-related activities. For example, the mind map can be easily converted into the traditional WBS. Furthermore, the mind map can be used to facilitate risk analysis, setting project team meeting agendas, allocating resources to project activities, and developing the project schedule (see Brown and Hyer, 2002, for additional details on the use of mind mapping for project management).

> From the Work Breakdown Structure, one can extract a list of all tasks arranged by task level. The WBS will show numeric identifiers for each task plus other information as desired. The WBS may take a wide variety of forms. From the WBS one can also develop the RACI Matrix which details the nature of responsibility of each individual or group involved in the project to the specific tasks required to complete the project. Mind mapping can greatly enrich the planning process.

3.5 RISK MANAGEMENT

Trade-Offs

PMBOK Guide

Risk

It was noted in Chapter 1 that the primary role of the project manager is managing trade-offs between time, budget, scope, and risk. As we discuss in this section, there are a host of activities that can be completed during the project planning phase that greatly facilitate managing project related risks.

The field of risk management has grown considerably over the last decade. The Project Management Institute's PMBOK (2013) devotes Chapter 11 to this topic. In general, risk management includes three areas: (1) risk identification, (2) risk analysis, and (3) response to risk. The process of accomplishing these three tasks is broken down into six subprocesses:

1. **Risk Management Planning** developing a plan for risk management activities.

2. **Risk Identification** finding those risks that might affect the project.

3. **Qualitative Risk Analysis** evaluating the seriousness of the risk and the likelihood it will affect the project.

4. **Quantitative Risk Analysis** developing measures for the probability of the risk and its impact on the project.

5. **Risk Response Planning** finding ways of reducing negative impacts on the project as well as enhancing positive impacts.

6. **Risk Monitoring and Control** maintaining records of and evaluating the subprocesses above in order to improve risk management.

1. Risk Management Planning   This planning process is like any other planning process. First, a method for carrying out steps 2 through 5 for any project must be designed. Care must be exercised to ensure that the necessary resources can be applied in a timely and well-organized manner. The planning process, just as the task of managing risk, is a continuous process. The factors that cause uncertainty appear, disappear, and change strength as time passes and the environment of a project changes. Note that planning how to deal with uncertainty is an organizational problem, not specifically a project problem. The result is that many firms create a formal, risk management group, whose job it is to aid the project management team in doing steps 2 through 5. The overall risk management group develops plans and maintains the database resulting from step 6.

Some of the inputs and outputs of steps 2 through 5 are unique to the project, and some are common for all projects. The overall group helps individual project risk teams with the necessary analytic techniques, information gathering, the development of options for response, and monitoring and evaluating the results.

2–3. Risk Identification and Qualitative Risk Analysis   We list these steps together because in practice they are often carried out together. As a risk is identified, an attempt to measure its timing, likelihood, and impact is often made concurrently.

Risk identification consists of a thorough study of all sources of risk in the project. Common sources of risk include the organization of the project itself; senior management of the project organization; the client; the skills and character of the project team members, including the PM; and acts of nature.

Scenario Analysis   Scenario analysis is a well-known method for identifying serious risks. It involves envisioning likely *scenarios* that may have major repercussions on the organization and then identifying the possible resulting outcomes of events such as a hurricane in New Orleans, an extended labor strike, the freezing of a river, or the failure of an oil well head 5000 feet below the water surface in the gulf of Mexico. These types of risk can often be identified and evaluated by project stakeholders or outside parties with previous experience in similar projects. Beyond this, a close analysis of the project plan, the WBS, and the RACI Matrix, as well as the PERT chart (Chapter 5) will often identify highly probable risks, extremely serious risks, or highly vulnerable areas, should anything go wrong.

After the major risks are identified, the following data should be obtained on each to facilitate further analysis: the probability of each risk event occurring, the range or distribution of possible outcomes if it does occur, the probabilities of each outcome, and the expected timing of each outcome. In most cases, good estimates will not be available, but getting as much data and as accurate estimates as possible will be crucial for the follow-on risk analysis. Above all, remember that a "best guess" is always better than no information.

Best Practice

Failure Mode and Effect Analysis (FMEA)   FMEA is a structured approach similar to the scoring methods discussed in Chapter 1 to help identify, prioritize, and better manage risk. Developed by the space program in the 1960s, FMEA can be applied to projects using the following six steps.

1. List ways the project might potentially fail.

2. List the consequences of each failure and evaluate its severity. Often severity, S, is ranked using a ten-point scale, where "1" represents failures with no effect and "10" represents very severe and hazardous failures that occur with no warning.

3. List the causes of each failure and estimate their likelihood of occurring. The likelihood of a failure occurring, L, is also customarily ranked on a ten-point scale, with a "1" indicating the failure is rather remote and not likely to occur and "10" indicating the failure is almost certain to occur.

4. Estimate the ability to detect each failure identified. Again, the detectability of failures, D, is customarily ranked using a ten-point scale, where a "1" is used when monitoring and control systems are almost certain to detect the failure and "10" where it is virtually certain the failure will not be detected.

5. Calculate the *Risk Priority Number* (*RPN*) by multiplying S, L, and D together.

6. Sort the list of potential failures by their RPNs and consider ways for reducing the risk associated with failures with high RPNs.

Table 3-6 illustrates the results of a FMEA conducted to assess the risk of a new drug development project at a pharmaceutical company. As shown in the table, five potential failures for the project were identified: (1) The new drug is not effective at treating the ailment in question, (2) the drug is not safe, (3) the drug interacts with other drugs, (4) another company beats it to the market with a similar drug, and (5) the company is not able to produce the drug in mass quantities. According to the results, the most significant risk is the risk of developing a new drug that is not effective. While it is unlikely that much can be done to reduce the severity of this outcome, steps can be taken to reduce the likelihood of this outcome as well as increase its detectability. For example, advanced computer technologies can be utilized to generate chemicals with more predicable effects. Likewise, perhaps earlier human clinical and animal trials can be used to help detect the effectiveness of new drugs sooner. In this case, if both L and D could each be reduced by one, the overall RPN would be reduced from 240 to 160.

Table 3-6   FMEA for New Product Development Project at Pharmaceutical Company

Failure	S	L	D	RPN
Not effective	8	6	5	240
Not safe	8	4	5	160
Drug interacts with other drugs	6	3	8	144
Beat to market	7	3	2	42
Can't produce	6	4	4	96

4. Quantitative Risk Analysis   Hertz and Thomas (1983) and Nobel prize winner Herbert Simon (1997) have written two classic books on this topic. As we noted in Chapter 1, the essence of risk analysis is to state the various outcomes of a decision as probability distributions and to use these distributions to evaluate the desirability of certain managerial decisions. The objective is to illustrate to the manager the distribution or *risk profile* of the outcomes (e.g., profits, completion dates, return on investment) of investing in some project. These risk profiles are one factor to be considered when making the decision, along with many others such as intangibles, strategic concerns, behavioral issues, fit with the organization, and so on.

A case in point is Sydney, Australia's M5 East Tunnel (PMI, March 2005). It was constructed under strict budgetary and schedule requirements, but given the massive traffic delays now hampering commuters, the requirements may have been seriously underestimated. Due to an inexpensive computer system with a high failure rate, the tunnel's security cameras frequently fail, requiring the operators to close the tunnel due to inability to react to an accident, fire, or excessive pollution inside the tunnel. The tunnel was built to handle 70,000 vehicles a day, but it carries 100,000 so any glitch can cause immediate traffic snarls. A risk analysis, including the risk of overuse, probably would have anticipated these problems and mandated a more reliable set of computers once the costs of failure had been included.

Estimates   Before discussing the risk analysis techniques, we need to discuss some issues concerning the input data coming out of the qualitative analysis of step 3. We assume here that estimating the range and timing of possible outcomes of a risky event is not a problem but that the probabilities of each may be harder to establish. Given no actual data on the probabilities, the best guesses of people familiar with the problem is a reasonable substitute. An example of such guesses (a.k.a. estimates) can be seen in Table 3-7.

Knowledgeable individuals are asked for three estimates of the cost of each activity, a normal estimate plus optimistic and pessimistic estimates of the cost for each. From these an expected value for the cost of an activity can be found, but we will delay discussing this calculation until Chapter 5 where we show such calculations for either cost or durations.

If approximations cannot be made, there are other approaches that can be used. One approach is to assume that all outcomes are equally probable, though there is no more justification for this assumption than assuming any other arbitrarily chosen probability values. Bear in mind that when using the common expected-value approach (see below) to help make a decision, the result can be misleading. For example, the probability of a disaster may be very low (resulting in a low expected value), but such risks must be carefully managed nonetheless, such as with insurance or extensive contingency planning.

Expected Value   When probability information is available or can be estimated, many risk analysis techniques use the concept of expected value of an outcome—that is, the value of an outcome multiplied by the probability of that outcome occurring. For example, in a coin toss using a quarter, there are two possible outcomes and the expected value of the game is the sum of the expected values of all outcomes. It is easily calculated. Assume that if the coin comes up "head" you win a quarter, but if it is "tails" you lose a quarter. We also assume that the coin being flipped is a "fair" coin and has a .5 probability of coming up either heads or tails. The expected value of this game is

$$E \text{ (coin toss)} = .5(\$.25) + .5(\$-.25) = 0$$

A decision table (a.k.a. a payoff-matrix), such as illustrated in Table 3-8, is a technique commonly used for single-period decision situations where there are a limited number of decision choices and a limited number of possible outcomes.

In the following decision table, there are four features:

1. Three decision choices or alternatives, A_i.

2. Four states of nature, S_j, that may occur.

3. Each state of nature has its own probability of occurring, p_j, but the sum of the probabilities must be 1.0.

4. The outcomes associated with each alternative and state of nature combination, O_{ij}, are shown in the body of the table.

If a particular alternative, A_i, is chosen, we calculate the expected value of that alternative as follows:

$$E (A_i) = p_1 (O_{i1}) + p_2 (O_{i2}) + p_3 (O_{i3}) \ldots \text{ for all values of } j$$

Table 3-7 Optimistic, Normal, and Pessimistic Cost Estimates for the Annual Tribute Dinner

Task Name	Optimistic Cost = a	Normal Cost = m	Pessimistic Cost = b	Expected Cost = (a + 4m + b)/6
Budget Information Annual Tribute Dinner				
Begin preparations for tribute dinner				
Select date & secure room				
Obtain corporate sponsorships for event	$100.00	$150.00	$350.00	$175.00
Identify potential businesses to sponsor				
Phone/write businesses	$100.00	$150.00	$350.00	$175.00
Event hosts/MC				
Identify and secure honoree of event				
Identify and secure master of ceremonies				
Identify/secure person to introduce honoree				
Identify/secure event hosts & hostesses				
Invitations				
Secure mailing lists				
Design invitation with PR firm	$1,250.00	$1,500.00	$2,200.00	$1,575.00
Print invitation	$2,300.00	$2,500.00	$3,000.00	$2,550.00
Mail invitation	$250.00	$300.00	$410.00	$310.00
RSVP's back				
Event entertainment secured	$750.00	$1,000.00	$1,250.00	$1,000.00
Food and drink				
Finalize menu				
Identify menu options				
Trial menus				
Select final menu	$700.00	$750.00	$800.00	$750.00
Identify company to donate wine				
Table decorations, gifts, cards, flowers, etc.	$2,200.00	$2,800.00	$3,250.00	$2,775.00
Identify and have made event gift to attendees	$2,000.00	$2,500.00	$3,000.00	$2,500.00
Find florist to donate table arrangements				
Hire calligrapher to make seating cards	$200.00	$300.00	$400.00	$300.00
Develop PR exhibit to display at event	$75.00	$150.00	$225.00	$150.00
Event and honoree publicity	$200.00	$325.00	$450.00	$325.00
Hire event photographer	$400.00	$450.00	$500.00	$450.00
Finalize seating chart				
Hold tribute dinner				
Send out "thank you's" to sponsors & donators	$75.00	$150.00	$225.00	$150.00

Each person responsible for a task in this project was asked to take the estimated costs and determine a more accurate budget. The spreadsheet includes the cost information. This project does not include any cost for staff time. Each member of the project team is considered part of General Salaries and Administration, and their associated time will not be expensed through this project.

Table 3-8   Decision Table (or payoff matrix) for Sample Problem

Alternatives	Probabilities States of Nature	0.1 High	0.4 Med.	0.3 Low	0.2 None	Expected Value
Fast		14	10	6	1	7.4
Average		10	12	9	5	9.5*
Slow		5	8	12	7	8.7

*Maximum

For example, using the data from Table 3-8 for alternative "Fast" we get

$$E \text{ (Fast)} = 0.1(14) + 0.4(10) + 0.3(6) + 0.2(1) = 7.4$$

The reader may recall that we used a similar payoff matrix in Chapter 1, when we considered the problem of buying a car. In that example, the criteria weights played the same role as probabilities play in the example above.

Best Practice

Simulation   We will demonstrate simulation in the next chapter (4) and will demonstrate it more in later chapters. In recent years, simulation software has made the process user friendly and far simpler than in the midtwentieth century. It has become one of the most powerful techniques for dealing with risks that can be described in numeric terms. The most difficult problems involved with the use of simulation are (1) explaining the power of using three point estimates (most likely, optimistic, and pessimistic) instead of the single point estimates decision makers have always used; and (2) explaining the notion of statistical distributions to people whose only acquaintance with statistical distributions is the (mistaken) notion that the grades in the classroom are, or should be, distributed by "the curve." Once the fundamental ideas behind a Monte Carlo simulation are understood, the power of the technique in dealing with risk is obvious. Even more potent is the notion that one can estimate the likelihood that certain risky outcomes will actually occur, such as the probability that project costs will be at or below a given limit, or the chance that a project will be completed as scheduled.

There is another problem with using simulation, or any process involving estimates of project costs, schedules, etc. It is convincing anyone connected to a project to make **honest** estimates of durations, costs, or any other variables connected with a project. The problem is the same whether one asks for single point or three point estimates. Asking individuals to be accountable for their estimates is always difficult for the askee, and project managers are advised to use their best interpersonal communication styles when seeking to improve project cost and time estimates. The PMI's code of ethics demands honesty, and PMs should strive to ensure it.

5. Risk Response Planning   Risk response typically involves decisions about which risks to prepare for and which to ignore and simply accept as potential threats. The main preparation for a risk is the development of a risk response plan. Such a plan includes contingency plans and logic charts detailing exactly what to do depending on particular events (Mallak, Kurstedt, and Patzak, 1997). For example, Iceland is frequently subjected to unexpected avalanches and has thus prepared a detailed response plan for such events, stating who is in charge, the tasks that various agencies are to do at particular times, and so on. Actually practicing those responses with dress rehearsals is particularly important if the risk is a potentially life-or-death emergency.

Contingency Plan   A contingency plan is a backup for some emergency or unplanned event, often referred to colloquially as "plan B," and there may also need to be a plan C and a plan D as well, for an even deeper emergency such as an oil spill in the gulf of Mexico, to give a wildly improbable example. The contingency plan includes who is in charge, what resources are available to the person, where backup facilities may be located, who will be supporting the person in charge and in what manner, and so on.

In another example, when Hurricane Katrina hit Mississippi and New Orleans in August 2005, Melvin Wilson of Mississippi Power, a subsidiary of 1250 employees, became "Director of Storm Logistics" for the duration. As a contingency, Mississippi Power subscribes to three weather forecasting services and in this case decided the most severe forecast was the right one. Wilson called for a retreat from the company's high-rise headquarters on the beach to a backup contingency office at a power plant 5 miles inland. By noon, the backup power plant flooded and lost power, which was not in the plan, and the cars in the parking lot were floating. A company security van made it through to take the storm team to a third option for a storm center—a service office in North Gulfport that had survived Hurricane Camille in 1969—there was no fourth option. The office was dry but without electricity or running water. The phone lines were down, and cell phones were useless but the company's own 1100 cell phones plus 500 extras to lend out had a unique radio function, and that worked. They were the only working communications for the first 72 hours on the gulf coast. The company's worst-case contingency plans had never imagined managing a repair crew of over 4000 from outside. But Wilson became responsible for directing and supporting 11,000 repairmen from 24 states and Canada, feeding and housing them in 30 staging areas including six full-service tent cities that housed 1800 each. He had to find 5000 trucks and 140,000 gallons of gasoline a day to help restore power to 195,000 customers. Within 12 days of the storm, power had been restored to all customers except a few thousand whose lines were too damaged to receive electricity. Clearly, Mississippi Power had not made contingency plans for such an extreme event, but the plans they had made, and the backups to those plans, were sufficient to give a smart team of emergency responders the chance to successfully handle this crisis.

Logic Chart Logic charts show the flow of activities once a backup plan is initiated. They force managers to think through the critical steps that will need to be accomplished in a crisis, and provide an overview of the response events and recovery operations. They include decisions, tasks, notifications, support needs, information flows, and other such activities. They are time independent and illustrate the many tasks as well as dependencies and interdependencies that emerge out of the initial response steps, such as: "If X has happened, do this; otherwise, do that."

6. Risk Monitoring and Control Like risk management planning, monitoring and control are tasks for the parent organization, as well as for the project. If the overall risk management group is not involved along with the project in performing the tasks of recording and maintaining records of what risks were identified, how they were analyzed and responded to, and what resulted from the responses, the records have a high probability of being lost forever when the project is completed (or abandoned). If records are lost or not easily available, the chance that other projects will "learn from the experiences of others" is very low.

It is the job of the risk management group to maintain records for how all projects deal with risks. The group, however, is not merely a passive record holder. It should be involved in the search for new risks, for developing new and better techniques of measuring and handling risk, and estimating the impact of risks on projects. Thus, the group should become an advisor to project risk management teams. It should provide an ongoing evaluation of current risk identification, measurement, analysis, and response techniques. Fundamentally, the group is devoted to the improvement of the organization's risk management activities.

> Risk management consists of risk planning and identification, qualitative and quantitative risk analysis, risk response, and risk monitoring and control. We deal with risk primarily through such means as decision tables, simulation, and response, which entail identifying which risks will be prepared for and which will be ignored and simply accepted.

In the next chapter, we use the project plan to develop a project budget. We discuss conflict surrounding the budgetary process. Then we deal with uncertainty, the project's (and PM's) constant companion.

REVIEW QUESTIONS

1. What are some benefits of setting up a project plan for similar, frequent projects?

2. Discuss the reasons for inviting the functional managers to a project launch meeting rather than their subordinates who may actually be doing the work.

3. Discuss the pros and cons of identifying and including the project team at the project launch meeting.

4. Why is participatory management beneficial to project planning? How does the process of participatory management actually work in planning?

5. What is the difference between the Resource column on the WBS (that would include personnel needed by the project) and the Assigned To column?

6. Under what circumstances is it sensible to do without a project launch meeting?

7. Distinguish among highly probable risks, extremely serious risks, and highly vulnerable areas in risk identification.

DISCUSSION QUESTIONS

8. For each one of the eight components of a project plan, discuss the problems that might be raised if the element was incomplete.

9. Give several examples of a type of project that would benefit from a template project plan being developed.

10. Why is the hierarchical planning process useful for project planning? How might it influence the plan if the hierarchical planning process was not used?

11. Develop a WBS with at least two levels for a project you are personally familiar with (e.g., moving away to college, registering for class, cleaning out a garage). (Hint: the plan will be more useful as a learning exercise if you have a subordinate or two, real or imaginary.) Be sure to include precedences, task durations, resource requirements, and milestones. Enter the plan in MSP.

12. Discuss the drawbacks of implementing a project plan without a RACI Matrix.

13. Pursuing a degree or certificate is a major project. Construct a brief "project plan" for this project that includes all nine elements described in the chapter.

14. Assume that your class instructor appointed you project manager to lead a dozen of your classmates in writing up the end-of-chapter pedagogy materials (i.e., Review Questions, Discussion Questions, Problems, Incidents for Discussion, and Cases) as an Instructor's Guide for this book. You plan to form subteams to work on each of these elements, each headed by a subteam leader. Of course, all the subteam materials will need to be integrated into the final Instructor's Guide at the end. Construct a WBS and RACI Matrix for this project.

15. You and your family and friends are planning to host a graduation party at the end of the school year. Construct a WBS for this party.

16. Construct a WBS for the project in Question 14.

17. Consider one or more projects (from this course or elsewhere) that you understand reasonably well. Identify situations where information learned from a later task of the project becomes important to an earlier task.

18. Contrast the Project Plan, and the Work Breakdown Structure.

PROBLEMS

19. Find the best alternative given the cost outcomes below. The probability of rain is 0.3, clouds is 0.2, and sun is 0.5.

Alternative	State		
	Rainy	Cloudy	Sunny
a	6	3	4
b	2	4	5
c	5	4	3
d	5	4	3

20. In Problem 19, base your decision instead on the *worst* possible outcome for each alternative.

21. A marketing firm is trying to win a major contract from a large retail company and is concerned with four major threats. (1) Competition: the probability of very competitive bids is high at 0.6, and the potential impact would be substantial at a value of 5 on a scale of 1–7 (where a 7 is a major negative impact and a 1 is slight). (2) Economy: probability of a recession is 0.4 and its impact would be 7 since the company would probably decide not to advertise. (3) Chance of a loss: a small probability of only 0.3 with a negative impact of 4. (4) Personnel loss (head of marketing is being courted by a competitor): probability of loss is 0.5 but negative impact is only 3. Use the FMEA technique to determine which risks are critical and which can be ignored.

22. A marketing analyst has investigated each of the four threats in Problem 21 in terms of NOT being able to ameliorate them and has come up with the following values (again, on a 7 point scale) for each of the threats: #1: 1, #2: 6, #3: 3, #4: 4. Recalculate the RPN and determine which risks are now critical and which can be ignored. How has this changed from before? Does this new ranking seem more realistic?

23. Vern Toney managed the small IT group of a growing business. Vern's boss, the CFO, was on Vern's back to cut costs in the IT group. The CFO felt Vern could cut a staff member or two and maintain their current service level. Vern was also receiving a steady flow of complaints about the response time to calls to the help desk. He had two people answering the help desk phones and three desktop support staff responding to the problems.

Vern had to do something. He thought that he might save money by outsourcing the group's help desk function. He called a few vendors, all of whom claimed they could save him money.

Vern was not sure if this would shorten the group's response time to help desk calls. He felt that he needed to do some research before he made a decision. He decided to construct a project plan for the research.

After closing the office door, he sat down at his computer using Microsoft Project software and started to identify all of the steps he needed to take before he phoned vendors for bids on taking over the help desk. The investigation would have to be a secret or his staff would worry about their job security.

First, Vern decided that he needed to identify the department's current level of service. This required knowing the current volume of calls, the length of time until the call ticket is assigned to a desktop support person, and the time it took to close the ticket. He thought that he could accomplish all of this in one week by doing all three steps simultaneously.

After he determined the current service level, Vern thought that he should informally poll all company managers to see what improvements in IT group service they would like. He figured 2 days to make all the phone calls. He could then call the finance department to get up-to-date payroll information on his staff's salary and overtime expenses. Vern thought that if he called right away, he would surely hear back in 1 day.

Vern also decided to call other IT managers in the city to try to establish a benchmark service level. He thought that step would take a week and he could start after finding the current service levels. Last, after every other step was completed, Vern could prepare a request for proposals to send to IT outsourcing vendors. He thought that the preparation of an RFP would take a week. He decided to start this planning project right away.

Question: Prepare a WBS using MSP with the steps that must be completed before Vern Toney can contact outsourcing vendors. If Vern starts on August 1, 2016, how long will it take to get ready to contact outsourcing vendors?

24. Develop a mind map to identify the tasks that need to be completed for a nonprofit organization's annual casino night charity event.

25. In addition to your regular responsibilities, your supervisor has just assigned you to be in charge of your organization's annual golf tournament. It is expected that 100 to 150 employees will enter the tournament. In addition to organizing the event, you are also responsible for promoting it. Your budget for the event is $25,000. Develop a mind map to identify the tasks that need to be completed for the golf tournament project.

INCIDENTS FOR DISCUSSION

Plymouth Zoo's Re-engineering Project

The Chief Operating Officer of the Plymouth Zoo, Avery Mitchell, was put in charge after the CEO unexpectedly died. Avery was named acting CEO and told by the zoo's Board of Directors that he would be considered for the position permanently if the next few months went smoothly. Avery was very nervous because he knew that the zoo was on the verge of financial troubles. He was not expecting to make the profits that had been projected for the next few months. He knew that admissions were down as a result of recent unrest in the city and nationally.

The deceased CEO had hired a consulting group to help identify cost savings for the zoo. The firm hired was unfamiliar to Avery, and there were rumors around the zoo that the lead consultant was a friend of the now deceased CEO.

The consulting group had been interviewing staff at the zoo for the last two weeks in order to prepare a proposal for work re-design to cut costs. Avery met with the consultants, and they presented him with their proposal. The proposal outlined the cost of the consultants and the projected savings the zoo could expect after the consultants' work was finished. Avery was unclear about precisely how the savings were determined and what would be the redesign project's specific deliverables.

Questions: What should Avery Mitchell do next? What information should he ask the consultants for before accepting their proposal? What project planning tools would you suggest Avery ask the consultants to use to outline the project more specifically and address his concerns?

Time Is Fleeting

A large privately owned retail discount store was having problems with their time clocks. There were six freestanding time clocks in the store for staff use. They were located conveniently at points where staff entered and exited the store. The staff could also clock in and out on the computer terminals that controlled the cash registers.

The time clocks were old and often in need of repair. The *Information Technology* (*IT*) department was responsible for the maintenance of the machines. The IT department could make minor repairs but had to call the clock vendor for the not infrequent major repairs.

The head of *Human Resources* (*HR*) wanted to launch a project to purchase and install new time clocks. He felt that because the current time clocks could not be counted on to work, the accuracy of the staff's working hours and the store's payroll was in question. This bothered him, and he felt the problem was getting worse as the clocks aged.

The head of the IT department wanted to launch a project to get rid of all the time clocks and have everyone clock in and out using the current computer terminals located at each register. This would greatly decrease the costs the department was incurring to maintain the current time clocks. The head of IT knew that the computer terminals were not conveniently located for anyone except the sales clerks, but he thought that he could add some terminals in other locations for less money than maintaining the current clocks. He also felt very confident in his staff's ability to maintain the computer terminals themselves, so the expense of calling in a vendor would disappear completely.

The head of HR did not like IT's idea at all. He had problems already with people clocking in for other staff and knew this would only get worse if every staff had to go to a designated computer terminal to clock in and out. The head of HR also knew he had several staff members who were not computer literate and would have trouble clocking in and out.

The two department heads went to the President, and each asked to set up and supervise a project to take care of the time clock problem.

Question: If you were the President how would you handle this problem?

C A S E

St. Dismas Assisted Living Facility—1

St. Dismas Medical Center, an urban, nonprofit, 450-bed rehabilitation hospital began to see a significant decline in admissions. St. Dismas' mission focuses on inpatient and outpatient rehabilitation of the severely injured and catastrophically ill. While the patient census varied from month to month, it appeared to the St. Dismas Board of Trustees that the inpatient population was slowly but steadily declining. The hospital's market researchers reported that fewer people were being severely injured due to the popularity of seat belts and bicycle/motorcycle helmets. In order to get a handle on the future of the organization, the Board, and the CEO, Fred Splient M.D. called for a major strategic planning effort to take place.

In January 1999, St. Dismas held a planning retreat to identify future opportunities. The outcome of the retreat was that the Medical Center needed to focus its efforts around two major strategic initiatives. The first, a short-run initiative, was to be more cost-effective in the delivery of inpatient care. The second, a long-run strategy, was to develop new programs and services that would capitalize on the existing, highly competent rehabilitation therapy staff and St. Dismas's excellent reputation in the region.

At the time of the retreat, Fred Splient's parents were living with him and his family. Fred was an active member of the "sandwich generation." His parents were aging and developing many problems common to the geriatric populace. Their increased medical needs were beginning to wear on Fred and his family. It crossed Fred's mind that life might be more pleasant if the hospital Board approved an expansion of the Medical Center's campus to include an assisted living facility.

In March 1999, Fred had his Business Development team prepare a rough estimate of the potential return on investment of an assisted living facility. He asked the team to identify different options for facility construction and the associated costs. The team also did a complete competitive analysis and examined the options for services to be offered based on St. Dismas's potential population base and catchment area. The Business Development team visited several facilities across the country. The team also interviewed companies that could oversee the design, building, and operation of the facility for St. Dismas. The development team produced a preliminary business plan based on the recommended structure for the facility, estimated capital expenditure needs, estimated income from operation of the facility, as well as projected revenues to other Medical Center programs resulting from the facility's population.

The plan was presented at the May 1999 meeting of the Board of Trustees. Fred Splient and his team introduced the Board to the concept of opening an assisted living facility on St. Dismas's campus. The facility would be set up as a for-profit subsidiary of the Medical Center so that it could generate a profit and not be subjected to the strict guidelines of the hospital's accrediting agencies. As a subsidiary organization, however, the Board would still have control.

The chosen facility design was a freestanding apartment-like facility with a sheltered connection to the Hospital for access to the kitchen and hospital services. The facility would have 100 units with 15 to 30 of the units classified as "heavy-assisted" and built to code to house the physically and medically disabled. The rest of the units would be "light-assisted," larger apartments. The population would be approximately 110 to 150 residents, with most being single occupants rather than couples.

The light-assisted apartments could hold residents who required only minor medical and social interventions. The residents of the heavy-assisted section would have more medical needs and would require assistance getting around. The Business Development team recommended this type of programming model, because many assisted living facilities were erected across the country, but few had a medical focus and offered the types of services that St. Dismas could offer—physical and occupational therapy programs, and behavior management programs to name a few.

The Board was assured that the facility would meet the strategic initiative of a growing business. The business plan projected an immediate increase in the number of referrals to the outpatient therapy programs. Another projected deliverable of the project was to enable St. Dismas to strengthen its focus on reimbursable preventive and wellness programs for the healthier geriatric population. The project's longer term goal was to increase the census in the hospital's inpatient units by having a location where people could age in place until they were in need of hospitalization, and then such a facility would be right next door.

Depending on the exact size of the apartments, their equipment, and the actual ratio of heavy- to light-assisted units, Fred estimated that the entire project would cost between $8,500,000 and $11,000,000 for the facility construction. That estimate included the cost of land, furnishings, and a sheltered connection to the hospital. When up and running, it was estimated that the net income would range between $9,000 and $12,000 per unit per year. The team estimated the net cash flow for the entire project to be around $1,500,000 per year.

Fred requested the Board to approve the concept and allow his team to prepare a pro forma plan to the Board for approval. The plan would include a recommended design for both heavy- and light-assisted apartments. It would also include all costs of land, construction, furnishings, and staffing. Income estimates would be included and would be conservatively biased. A timetable would also be included.

The Board conducted several executive sessions, and by the middle of May voted to approve the concept. They approved the architectural-construction-management firm recommended by the team, and they requested Splient to proceed with developing a complete project plan. The Board appointed two Board members to sit on Fred's planning group.

In June, Dr. Splient gathered his executive team together and presented the project mission, and scope. He reported that the board had approved a small budget to finance the planning process. The Board also stipulated that construction could not begin until after the November 1999 city elections because two of the

Board Members were running in that election, one for a city council seat and one as a county commissioner. The Board also stated that they would like a plan that would allow the facility to open by July 2000, as research has shown that many adult children find the summer the easiest time to assist their parents in finding an alternative to independent living arrangements. The CEO and executive team were now confident that they were ready to launch the project to plan, build, and open an assisted living facility at St. Dismas.

A few days later, Fred decided that it was time to set up the team that would take responsibility for what he called the ALF project. He quickly decided to include the following staff at the launch meeting:

- Chief Financial Officer (CFO)
- Vice President of Business Development and Marketing
- Rehab Services Medical Director
- Construction Project Manager for capital facilities projects
- Chief Operations Officer (COO) (nursing, facilities, food services, and housekeeping)
- Director of Information Services
- Director of Support Services (central supply, purchasing, and security)
- Two members of the Board of Trustees, one with construction experience and the other a probable electee to the city council.

Even though the department directors from Support Services and Information Services would not be involved until later, Fred decided to include them from the beginning. Fred knew some members of his team had a tendency to become obstacles to progress if they felt left out.

Fred named the group the ALF Project Steering Committee and held the first meeting. Fred presented his vision for the facility. He told the group that he personally would be managing this project. He led a discussion of all the major steps that must be included in the project plan, and asked each team member to identify the areas for which they would accept responsibility. The hospital's Construction Project Manager took responsibility for the construction of the facility, and the COO volunteered to oversee the building design, as well as define the needs for food services, housekeeping, staffing, and policy and procedure development. The CFO agreed to develop the budgets for each area of the project as well as the operating budget for the facility. The CFO also agreed to create the payroll and accounting systems necessary to operate the facility.

The IS director accepted responsibility to define and set up all the telecommunications and information system needs of the facility. The VP of Business Development agreed to create a preliminary marketing plan, and a communication package for the community and hospital staff. In addition, she discussed organizing a major ground breaking event. The Medical Director said that he would design an assessment tool for determining residents' level of medical needs upon moving in to the facility. He felt this was the first step in defining what clinical services should be offered to residents. Fred told the team that he would develop the management structure for the new facility and work with in-house counsel to identify all governmental regulations as well as all industry standards that pertain to an assisted living facility and govern the facility's practices. Splient gave the team 2 months to come back with their detailed action plans for their areas of responsibility.

QUESTIONS

1. Define project deliverables.
2. Define project constraints and assumptions.
3. Develop a preliminary Level 1 WBS.

4. Is Dr. Splient a good choice for project manager? Support your position.

C A S E

John Wiley & Sons

John Wiley & Sons, Inc. publishes books, journals, and electronic products for the educational, professional, scientific, technical, and consumer markets. The oldest independent publisher in North America, Wiley is in the forefront of electronic publishing, with more than 200 products and services on disk, on CD-ROM, or available by network. Wiley has more than 11,000 active book titles and 400 journals. The company publishes 1500 new titles in a variety of formats each year. The company has approximately 2000 employees worldwide.

Wiley has U.S. publishing, marketing, and distribution centers in New York, Colorado, Maryland, New Jersey, and Illinois. A substantial portion of Wiley's business comes from international markets. In addition to offices in the United States, it has operations in Europe (England and Germany), Canada, Asia, and Australia to serve the needs of the local markets and explore opportunities for expanding its publishing programs.

In the early years, Wiley was best known for the works of Washington Irving, Edgar Allan Poe, Herman Melville, Nathaniel Hawthorne, and other nineteenth-century American literary giants. But by the turn of the century, the company was established as a leading publisher of works on science and technology.

Today its areas of specialization include the sciences, engineering, technology, mathematics, accounting, and business management, with a growing presence in general interest titles. Wiley is committed to providing information in those formats most accessible to its readers and is taking advantage of the rapid advances in digital information technology to enhance the speed and flexibility with which it delivers print publications as well as to develop a range of offerings in electronic formats.

The consulting firm you work for has been contacted by Wiley to support its textbook *Project Management in Practice*. Specifically, John Wiley and Sons is interested in contracting your consulting firm to develop the state-of-the-art website described above. Furthermore, Wiley would also like your firm to benchmark website state-of-the-art in terms of content, capabilities, and functionality prior to designing and developing this website.

QUESTIONS

1. Develop a mind map for this project.
2. Convert your mind map into a WBS.
3. Discuss how your mind map might be used to facilitate other project planning activities such as resource allocation, schedule development, and risk analysis.

C A S E

Samson University

Samson University is a small liberal arts university located in the northeast of the country. Recently, QBS Inc., a large multinational corporation headquartered in the same city, made a large gift to the university to develop a 1-year Master of Science program in Project Management. To develop the new Project Management program, Samson's business school dean, Dr. Ryan, asked Professor Scott to chair a taskforce to develop the new degree program. Together, Dean Ryan and Professor Scott decided that Professors Samuelson, Kacy, Regan, and Lee should also serve on the taskforce

At the taskforce launch meeting, Dean Ryan acknowledged how much she appreciated everyone's willingness to serve on the taskforce given all their other responsibilities. She went on to explain how developing this program would significantly enhance the university's relationships with QBS, lead to important job opportunities for its graduates, and ultimately enhance the university's reputation. She then turned the meeting over to Professor Scott.

Professor Scott began:

I would also like to echo Dean Ryan's appreciation for your willingness to serve on this taskforce. Personally, I am very excited about this opportunity and I truly believe we can develop a program that is unique and will attract great students and major employers. Today, my goal is to have us brainstorm about what work we need to undertake to complete our charge. I will record the ideas you come up with on the flip chart and then use this to develop a draft project schedule for your review. So without further delay, what ideas come to mind regarding the work we need to do to complete our charge?

Professor Lee was the first to respond:

In my view, the first thing we need to do is benchmark other Project Management programs and find out what courses these programs offer. Also, I think we need to decide what our goal is. In particular, are we trying to develop a program that achieves parity with other programs or are we trying to reinvent the way project management is taught?

Professor Kacy next chimed in:

I agree with Dr. Lee that benchmarking is an important step. Based on what we learn from benchmarking other programs, we will then need to develop the curriculum for our program.

Dean Ryan added:

From an administrative perspective, as you develop the curriculum you will need to consider faculty related issues. For example, does our current faculty have the background to teach the new courses? And if so, is there sufficient slack that we can accommodate the new courses in the faculty's current teaching loads?

Professor Samuelson suggested:

In addition to benchmarking other programs, I think it is important to solicit input from key stakeholder groups including potential students, our faculty, and companies that would recruit graduates of the program.

Dr. Lee agreed:

I completely agree with Dr. Samuelson. My suggestion is we create an online survey to solicit recruiter opinions.

Dean Ryan added:

Speaking of recruiters, we also need to evaluate whether we have sufficient resources in our Career Management Center to handle the coaching and placement needs of this new group of students.

Professor Scott next suggested:

There are a lot of issues that come to mind regarding the curriculum. For example, should we develop a skills matrix? How much hands-on experience should be emphasized? Should the program be organized around modules or should we have standard semester length courses?

Building on Professor Scott's comments, Professor Kacy remarked:

Yes, getting the curriculum right is critical. Also, we need to determine the split between hard analytical skills and softer skills. And if we were to go with modules, would there be themes for each module?

Professor Regan then commented:

Another issue we need to address is what would be the admissions criteria for the program? For example, would students need to have some number of years of work experience?

As the discussion died down, Professor Scott wrapped up the meeting:

This has been a productive meeting. I think we have done an excellent job identifying the work ahead of us. I greatly appreciate the passion each of you has demonstrated and the contributions all of you have made. I will take the list we generated, organize it a bit, and then develop a tentative schedule for your review. I will also have my staff assistant send out a poll to identify a weekly meeting time.

QUESTIONS

1. Critique the launch meeting. Are there aspects you think are worth emulating? Are there aspects you would do differently?

2. Develop a mind map for this project using the ideas shared in the meeting and other ideas that occur to you.

3. Convert your mind map into a WBS.

4. Review your mind map and identify risky potential failure points. Which are the most serious? Which are the most likely? Determine the most critical failure points by calculating all their RPNs. Develop a contingency plan for each of the most critical failure points you identify.

BIBLIOGRAPHY

AARON, J. M., C. P. BRATTA, and D. P. SMITH. "Achieving Total Project Control Using the Quality Gate Method." *Proceedings of the Annual Symposium of the Project Management Institute*, San Diego, October 4, 1993.

BAILETTI, A. J., J. R. CALLAHAN, and P. DIPIETRO. "A Coordination Structure Approach to the Management of Projects." *IEEE Transactions on Engineering Management*, November 1994.

BAILEY, D. E. "Comparison of Manufacturing Performance of Three Team Structures in Semiconductor Plants." *IEEE Transactions on Engineering Management*, February 1998.

BOWEN, H. K. *Project Management Manual*. Cambridge, MA: Harvard Business School, 9–697–034, October 6, 1997.

Brown, K. A., and N. L. Hyer. "Whole-Brain Thinking for *Project Management*." *Business Horizons*, May–June 2003.

Ford, R. C., and F. S. McLaughlin. "Successful Project Teams: A Study of MIS Managers." *IEEE Transactions on Engineering Management*, November 1992.

Hambleton, L. *Treasure Chest of Six Sigma Growth Methods, Tools, and Best Practice*. Prentice Hall, Upper Saddle River, NJ, 2008.

Hauptman, O., and K. K. Hirji. "The Influence of Process Concurrency on Project Outcomes in Product Development: An Empirical Study of Cross-Functional Teams." *IEEE Transactions on Engineering Management*, May 1996.

Knutson, J. "How to Manage a Project Launch Meeting." *PM Network*, July 1995.

Langley, A. "Between 'Paralysis by Analysis' and 'Extinction by Instinct.'" *IEEE Engineering Management Review*, Fall 1995, reprinted from Sloan Management Review, Spring 1995. (This is a thoughtful article that speaks to both sides of the "How much planning should we do?" issue.)

Lencioni, P., *The Five Dysfunctions of a Team: A Leadership Fable*. San Francisco, Jossey-Bass, A Wiley Company, 2002. (Much like Goldratt's *The Goal*, this work is fictional and tells the story of a new senior manager who takes over a team of subordinates. It is a quick and easy read and well worth the brief time.)

Martin, P. K., and K. Tate. "Kick Off the Smart Way." *PM Network*, October 1998.

Pells, D. L. "Project Management Plans: An Approach to Comprehensive Planning for Complex Projects," in P. C. Dinsmore, ed., *The AMA Handbook of Project Management*, New York: Amacom, 1993.

PMI, "Mutual Disagreement," *PM Network*, February 2005.

PMI, "A Derailed Vision," *PM Network*, April 2004.

Prentis, E. L. "Master Project Planning: Scope, Time and Cost." *Project Management Journal*, March 1989.

Webster, J. L., W. E. Reif, and J. S. Bracker. "The Manager's Guide to Strategic Planning Tools and Techniques," *Planning Review*, November/December 1989. Reprinted in *IEEE Engineering Management Review*, December 1990. (A fascinating compilation of planning techniques including such methods as the Delphi method, stakeholder analysis, benchmarking, critical success factors, focus group, and many others—30 in all. It also has a short history of strategic planning.)

4

Budgeting the Project

PMBOK Guide

Having finished the planning for the technical aspects of the project, there is one more important element of planning to finish that will then result in the final go-ahead from top management to initiate the project. A budget must be developed in order to obtain the resources needed to accomplish the project's objectives. A budget is simply a plan for allocating organizational resources to the project activities. PMBOK covers the topic of budgeting in Chapter 7 on Cost.

But the budget also serves another purpose: It ties the project to the organization's aims and objectives through organizational policy. For example, NASA's Mars Pathfinder-Rover mission embedded a new NASA policy—to achieve a set of limited exploration opportunities at extremely limited cost. In 1976, NASA's two Viking-Mars Lander missions cost $3 billion to develop. In 1997, however, the Pathfinder-Rover mission cost only $175 million to develop, a whopping 94 percent reduction. The difference was the change in organizational policy from a design-to-performance orientation to a design-to-cost orientation.

In Chapter 3, we described the project planning process as a set of steps that began with the overall project plan and then divided and subdivided the plan's elements into smaller and smaller pieces that could finally be sequenced, assigned, scheduled, and budgeted. Hence, the project budget is nothing more than the project plan, based on the WBS, expressed in monetary terms and it becomes a part of the Project Charter.

Once the budget is developed, it acts as a tool for upper management to monitor and guide the project. As we will see later in this chapter, it is a necessary managerial tool, but it is not sufficient. Appropriate data must be collected and accurately reported in a timely manner or the value of the budget to identify current financial problems or anticipate upcoming ones will be lost. This collection and reporting system must be as carefully designed as the initial project plans because late reporting, inaccurate reporting, or reporting to the wrong person will negate the main purpose of the budget. In one instance, the regional managers of a large computer company were supposed to receive quarterly results for the purpose of correcting problems in the following quarter. The results took 4 months to reach them, however, completely negating the value of the budgeting-reporting system.

In this chapter, we will first examine some different methods of budgeting and cost estimating, as used for projects. Then we will consider some ways to improve the cost estimation process, including some technical approaches such as learning curves and tracking signals. We will also discuss some ways to misuse the budget that are, unfortunately, common. Last, we discuss the problem of budget uncertainty and the role of risk management when planning budgets.

Risk

METHODS OF BUDGETING

Budgeting is simply the process of forecasting what resources the project will require, what quantities of each will be needed, when they will be needed, and how much they will cost. Tables 4-1 and 4-2 depict the direct costs involved in making a short documentary film. Table 4-1 shows the cost per unit of usage (cost/hour) of seven different personnel categories and one facility. Note that the facility does not charge by the hour, but has a flat rate charge. Table 4-2 shows the resource categories and amounts used for each activity required to make the DVD. The resource costs shown become part of the budget for producing the documentary film. As you will see below, overhead charges may be added to these direct charges.

Most businesses and professions employ experienced estimators who can forecast resource usage with amazingly small errors. For instance, a bricklayer can usually estimate within 1 or 2 percent the number of bricks required to construct a brick wall of given dimensions. In many fields, the methods of cost estimation are well documented based on the experience of estimators gathered over many years. The cost of a building, or house, is usually estimated by the square feet of floor area multiplied by an appropriate dollar value per square foot and then adjusted for any unusual factors.

Budgeting a project such as the development of a control system for a new computer, however, is often more difficult than budgeting more routine activities—and even more difficult than regular departmental budgeting which can always be estimated as: "Same as last year plus X percent." But project budgeters do not usually have tradition

Table 4-1   Resource Cost per Unit for Producing a Short Documentary Film

			Producing a DVD Resource Cost			
ID	Resource Name	Max. Units	Std. Rate	Ovt. Rate	Cost/Use	Accrue At
1	Scriptwriter	1	$75.00/hr	$100.00/hr	$0.00	Prorated
2	Producer	1	$100.00/hr	$150.00/hr	$0.00	Prorated
3	Client	0.2	$0.00/hr	$0.00/hr	$0.00	Prorated
4	Secretary	1	$25.00/hr	$40.00/hr	$0.00	Prorated
5	Editor	1	$50.00/hr	$85.00/hr	$0.00	Prorated
6	Production staff	1	$40.00/hr	$70.00/hr	$0.00	Prorated
7	Editing staff	1	$40.00/hr	$70.00/hr	$0.00	Prorated
8	Editing room	1	$0.00/hr	$0.00/hr	$250.00	Start

Table 4-2   Budget by Resource for Producing a Short Documentary Film

Producing a DVD
Budget by Resource

ID	Task Name	Resource Work Hours	Cost	Task Duration
1	**Project approval**	0 hr	$0.00	0 days
2	**Scriptwriting**	112 hr	$8,400.00	14 days
	Scriptwriter	112 hr	$8,400.00	
3	**Schedule shoots**	240 hr	$5,400.00	15 days
4	**Begin scheduling**	0 hr	$0.00	0 days
5	**Propose shoots**	120 hr	$7,000	5 days
	Scriptwriter	40 hr	$3,000.00	
	Producer	40 hr	$4,000.00	
	Client	40 hr	$0.00	
6	**Hire secretary**	40 hr	$4,000.00	5 days
	Producer	40 hr	$4,000.00	
7	**Schedule shoots**	80 hr	$2,000.00	10 days
	Secretary	80 hr	$2,000.00	
8	**Scheduling comp**	0 hr	$0.00	0 days
9	**Script approval**	80 hr	$4,000.00	5 days
	Producer	40 hr	$4,000.00	
	Client	40 hr	$0.00	
10	**Revise script**	80 hr	$7,000.00	5 days
	Scriptwriter	40 hr	$3,000.00	
	Producer	40 hr	$4,000.00	
11	**Shooting**	160 hr	$7,200.00	10 days
	Editor	80 hr	$4,000.00	
	Production staff	80 hr	$3,200.00	
12	**Editing**	168 hr	$5,290.00	7 days
	Editor	56 hr	$2,800.00	
	Editing staff	56 hr	$2,240.00	
	Editing room	56 hr	$250.00	
13	**Final approval**	160 hr	$6,250.00	5 days
	Producer	40 hr	$4,000.00	
	Client	40 hr	$0.00	
	Editor	40 hr	$2,000.00	
	Editing room	40 hr	$250.00	
14	**Deliver DVD to client**	0 hr	$0.00	0 days

to guide them. Projects are, after all, unique activities. Of course, there may be somewhat similar past projects that can serve as a model, but these are rough guides at best. Forecasting a budget for a multiyear project such as a large product line or service development project is even more hazardous because the unknowns can escalate quickly with changes in technology, materials, prices, and even the findings of the project up to that point.

Organizational tradition also impacts project budgeting. Every firm has its own rules about how overhead and other indirect costs are charged against projects. Every firm has its ethical codes. Most firms must comply with the Sarbanes-Oxley Act (SOX) and the Health Insurance Portability and Accountability Act (HIPAA). Most firms have their own accounting idiosyncrasies, and the PM cannot expect the accounting department to make special allowances for his or her individual project. Although accounting will charge normal expenditures against a particular activity's account number, as identified in the WBS, unexpected overhead charges, indirect expenses, and usage or price variances may suddenly appear when the PM least expects it, and probably at the worst possible time. (Price variances due to procurement, and the entire procurement process, are discussed in Chapter 12 of PMBOK, 2013.) There is no alternative—the PM must simply become completely familiar with the organization's accounting system, as painful as that may be.

PMBOK Guide

In the process of gaining this familiarity, the PM will discover that cost may be viewed from three different perspectives (Hamburger, 1986). The PM recognizes a cost once a commitment is made to pay someone for resources or services, for example when a machine is ordered. The accountant recognizes an expense when an invoice is received—not, as most people believe, when the invoice is paid. The controller perceives an expense when the check for the invoice is mailed. The PM is concerned with commitments made against the project budget. The accountant is concerned with costs when they are actually incurred. The controller is concerned with managing the organization's cash flows. Because the PM must manage the project, it is advisable for the PM to set up a system that will allow him or her to track the project's commitments.

Another aspect of accounting that will become important to the unaware PM is that accountants live in a linear world. When a project activity has an $8,000 charge and runs over a four-month period, the accounting department (or worse, their software) sometimes simply spreads the $8,000 evenly over the time period, resulting in a $2,000 allocation per month. If expenditures for this activity are planned to be $5,000, $1,000, $1,000, and $1,000, the PM should not be surprised when the organization's controller storms into the project office after the first month screaming about the unanticipated and unacceptable cash flow demands of the project!

Next, we look at two different approaches for gathering the data for budgeting a project: top-down and bottom-up.

Top-Down Budgeting

The top-down approach to budgeting is based on the collective judgments and experiences of top and middle managers concerning similar past projects. These managers estimate the overall project cost by estimating the costs of the major tasks, which estimates are then given to the next lower level of managers to split up among the tasks under their control, and so on, until all the work is budgeted.

The advantage of this approach is that overall budget costs can be estimated with fair accuracy, though individual elements may be in substantial error.

Another advantage is that errors in funding small tasks need not be individually identified because the overall budget allows for such exceptions. Similarly, the good chance that some small but important task was overlooked does not usually cause a serious budgetary problem. The experience and judgment of top management are presumed to include all such elements in the overall estimate. In the next section, we will note that the assumptions on which these advantages are based are not always true.

Bottom-Up Budgeting

In bottom-up budgeting, the WBS identifies the elemental tasks, whose resource requirements are estimated by those responsible for executing them (e.g., programmer-hours in a software project). This can result in much more accurate estimates, but it often does not do so for reasons we will soon discuss. The resources, such as labor and materials, are then converted to costs and aggregated to different levels of the project, eventually resulting in an overall direct cost for the project. The PM then adds, according to organizational policy, indirect costs such as general and administrative, a reserve for contingencies, and a profit figure to arrive at a final project budget.

Bottom-up budgets are usually more accurate in the detailed tasks, but risk the chance of overlooking some small but costly tasks. Such an approach, however, is common in organizations with a participative management philosophy and leads to better morale, greater acceptance of the resulting budget, and heightened commitment by the project team. It is also a good managerial training technique for aspiring project and general managers.

Unfortunately, true bottom-up budgeting is rare. Upper level managers are reluctant to let the workers develop the budget, fearing the natural tendency to overstate costs, and fearing complaints if the budget must later be reduced to meet organizational resource limitations. Moreover, the budget is upper management's primary tool for control of the project, and they are reluctant to let others set the control limits. Again, we will see that the budget is not a sufficient tool for controlling a project. Top-down budgeting allows the budget to be controlled by people who play little role in designing and doing the work required by the project. It should be obvious that this will cause problems—and it does.

Best Practice

We recommend that organizations employ both forms of developing budgets. They both have advantages, and the use of one does not preclude the use of the other. Making a single budget by combining the two depends on setting up a specific system to negotiate the differences. We discuss just such a system below. The only disadvantage of this approach is that it requires some extra time and trouble, a small price to pay for the advantages. A final warning is relevant. Any budgeting system will be useful only to the extent that all cost/revenue estimates are made with scrupulous honesty.

Project budgeting is a difficult task due to the lack of precedent and experience with unique project undertakings. Yet, understanding the organization's accounting system is mandatory for a PM. The two major ways of generating a project budget are top-down and bottom-up. The former is usually accurate overall but possibly includes significant error for low-level tasks. The latter is usually accurate for low-level tasks but risks overlooking some small but potentially costly tasks. Most organizations use top-down budgeting in spite of the fact that bottom-up results in better acceptance and commitment to the budget.

4.2 COST ESTIMATING

In this section, we look at the details of the process of estimating costs and some dangers of arbitrary cuts in the project budget. We also describe and illustrate the difference between activity budgeting and program budgeting.

Work Element Costing

The task of building a budget is relatively straightforward but tedious. Each work element is evaluated for its resource requirements, and its costs are then determined. For example, suppose a certain task is expected to require 16 hours of labor at $10 per hour, and the required materials cost $235. In addition, the organization charges overhead for the use of utilities, indirect labor, and so forth at a rate of 50 percent of direct labor. Then, the total task cost will be

$$\$235 + [(16 \text{ hr} \times \$10/\text{hr}) \times 1.5] = \$475$$

In some organizations, the PM adds the overhead charges to the budget. In others, the labor time and materials are just sent to the accounting department and they run the numbers, add the appropriate overhead, and total the costs. Although overhead was charged here against direct labor, more recent accounting practices such as activity-based costing may charge portions of the overhead against other cost drivers such as machine time, weight of raw materials, or total time to project completion.

Direct resource costs such as for materials and machinery needed solely for a particular project are usually charged to the project without an overhead add-on. If machinery from elsewhere in the organization is used, this may be charged to the project at a certain rate (e.g., $/hr) that will include depreciation charges, and then will be credited to the budget of the department owning and paying for the machine. On top of this, there is often a charge for GS&A (general, sales, and administrative) costs that includes upper management, staff functions, sales and marketing, plus any other costs not included in the overhead charge. GS&A may be charged as a percentage of direct costs, all direct and indirect costs, or on other bases including total time to completion.

Thus, the fully costed task will include direct costs for labor, machinery, and resources such as materials, plus overhead charges, and finally, GS&A charges. The full cost budget is then used by accounting to estimate the profit to be earned by the project. The wise PM, however, will also construct a budget of direct costs for his or her own use. This budget provides the information required to manage the project without being confounded with costs over which he or she has no control.

Note that the overhead and GS&A effect can result in a severe penalty when a project runs late, adding significant additional and possibly unexpected costs to the project. Again, we stress the importance of the PM thoroughly understanding the organization's accounting system, and especially how overhead and other such costs are charged to the project.

Of course, this process can also be reversed to the benefit of the PM by minimizing the use of drivers of high cost. Sometimes clients will even put clauses in contracts to foster such behavior. For example, when the state of Pennsylvania contracted for the construction of the Limerick nuclear power generating facility in the late 1980s, they included such an incentive fee provision in the contract. This provision stated that any savings that resulted from finishing the project early would be split between the state and the contractor. As a result, the contractor went to extra expense and trouble to make sure the project was completed early. The project came in 8 months ahead of its 49-month due date and the state and the contractor split the $400 million savings out of the total $3.2 billion budget.

The Impact of Budget Cuts

In the previous chapter on planning, we described a process in which the PM plans Level 1 activities, setting a tentative budget and duration for each. Subordinates (and this term refers to anyone working on the project even though such individuals may not officially report to the PM and may be "above" the PM on the firm's organizational chart) then take responsibility for specifying the Level 2 activities required to produce the Level 1 task. As a part of the Level 2 specifications, tentative budgets and durations are noted for each Level 2 activity. The PM's initial budget and duration estimates are examples of top-down budgeting. The subordinate's estimates of the Level 2 task budgets and durations are bottom-up budgeting. As we promised, we now deal with combining the two budgets.

We will label the Level 1 task estimate of duration of the ith task as t_i, and the respective cost estimate as r_i, the t standing for "time" and the r for "resources." In the meantime, the subordinate has estimated task costs and durations for each of the Level 2 tasks that comprise Level 1 task i. We label the *aggregate* cost and duration of these Level 2 activities as r'_i and t'_i, respectively. It would be nice if r_i equaled r'_i, but the reality is rarely that neat. In general, $r_i << r'_i$ (The same is true of the time estimates, t_i and t'_i.) There are three reasons why this happens. First, jobs always look easier, faster, and cheaper to the boss than to the person who has to do them (Gagnon and Mantel, 1987). Second, bosses are usually optimistic and never admit that details have been forgotten or that anything can or will go wrong. Third, subordinates are naturally pessimistic and want to build in protection for everything that might possibly go wrong.

It is important that we make an assumption for the following discussion. We assume that both boss and subordinate are reasonably honest. What follows is a win-win negotiation, and it will fail if either party is dishonest. (We feel it is critically important to remind readers that it is never smart to view the other party in a negotiation as either stupid or ignorant. Almost without fail, such thoughts are obvious to the other party and the possibility of a win-win solution is dead.) The first step in reducing the difference between the superior's and subordinate's estimates occurs when the worker explains the reality of the task to the boss, and r_i rises. Encouraged by the fact that the boss seems to understand some of the problems, the subordinate responds to the boss's request to remove some of the protective padding. The result is that r'_i falls.

The conversation now shifts to the technology involved in the subordinate's work and the two parties search for efficiencies in the Level 2 work plan. If they find some, the two estimates get closer still, or, possibly, the need for resources may even drop below either party's estimate.

To complete our discussion, let's assume that after all improvements have been made, r'_i is still somewhat higher than r_i. Should the boss accept the subordinate's cost estimate or insist that the subordinate accept the boss's estimate? To answer this question, we must recall the discussion of project life cycles from Chapter 1. We discussed two different common forms of life cycles, and these are illustrated again, for convenience, in Figure 4-1. One curve is S-shaped, and the other is J-shaped . As it happens, the shapes of these curves hold the key to our decision.

Figure 4-1   Two project life cycles (cf. Figures 1-2 and 1-3).

If the project life cycle is S-shaped, then with a somewhat reduced level of resources, a smaller than proportional cut will be made in the project's objectives or performance, likely not a big problem. If the project's life cycle is J-shaped , the impact of inadequate resources will be serious, a larger than proportional cut will be made in the project's performance. The same effect occurs during an "economy drive" when a senior manager decrees an across-the-board budget cut for all projects of, say, 5 or 10 percent. For a project with a J-shaped life cycle, the result is disaster. It is not necessary to know the actual shape of a project's life cycle with any precision. One needs merely to know the probable curvature (concave or convex to the baseline) of the last stage of the cycle for the project being considered.

The message here is that for projects with S-shaped life cycles, the top-down budgeting process is probably acceptable. For J-shaped life-cycle projects, it is dangerous for upper management not to accept the bottom-up budget estimates. At the very least, management should pay attention when the PM complains that the budget is insufficient to complete the project. An example of this problem is NASA's Space Shuttle Program, projected by NASA to cost $10–13 billion but cut by Congress to $5.2 billion. Fearing a cancellation of the entire program if they pointed out the overwhelming developmental problems they faced, NASA acquiesced to the inadequate budget. As a result, portions of the program fell 3 years behind schedule and had cost overruns of 60 percent. As the program moved into the operational flight stage, problems stemming from the inadequate budget surfaced in multiple areas, culminating in the Challenger explosion in January 1986.

Finally, in these days of increasing budget cuts and great stress on delivering project value, cuts to the organization's project portfolio must be made with care. Wheatly (2009) warns against the danger of focusing solely on ROI when making decisions about which projects will be kept and which will be terminated. We will have considerably more to say about this subject in Chapter 8.

An Aside

Here and elsewhere, we have preached the importance of managers and workers who are willing to communicate with one another frequently and honestly when developing budgets and schedules for projects. Such communication is the exception, not the rule. The fact that only a small fraction of software development projects are completed even approximately on time and on budget is so well known as to be legend, as is the record of any number of high technology industries. Sometimes the cause is scope creep, but top-down budgeting and scheduling are also prime causes. Rather than deliver another sermon on the subject, we simply reprint Rule #25 from an excellent book by Jim McCarthy, *Dynamics of Software Development* (1995).

Don't Accept Dictation

I am amazed at the extent to which the software development community accepts bogus dictates, especially when it comes to scheduling. This astonishing passivity is emblematic of Old World behavior applied to New World problems. Given that it's extremely difficult (probably impossible) for a team of committed professionals to create a schedule that even approximates the rate at which the product ultimately materializes, it's utter madness that in many organizations the dates, the features, and the resources—the holy triangle—of a software development project are dictated by people unfamiliar with developing software. Too often people like "Upper Management" or "Marketing" or some other bogeymen conjure up the date. What's worse, by some malignant and pervasive twist of illogic, otherwise competent development managers accept this sort of folly as standard operating procedure.

I have polled dozens of groups of development managers, and my informal data gathering suggests that somewhere in the neighborhood of 30 to 40 percent of all development efforts suffer from dictated features, resources, and schedules. It should be a fundamental dogma that the person who has to do the work should predict the amount of time it will take. Of course, if accuracy isn't a goal, anybody can make foolish predictions.

In some ways, the root of all scheduling evil is that software developers and their managers abdicate their responsibility to determine the probable effort required to achieve a given set of results. The ultimate act of disempowerment is to take away the responsibility for the schedule from those who must live by it. To accept this treatment under any circumstances is no less heinous an act than imposing a bogus scheduling imperative on a team to begin with.

It's easy to sympathize with the urge for control and predictability that this phenomenon manifests, but why on earth should such organizational goofiness persist in the face of what always follows, repeated software calamity?

Often people and organizations have a hard time learning from their mistakes. We tend to be a bit thick sometimes. Our diagnosis of what went wrong the last time can be utterly erroneous, and so we gear up to do it all again—without ever even beginning to experience the core insights required for successful software development.

This blindness is especially likely after a disastrously late software project. Many team members want desperately never to repeat such a death march, so they leave the group. As evidenced by their urge to survive, these people are often the most vital members of the team. The remnant is left lurching about in a fog of blame. Like the Angel of Death, Guilt visits every cubicle. The managers are choking on their own failure, so their ability to lead is smothered. The marketing people have been made to look foolish, their promises just so much gas, and cynicism creeps into their messages. The executives are bewildered, embarrassed, and angry. The customers have been betrayed yet another time.

Slowly the fog dissipates, and a modicum of hope materializes. New team members re-inject a measure of the lost vitality into the team, and new (or forgetful) managers take the helm. The technological siren seduces the group once again. The executives, chastened but unlearning, plunk down enough dough and tell the team when the new project must be done. The cycle repeats.

How is a person to cope with such folly? If you find yourself in such an organizational situation, how should you respond? Keep in mind that in an asylum, the sane are crazy. And in an organization in which irrationality prevails, the irrationality tends to concentrate the further up you go. Your situation might be hopeless because the extent to which you are viewed as crazy will tend to intensify in direct proportion to the power of the observer. You might be able to cope with irrational and self-destructive organizational values, but you're unlikely to prosper in such a setting. A situation this gravely out of whack must be resolved, however. So you steel yourself and inform your dictators that, much as you would like to accept their dictates, you are unable to do so because reality requires otherwise. You remind them (tactfully) that their power is not magic, that their wishes don't make software. You help them envision a future in which people are striving to meet *their own* goals, things they've proposed to do over a certain interval and things that have a chance of being done even sooner than anticipated.

You need to build schedules meticulously from the bottom up. Each person who has a task to do must own the design and execution of that task and must be held accountable for its timely achievement. Accountability is the twin of empowerment. The two together can create a reasonable software development plan.

Reprinted with the kind permission of Jim McCarthy, copyright holder, from *Dynamics of Software Development* by Jim McCarthy, Microsoft Press, Redmond, WA, 1995, pp. 88–89.

Activity vs. Program Budgeting

Traditional organizational budgets are typically *activity* oriented and based on historical data accumulated through an activity-based accounting system. Individual expenses are classified and assigned to basic budget *lines* such as phone, materials, fixed personnel types (salaried, exempt, etc.), or to production centers or processes. These lines are then aggregated and reported by organizational units such as departments or divisions.

Project budgets can also be presented as activity budgets, such as in Table 4-3 where one page of a six-page monthly budget report for a real estate management project is illustrated. When multiple projects draw resources from several different organizational units, the budget may be divided between these multiple units in some arbitrary fashion, thereby losing the ability to control project resources as well as the reporting of individual project expenditures against the budget.

This difficulty gave rise to *program budgeting*, illustrated in Table 4-4. Here the program-oriented project budget is divided by task and expected time of expenditure, thereby allowing aggregation across projects. Budget reports are shown both aggregated and disaggregated by "regular operations," and each of the projects has its own budget. For example, Table 4-3 would have a set of columns for regular operations as well as for each project.

Cost estimating is more tedious than complex except where overhead and GS&A expenses are concerned. Thus, the wise PM will learn the organization's accounting system thoroughly. Low budget estimates or budget cuts will not usually be too serious for S-shaped life-cycle projects but can be disastrous for exponential life-cycle projects. Two kinds of project budget exist, usually depending on where projects report in the organization. Activity budgets show lines of standard activity by actual and budget for given time periods. Program budgets show expenses by task and time period. Program budgets are then aggregated by reporting unit.

Table 4-3   Typical Monthly Budget for a Real Estate Project (page 1 of 6)

	\multicolumn{3}{c}{Current}		
	Actual	Budget	Variance	Pct.
Corporate—Income Statement				
Revenue				
8430 Management fees	.00	.00	.00	.0
8491 Prtnsp. reimb.—property mgmt.	7,410.00	6,222.00	1,188.00	119.0
8492 Prtnsp. reimb.—owner acquisition	.00	3,750.00	3,750.00—	.0
8493 Prtnsp. reimb.—rehab	.00	.00	.00	.0
8494 Other income	.00	.00	.00	.0
8495 Reimbursements—others	.00	.00	.00	.0
Total revenue	7,410.00	9,972.00	2,562.00—	74.3
Operating expenses				
Payroll & P/R benefits				
8511 Salaries	29,425.75	34,583.00	5,157.25	85.0
8512 Payroll taxes	1,789.88	3,458.00	1,668.12	51.7
8513 Group ins. & med. reimb.	1,407.45	1,040.00	387.45—	135.3
8515 Workers' compensation	43.04	43.00	.04—	100.0
8516 Staff apartments	.00	.00	.00	.0
8517 Bonus	.00	.00	.00	.0
Total payroll & P/R benefits	32,668.12	39,124.00	6,457.88	83.5
Travel & entertainment expenses				
8512 Travel	456.65	300.00	156.65—	152.2
8522 Promotion, entertainment & gift	69.52	500.00	430.48	13.9
8523 Auto	1,295.90	1,729.00	433.10	75.0
Total travel & entertainment exp.	1,822.07	2,529.00	706.93	72.1
Professional fees				
8531 Legal fees	419.00	50.00	369.00—	838.0
8532 Accounting fees	289.00	.00	289.00—	.0
8534 Temporary help	234.58	200.00	34.58—	117.2

4.3   IMPROVING COST ESTIMATES

At the end of his *"Don't Accept Dictation,"* reprinted above, McCarthy wrote "Each person who has a task to do must own the design and execution of that task and must be held accountable for its timely achievement. Accountability is the twin of empowerment." If empowerment is to be trusted, it must be accompanied by account-ability. Fortunately, it is not difficult to do this. This section deals with a number of ways for improving the process of cost estimating and an easy way of measuring its accuracy. These improvements are not restricted to cost estimates, but can be applied to almost all of the areas in project management that call for estimating or forecast-ing any aspect of a project that is measured numerically; e.g., task durations, the time for which specialized personnel will be required, or the losses associated with specific types of risks should they occur. These improvements range from better formalization

Risk

Table 4-4 Project Budget by Task and Month

Task	Start Node (I)	End Node (J)	Estimate (£)	Monthly Budget (£)							
				1	2	3	4	5	6	7	8
A	1	2	7000	5600	1400						
B	2	3	9000		3857	5143					
C	2	4	10000		3750	5000	1250				
D	2	5	6000		3600	2400					
E	3	7	12000				4800	4800	2400		
F	4	7	3000				3000				
G	5	6	9000			2571	5143	1286			
H	6	7	5000					3750	1250		
I	7	8	8000						2667	5333	
J	8	9	6000								6000
			75000	5600	12,607	15,114	14,193	9836	6317	5333	6000

of the estimating/forecasting process, using forms and other simple procedures, to straightforward quantitative techniques involving learning curves and tracking signals. We conclude with some miscellaneous topics, including behavioral issues that often lead to incorrect budget estimates.

Forms

The use of simple forms such as that in Figure 4-2 can be of considerable help to the PM in obtaining accurate estimates, not only of direct costs, but also when the resource is needed, how many are needed, who should be contacted, and if it will be available when needed. The information can be collected for each task on an individual form and then aggregated for the project as a whole.

Learning Curves

Suppose a firm wins a contract to supply 25 units of a complex electronic device to a customer. Although the firm is competent to produce this device, it has never produced one as complex as this. Based on the firm's experience, it estimates that if it were to build many such devices it would take about 4 hours of direct labor per unit produced. With this estimate, and the wage and benefit rates the firm is paying, the PM can derive an estimate of the direct labor cost to complete the contract.

Unfortunately, the estimate will be in considerable error because the PM is underestimating the labor costs to produce the initial units that will take much longer than 4 hours each. Likewise, if the firm built a prototype of the device and recorded the direct labor hours, which may run as high as 10 hours for this device, this estimate applied to the contract of 25 units would give a result that is much too high.

In both cases, the reason for the error is the learning exhibited by humans when they repeat a task. In general, it has been found that unit performance improves by a fixed percent each time the total production quantity doubles. More specifically, *each time the output doubles, the worker hours per unit decrease by a fixed percentage of their previous value.* This percentage is called the learning rate, and typical values run

Project name_____

Date_____

Task number_____

RESOURCES NEEDED

Resources	Person to Contact	How Many/ Much Needed	When Needed	Check (√) If Available
People: Managers, Supervisors				
Professional & Technical				
Nontechnical				
Money				
Materials: Facilities				
Equipment				
Tools				
Power				
Space				
Special Services: Research & Test				
Typing/clerical				
Reproduction				
Others				

Figure 4-2 Form for gathering data on project resource needs.

between 70 and 95 percent. The higher values are for more mechanical tasks, while the lower, faster-learning values are for more mental tasks such as solving problems. A common rate in manufacturing is 80 percent. For example, if the device described in the earlier example required 10 hours to produce the first unit and this firm generally followed a typical 80 percent learning curve, then the second unit would require $.80 \times 10 = 8$ hours, the fourth unit would require 6.4 hours, the eighth unit 5.12 hours, and so on. Of course, after a certain number of repetitions, say 100 or 200, the time per unit levels out and little further improvement occurs.

Mathematically, this relationship we just described follows a negative exponential function. Using this function, the time required to produce the nth unit can be calculated as

$$T_n = T_1 n^r$$

where T_n is the time required to complete the nth unit, T_1 is time required to complete the first unit, and r is the exponent of the learning curve and is calculated as the log(learning rate)/log(2). Tables are widely available for calculating the completion time of unit n and the cumulative time to produce units one through n for various learning rates; for example, see Meredith and Shafer (2013). The impact of learning can also be incorporated into spreadsheets developed to help prepare the budget for a project as is illustrated in the example at the end of this section.

⭐
Best Practice

The use of learning curves in project management has increased greatly in recent years. For instance, methods have been developed to approximate composite learning curves for entire projects (Amor and Teplitz, 1998), for approximating total costs from the unit learning curve (Camm, Evans, and Womer, 1987), and for including learning curve effects in critical resource diagramming (Badiru, 1995). The conclusion is that the effects of learning, even in "one-time" projects, should not be ignored. If costs are underestimated, the result will be an unprofitable project and senior management will be unhappy. If costs are overestimated, the bid will be lost to a savvier firm and senior management will be unhappy.

Media One Consultants

Media One Consultants is a small consulting firm that specializes in developing the electronic media that accompany major textbooks. A typical project requires the development of an electronic testbank, PowerPoint lecture slides, and a website to support the textbook.

A team consisting of three of the firm's consultants just completed the content for the first of eighteen chapters of an operations management textbook for a major college textbook publisher. In total, it took the team 21 hours to complete this content. The consultants are each billed out at $65/ hour plus 20 percent to cover overhead. Past experience indicates that projects of this type follow a 78 percent learning curve.

The publisher's developmental editor recently sent an email message to the team leader inquiring into when the project will be complete and what the cost will be. Should the team leader attempt to account for the impact of learning in answering these questions? How big a difference does incorporating learning into the budget make? What are the managerial implications of not incorporating learning into the time and cost estimates?

The team leader developed the spreadsheet below to estimate the budget and completion time for this project. The top of the spreadsheet contains key parameters such as the learning rate, the consultants' hourly billout rate, the overhead rate, and the time required to complete the first chapter. The middle of the spreadsheet contains formulas to calculate both the unit cost and time of each chapter and the cumulative cost and time.

According to the spreadsheet, the cost of the project is $14,910 and will require in total 191.2 hours. Had the impact of learning not been considered, the team leader would have likely grossly overestimated the project's cost to be $29,484 (1,638 × 18) and its duration to be 278 (21 × 18) hours. Clearly, several negative consequences could be incurred if these inflated time and cost estimates were used. For example, the publisher might decide to reevaluate its decision to award the contract to Media One. Furthermore, the time when the team members would be able to start on their next assignment would be incorrectly estimated. At a minimum, this would complicate the start of future projects. Perhaps more damaging, however, is that it could lead to lost business if potential clients were not willing to wait for their project to begin based on the inflated time estimates.

	A	B	C	D	E	F
1	Learning Rate	78.0%				
2	Hourly Rate	$65				
3	Overhead Rate	20.0%				
4	Time for First Unit	21				
5						
6			Cumulative	Chapter	Cumulative	
7	Chapter Number	Unit Time	Time	Cost	Cost	
8	1	21.0	21.0	$1,638	$1,638	
9	2	16.4	37.4	$1,278	$2,916	
10	3	14.2	51.5	$1,105	$4,020	
11	4	12.8	64.3	$997	$5,017	
12	5	11.8	76.1	$920	$5,937	
13	6	11.0	87.2	$862	$6,799	
14	7	10.5	97.6	$815	$7,614	
15	8	10.0	107.6	$777	$8,391	
16	9	9.6	117.1	$745	$9,137	
17	10	9.2	126.3	$718	$9,854	
18	11	8.9	135.2	$693	$10,548	
19	12	8.6	143.8	$672	$11,220	
20	13	8.4	152.2	$653	$11,873	
21	14	8.2	160.4	$636	$12,509	
22	15	8.0	168.3	$620	$13,130	
23	16	7.8	176.1	$606	$13,736	
24	17	7.6	183.7	$593	$14,329	
25	18	7.5	191.2	$581	$14,910	
26						
27	*Key Formulas:*					
28	B8	=B4				
29	B9	=B$8*(A9^(LOG(B$1)/LOG(2))) {copy to cells B10:B25}				
30	C8	=B8				
31	C9	=B9 + C8 {copy to cells C10:C25}				
32	D8	=(B8*B$2)*(1 + B$3)				
33	D9	=(B9*B$2)*(1 + B$3) {copy to cells D10:D25}				
34	E8	=D8				
35	E9	=D9 + E8 {copy to cells E10:E25}				

Tracking Signals

In Chapter 3, we noted that people do not seem to learn by experience, no matter how much they urge others to do so. PMs and others involved with projects spend much time estimating—activity costs and durations, among many other things. There are two types of error in those estimates. First, there is *random error*. Errors are random when there is a roughly equal chance that estimates are above or below the true value of a variable, and the average size of the error is approximately equal for over and under estimates. (Naturally, we try to devise ways of estimating that minimize the size of these random errors.) If either of the above is not true for an estimator—either the chance of over or under estimates are not about equal or the size of over or under estimates are not approximately equal—the estimates are said to be *biased*. Random errors cancel out, which means that if we add them up the sum will approach zero. Errors caused by bias do not cancel out. They are *systematic* errors.

Best Practice

Calculation of a number called the *tracking signal* can reveal if there is systematic bias in cost and other estimates and whether the bias is positive or negative. Knowing this can then be quite helpful to a PM in making future estimates or on the critically important task of judging the quality of estimates made by others. Consider the spreadsheet data in Figure 4-3 where estimated and actual values for some factor are listed in the order they were made, indicated for ease of reference by "period." In order to compare estimates of different resources measured in units and of different magnitudes, we will derive a tracking signal based on the *ratio* of actual to estimated values rather than the usual *difference* between the two.

To calculate the first period ratio in Figure 4-3, for example, we would take the ratio $163/155 = 1.052$. This means that the actual was 5.2 percent higher than the estimate, a

	A	B	C	D	E	F	G
1	This is a template for improving one's estimating skills.						
2							
3	MAR = Sum[|(At / Et)−1|] / n						
4	Tracking Signal = Sum[(At / Et)−1] / MAR						
5							Tracking
6	Period	Estimate	Actual	$(A_t / E_t) - 1$	$\|(A_t / E_t) - 1\|$	MAR	Signal
7	1	155	163	.052	.052		
8	2	242	240	−.008	.008	0.030	1.448
9	3	46	67	.457	.457	0.172	2.904
10	4	69	78	.130	.130	0.162	3.898
11	5	75	71	−.053	.053	0.140	4.120
12	6	344	423	.230	.230	0.155	5.205
13	7	56	49	.125	.125	0.151	4.523
14	8	128	157	.227	.227	0.160	5.670
15							
16	Total			.908	1.281		
17							
18	Formulas:						
19	Cell D7	=(C7/B7)−1 {copy to cells D8:D14}					
20	Cell D7	=(ABS)D7 {copy to cells E8:E14}					
21	Cell F8	=SUM(E$7:E8)/COUNT(E$7:E8) {copy to cells F9:F14}					
22	Cell G8	=SUM(D$7:D8)/F8 {copy to cellsG9:G14}					
23	Cell D16	=SUM(D7:D14) {copy to cells E16}					

Figure 4-3 Excel® template for finding bias in estimates.

forecast that was low. In column D, we list these errors for each of the periods and then cumulate them at the bottom of the spreadsheet. Note that in columns D and E we subtract 1 from the ratio. This centers the data around zero rather than 1.0, which makes some ratios positive, indicating an actual greater than the forecast, and other ratios negative, indicating an actual less than the forecast. If the cumulative percent error at the bottom of the spreadsheet is positive, which it is in this case, it means that the actuals are usually greater than the estimates. The forecaster underestimates if the ratio is positive and overestimates if it is negative. The larger the percent error, the greater the forecaster's bias, systematic under- or overestimation.

Column E simply shows the absolute value of column D. Column F is the "mean absolute ratio," abbreviated MAR, which is the running average of the values in column E up to that period. (Check the formulas in the spreadsheet of Figure 4-3.) The tracking signal listed in column G is the ratio of the running sum of the values in column D divided by the MAR for that period. If the estimates are unbiased, the running sum of ratios in column D will be about zero, and dividing this by the MAR will give a very small tracking signal, possibly zero. On the other hand, if there is considerable bias in the estimates, either positive or negative, the running sum of the ratios in column D will grow quite large. Then, when divided by the mean absolute ratio this will show whether the tracking signal is > 1 or < 1, and therefore greater than the variability in the estimates or not. If the bias is large, resulting in large positive or negative ratios, the resulting tracking signal will be correspondingly positive or negative.

It should be noted that it is not simply the bias that is of interest to the PM, although bias is very important. The MAR is also important because this indicates the variability of the estimates compared with the resulting actual values. With experience, the MAR should decrease over time though it will never reach zero. We strive to find a forecasting technique that minimizes both the bias *and* the MAR. By observing her own errors, the PM can learn to make unbiased estimates. When meeting with her subordinates in order to coach them on improving their estimates, it is important to recognize that most overestimates of duration or resource requirements are the result of an attempt by the subordinate to make "safe" estimates, and underestimates result from overoptimism. If subordinates overcorrect, the PM should avoid sharp criticism. Reasonable accuracy is the goal, but the uncertainty surrounding all projects does not allow random estimate errors to vanish.

Other Factors

Studies consistently show that between 60 and 85 percent of projects fail to meet their time, cost, and/or performance objectives. The record for information system (IS) projects is particularly poor, it seems. For example, there are at least 45 estimating models available for IS projects but few IS managers use any of them (Lawrence, 1994; Martin, 1994). While the variety of problems that can plague project cost estimates seem to be unlimited, there are some that occur with high frequency; we will discuss each of these in turn.

Changes in resource prices, for example, are a common problem. The most common managerial approach to this problem is to increase all cost estimates by some fixed percentage. A better approach, however, is to identify each input that has a significant impact on the costs and to estimate the rate of price change for each one. The Bureau of Labor Statistics (BLS) in the U.S. Department of Commerce publishes price data and "inflators" (or "deflators") for a wide range of commodities, machinery, equipment, and personnel specialities. (For more information on the BLS, visit http://stats.bls.gov or www.bls.gov.)

Another problem is overlooking the need to factor into the estimated costs an adequate allowance for waste and spoilage. Again, the best approach is to determine the individual rates of waste and spoilage for each task rather than to use some fixed percentage.

A similar problem is not adding an allowance for increased personnel costs due to loss and replacement of skilled project team members. Not only will new members go through a learning period, which increases the time and cost of the relevant tasks, but professional salaries usually increase faster than the general average. Thus, it may cost substantially more to replace a team member with a newcomer who has about the same level of experience.

Then there is also the Brooks's "mythical man-month" effect* which was discovered in the IS field but applies just as well in projects. As workers are hired, either for additional capacity or to replace those who leave, they require training in the project environment before they become productive. The training is, of course, informal on-the-job training conducted by their coworkers who must take time from their own project tasks, thus resulting in ever more reduced capacity as more workers are hired.

And there is the behavioral possibility that, in the excitement to get a project approved, or to win a bid, or perhaps even due to pressure from upper management, the project cost estimator gives a more "optimistic" picture than reality warrants. Inevitably, the estimate understates the cost. This is a clear violation of the PMI's Code of Ethics. It is also stupid. When the project is finally executed, the actual costs result in a project that misses its profit goals, or worse, fails to make a profit at all—hardly a welcome entry on the estimator's résumé.

Even organizational climate factors influence cost estimates. If the penalty for overestimating costs is much more severe than underestimating, almost all costs will be underestimated, and vice versa. A major manufacturer of airplane landing gear parts wondered why the firm was no longer successful, over several years, in winning competitive bids. An investigation was conducted and revealed that, 3 years earlier, the firm was late on a major delivery to an important customer and paid a huge penalty as well as being threatened with the loss of future business. The reason the firm was late was because an insufficient number of expensive, hard to obtain parts was purchased for the project and more could not be obtained without a long delay. The purchasing manager was demoted and replaced by his assistant. The assistant's solution to this problem was to include a 10 percent allowance for additional, hard to obtain parts in every cost proposal. This resulted in every proposal from the firm being significantly higher than their competitors' proposals in this narrow margin business.

There is also a probabilistic element in most projects. For example, projects such as writing software require that every element work 100 percent correctly for the final product to perform to specifications. In programming software, if there are 1000 lines of code and each line has a .999 probability of being accurate, the likelihood of the final program working is only about 37 percent!

Sometimes, there is plain bad luck. What is indestructible, breaks. What is impenetrable, leaks. What is certified, guaranteed, and warranted, fails. The wise PM includes allowances for "unexpected contingencies."

There are many ways of estimating project costs; we suggest trying all of them and then using those that "work best" for your situation. The PM should take into consideration as many known influences as can be predicted, and those that cannot be predicted must then simply be "allowed for."

---

*This is from another classic work, Brooks (1975), that had a major impact on managers, particularly in the Information Systems area.

Finally, a serious source of inaccurate estimates of time and cost is the all too common practice of some managers arbitrarily to cut carefully prepared time and cost estimates. Managers rationalize their actions by such statements as "I know they have built a lot of slop in those estimates," or "I want to give them a more challenging target to shoot at." This is not effective management. It is not even good common sense. (Reread the excerpt from McCarthy, 1995 appearing above.) Cost and time estimates should be made by the people who designed the work and are responsible for doing it. As we argued earlier in this chapter, the PM and the team members may negotiate different estimates of resources needs and task durations, but managerially dictated arbitrary cuts in budgets and schedules almost always lead to projects that are late and over budget. We will say more about this later.

Boston's Big Dig highway/tunnel project is one of the largest, most complex, and technologically challenging highway projects in U.S. history. The "Big Dig," originally expected to cost less than $3 billion, was declared complete after two decades and $14.6 billion for planning and construction, almost a 500 percent cost overrun (Abrams, 2003 and PMI, August 2004). With an estimated benefit of $500 million per year in reduced congestion, pollution, accidents, fuel costs, and lateness, the project has an undiscounted payback of almost 30 years. This project was clearly one that offered little value to the city if it wasn't completed, and so it continued far past what planners thought was a worthwhile investment, primarily because the federal government was paying 85 percent of its cost. One clear lesson from the project has been that unless the state and local governments are required to pay at least half the cost of these megaprojects, there won't be serious local deliberation of their pros and cons. The overrun is attributed to two major factors: (1) underestimates of the initial project scope, typical of government projects; and (2) lack of control, particularly costs, including conflicts of interest between the public and private sectors.

> There are numerous ways to improve the process of cost estimation ranging from simple but useful forms and procedures to special techniques such as learning curves and tracking signals. Most estimates are in error, however, because of simpler reasons such as not using available tools, common sense, or failing to allow for problems and contingencies, such as having to replace workers midstream. In addition, there are behavioral and organizational reasons, such as informal incentive systems that reward inaccurate estimates.

4.4   BUDGET UNCERTAINTY AND PROJECT RISK MANAGEMENT

Risk

PMBOK Guide

In spite of the care and effort expended to create an accurate and fair budget, it is still only an estimate made under conditions of uncertainty. Because projects are unique, risk pervades all elements of the project, and particularly the project's goals of performance, schedule, and budget. We will discuss these issues of uncertainty and risk here, and offer some suggestions for dealing with them. PMBOK covers the topic of risk in Chapter 11 on Risk.

Budget Uncertainty

Perceptually, the PM sees the uncertainty of the budget like the shaded portion of Figure 4-4, where the actual project costs may be either higher or lower than the estimates the PM has derived. As we will describe later, however, it seems that more

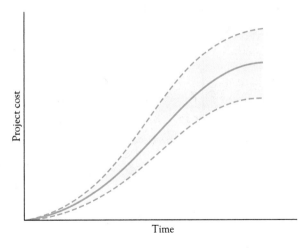

Figure 4-4   Estimate of project cost: estimate made at project start.

things can go wrong in a project and drive up the cost than can go right to keep down the cost. As the project unfolds, the cost uncertainty decreases as the project moves toward completion. Figures 4-5 (a), (b), and (c) illustrate this. An estimate at the beginning of the project as in Figure 4-4 is shown as the t_0 estimate in Figure 4-5(a). As work on the project progresses, the uncertainty decreases as the project moves toward completion. At time t_1 the cost to date is known and another estimate is made of the cost to complete the project, Figure 4-5(b). This is repeated at t_2, Figure 4-5(c). Each estimate, of course, begins at the actual cost to date and estimates only the remaining cost to completion. The further the project progresses, the less the uncertainty in the final project cost. It is common in project management to make new forecasts about project completion time and cost at fixed points in the project life cycle, or at special milestones.

The reasons for cost uncertainty in the project are many: prices may escalate, different resources may be required, the project may take a different amount of time than we expected, thereby impacting overhead and indirect costs, and on and on. Earlier, we discussed ways to improve cost estimates, to anticipate such uncertainty, but change is a fact of life, including life on the project, and change invariably alters our previous budget estimates.

Three Causes for Change   There are three basic causes for change in projects and their budgets and/or schedules. Some changes are due to errors the cost estimator made about how to achieve the tasks identified in the project plan. Such changes are due to technological uncertainty: a building's foundation must be reinforced due to a fault in the ground that wasn't identified beforehand; a new innovation allows a project task to be completed easier than was anticipated, and so on.

Other changes result because the project team or client learns more about the nature of the scope of the project or the setting in which it is to be used. This derives from an increase in the team's or client's knowledge or sophistication about the project deliverables. The medical team plans to use a device in the field as well as in the hospital. The chemists find another application of the granulated bed process if it is altered to include additional minerals.

The third source of change is the mandate: A new law is passed, a trade association sets a new standard, a governmental regulatory agency adopts a new policy. These changes alter the previous "rules of conduct" under which the project had been operating, usually to the detriment of the budget.

(a)

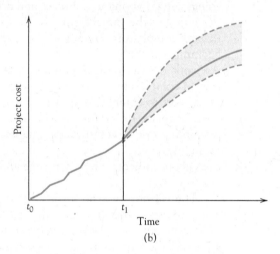

(b)

Figure 4-5 (a), (b), and (c) Estimates of project cost: estimates made at time t_0, t_1, and t_2.

(c)

Best Practice

Handling Changes   There are different ways to handle such changes. The least preferred way is simply to accept a negative change and take a loss on the project. The best approach is to prepare for change ahead of time by including provisions in the original contract for such changes. The easiest change to handle is when the change is the result of an increased specification by the client, yet even these kinds of changes are often mishandled by the project organization. The best practice is to include in the contract a formal change control procedure that allows for renegotiation of price and schedule for client-ordered changes in performance.

More difficult changes are those resulting from misunderstood assumptions, technological uncertainty, and mandates. Assumptions and some technological uncertainties are most easily handled by carefully listing all the assumptions, including those regarding technology, in the contract and stating that if these assumptions fail to hold, the project's cost and schedule may have to be adjusted.

Mandates are the most difficult to accommodate because they can affect anything about the project and usually come without warning. The shorter the project duration, however, the less likely an unexpected mandate will impact the project. Thus, when contracting for a project of extended duration, it is best to divide it into shorter segments and contract for only one segment at a time. Of course, this also gives clients the opportunity to reconsider whether they want to complete the full project, as well as giving the competition an opportunity to steal the remainder of the project from you. Nevertheless, if a client wants to cancel a contract and is locked into a long-term agreement, the project will not have a happy ending anyway. At least with shorter segments the client may be willing to finish a segment before dropping the project. In any event, if the client is pleased with your performance on one segment of the contract, it is unlikely that a competitor will have the experience and cost efficiencies that you have gained and will be able to steal the next segment. At the least, the client would be obligated to give you an opportunity to match their bid.

As changes impact the project's costs, the budget for the remainder of the project will certainly have to be revised. There are three ways to revise a budget during the course of a project, each depending on the nature of the changes that have been experienced. If the changes are confined to early elements of the project and are not seen to impact the rest of the project, then the new budget can be estimated as the old budget plus the changes from the early elements.

More frequently, something systemic has changed that will impact the costs of the rest of the project tasks as well, such as a higher rate of inflation. In this case, the new budget estimate will be the accumulated costs to date plus the previous estimates of the rest of the budget multiplied by some correction factor for the systemic change. Recall that the BLS is an excellent source for such historical data that will aid the PM in estimating an appropriate correction factor.

Last, there may be some individual changes now perceived to impact specific elements of the remaining project tasks. The new budget estimate will then be the actual costs to date plus the expected costs for the remaining project tasks. Generally, both systematic and individual changes in the project will be revised in all three ways at once.

Project Budgeting in Practice

According to the *Oxford Review of Economic Policy*, a study of 258 projects in 20 countries showed that nine out of ten projects experience cost overruns, and sometimes by over 100 percent! You might wonder how this can possibly happen, but it turns out that it happens quite easily, primarily due to the dynamics of people and groups making decisions in an organization over some period of time. Let's go through what happens in a typical project to see how this occurs.

To determine a project budget,* the project manager (PM) starts with the project plan or WBS to determine the various steps required in the project, the resource needs, labor hours, and associated costs. This cost estimate, plus a "contingency" of up to 25 percent added to either the labor hours or total cost, is then used as the project budget for both obtaining approval for the project and as a placeholder in the department's budget so the funds will be encumbered and unavailable for other purposes. (The addition of a contingency is standard practice and expected.)

However, top management is also responsible for constructing a budget for the company and may have also calculated some cost for this project, or the department that will be funding it. In the process, they will be using their own methods, such as the budget or cost of a previous but similar project, the amount of money the department was budgeted for last year, the amount of monies available for them to spend, the amount the project manager or department spent last year, gut-feel, and other such approaches. When this is aggregated by department, the totals are compared to what each department spent the previous year, what the company's departmental priorities are for this year, how the total budget compares with the total money available, and then the department is given an appropriate lump sum budget for the year. The department then allocates their departmental budget according to their priorities, and increments or decrements the project budgets by an amount to meet the department's budget. Thereupon the project's plan is adjusted, if possible, by the assigned budget rather than vice-versa, but typically the scope cannot be reduced so the PM tries to adjust the plan to suit.

But the dynamics are still not over. At some point(s) in the future, the department's budget may well be cut further, so all the projects' placeholder budgets are decremented even more, requiring additional "adjustments" to the project plan (but again without allowing a reduction in scope). According to one expert in project management (Swanson, 2011), due to natural optimism at project start most PMs underestimate their projects' costs by 30 percent or more. Given that their expense contingency was less than 25 percent even before these factors impacted the budget, it is no wonder that the great majority of projects have cost overruns.

4.5   PROJECT RISK SIMULATION WITH CRYSTAL BALL®

Risk

PMBOK Guide

At this point, we will deal with one of the more quantitative methods of dealing with risk as it applies to the task of simulating budgets and cash flows. The essence of risk analysis is to make estimates or assumptions about the probability distributions associated with key parameters and variables and to use analytic decision models or Monte Carlo simulation models based on these distributions to evaluate the desirability of certain managerial decisions. Real-world problems are usually large enough that the use of analytic models is very difficult and time consuming. With modern computer software, simulation is not difficult. PMBOK describes the simulation process in Chapter 11 on Risk.

A mathematical model of the situation is constructed, and a simulation is run to determine the model's outcomes under various scenarios. The model is run (or

*A useful reference for estimating the costs for a project budget is the Project Management Institute's 2010 publication: *The Practice Standard for Project Estimating.*

replicated) repeatedly, starting from a different point each time based on random choices of values from the probability distributions of the input variables. Outputs of the model are used to construct statistical distributions of items of interest to decision makers, such as costs, profits, completion dates, or return on investment. These distributions are the *risk profiles* of the outcomes associated with a decision. Risk profiles can be considered by the manager when considering a decision, along with many other factors such as strategic concerns, behavioral issues, fit with the organization, cost and scheduling issues, and so on.

In the following section, using an example we have examined earlier in Chapter 1, we illustrate how Oracle Crystal Ball® 11.1.2.2 (CB), a widely used Excel® Add-In that is available with this book, can be used to improve the PM's understanding of the risks associated with managing projects.

Reconsider the PsychoCeramic Sciences example we solved in Chapter 1 in the section devoted to finding the discounted cash flows associated with a project. Setting this problem up in Excel® is straightforward, and the earlier analytic solution is shown here for convenience as Table 4-5. We found that the project cleared the barrier of a 13 percent hurdle rate for acceptance. The net cash flow over the project's life is just under $400,000, and discounted at the hurdle rate plus 2 percent annual inflation, the net present value of the cash flow is about $18,000. The rate of inflation is shown in a separate column because it is another uncertain variable that should be included in the risk analysis.

Assume that the expenditures in this example are fixed by contract with an outside vendor so that there is no uncertainty about the outflows; there is, of course, uncertainty about the inflows. Suppose that the estimated inflows are as shown in Table 4-6 and include a minimum (pessimistic) estimate, a most likely estimate, and a maximum (optimistic) estimate. (In Chapter 5, "Scheduling the Project," we will deal in more detail with the methods and meaning of making such estimates. Shortly, we will deal with the importance of ensuring the honesty of such estimates.) Both the beta and the triangular statistical distributions are well suited for modeling variables with these three parameters. In earlier versions of CB the beta distribution was complicated and not particularly intuitive to use, so the triangular distribution was used as a reasonably good approximation of the beta. Use of a new beta distribution, labeled "BetaPERT" by CB in its distribution Gallery, has been simplified in version CB 11.1.2.2; we will use it in this example, and the simulations run elsewhere in this book.[*]

The hurdle rate of return is typically fixed by the firm, so the only remaining variable is the rate of inflation that is included in finding the discount factor. We have assumed a 2 percent rate of inflation with a normal distribution, plus or minus 1 percent (i.e., 1 percent represents ± 3 standard deviations).

It is important to point out that approaches in which only the most likely estimate of each variable is used are equivalent to assuming that the input data are known with certainty. The major benefit of simulation is that it allows all possible values for each variable to be considered. Just as the distribution of possible values for a variable is a better reflection of reality than the single "most likely" value, the distribution of outcomes developed by simulation is a better forecast of an uncertain future reality than is a forecast of a single outcome. In general, precise forecasts will be "precisely wrong."

---

[*]The instructions for its use are the same for either the beta or triangular distributions, so the reader (or teacher) may select either.

Table 4-5   Single-Point Estimates of the Cash Flows for PsychoCeramic Sciences, Inc.

	A	B	C	D	E	F	G
1					Discount	Net Present	Inflation
2	Year	Inflow	Outflow	Net Flow	Factor	Value	Rate, p
3				B−C	$1/(1 + k + p)^t$	D × E	
4	2013*	0.00	125,000.00	−125,000.00	1	−125,000.00	0.0200
5	2013	0.00	100,000.00	−100,000.00	0.8696	−86,956.52	0.0200
6	2014	0.00	90,000.00	−90,000.00	0.7561	−68,052.93	0.0200
7	2015	50,000.00	0.00	50,000.00	0.6575	32,875.81	0.0200
8	2016	120,000.00	15,000.00	105,000.00	0.5718	60,034.09	0.0200
9	2017	115,000.00	0.00	115,000.00	0.4972	57,175.32	0.0200
10	2018	105,000.00	15,000.00	90,000.00	0.4323	38,909.48	0.0200
11	2019	97,000.00	0.00	97,000.00	0.3759	36,465.89	0.0200
12	2020	90,000.00	15,000.00	75,000.00	0.3269	24,517.63	0.0200
13	2021	82,000.00		82,000.00	0.2843	23,309.52	0.0200
14	2022	65,000.00		65,000.00	0.2472	16,067.01	0.0200
15	2022	35,000.00		35,000.00	0.2472	8,651.46	0.0200
16							
17	Total	759,000.00	360,000.00	399,000.00		17,997.00	
18							
19				*t = 0 at the beginning of 2013			
20							
21	Formulae						
22	Cell B17		=Sum(B4:B15) copy to C17, D17, F17				
23	Cell D4		=(B4−C4) copy to D5:D15				
24	Cell E4		=1/(1 +.13 + G4)^0				
25	Cell E5		=1/(1 +.13 + G5)^1				
26	Cell E6		=1/(1 + .13 + G6)^(A6 − 2012) copy to E7:E15				
27	Cell E15		=E14				
28	Cell F4		=D4*E4 copy to F5:F15				
29							

Using CB to run a Monte Carlo simulation requires us to define two types of cells in the Excel® spreadsheet.* The cells that contain variables or parameters that we make assumptions about are defined as *assumption cells*. For the PsychoCeramic Sciences case, these are the cells in Table 4-5, columns B and G, the cash inflows and

---

*It is generally helpful for the reader to work the problem as we explain it. If the CB Add - In has not been installed on your computer, consult the instructions that accompany this book. For those who wish to access additional instruction on the use of CB, you may use the following link to the CB Users Group (CBUG): http://tech. groups.yahoo.com/group/cbug2/ .

Table 4-6 Pessimistic (Minimum), Most Likely, and Optimistic (Maximum) Estimates for Cash Inflows for PsychoCeramic Sciences, Inc.

	A	B	C	D
		Minimum	Most Likely	Maximum
1		Inflow	Inflow	Inflow
2	Year			
3	2015	$35,000	$50,000	$60,000
4	2016	95,000	120,000	136,000
5	2017	100,000	115,000	125,000
6	2018	88,000	105,000	116,000
7	2019	80,000	97,000	108,000
8	2020	75,000	90,000	100,000
9	2021	67,000	82,000	91,000
10	2022	51,000	65,000	73,000
11	2022	30,000	35,000	38,000
12				
13	Total	$621,000	$759,000	$847,000

the rate of inflation, respectively. As noted above, we assume that the rate of inflation is normally distributed with a mean of 2 percent and a standard deviation of .33 percent. Likewise, we assume that yearly inflows can be modeled with a BetaPERT (or a triangular) distribution.

The cells that contain the outcomes (or results) we are interested in forecasting are called *forecast cells*. In PsychoCeramic's case we want to predict the NPV of the project. Hence, cell F17 in Table 4-5 is defined as a forecast cell. Each forecast cell typically contains a formula that is dependent on one or more of the assumption cells. Simulations may have many assumption and forecast cells, but they must have at least one of each. Before proceeding, open Crystal Ball® and make an Excel® spreadsheet copy of Table 4-5, adding column G for the inflation rate.

To illustrate the process of defining an assumption cell, consider cell B7, the cash inflow estimate for 2015. We can see from Table 4-6 that the minimum expected cash inflow is $35,000, the most likely cash flow is $50,000, and the maximum is $60,000.

If you have not already done so, load the Excel program on your computer. If prompted, click on "Use Crystal Ball" and then open the spreadsheet you made of Table A in Chapter 1 (also shown in Table 4-5). Given the information in Table 4-6, the process of defining the assumption cells and entering the pessimistic and optimistic data is straightforward and involves six steps:[*]

1. Click on cell **B7** to select it as the relevant assumption cell.
2. Select the Crystal Ball tab in Excel and from the Crystal Ball ribbon, select "Define Assumption" at the very left of the Crystal Ball ribbon. CB's **Distribution Gallery** is now displayed as shown in Figure 4-6.

---

*It is generally helpful for the reader to work the problem as we explain it.

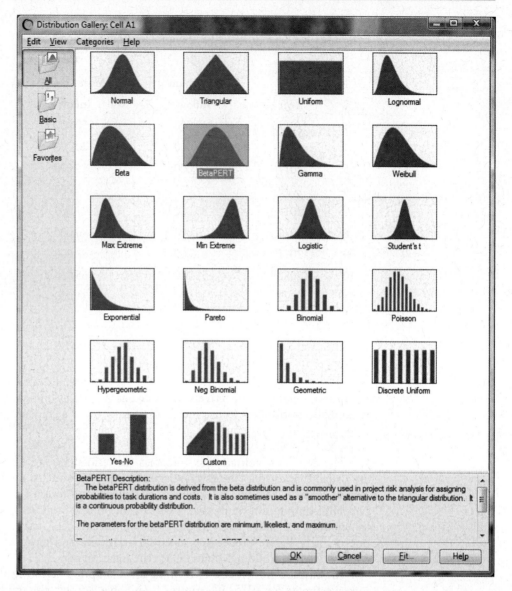

Figure 4-6   Crystal Ball® Distribution Gallery.

3. CB allows you to choose from a wide variety of probability distributions. Click on the **BetaPERT** box and then click "OK" button to select it.

4. CB's BetaPERT Distribution dialog box is displayed as in Figure 4-7. It may have numbers in the boxes but ignore them. If it does not otherwise appear exactly like Figure 4-7, click "Parameters" on the menu at the top of the BetaPERT Distribution dialog box, and then select "Minimum, Most Likely, Maximum" at the top of the drop-down menu.

5. In the **Name:** textbox at the top of the dialog box enter a descriptive label, for example, *Cash Inflow 2015*. Then, enter the pessimistic, most likely, and optimistic estimates from Table 4-6 in the appropriate cells below the distribution.

6. Click on the "Enter" button and then on the **"OK"** button.

Now repeat steps 1 through 6 for the remaining cash inflow assumption cells (cells B8:B15), using the information in Table 4-6.

Figure 4-7 Crystal Ball® dialog box for model inputs assuming the BetaPERT distribution.

When finished with the cash inflow cells, assumption cells for the inflation values in column G need to be defined. For these cells select the **Normal** distribution. We decided earlier to use a 2 percent inflation rate, plus or minus 1 percent. Recall that the normal distribution is bell-shaped and that the mean of the distribution is its center point. Also recall that the mean, plus or minus three standard deviations, includes 99+ percent of the data. The Normal Distribution dialog box, Figure 4-8, calls

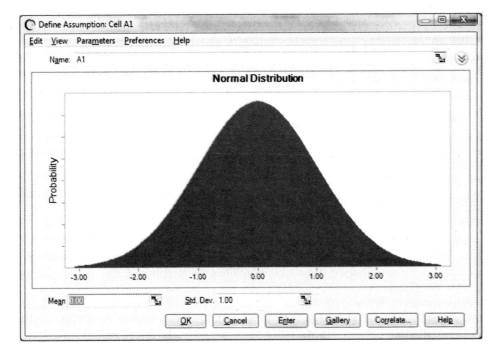

Figure 4-8 Crystal Ball® dialog box for model inputs assuming the normal distribution.

for the distribution's mean and its standard deviation. The mean will be 0.02 (2 percent) for all cells. The standard deviation will be .0033 (one-third of the ± percent range). (Note that Figure 4-8 displays only the first two decimal places of the standard deviation. The actual standard deviation of .0033 is used by the program, but if you wish to see the .0033 you may click on "Preferences" at the top of the box. Then click on "Chart," "Axis," "Cell format," "Number," and change the "2" to "4." "OK" your way back to the input data sheet.) As you enter these data, the distribution will show a mean of 2 percent and a range from 1 percent to 3 percent.

Notice that there are two cash outflows for the year 2013, but one of those occurs at the beginning of the year and the other at the end of the year. The entry at the beginning of the year is not discounted, so there is no need for an entry in G4. (Some versions of CB insist on an entry, however, so go ahead and enter 2 percent with zero standard deviation.) Move on to cell G5, in the **Name:** textbox for the cell G5 enter *Inflation Rate*. Then enter .02 in the **Mean** textbox and .0033 in the **Std. Dev.** textbox. While the rate of inflation could be entered in a similar fashion for the following years, a more efficient approach is to copy the assumption cell G5 to G6. Since CB is an add-in to Excel®, simply using Excel®'s copy and paste commands will not work. Rather, CB's own copy and paste commands must be used to copy the information contained in both assumption and forecast cells. The following steps are required:

1. Place the cursor on cell **G5**.
2. Click on "Copy"in the Crystal Ball ribbon.
3. Highlight the range **G6:G14**.
4. Click on "Paste" in the Crystal Ball ribbon.

Note that 2022 has two cash inflows, both occurring at the end of the year. Because we don't want to generate two different rates of inflation for 2022, the value generated in cell G14 should be used for both 2022 entries. Type =G14 in the G15 cell. Now we consider the forecast or outcome cell. In this example we wish to find the net present value of the cash flows we have estimated. The process of defining a forecast cell involves four steps.

1. Click on the cell **F17** to select it as containing an outcome that interests us.
2. Select the menu option Define Forecast from the Crystal Ball ribbon at the top of the screen.
3. CB's Define Forecast dialog box is now displayed. In the **Name:** textbox, enter a descriptive name such as *Net Present Value of Project*. Then enter a descriptive label such as *Dollars* in the **Units:** textbox.
4. Click **OK**. There is only one Forecast cell in this example, but in other situations there may be several. Use the same four steps to define each of them.

When you have completed all entries, what was Table 4-5 is now changed and appears as Table 4-7.

We are ready to simulate. CB randomly selects a value for each assumption cell based on the probability distributions which we specified and then calculates the net present value of the cell values selected. By repeating this process many times, we can get a sense of the distribution of possible outcomes, or in this case the distribution of NPVs for this project.

Approximately in the center of the CB ribbon, you will see the **Run Preferences**. Below it is the "**Trials**" box. It should be set to "1000." If not, simply enter 1000 in the box. To run the simulation, click the green Start Arrow in the CB ribbon.

Table 4-7 Three-Point Estimate of Cash Flows and Inflation Rate for PsychoCeramic Sciences, Inc. All Assumption and Forecast Cells Defined

	A	B	C	D	E	F	G
1					Discount	Net Present	Inflation
2	Year	Inflow	Outflow	Net Flow	Factor	Value	Rate
3				B−C	$1/(1+k+p)^t$	D × E	
4	2013*	0.00	125,000.00	−125,000.00	1	−125,000.00	0.02
5	2013	0.00	100,000.00	−100,000.00	0.86957	−86,956.52	0.02
6	2014	0.00	90,000.00	−90,000.00	0.75614	−68,052.93	0.02
7	2015	50,000.00	0.00	50,000.00	0.65752	32,875.81	0.02
8	2016	120,000.00	15,000.00	105,000.00	0.57175	60,034.09	0.02
9	2017	115,000.00	0.00	115,000.00	0.49718	57,175.32	0.02
10	2018	105,000.00	15,000.00	90,000.00	0.43233	38,909.48	0.02
11	2019	97,000.00	0.00	97,000.00	0.37594	36,465.89	0.02
12	2020	90,000.00	15,000.00	75,000.00	0.32690	24,517.63	0.02
13	2021	82,000.00	0.00	82,000.00	0.28426	23,309.52	0.02
14	2022	65,000.00	0.00	65,000.00	0.24718	16,067.01	0.02
15	2022	35,000.00	0.00	35,000.00	0.24718	8,651.46	
16							
17	Total	759,000.00	360,000.00	399,000.00		17,996.77	
18							
19		*t = 0 at the beginning of 2013					
20							
21	Formulae						
22	Cell B17		=Sum(B4:B15) copy to C17, D17, F17				
23	Cell D4		=(B4 − C4) copy to D5:D15				
24	Cell E4		=1/(1 + .13 + G4)^0				
25	Cell E5		=1/(1 + .13 + G5)^1				
26	Cell E6		=1/(1 + .13 + G6)^(A6–2012) copy to E7:E15				
27	Cell E15		= E14				
28	Cell F4		=D4*E4 copy to F5:F15				

The distribution of NPVs resulting from simulating this project 1,000 times is displayed in Figure 4-9. Statistical information on the distribution is shown in Figure 4-10. The NPVs had a mean of $11,086 and a standard deviation of $8,115. We can use this information to make probabilistic inferences about the NPV of the project such as what is the probability the project will have a positive NPV, what is the probability the project's NPV will exceed $10,000, or what is the probability the project's NPV will be between $5,000 and $10,000?

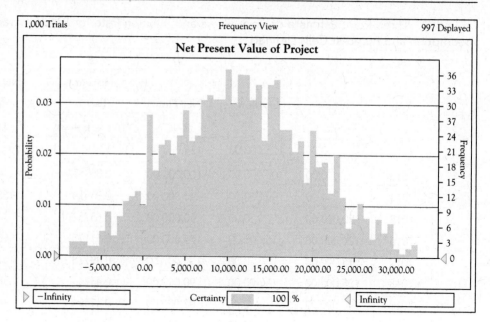

Figure 4-9 Frequency chart of the simulation output for net present value of Psycho-Ceramic Sciences, Inc. Project.

CB provides considerable information about the forecast cell in addition to the frequency chart including percentile information, summary statistics, a cumulative chart, and a reverse cumulative chart. For example, to see the summary statistics for a forecast cell, click on the Extract Data button in the CB ribbon and check Statistics in the dialog box that is displayed. The Statistics view for the frequency chart (Figure 4-9) is illustrated in Figure 4-10.

Figure 4-10 contains some interesting information. There are, however, several questions that are more easily answered by using Figure 4-9, the distribution of the simulation's outcomes. What is the likelihood that this project will achieve an NPV at least $10,000 above the hurdle rate including inflation? It is easy to answer this question. Note that there are black triangles at either end of the baseline of the distribution in Figure 4-9. By placing the cursor on the triangle on the left end of the simulation distribution baseline and sliding it to the $10,000 mark, the probability of a $10,000 or greater outcome can be read in the "Certainty" box. One can also find the same answer by deleting the "–Infinity" in the box in the lower left corner of the Frequency View and entering $10,000 in it.

Figure 4-10 Summary statistics of the PsychoCeramic Sciences, Inc. simulation.

Statistics	Net Present Value of Project
Trials	1000
Mean	11,086.17
Median	11,017.84
Mode	---
Standard Deviation	8,114.60
Variance	65,846,681.91
Skewness	0.1293
Kurtosis	2.69
Coeff. of Variability	0.7320
Minimum	−8,897.91
Maximum	37,689.89
Range Width	46,587.79
Mean Std. Error	256.61

Even in this simple example, the power of including uncertainty in project budgets should be obvious. Because a manager is always uncertain about the amount of uncertainty, it is also possible to examine various levels of uncertainty quite easily using CB. We could, for instance, alter the degree to which the inflow estimates are uncertain by expanding or contracting the degree to which optimistic and pessimistic estimates vary around the most likely estimate. We could increase or decrease the level of inflation. Simulation runs made with these changes provide us with the ability to examine just how sensitive the outcomes (forecasts) are to possible errors in the input data. This allows us to focus on the important risks and to ignore those that have little effect on our decisions.

Considering Disaster

Risk

In our consideration of risk management in the PsychoCeramic Sciences example, we based our analysis on an "expected value" approach to risk. The expected cost of a risk is the estimated cost of the risk if it does occur times the probability that it will occur. How should we consider an event that may have an extraordinarily high cost if it occurs, but has a very low probability of occurring? Examples come readily to mind: the World Trade Center destruction of 9/11, Hurricane Katrina, the BP oil spill in the Gulf of Mexico, the Hurricane Sandy floods of 2012 (a supposedly 500-year event!). The probability of such events occurring is so low that their expected value may be much less than some comparatively minor misfortunes with a far higher probability of happening.

If you are operating a business that uses a "just in time" input inventory system, how do you feel about a major fire at the plant of your sole supplier of a critical input to your product? The supplier reports that their plant has never had a major fire, and has the latest in fire prevention equipment. Does that mean that a major plant fire is impossible? Might some other disaster close the plant—a strike, an al Qaeda bomb? Insurance comes immediately to mind, but getting a monetary pay-back is of little use when you are concerned with the loss of your customer base or the death of your firm.

In an excellent book, *The Resilient Enterprise*, Yossi Sheffi (Sheffi, 2005) deals with the risk management of many different types of disasters. He details the methods that creative businesses have used to cope with disasters that struck their facilities, supply chains, customers, and threatened the future of their firms. The subject is more complex than we can deal with in these pages, but we strongly recommend the book, a "good read," to use a reviewer's cliché.

> In spite of the effort taken to make realistic budget estimates, it can still be useful to prepare for changes in the budget as the project unfolds. Such changes derive from multiple sources, including technology, economics, improved project understanding, and mandates. To the extent possible, it is best to include these contingencies in the contract in case they come to pass. Simulation is one excellent approach for determining the distribution of various possible outcomes occurring when risk is present in a project.

We are now ready to consider the scheduling problem. Because durations, like costs, are uncertain, we will continue our discussion of the matter, adding some powerful but reasonably simple techniques for dealing with the uncertainty surrounding both project schedule and cost.

REVIEW QUESTIONS

1. Contrast the disadvantages of top-down budgeting and bottom-up budgeting.

2. What is the logic in charging administrative costs based on total time to project completion?

3. Would you expect a task in a manufacturing plant that uses lots of complex equipment to have a learning curve rate closer to 70 percent or 95 percent?

4. How does a tracking signal improve budget estimates?

5. Are there other kinds of changes in a project in addition to the three basic types described in Section 4.4? Might a change be the result of two types at the same time?

DISCUSSION QUESTIONS

6. Given the tendency of accountants to allocate a project's estimated costs evenly over the duration of the task, what danger might this pose for a project manager who faces the following situation? The major task for a $5 million project is budgeted at $3 million, mostly for highly complex and expensive equipment. The task has a six-month duration, and requires the purchase of the equipment at the beginning of the task to enable the project team to conduct the activities required to complete the task. The task begins December 1.

7. The chapter describes the problems of budgeting projects with S-shaped and J-shaped life-cycle curves. What might be the budget problems if the life cycle of a project was just a straight diagonal line from 0 at project start to 100 percent at project completion?

8. If a firm uses program budgeting for its projects, is an activity budget not needed? If it is, then of what value is the program budget?

9. As a senior manager, you oversee a project with a total estimated cost of 245 engineer-months of effort. Three months ago, however, the project had fallen behind by about 25 engineer-months so you authorized the hiring of three additional engineers, which you felt should more than make up for the delay in the remaining year of the project (3×12 months = 36 engineer-months). You have just received the latest quarterly project status report and are surprised to learn that the project is now 40 engineer-months behind schedule! Your first reaction is to calculate how many more engineers need to be hired to make up for the increased delay. Using Brooks's concept of the "mythical man month," explain what might be happening here.

10. So what was wrong with the purchasing manager's assistant's solution (outlined in Section 4.3) to the problem of having an inadequate supply of hard-to-obtain parts?

11. Contrast simulation to other risk analysis tools discussed in Chapter 3 such as decision tables, FMEA, logic charts, and contingency planning. What are its advantages and disadvantages? If you were to do an important risk analysis, which tool would you prefer?

PROBLEMS

12. Your firm designs PowerPoint slides for computer training classes, and you have just received a request to bid on a contract to produce the slides for an 8-session class. From previous experience, you know that your firm follows an 85 percent learning rate. For this contract it appears the effort will be substantial, running 50 hours for the first session. Your firm bills at the rate of $100/hour and the overhead is expected to run a fixed $600 per session. The customer will pay you a flat fixed rate per session. If your nominal profit margin is 20 percent, what will be the total bid price, the per session price, and at what session will you break even?

13. In the template for finding bias (Fig. 4.3), using the Actuals as shown, compare the estimating model shown in the figure with the following estimates:

Period:	1	2	3	4	5	6	7	8
Estimate:	179	217	91	51	76	438	64	170

Base your comparison on the mean bias and the MAR. Comment.

14. The IT unit of a company has been asked to prepare a budget for a special software package project. The group has considerable experience with similar tasks and submits the costs in the following table. The group also thinks that the distribution of the hours worked for each phase is normal. The wage rate for the software engineers employed on each phase is $60 per hour. Using simulation, find the distribution of total engineering costs for all the phases. What is the average

engineering cost? Also, find the probability that the total engineering cost will be less than $85,000.

Phase	Average Time (hours)	Standard Deviation
Requirements Planning	80	15
Design	160	25
Prototype Development	320	70
Final Development	640	100
Test	120	20

15. Reconsider the following problem from Chapter 1: A 4-year financial project is forecast to have net cash inflows of $20,000; $25,000; $30,000; and $50,000 in the next 4 years. It will cost $75,000 to implement the project, payable at the beginning of the project. If the required rate of return is 0.2, conduct a discounted cash flow calculation to determine the NPV. Now, however, assume that the net cash inflows are probabilistic variables. Further assume that each forecast net cash inflow is normally distributed with standard deviations of $1,000, $1,500, $2,000, and $3,500, respectively. Given a required rate of return of 0.2, find the mean forecast NPV using Crystal Ball®. What is the probability that the actual NPV will be positive?

16. What would happen to the NPV of the above project if the inflation rate was expected to be 4 percent in each of the next 4 years? You may use either Excel® or Crystal Ball® to determine your answer.

17. Information about the cash flows for a 4-year financial project is listed in the following table. The cash flows are assumed to follow a triangular distribution. The cost of implementing the project is expected to be between $60,000 and $70,000, with all values in this range being equally likely. Analysis of changes in the Consumer Price Index suggests that the annual rate of inflation can be approximated with a normal distribution with a mean of 4 percent and standard deviation of 1.5 percent. The organization's required rate of return is 20 percent. Develop a model in Crystal Ball® to analyze this situation and answer the following questions.

Year	Minimum Inflow	Most Likely Inflow	Maximum Inflow
1	$15,000	$20,000	$30,000
2	$20,000	$25,000	$35,000
3	$20,000	$30,000	$35,000
4	$40,000	$50,000	$60,000

(a) What is the expected NPV of this project?

(b) What is the range of NPVs?

(c) How would you characterize the level of risk associated with this project?

(d) Would you recommend undertaking the project? Why or why not?

18. Server Farm Inc. (SFI) needs to upgrade its server computers. Company management has identified the following two options: (1) shift to a Windows-based platform from its current Unix-based platform, or (2) stick with a Unix-based platform. It is standard practice at SFI to use a triangular distribution to model uncertain costs.

Along these lines, the company estimates that if it migrates to Windows, the new server hardware could cost as little as $100,000 or as much as $200,000. The technical group's best estimate is that the hardware costs will be $125,000 if the Window's option is pursued. Likewise, the company's best guess regarding the cost to upgrade and convert its software to Windows is $300,000 with a range of $275,000 to $500,000. Finally, if the company converts to Windows, employee training costs are estimated to range between $9,000 and $15,000, with the best guess being $10,000. If the company sticks with Unix, the new server hardware will most likely cost $100,000, but could cost as little as $80,000 or as much as $210,000. Software conversion and upgrade costs are expected to be $300,000 but could be as low as $250,000 and as high as $525,000. Employee training costs should fall between $8,000 and $17,500, with a best guess of $10,000. Develop a model to simulate this situation using Crystal Ball® and answer the following questions.

(a) What is the expected cost of each project?

(b) What is the probability that each project's cost will exceed $575,000?

(c) Which project would you consider to be the most risky?

(d) Which project would you recommend SFI undertake? Why?

19. A light manufacturing firm has set up a project for developing a new machine for one of its production lines. The most likely estimated cost of the project itself is $1,000,000, but the most optimistic estimate is $900,000 while the pessimists predict a project cost of $1,200,000. The real problem is that even if the project costs are within those limits, if the project itself plus its implementation costs exceed $1,425,000, the project will not meet the firm's NPV hurdle. There are four cost categories involved in adding the prospective new machine to the production line: (1) engineering labor cost, (2) nonengineering labor cost, (3) assorted material cost, and (4) production line down-time cost.

The engineering labor requirement has been estimated to be 600 hours, plus or minus 15 percent at a cost of $80 per hour. The nonengineering labor requirement is estimated to be 1500 hours, but could be as low as 1200 hours or as high as 2200 hours at a cost of $35 per hour. Assorted material may run as high as $155,000 or as low as $100,000, but is most likely to be about $135,000. The best guess of time lost on the production line is 110 hours, possibly as low as 105 hours and as high as 120 hours. The line contributes about $500 per hour to the firm's profit and overhead. What is the probability that the new machine project will meet the firm's NPV hurdle?

INCIDENTS FOR DISCUSSION

A Budgeting Novice

Alexander Jones was an experienced project manager of a small machine shop. He had always had complete authority when working with the clients on specifications of the projects as well as when working with the project team on the schedule. His boss, however, did not feel comfortable letting Alex determine project budgets. The boss always did that himself.

A client approached Alex about designing a piece of surgical equipment. Alex was excited about this project because his usual job was to design and make parts of factory equipment. He was delighted to have a chance to do something that might directly affect humankind. Alex knew what the surgical tool was intended to do and had figured out what had to be done to design and manufacture it. He had even estimated the labor-hour requirement. He wanted to do all the planning discussions with the client, including discussions on the budget.

Questions: What do you think Alex should show to his boss so that the boss would feel more comfortable letting Alex determine and monitor the project's budget? What should Alex say to persuade the boss?

Stealth Electronics

Stealth Electronics manufactures secret electronic weapon systems. They have just engineered a new system. They bid for and won a contract with DARPA (Defense Advanced Research Projects Agency). Stealth Electronics negotiated a cost plus contract for development of the prototype. The prototype project was approximately on time and on budget. They are about to submit a bid to produce the first 25 electronic weapon systems. The production contract will be a fixed fee. The CFO of Stealth Electronics has examined the costs associated with building the prototype and thinks the proposed bid for production of the first 25 systems is significantly too low.

Question: What should the CFO do?

General Sensor Company

Justin Jordan has been named Project Manager of the General Sensor Company's new sensor manufacturing process project. Sensors are extremely price sensitive. General has done a great deal of quantitative work to be able to accurately forecast changes in sales volume relative to changes in pricing.

The company president, Guy General, has faith in the sensitivity model that the company uses. He insists that all projects affecting the manufacturing costs of sensors be run against the sensitivity model to generate data to calculate the return on investment. The net result is that project managers, like Justin, are under a great deal of pressure to submit realistic budgets so go/no-go project decisions can be made quickly. Guy has canceled several projects that appeared marginal during their feasibility stages and recently fired a project manager for overestimating project costs on a new model sensor. The project was killed early in the design stages, and 6 months later a competitor introduced a similar sensor that proved to be highly successful.

Justin's dilemma is how to construct a budget that accurately reflects the costs of the proposed new process. Justin is an experienced executive and feels comfortable with his ability in estimating costs of projects. However, the recent firing of his colleague has made him a little gun-shy. Only one stage of the four-stage sensor manufacturing process is being changed. Justin has detailed cost information about the majority of the process. Unfortunately the costs and tasks involved in the new modified process stage are unclear at this point. Justin also believes that the new modifications will cause some minor changes in the other three stages, but these potential changes have not yet been clearly identified. The stage being addressed by the project represents almost 50 percent of the manufacturing cost.

Questions: Under these circumstances, would Justin be wise to pursue a top-down or a bottom-up budgeting approach? Why? What factors are most relevant here?

C A S E

St. Dismas Assisted Living Facility Project Budget Development—2

Fred Splient gave his ALF Project Steering Committee 2 months to develop an action plan for their area of responsibility in the project. Each member was told to include the tasks, predecessors and successors, resources needed, responsible person, and an estimated cost. He asked that these be presented to the steering team on August 31.

All through July the ALF project team scrambled to identify the steps required to open the facility and to determine what it would cost. Each team member met with his or her departmental staff to get help in identifying what was needed. For example, the COO spoke with the Dietary Department head and asked that she develop a plan to meet all requirements to set up the facility to feed the residents. The COO then asked the Facilities Manager to develop an action plan to prepare the building and maintain it. The COO also met with the Rehab Services Medical Director and his clinical staff to identify the residents' probable medical needs based on the projected population, and to develop an action plan to prepare to meet the residents' health needs. The COO asked the therapy manager to prepare a plan to develop social activities for the residents.

Everyone on the team called the Chief Financial Officer for help in determining the budgets for their action plans. The CFO also had to validate the estimates of cost and revenue from facility operations, and to project earnings and return on the investment. Like any good administrator, when the CFO realized he had no expertise in this area, he hired a consultant to help him determine the project costs and budget. Dr. Sara Sharf was chosen as the consultant—she had over 5 years' experience in developing business plans for assisted living facilities.

Dr. Sharf recommended that St. Dismas target the middle income geriatric population since there were many up-scale facilities in the area. Dr. Sharf and the market researchers determined what level of rent people in that population could and would pay. They then looked at what needed to be in the facility to meet the needs of their targeted population. After additional site visits of facilities and meetings with the selected construction contractor, they finalized the layout of units and common space areas that would be included in the design. The Construction Project Manager requested and received an action plan and cost estimate from the construction contractor. The contractor had estimated that construction cost would probably run about $70 per square foot with a standard deviation of $3.67. He could not be absolutely sure because of potential change orders. He emphasized that the estimates assumed that the project would be completed without further changes in its design concept.

While the CFO was haggling with the construction contractor about determining a more accurate cost estimate, he received a phone call from Dr. Zen Link, the Head of Geriatric Medicine at St. Dismas. Dr. Link's secretary had seen men measuring the land behind the parking lot and she wanted to know what was going on; so did Dr. Link. Since Dr. Link was one of the hospital's best referrers, the CFO told him about the potential project. Dr. Link felt that his input was needed up front as he was the only person on staff who would know the health needs of the facility's residents and appropriate equipment needs and staffing models that should be set up. With Dr. Link's input, the CFO estimated the operating costs to run the facility and projected the occupancy rates needed to cover those costs. The Rehab Services Medical Director, who was a member of the original project team, was quite upset when he saw Dr. Link's budget for the medical equipment that was to be purchased for the facility. The Medical Director felt that Dr. Link wanted to purchase too much expensive equipment, which was not necessary to have on site. The hospital had the majority of the equipment that was necessary and there was no need to duplicate it, thus inflating that portion of the budget. The CFO did not want to get in the middle of their argument so he left Link's budget just as Link submitted it and hoped someone would raise the issue at the next Steering Team Meeting. The CFO was quite concerned about the lack of experience of the team in developing such a budget, and he felt that there was far more uncertainty in the budget than the estimates reflected.

With the construction cost estimate and an outline of the services to be provided, the following projected capital expenditure was developed.

Preliminary Project Budget

Apartment Type	Net Sq Ft	Units	Total Sq Ft
Studio units	450	20	9,000
1 BR/bath units	600	80	48,000
		100	57,000

Apartment Type	Net Sq Ft	Units	Total Sq Ft
Common space	0.3		17,100
Net to gross	1.3		22,230
Total gross sq ft			96,330

Square feet	96,330
Est cost per sq ft	$70.00

Construction Costs

Building	$6,743,000
Contingency	674,300
Land	600,000
Program development & equipment costs	405,000
Furniture	400,000*(see below)
A&E fees @ 5%	347,000
Financing costs	202,000
Capitalized interest	135,000
Site improvements	125,000
Phone & IS system	30,000
Kitchen equipment	30,000
Total	$ 9,991,300

Organizational costs:

Legal and accounting	25,000
Initial marketing	250,000 $2,500/unit
Project consultant	80,000
Follow-up market survey	20,000
Total organizational costs	375,000
Total	$10,066,300

*	Heavy Asst.		Light Asst.	
Studio	5 units		15 units	
	$4,160/unit		$3,280/unit	
1 BR/bath	20 units		60 units	
	$5,460/unit		$3,780/unit	

The CFO developed an income statement for the next 20 years. The first 3 years are shown below.

St. Dismas Assisted Living Pro Forma

	Year 1	Year 2	Year 3
Service Revenues			
Studios	$ 256,662	$ 414,012	$ 430,572
One bedroom	408,564	1,398,197	2,077,321
Additional person revenue	30,866	72,291	98,841
Ancillary revenue	28,969	67,656	92,417
Total service revenues	725,061	1,952,155	2,699,151
Operating Expenses			
Salaries and wages	376,657	649,606	692,734
Employee benefits	82,865	142,913	152,401

	Year 1	Year 2	Year 3
Supplies	69,571	55,910	73,434
Purchased services	76,177	50,000	50,000
Utilities	217,516	—	—
Insurance	48,000	—	—
Other	29,002	78,086	107,966
Total operating expenses	899,788	976,515	1,076,535
Income (Loss) Before Other Expenses	(174,727)	975,640	1,622,616
Other Expenses (Income)			
Depreciation and amortization	560,200	560,700	561,200
Interest expense	—	—	—
Interest income	(1,226)	11,321	47,451
Total other expenses (income)	558,974	572,021	608,651
Net Income (Loss)	$(733,701)	$ 403,619	$1,013,965
Internal Rate of Return	10.1		
Average Occupied Units			
20 units	12.3	19.0	19.0
80 units	19.6	52.6	75.0
	46.0		
Total	31.9	71.6	94.0
Resident Days			
20 units	4,488	6,935	6,935
80 units	7,146	19,191	27,380
Total	11,634	26,126	34,315
Full-time Equivalents	21.8	37.8	38.8
Cash Flow:			
Net income (loss)	$ (733,701)	$ 403,619	$1,013,965
Minus: capital investment	(10,079,000)	(5,000)	(5,500)
Add: depreciation and amortization	560,200	560,700	561,200
Add: working capital change	130,656	82,500	18,638
Net cash flow	$(10,121,845)	$1,041,819	$1,588,302

The CFO, Dr. Sharf, and the Projct Steering Team were ready to combine their individual plans and costs into a composite plan and budget.

QUESTIONS

1. The cost per square foot for the units is given in the text together with its standard deviation. What other areas of cost or revenue are likely to have cost uncertainty? How should these uncertainties be handled?

2. How would you suggest the team handle the issue of Dr. Link's supposedly inflated medical equipment costs?

C A S E

Photstat Inc.

Photstat Inc. is contemplating the formation of a project team to develop a new service. Briefly, the service would allow customers to order customized mouse pads over the Internet based on photographs or other artwork sent electronically to the firm.

The company estimates that the price of the mouse pad will be between $10 and $15 per unit, with all prices in this range equally likely. Based on historical data, Photstat estimates that the total market size for these types of products in their first year follows a normal distribution with a mean of 100,000 units and a standard deviation of 10,000. Again, according to historical data, Photstat's market share tends to be normally distributed with a mean of 30 percent and standard deviation of 3 percent. Market growth tends to follow a normal distribution growing an average of 10

percent per year with a standard deviation of 3 percent. Estimates from the equipment manufacturer selected to design and produce the required equipment indicate that the cost of the equipment is normally distributed with a mean of $500,000 and a standard deviation of 60,000. Historical data indicate there is a 10 percent chance that the equipment will last for only 3 years. Similarly, there is a 60 percent chance the equipment will last 6 years, a 20 percent chance it will last 8 years, and a 10 percent chance the equipment will last 10 years. The variable costs of similar products were found to be normally distributed with a mean of $3 and a standard deviation of $0.25. Finally, an economic analysis undertaken by the firm suggests that the rate of inflation in any given year is normally distributed with a mean of 3 percent and a standard deviation of 0.5 percent.

QUESTIONS

1. What is the expected value of the project?

2. Simulate this project 1000 times and compute the average profit over the 1000 replications. Plot a histogram of the outcomes of the 1000 replications.

3. How does the average of the simulation compare to the expected value you calculated? What are the managerial implications of this difference?

C A S E

Building the Geddy's dream house

Neil and Alexis Geddy graduated from college 5 years ago. Since graduating, Neil has been working as an engineer while Alexis has been working in marketing. Initially, the young couple focused on paying off their student loans which they were able do in a little more than 2 years. Since paying off their student loans, the couple

have been diligently saving for the downpayment on a house which they would like to build. Neil and Alexis feel they currently have ample savings for the downpayment and are excited to start building their dream house.

Based on their current incomes and the amount they have saved for the down payment, Neil and Alexis would like to spend no more than $350,000 on the construction of their house, but believe they could swing spending as much as $375,000. For the past couple of months the couple have been talking to people they know who have built houses, researching homebuilding websites, and visiting building supply stores to better understand the costs and process associated with building a custom home. Table A summarizes the couple's cost estimates based on what they have learned.

As shown in the table, Neil and Alexis developed three cost estimates for each expense category. The most likely estimate corresponds to the option they would choose (e.g., doors, cabinets) or what the expected costs of an activity would be baring unforeseen difficulties. The pessimistic cost estimates represent the cost if they decided to splurge or if particular challenges were encountered. Finally, the optimistic costs represent opportunities for them to go with lower cost options or in cases where the progress on the activity goes better than expected.

Table A   Construction Cost Estimates

Expense	Optimistic Cost Estimate	Most Likely Cost Estimate	Pessimistic Cost Estimate
Architect	$27,000	$40,000	$51,000
Bath Fixtures	$7,000	$8,000	$12,000
Built-in Appliances	$1,600	$2,000	$3,500
Cabinets	$5,000	$6,000	$10,000
Carpeting	$4,000	$5,000	$7,000
Countertops	$4,000	$6,000	$9,000
Doors	$3,500	$4,000	$8,000
Excavation	$2,500	$2,500	$5,000
Finish Carpentry	$7,000	$7,500	$10,000
Finish Hardware	$1,250	$1,500	$2,000
Flooring	$9,000	$10,000	$13,000
Foundation	$22,000	$25,000	$30,000
Garage Doors	$2,700	$3,000	$4,500
Gas Fireplaces	$1,700	$2,000	$3,000
General Contractor	$30,000	$40,000	$55,000
Heating and Cooling	$10,000	$12,000	$15,000
Insulation	$3,750	$4,000	$5,500
Lighting Fixtures	$2,750	$3,000	$6,000
Painting	$2,750	$3,000	$4,500
Plumbing	$6,200	$7,000	$8,500
Roofing	$11,500	$12,000	$15,000
Rough Carpentry	$110,000	$120,000	$150,000
Windows	$18,500	$20,000	$27,000
Wiring	$6,000	$6,500	$8,500

QUESTIONS

1. Based on only the couple's most likely cost estimates, what would you estimate the cost of building the house to be? How does this value compare to what the Geddys budgeted?

2. Simulate this project 10,000 times assuming the expenses follow a triangular distribution. Based on simulation analysis, what is the expected cost of building the house? How does the expected value from the simulation compare to your answer in the previous question? How do you reconcile any differences between the two? Which estimate do you have more confidence in?

3. What are the maximum and minimum amounts the couple can expect to spend on the house?

4. What is the probability that constructing the house will exceed $350,000? What is the probability

the costs will be less $375,000? What is the probability that constructing the house will cost between $350,000 and $375,000? Based on your analysis how concerned should the couple be?

5. Assume that 2 months into the construction of the house, the couple decide they need the services of an interior designer to help them with making the right choices. After making a few calls, the couple estimate that, most likely, hiring an interior designer will cost $2,500. However, if they use the interior designer minimally, they could reduce the cost to $1,500 while if they need to rely on the interior designer more than they expect, the cost could reach $5,000. Modify your simulation model to incorporate the cost of an interior designer. What impact does this change have on the construction budget?

BIBLIOGRAPHY

ABRAMS, S. "The Big Dig," *Kennedy School Bulletin*, Harvard University, Cambridge, MA Spring 2003.

AMOR, J. P., and C. J. TEPLITZ. "An Efficient Approximation for Project Composite Learning Curves." *Project Management Journal*, September 1998.

BADIRU, A. B. "Incorporating Learning Curve Effects into Critical Resource Diagramming." *Project Management Journal*, June 1995.

BREYFOGLE, F. W., III. *Implementing Six Sigma: Smarter Solutions Using Statistical Methods.* 2nd ed., Hoboken: John Wiley, 2003.

BROOKS, F. P. *The Mythical Man-Month.* Reading, MA: Addison-Wesley, 1975.

CAMM, J. D., J. R. EVANS, and N. K. WOMER. "The Unit Learning Curve Approximation of Total Cost." *Computers in Industrial Engineering.* Vol. 12, No. 3, 1987.

EVANS, J. R., and D. L. OLSON. *Introduction to Simulation and Risk Analysis.* Upper Saddle River, NJ: Prentice Hall, 1998. (An excellent book using Crystal Ball® software.)

GAGNON, R. J., and S. J. MANTEL, Jr. "Strategies and Performance Improvement for Computer-Assisted Design." *IEEE Transactions on Engineering Management*, November 1987.

HAMBURGER, D. H. "Three Perceptions of Project Cost—Cost Is More Than a Four Letter Word." *Project Management Journal*, June 1986. (Recommended reading for any project manager who is not familiar with accounting.)

HERTZ, D. B., and H. THOMAS. *Risk Analysis and Its Applications.* New York: Wiley, 1983. (The name "Hertz" is almost synonymous with risk analysis, particularly strong in the area of financial risk.)

LAWRENCE, A. O. "Using Automated Estimating Tools to Improve Project Estimating." *PM Network*, December 1994.

LIBERATORE, M. J., and G. J. TITUS. "The Practice of Management Science in R & D Project Management." *Management Science*, August 1983.

MALLAK, L. M., H. A. KURSTEDT, Jr., and G. A. PATZAK. "Planning for Crises in Project Management." *Project Management Journal*, June 1997.

MARTIN, J. E. "Selecting an Automated Estimating Tool for IS Development Projects." *PM Network*, December 1994.

MCCARTHY, J. *Dynamics of Software Development.* Redmond, WA: Microsoft Press, 1995. (An excellent read-and-enjoy book that is not just for software projects. It is packed with irreverent good sense.)

MEREDITH, J. R. and S. M. SHAFER. Operations Management for MBAs. Hoboken, NJ: Wiley, 2003.

PMI. "Digging Deep," *PM Network*, August 2004.

PMI. "Polluted Progress," *PM Network*, March 2005.

PMI Standards Committee. *A Guide to the Project Management Body of Knowledge, 5th ed.* Newtown Square, PA: Project Management Institute, 2013.

PYZDEK, T. *The Six Sigmas Handbook, Revised and Expanded: The Complete Guide for Greenbelts, Blackbelts, and Managers at All Levels.* New York: McGraw Hill, 2003.

Rath & Strong's Six Sigma Pocket Guide. Rath & Strong Management Consultants, Lexington, MA: 2000.

SIMON, H. *The New Science of Management Decisions*, rev. ed. Englewood Cliffs, NJ: Prentice Hall, 1997. (An excellent and readable classic on management science with a particularly good introduction to risk analysis.)

SWANSON, S. A. "Estimating Errors," *PM Network*, October 2011.

WHEATLEY, M. "Making the Cut." *PM Network*, June 2009.

5

Scheduling the Project

Consider the job of planning a project, developing a budget for it, and scheduling all of the many tasks involved. It should be obvious that these three activities are not actually separable. Because a budget must include both the amounts and timing of resources received or expended, one cannot prepare a budget without knowing the specifics of each task and the time period(s) during which the task must be undertaken. Similarly, the project plan implies a schedule just as a schedule implies a plan. It is useful to begin study of these interdependent, partial descriptions of a project with an examination of the planning process because this process is the foundation of all that follows. The decision about whether to turn our attention first to the budget or the schedule is arbitrary. We chose the budget largely because most readers have some familiarity with the subject. The problem is that planning, budgeting, and scheduling are parts of the same basic process. They are considered separately only because we cannot write about all three at the same time.

PMBOK Guide

Risk

The project schedule is simply the project plan in an altered format. It is a convenient form for monitoring and controlling project activities. Actually, the schedule itself can be prepared in several formats. PMBOK covers some of these in Chapter 6 on Project Time Management. In this chapter, we describe the most common formats—Gantt charts and PERT/CPM networks—and demonstrate how to convert a project plan or WBS into these formats. We also note some of the strengths and weaknesses of the different displays. In addition, we apply risk management directly to the project schedule. From this analysis we show how to estimate the likelihood that a project can be completed on or before a specific time. (In Chapter 6, we explore what to do if it appears that the project will not be completed on schedule.) In addition to standard analytic methods for risk management, we once again demonstrate simulation methods.

We start with simple plans and schedule them manually. After scheduling by hand, we turn to the computer and use MSP to do our scheduling and many other tasks for us. The same approach is used for risk management. First, problems involving risk will be solved by hand. Once the theory is understood, we use the computer to handle the same problems without so much arithmetic.

5.1 PERT AND CPM NETWORKS

In the late 1950s, the Program Evaluation and Review Technique (PERT) and the Critical Path Method (CPM) were independently developed. PERT was developed by the U.S. Navy, Booz-Allen Hamilton (a business consulting firm), and Lockheed Aircraft (now Lockheed Martin Corp.); and CPM was developed by Dupont De Nemours Inc. When they were developed, there were significant differences in the methods. For example, PERT used probabilistic (or uncertain) estimates of activity durations and CPM used deterministic (or certain) estimates but included both time and cost estimates to allow time/cost trade-offs to be used. Both methods employed networks to schedule and display task sequences. (Throughout this chapter, we will use the words "activity" and "task" as synonyms to avoid constant repetition of one or the other.) Both methods identified a *critical path* of tasks that could not be delayed without delaying the project. Both methods identified activities with *slack* (or *float*) that could be somewhat delayed without extending the time required to complete the project. While PERT and CPM used slightly different ways of drawing the network of activities, anything one could do with PERT, one could also do with CPM and vice versa. When writing about the history of project management, differentiating PERT and CPM is important and interesting. When managing projects, the distinction is merely fussy. Traditional PERT is used less often than CPM; but CPM can be used with three-time estimates, and we can do things with PERT that were restricted to CPM in "olden times." We use both names because users in the real world are apt to use either.

The Language of PERT/CPM

Several terms used in discussing PERT/CPM analysis have been adopted from everyday language but have quite different meanings than in common usage. These terms are defined here as used in PERT/CPM.

Activity—A task or set of tasks required by the project. Activities use resources and time.

Event—An identifiable state resulting from the completion of one or more activities. Events consume no resources or time. Before an event can be *achieved* or *realized*, all its predecessor activities must be completed.

Milestones—Identifiable and noteworthy events marking significant progress on the project.

Network—A diagram of nodes (may represent activities or events) connected by directional arcs (may represent activities or simply show technological dependence) that defines the project and illustrates the technological relationships of all activities. Networks are usually drawn with a "Start" node on the left and a "Finish" node on the right. Arcs are always tipped with an arrowhead to show the direction of precedence, that is, from predecessors to successors.

Path—A series of connected activities (or intermediate events) between any two events in a network.

Critical path—The set of activities on a path from the project's start event to its finish event that, if delayed, will delay the completion date of the project.

Critical time—The time required to complete all activities on the critical path.

In Chapter 3, on planning, we noted that tasks may be divided into subtasks and each of the subtasks may be further divided. To carry out this process, it is necessary to know which tasks are immediate predecessors or successors of which others. The predecessor/successor relationship defines technological dependence. (See Chapter 3, Section 3.3.)

Building the Network

There are two ways of displaying a project network. In one we depict the activities as arrows and events as nodes. This gives an activity-on-arrow (AOA) network, usually associated with PERT. Alternatively, we can create an activity-on-node (AON) network by showing each task as a node and linking the nodes with arrows that show their technological relationship. The AON network is often associated with CPM. To understand the distinction, let us assume a small project represented by the tasks and precedences shown in Table 5-1.

Because it is easiest to draw, we start with the AON network. Because tasks **a** and **b** have no predecessors, they follow the **Start** node. We connect them to the starting node with arrows as in Figure 5-1.

Note that task **c** has **a** as a predecessor and that tasks **d** and **e** have **b** as their common predecessor as shown in Figure 5-2.

The network is easily completed. Task **f** has both **c** and **d** as predecessors, while **g** follows **e**. Because there are no more tasks, we can tie all loose ends to a node labeled **Finish** as in Figure 5-3.

The AOA network is generally more difficult to draw, but depicts the technical relationships of the activities quite well. Beginning the same way, we create a **Start** node from which flow all activities that have no predecessors, in this case **a** and **b**. The completion of these activities results in events (nodes, often drawn as circles) numbered **1** and **2** for easy identification as in Figure 5-4.

Table 5-1   A Sample Set of Project Activities and Precedences

Task	Predecessor
a	—
b	—
c	a
d	b
e	b
f	c, d
g	e

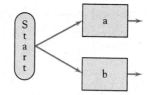

Figure 5-1   Stage 1 of a sample AON network from Table 5-1.

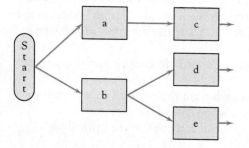

Figure 5-2   Stage 2 of a sample AON network from Table 5-1.

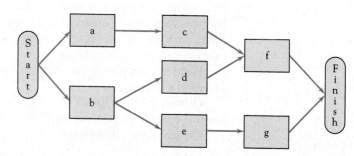

Figure 5-3   A completed sample AON network from Table 5-1.

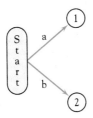

Figure 5-4 Stage 1 of sample AOA network from Table 5-1.

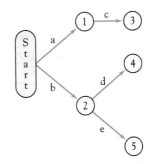

Figure 5-5 Stage 2 of a sample AOA network from Table 5-1.

Table 5-1 indicates that task **a** precedes task **c**, and that task **b** precedes both tasks **d** and **e**. Figure 5-5 shows these additions with event nodes **3**, **4**, and **5**, as indicated.

We are left with two activities, **f** and **g**. Task **f** has two predecessors, **c** and **d**. This means that tasks **c** and **d** actually finish at the same node (or event) and that **f** cannot start until this event is achieved, that is, until both **c** and **d** are completed. Task **g** is preceded by **e**. Table 5-1 shows no more tasks, and as in the case of the AON network this means that all tasks with no successors should go to a node labeled **Finish**. See Figure 5-6(a) in which the nodes have been renumbered and some combined for viewing simplicity.

We can handle **f** in a simpler though equivalent way by connecting the nodes following **c** and **d** in Figure 5-5 with an arrow drawn with a dashed line, see Figure 5-6(b). This is called a *dummy activity* and merely shows a technological linkage. Generally speaking, dummy tasks are used in situations where two activities have the same starting and finishing nodes or where a single activity connects to two or more nodes. The problem with two activities sharing the same starting and finishing nodes is that it becomes difficult to distinguish the tasks from one another. One solution to this problem is to add an extra ending node for one of the tasks and then draw a dummy task from the new node to the previously shared node. Adding a dummy task in this situation ensures that the tasks have unique identities while at the same time maintaining the correct technological precedence relationships. Dummy tasks require no time and no resources.

With occasional exceptions for clarity, we will use AON networks throughout this book because they are used by most of the popular project management software. An important advantage of AON notation is that the networks are easy to draw. AOA networks, particularly when they have more than 15 or 20 activities, are difficult to draw by hand. With modern software this is not a serious problem, but the software that generates AOA networks is quite expensive. AON networks often do not show events,

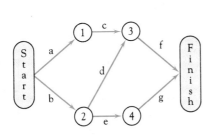

Figure 5-6(a) A completed sample AOA network from Table 5-1.

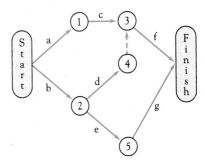

Figure 5-6(b) A completed sample AOA network showing the use of a dummy task, Table 5-1.

Table 5-2   A Sample Problem for Finding the Critical Path and Critical Time

Activity	Predecessor	Duration
a	—	5 days
b	—	4
c	a	3
d	a	4
e	a	6
f	b, c	4
g	d	5
h	d, e	6
i	f	6
j	g, h	4

but it is simple enough to add them by showing the event (usually a milestone) exactly as if it were an activity but with zero time duration and no resources. The PM should be familiar with both types of networks.

Finding the Critical Path and Critical Time

Let us now consider a more complicated example. Given the data in Table 5-2, we can start drawing the associated AON network as in Figure 5-7. The activity names and durations are shown in the appropriate nodes.

Note that activity **f** follows both **b** and **c**. If we redraw Figure 5-7 and place the **c** node below the **d** and **e** nodes, we will avoid having several of the arrows crossing one another; see Figure 5-8 for the complete network. This kind of rearrangement is quite common when drawing networks, and most software will allow the user to click and drag nodes around to avoid the confusion of too many crossing arrows.

We can add information to the nodes in the network. Just above each node it is common practice to show what is called the *earliest start time* (ES) and *earliest finish time* (EF) for the associated activity. Just below each node is shown the *latest start time* (LS) and *latest finish time* (LF) for the activity. The node would appear as in Figure 5-9. The corresponding information for Figure 5-8 is shown in Figure 5-10 and its derivation is described in detail just below.

Activities **a** and **b** may start on Day 0, their ESs. Their EFs will be equal to their durations, 5 and 4 days, respectively. Tasks **c**, **d**, and **e** cannot start before **a** is completed

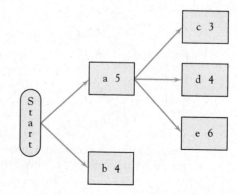

Figure 5-7   Stage 1 of a sample network from Table 5-2.

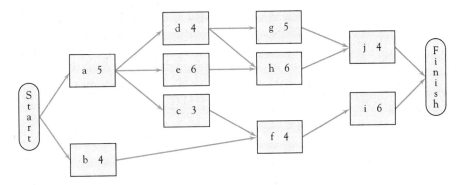

Figure 5-8   A complete network from Table 5-2.

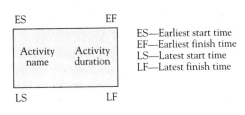

ES—Earliest start time
EF—Earliest finish time
LS—Latest start time
LF—Latest finish time

Figure 5-9   Information contents in an AON node.

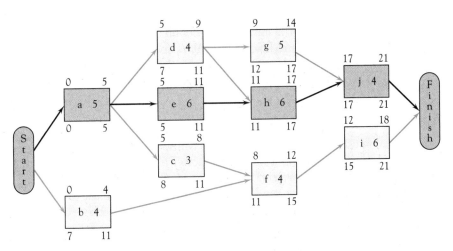

Figure 5-10   The critical path and time for sample project in Table 5-2.

on Day 5. Adding their respective durations to their ESs gives us their EFs, **c** finishing on Day 8, **d** on Day 9, and **e** on Day 11. Task **f** cannot start before *both* **b** and **c** are finished on Day 8, resulting in the EF for **f** on Day 12. Similarly, we find EFs for tasks **g** (9 + 5 = 14) and **h** (11 + 6 = 17). Recall that a successor cannot be started until all predecessors are completed. Thus, **h** cannot start until Day 11 when both **d** and **e** are finished—Days 9 and 11, respectively. The same situation is true for task **j**. It cannot be started until both **g** and **h** are completed on Day 17, giving an EF of 17 + 4 = 21. Task **i**, following **f**, has an EF of 12 + 6 = 18. No tasks follow **i** and **j**, completed on Days 18 and 21, respectively. When they are both finished, the project is finished. That event occurs on Day 21.

All activities, and thus all paths, must be completed to finish the project. The shortest time for completion of the network is equal to the longest path through the network, in this case **a-e-h-j**. If any activity on the **a-e-h-j** path is even slightly delayed, the project will be delayed and that identifies **a-e-h-j** as the critical path and 21 days as the critical time. In Figure 5-10 the critical path is depicted by a bold line—a common practice with PERT/CPM networks. We found the ES and EF for each activity quite easily by beginning at the start node and moving from left to right through the network, calculating as we go from node to node. This is called a "forward pass" (or "left-to-right pass") and makes it simple to find the critical path and time for PERT/CPM networks.

In a similar fashion, we can perform a "backward pass" (or "right-to-left pass") to calculate the LS and LF values for each activity. Referring to Figure 5-10, we begin by assuming that we would like to complete the project within the critical time identified in the forward pass, 21 days in our example. Clearly, activities **i** and **j** must be completed no later than Day 21 in order not to delay the entire project. Therefore, these activities both have LFs of 21.

Given a task time of 4 days, **j** must be started no later than Day 17 in order to be completed by Day 21. Likewise, task **i** can be started as late as Day 15 and still finished by Day 21 given its 6-day task time. Because task **j** cannot be started any later than Day 17, tasks **g** and **h** must be completed by Day 17. In a similar fashion, task **f** must be completed by Day 15 so as not to delay task **i** beyond its LS. Subtracting the task times from the LF for each of the tasks yields LSs of 11, 11, and 12 for tasks **f**, **h**, and **g**, respectively.

Now consider task **d**. Task **d** precedes both tasks **g** (LS = 12) and **h** (LS = 11). The question is, should **d**'s LF be 11 or 12? The correct answer is 11. The reason being, if task **d** were completed on Day 12, task **h** could not start on its LS of Day 11. Therefore we note that in situations where a particular activity precedes more than one task, its LF is equal to the minimum LSs of all activities it precedes.

The LFs and LSs for tasks **b**, **c**, and **e** are easily calculated since each of these tasks precedes a single task. Task **a** precedes tasks **c**, **d**, and **e**. Because task **e** has the lowest LS of 5 days, the LF for task **a** is calculated to be 5 days.

Calculating Activity Slack

If activities on the critical path cannot be delayed without causing the entire project to be delayed, does it follow that activities not on the critical path can be delayed without delaying the project? As a matter of fact, it does—within limits. The amount of time a noncritical task can be delayed without delaying the project is called *slack* or *float*. The slack for any activity is easily calculated as LS − ES = LF − EF = slack.

It should be clear that for any task on the critical path, its LF must be the same as its EF. It therefore has zero slack. If it finishes later than its EF, the activity will be late, causing a delay in the project. (Of course, the statement is equally true for its LS and ES.) This rule holds for activities **a**, **e**, **h**, and **j**, all on the critical path. But for activities not on the critical path the LF and EF (or the LS and ES) will differ and this difference is the activity slack. Take activity **i**, for example. It could be completed as early as Day 18 because its ES is Day 12 and it has a 6-day duration. It must, however, be completed by Day 21 or the project will be delayed. Because **i** has a duration of 6 days, it cannot be started later than Day 15 (21 − 6). Given an LS of 15 and an ES of 12, task **i** could be delayed up to 3 days (LS − ES or LF − EF) without affecting project completion time. Thus, activity **i** has 3 days of slack.

For another example, consider task **g**. It is a predecessor to task **j** that is on the critical path. Task **j** *must* start on Day 17, which gives task **g** an LF of 17. It has an EF of Day 14 and thus has 3 days of slack.

Now consider a more complex situation: task **d**. First, task **d** must be completed by Day 12 so as not to make **g** late and thus **j** late and thereby the whole project late! Thus, along this path task **d** has 3 days of slack in the role as a predecessor of task **g**. But **d** is *also* a predecessor of critical activity **h**, and along this path task **d** must be completed by Day 11 or **h** will be late to start. Task **d**, therefore, has only 2 days of slack, not 3.

Slack for other tasks are determined in the same way. Task **f** precedes **i**, and the latter has an LS of Day 15. Given an LF of 15, **f** must start no later than Day 11. Its ES of Day 8 means that **f** has 3 days of slack. Task **c** is a predecessor of **f**, and because the latter's LS is Day 11, **c** must be completed by then. With an LF of 11 and an EF of 8, **c** has 3 days of slack. The only remaining task to be considered is **b**. This task is linked to **f** and, like **c**, must be complete by **f**'s LS, Day 11. With an EF of Day 4, **b** has 7 days of slack.

Throughout this discussion of calculating slack, we have made two assumptions that are standard in these analyses. First, when calculating slack for a set of activities on a noncritical path, the calculation for any given activity assumes that no other activity on the path will use any of the slack. Once a project is underway, if a predecessor activity uses some of its slack, its EF is adjusted accordingly and the ESs of successor activities must also be corrected. We have also assumed that the critical time for the project is also the project's due date, but it is not uncommon for a project to have "project slack" (or "network slack"). Our 21-day project might be started 23 days before its promised delivery date, in which case activities on the "critical path" would have 2 days of slack and noncritical activities would have an additional 2 days of slack.

Milestones may be added to the display quite easily: Add the desired milestone event as a node with zero duration. Its ES will equal its EF, and its LS and LF will be equal. Milestones should, of course, be immediate successors of the activities that result in the milestone events. Finally, if a starting date has been selected for the project, it is common to show ES, EF, LS, and LF as actual dates.

Before continuing, a pause is in order to consider the managerial implications of the critical path and slack. The PM's primary attention must be paid to activities on the critical path. If anything delays one of these activities, the project will be late. At the start of the project, the PM correctly notes that activity **a** is on the critical path and **b** is not. This raises an interesting question. Can any resources reserved for use on **b** be borrowed for a few days to work on **a** and thereby shorten its duration? The nature of **b**'s resources and **a**'s technology will dictate whether or not this is possible. If **a**, for example, could be shortened a day by using **b**'s resources for 4 days, the critical path would be shortened by a day. This would cause no problem for **b**, which had 7 days of slack. If the delivery date for the project remains the same, the entire project would then have a day of slack. The presence of project slack tends to lower the PM's pulse rate and blood pressure.

Doing It the Easy Way—Microsoft Project (MSP)

As promised, once the reader understands how to build a network by hand, we can introduce tools provided through project management software. The first task is transferring information from the project plan into the software, MSP in this case. This is not difficult. MSP presents a tab entry table much like the project plan template shown in Table 5-3. It has spaces where the tasks can be identified, plus spaces for activity durations and predecessors. The software automatically numbers each activity that is entered. MSP offers a great number of options for viewing the data once it is entered into the project plan or entry view. If a specific start date or finish date is already determined for an activity, MSP allows you to enter it as well.

Once the project plan data are entered, MSP will automatically draw an AON PERT/CPM network as shown in Figure 5-11. Note that the figure lacks start and finish nodes because they were not entered on the activity list. Note also that the tasks in the network appear with ID numbers in order, flowing from left to right and from the top to

Table 5-3   An MSP Version of Sample Problem in Table 5-2

ID	TaskName	Duration	Predecessors
1	a	5 days	
2	b	4 days	
3	c	3 days	1
4	d	4 days	1
5	e	6 days	1
6	f	4 days	2, 3
7	g	5 days	4
8	h	6 days	4, 5
9	i	6 days	6
10	j	4 days	7, 8

the bottom. In Figure 5-11 several arrows cross, which may be confusing. The nodes show the activity name, ID number, duration, and start and finish times. These nodes are easily customized to show many different things concerning each specific activity.

It is simple to add Start and Finish nodes as milestones to make the network easier to understand. An activity named "Start" is entered at the top of the list, and an activity named "Finish" at the bottom. We want these activities to appear as milestones, significant events in the life of the project. In MSP a milestone is an activity with a duration of 0. Because we want the Start and Finish milestones to be linked to the beginning and ending activities of the project, all predecessors will have to be changed in light of these additions. For example, **a** and **b** will now have Start as a predecessor, and the last two activities, **i** and **j**, are predecessors to Finish. (In MSP, predecessors are indicated by task ID numbers rather than the task names used here for clarity.)

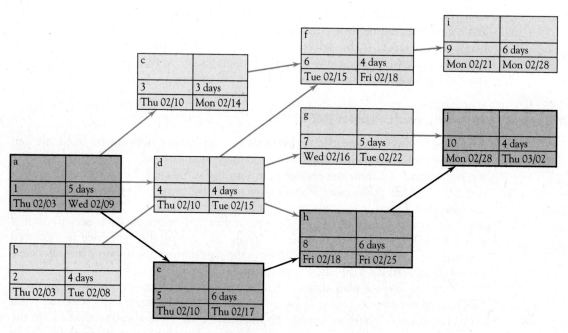

Figure 5-11   An MSP version of PERT/CPM network from Table 5-3.

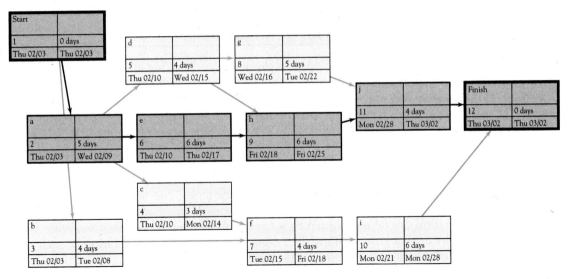

Figure 5-12   A modified version of MSP network from Figure 5-11.

Redrawing the network to get rid of the crossing arrows is also simple. As we noted when drawing the network manually, this is corrected by moving the **c**, **f**, and **i** nodes down to the bottom of the network. In MSP, that is easily done by simply dragging the nodes to whatever location you wish. See Figure 5-12 for the results of both changes. Notice in Figure 5-12 that because we added Start and Finish to the activity list, the other activities have been renumbered to conform to the changed list.

MSP will also calculate slack. (For details, click on MSP's "**Help**," type "Slack," and follow the directions.) MSP, and some writers, differentiate between "total slack" and "free slack." Total slack is LF − EF or LS − ES as we explained in the section just above. Free slack is defined as the time an activity can be delayed without affecting the start time of *any* successor activity. Take activity **b** for example. Its EF is 4 days, but it could be finished as late as 8 days without affecting task **f** in any way. It is thus said to have 4 days of free slack. Using **b** as an example, the rule for calculating free slack for an activity is

$$\text{Free slack for b} = \text{ES of earlier successor} - \text{b's ES} - \text{b's duration}$$
$$4 = 8 - 0 - 4.$$

The total slack for **b** is seven days, as we calculated in the section on finding slack.

These same calculations can be done by using the Solver in Excel®. To see how this is accomplished, refer to Lawrence and Pasternak (1998, Chapters 5 and 6). Finding the critical path is a fairly straightforward problem in linear programming, but it often takes more time than doing the same problem by hand, and certainly much more time (entering the required information) than letting MSP solve the problem.

Following the definition of some terms commonly used in PERT/CPM analysis, both AON and AOA networks are illustrated. ES and EF are found for all network activities, and the critical time and critical path are identified by the forward-pass method. LS and LF are calculated for all activities by the backward-pass method, and slack is defined as either LS − ES or LF − EF. The managerial implications of the critical path and of project slack are briefly discussed. The same problem used for illustrating networks is entered into MSP and shown as an output of the software.

5.2   PROJECT UNCERTAINTY AND RISK MANAGEMENT

Risk

In Chapter 4, Section 4.5 on risk analysis mentioned making most likely (or normal), optimistic, and pessimistic cost estimates for project tasks. Such estimates were shown in Table 4-6, and we promised to illustrate how to use these and similar estimates of task duration to determine the likelihood that a project can be completed by some predetermined time or cost. It is now time to keep that promise.

Calculating Probabilistic Activity Times

First, it is necessary to define what is meant by the terms "pessimistic," "optimistic," and "most likely" (or "normal"). Assume that all possible durations (or all possible costs) for some task can be represented by a statistical distribution as shown in Figure 5-13. The individual or group making the estimates is asked for a task duration, a, such that the actual duration of the task will be a or lower less than 1 percent of the time. Thus a is an optimistic estimate. The pessimistic estimate, b, is an estimated duration for the same task such that the actual finish time will be b or greater less than 1 percent of the time. (These estimates are often referred to as "at the .99 or the 99 percent level" or at the "almost never level.") The most likely or normal duration is m, which is the mode of the distribution shown in Figure 5-13.

The mean of this distribution, also referred to as the "expected time," T_E, can easily be found in the following way:*

$$T_E = (a + 4m + b)/6$$

For the statisticians among our readers, this calculation gives an approximation of the mean of a beta distribution. The beta distribution is used because it is far more flexible than the more common normal distribution and because it more accurately reflects actual time and cost outcomes. (For the derivation of the approximation, see Kamburowski, 1997; Keefer and Verdini, 1993).** The calculation itself is merely a weighted average of the three time estimates, a, m, and b using weights of 1-4-1, respectively. (For those favoring the triangular distribution, its true mean is $(a + m + b)/3$ which is another weighted average but with equal weights for the three estimates.)

We can also approximate the standard deviation, σ, of the beta distribution as

$$\sigma = (b - a)/6$$

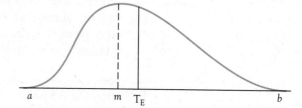

Figure 5-13   The statistical distribution of all possible times for an activity.

---

*MSP refers to the typical or "most likely" time as the "expected" time. After one has entered the optimistic, pessimistic, and "expected" times in MSP, it will calculate the "duration," which is T_E in our notation. In most works on project management, T_E is denoted as the expected time or the mean time.

**For readers who have never studied statistics or who have forgotten what they learned, there is a brief appendix on statistics and probability at the end of this book.

In this case, the "6" is not a weighted average but rather an assumption that the range of the distribution covers six standard deviations (6σ). It follows that the variance of this distribution is estimated as

$$\text{Var} = \sigma^2 = ((b - a)/6)^2$$

The assumption that the range of the distribution, $b - a$, covers six standard deviations is important. It assumes that the estimator actually attempted to judge a and b so that 99.7 percent of all cases were greater than a and less than b; that is, less than 1 percent lay outside of these estimates. We have never met a PM who was comfortable with such extreme levels of likelihood. 99.7 percent translates to "almost never outside the range," (three standard deviations) leading to estimates of a and b that are so small and large, respectively, as to be nearly useless.

But estimators are not so uncomfortable making estimates at the 95 (or 90) percent levels where a is estimated so that 5 (or 10) percent of all cases are less than a, and 5 (or 10) percent are greater than b. These estimates are within the range of everyday experience. These levels, however, do not cover 6σ, so using the above formula for finding the standard deviation will result in a significant underestimation of the uncertainty associated with activity durations and cost estimates. Correcting for such errors is simple. If a and b estimates are made at the 95 percent level, the following should be used to find σ (and squared to find the variance):

$$\sigma = (b - a)/3.3$$

If estimates of a and b are made at the 90 percent level

$$\sigma = (b - a)/2.6$$

The Probabilistic Network, an Example

Table 5-4 shows a set of tasks, their predecessors, and optimistic, most likely, and pessimistic durations for each activity, plus the expected time and activity duration variance. (If the project had been more realistic, that is, much larger, we would have used an Excel® spreadsheet to handle all the calculations.)

The expected time for each activity was calculated by using the previously noted weighted average of the three time estimates. (The fractional remainders for these calculations are left in sixths for convenience because each T_E will be added to others.) For example, to find T_E for activity **a**, we have

$$T_E = (a + 4m + b)/6$$
$$= (8 + 4(10) + 16)/6$$
$$= 64/6$$
$$= 10\ 4/6\ \text{days}$$

The variance for **a** is also easily found as

$$\text{Var} = ((b - a)/6)^2$$
$$= ((16 - 8)/6)^2$$
$$= (8/6)^2$$
$$= (1.33)^2$$
$$= 1.78$$

Table 5-4   A Sample Set of Project Activities with Uncertain Durations

Activity	Pred	Opt. a	M. Likely m	Pess. b	T_E (a + 4m + b)/6	Var. $((b - a)/6)^2$
a	—	8	10	16	10 4/6	1.78
b	a	11	12	14	12 1/6	.25
c	b	7	12	19	12 2/6	4.00
d	b	6	6	6	6	.00
e	b	10	14	20	14 2/6	2.78
f	c, d	6	10	10	9 2/6	.44
g	d	5	10	17	10 2/6	4.00
h	e, g	4	8	11	7 5/6	1.36

(The traditional $((b - a)/6)^2$ was used to calculate the variance, solely because it is traditional. A problem at the end of this chapter will ask the reader to recalculate the variance assuming 95 and 90 percent estimations, thereby repeating some of the calculations shown in this section.)

The network associated with the data in Table 5-4 appears in Figure 5-14. Note that the entries inside the nodes are the activity identifier, T_E, and variance, in that order. Some activities are known with certainty (i.e., $a = m = b$), as in task **d** that takes 6 days in this example. (A real-world example of such an activity would be a 60-day toxicity test of a new drug. In that case, $a = m = b = 60$ days, not more and not less.) Once in a great while the test may get fouled up and the estimate will be wrong, but our drug manufacturing friends tell us this is quite rare.) In some cases, the optimistic and most likely times are the same, $a = m$. We might, for instance, allow a specific time for paint to dry, a time that is usually sufficient, but may not be if the weather is very humid. Occasionally, the most likely and the pessimistic times may be the same, $m = b$, as in **f**. Sometimes the range may be symmetric, $(m - a) = (b - m)$, but more often it is not. Some activities have little uncertainty in duration, which is to say, low variance. Some have high uncertainty, high variance.

The expected time for each activity can be used to find the critical path and critical time for the network. A forward pass is made, and the critical path is found to be **a-b-d-g-h**. The critical time is 47 days. Because the mean time (T_E) is used for all activities, there is a 50–50 probability of completing the project in 47 days or less—and also, 47 days or more. Activity slack is calculated by using a backward pass, exactly as we did in the previous section.

There are several problems with conducting the risk analysis in the way that we are demonstrating. For example, given the uncertainty in path durations, we cannot be sure that **a-b-d-g-h** is actually the critical path. One of the other paths, **a-b-c-f**, for example, may turn out to be longer when the project is actually carried out. Remember that a, m, and b are estimates, and remember also that the durations are ranges, not point estimates. We refer to **a-b-d-g-h** as the critical path solely because it is customary to call the path with the longest expected time the "critical path." Again, *only after the fact do we know which path was actually the critical path*. The managerial implication of this caveat is that the PM must carefully manage all paths that have a reasonable chance of being the actual critical path. It is also well to remember that in reality all projects are characterized by uncertainty. Sometimes, with routine maintenance projects, for example, activity variances are quite small, but they are rarely zero.

There are also problems with conducting the same type analysis by use of simulation. We will delay discussions of the assumptions behind these methods and a comparison of

Table 5-5 An MSP Version of a Sample Problem from Table 5-4

ID	Task Name	Predecessors	Expected Duration	Optimistic Duration	Most Likely Duration	Pessimistic Duration
1	Start		0 days	0 days	0 days	0 days
2	a	1	10.67 days	8 days	10 days	16 days
3	b	2	12.17 days	11 days	12 days	14 days
4	c	3	12.33 days	7 days	12 days	19 days
5	d	3	6 days	6 days	6 days	6 days
6	e	3	14.33 days	10 days	14 days	20 days
7	f	4, 5	9.33 days	6 days	10 days	10 days
8	g	5	10.33 days	5 days	10 days	17 days
9	h	6, 8	7.83 days	4 days	8 days	11 days
10	Finish	7, 9	0 days	0 days	0 days	0 days

the pros and cons of such analyses until we have completed descriptions of both methods. In the meantime, it is helpful to bear in mind that the analysis started in Table 5-4, and continued in Table 5-5, and the simulation methods we then discuss are simply two different methods of accomplishing essentially the same thing.

Once More the Easy Way

Just as it did for the deterministic sample network, MSP can easily handle the probabilistic network, though as we will see, it does not do some of the calculations that we demonstrate. Those can be done easily enough in Excel®. The stochastic (a fancy synonym for "probabilistic," from the Greek word for "conjectural" and pronounced "sta kas' tic" or "stō kas' tic") network used for the preceding discussion is shown as a product of MSP. Table 5-4 becomes MSP Table 5-5, and Figure 5-14 becomes MSP Figure 5-15.

While Figure 5-14 shows the total elapsed time from Day 0 to Day 47 as one proceeds from left to right, the MSP equivalent, Figure 5-15, shows time as start and finish

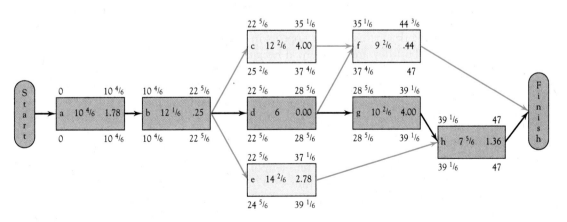

Figure 5-14 An AON network from Table 5-4.

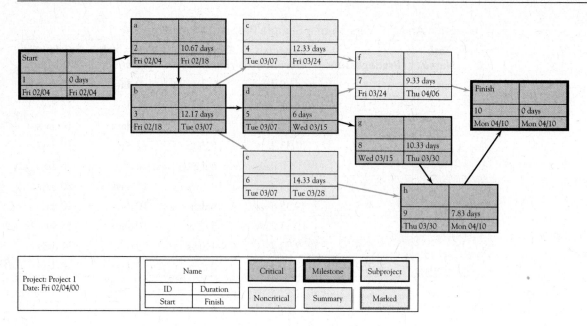

Figure 5-15 An MSP version of a sample problem network in Figure 5-14.

calendar dates. The project starts on February 4 and is completed on April 10. That is a total elapsed calendar time of 67 days. The time appears significantly different from the 47 days that we determined above as being the expected time for the project. The difference is caused by the fact that MSP assumes (defaults to) a 5-day work week. If you count out the work days on a calendar, you may find that the project seems to take 48 or even 49 days, not 47. That anomaly results from the fact that MSP operates on a real-world calendar. It remembers that February has a national holiday, President's Day. It also remembers that February has 29 days on leap years, and it was on a leap year that we created this example. (It is not difficult to change the work week assumption or to add or delete holidays.) Not counting Saturdays, Sundays, holidays, and remembering the leap year, the project has an expected duration of 47 days, as we thought it should.

Table 5-6 shows a project plan for development and approval of a project proposal directed to the YMCA for sponsoring a day care service. The project plan covers the process from the investigation of the need for the service through the creation of an implementation plan, given that the YMCA accepts the proposal. In addition to the *a*, *m*, and *b* results, the personnel resource requirements for each activity are shown.

The network for this project appears in Figure 5-16. Note that there is no Start or Finish node, but they are not needed because the start and finish dates for each activity are shown in the activity nodes. In addition to the network, the project calendar for the period from April 16 to May 27 is also shown; see Figure 5-17. This view simply shows the relevant project activities laid out on a standard calendar.

The Probability of Completing the Project on Time

Let us now return to our sample problem of Table 5-4 and Figure 5-14. Recall that the project has an expected critical time of 47 days (i.e., path **a-b-d-g-h**). How would you respond if your boss said, "The client just called and wants to know if we can deliver the project on April 30, 51 working days from today. I've checked, and we can start tomorrow morning."

Table 5-6   Three-Time Duration Example for a Day Care Project, with T_E and Resources Shown (MSP)

Day Care Service Investigation Project Plan

ID	TaskName	Predecessors	T_E	a	m	b	Resource Names
1	Develop employee survey to assess need and desire		2 wks	1 wk	2 wks	3 wks	Proj Mgr
2	Send survey out to staff	1	0 wks	0 wks	0 wks	0 wks	HR
3	Develop ad campaign to get staff to participate in survey	1	1.67 wks	1 wk	1.5 wks	3 wks	Marketing
4	Surveys returned	2, 3	2.33 wks	2 wks	2 wks	4 wks	
5	Analyze results	4	1.27 wks	4 days	6 days	10 days	Proj Mgr
6	Meet with YMCA to assess and verify proposal for service		2.83 wks	3 wks	3 wks	2 wks	HR, Proj Mgr
7	Identify other centers in the area (usage, fee structure, etc.)		5.83 wks	4 wks	6 wks	7 wks	HR
8	Cost/Benefit analysis complete	6, 7, 5	1.5 wks	1 wk	1.5 wks	2 wks	Finance, Proj Mgr
9	Go/No Go decision	8	1.07 wks	2 days	1 wk	2 wks	Exec Team
10	If Go, develop implementation plan	9	3 wks	1 wk	3 wks	5 wks	HR, Proj Mgr, Marketing

PERT view

Figure 5-16 A PERT/CPM network for the day care project (MSP).

You know that path **a-b-d-g-h** has an expected duration of 47 days, but if you promise delivery in 47 days there is a 50 percent chance that this path will be late, not to mention the possibility that one of the other three paths will take longer than 47 days to complete. That seems to you to be too risky. Tomorrow morning will be 50 working days before April 30, so you wonder: What is the probability that the project will be completed in 50 days or less?

This question can be answered with the information available concerning the level of uncertainty for the various project activities. First, there is an assumption that should be noted. The individual variances of the activities in a series of activities (such as a path through a network) may be summed to find the variance of the set of activities on the path itself, if the various activities in the set are *statistically independent*. In effect, statistical independence means the following in this example: If **a** is a predecessor of **b**, and if **a** is early or late, it will not affect the *duration* of **b**. Note what this does *not* say. It does *not* say that the date when **b** is completed will not be affected. If **a** is late, **b** is also likely to be late, but the time required to accomplish **b**, its duration, will not be affected. This may be a subtle distinction, but it is important because the condition of statistical independence is usually met by project activities, and this allows us to answer the boss's question seriously.

There are times when the assumption of statistical independence is not met. For example, assume two activities require some software code to be written. If during the project the code writer originally assigned to the project becomes unavailable and a less experienced code writer is assigned to the tasks, the times to complete these two tasks are clearly not independent of one another. If the lack of experience increases the task time and/or variance of one task, it is likely to impact other tasks in the same fashion. In this case, one should deal with the problem by reestimating the duration of both tasks. In general, this should be done anytime the resources supplied to a project are different from those presumed when the duration of project activities was originally estimated.

Project started date: 04/21
Project completion date: 07/20

Day Care Center Investigation

Apr 16 – May 27

Sunday	Monday	Tuesday	Wednesday	Thursday	Friday	Saturday
16	17	18	19	20	21	22
					Develop employee survey to assess ne	
					Meet with YMCA to assess and verify p	
23	24	25	26	27	28	29
		Develop employee survey to assess need and desire, 2 wks				
		Meet with YMCA to assess and verify proposal for service, 2.83 wks				
30	01	02	03	04	05	06
	Develop employee survey to assess need and desire, 2 wks				Develop employee survey to assess ne	
			Send survey out t			
		Meet with YMCA to assess and verify proposal for service, 2.83 wks				
07	08	09	10	11	12	13
	Develop ad campaign to get staff to participate in survey, 1.67 wks					
	Meet with YMCA to assess and verify proposal for service, 2.83 wks					
14	15	16	17	18	19	20
Develop ad campaign to get staff to participate in survey, 1.67 wks				Surveys returned, 2.33 wks		
21	22	23	24	25	26	27
		Surveys returned, 2.33 wks				

Project plan calendar view

Figure 5-17   An MSP project calendar for the day care project, for the period 4/16 to 5/27.

To complete a project by a specified time requires that all the paths in the project's network be completed by the specified time. Therefore, determining the probability that a project is completed by a specified time requires calculating the probability that all paths are finished by the specified time. Then based on our assumption that the paths are independent of one another, we can calculate the probability that the entire project is completed within the specified time by multiplying these probabilities together. Again, recall from basic statistics that the probability of multiple independent events all occurring is equal to the product of each event's individual probability of occurrence.

To begin, let's evaluate the probability that path **a-b-d-g-h**, which is apparently the critical path, will be completed on or before 50 days after the project is started. We can find the probability by finding Z in the following equation:

$$Z = (D - \mu)/\sqrt{\sigma_\mu^2}$$

where:

  D = the desired project completion time.

  μ = the sum of the T_E activities on the path being investigated.

  σ_μ^2 = the variance of the path being considered (the sum of the variances of the activities on the path).

The exact nature of Z will become clear shortly. Using the problem at hand, $\mu = 47$ days, $D = 50$ days, and $\sigma_\mu^2 = 1.78 + .25 + .00 + 4.00 + 1.36 = 7.39$ days. (The square root of $7.39 = 2.719$.) Using these numbers, we find

$$Z = (50 - 47)/2.719$$
$$= 1.10$$

Because the square root of the variance of a statistical distribution equals the standard deviation of that distribution, Z is the number of standard deviations separating D and μ. The distribution in question is the distribution of the times required to complete the path **a-b-d-g-h**. Consider all possible combinations of the activity times of the tasks on this path. This would include all possibilities from a combination of all optimistic times to a combination of all pessimistic times and everything in between. And even this does not include the highest and lowest project duration outcomes because the estimates do not cover 100 percent of all possible activity times; they cover only 99 + percent. We can illustrate the frequency distribution of the critical path completion times in Figure 5-18. (The Central Limit theorem allows the use of a normal distribution.)

The calculation of Z made above shows the desired date, D, to be approximately 1.1 standard deviations above the expected critical time, μ, for the project. If we define the total area under the curve as 1.0 (100 percent of all times), then the area under the curve to the left of 50 days is equivalent to the probability that the path **a-b-d-g-h** will be completed in 50 days or less.

Table 5-7 shows the probability associated with a wide range of values of Z. For $Z = 1.10$, the probability is .8643 or about 86 percent that this path will be finished on or before Day 50. Again, we remind you that because of uncertainty, other paths may turn out to be critical, possibly delaying the project. Therefore, calculating the probability that the entire project is completed by some specified date requires calculating the probability that all paths that comprise the project are finished by the specified time.

Similar calculations are next done for paths **a-b-c-f**, **a-b-e-h**, and **a-b-d-f**. The probabilities of each of these paths being completed by Day 50 are 98.5 percent, 97.8 percent, and virtually 100 percent, respectively. Based on this, the probability that the entire project is completed by Day 50 is calculated as $.864 \times .985 \times .978 \times 1.000 = .832$ or 83.2 percent.

A few comments are relevant at this point. First, to simplify the task of calculating the probability that a project is completed by a specified time, for practical purposes it is reasonable to consider only those paths whose expected completion times have a reasonable chance of being greater than the specified time. For example, if the sum of a path's expected time and 2.33 of its standard deviations is less than the specified time, then the

Figure 5-18   The statistical distribution of completion times of the path **a-b-d-g-h** in Table 5-4.

probability of this path taking longer than the specified time is quite small, less than 1 percent (2.06 standard deviations would be less than 2 percent). We simply assume that there is a negligible probability that the path will cause the project to be late. For example, path **a-b-d-f**'s expected time and standard deviation are 38.2 and 1.57, respectively. Using this rule of thumb, we get $38.2 + (2.33 \times 1.57) = 41.9$, which is much less than 50. Since there is less than a 1 percent chance this path will take longer than 41.9 days, there is no need to consider the possibility that it will take longer than 50 days.

Table 5-7 The Cumulative (Single Tail) Probabilities of the Normal Probability Distribution (Areas under the Normal Curve from $-\infty$ to Z)

Example: the area to the left of Z = 1.34 is found by following the left Z column down to 1.3 and moving right to the .04 column. At the intersection read .9099. The area to the right of Z = 1.34 is 1 − .9099 = .0901. The area between the mean (dashed line) and Z = 1.34 is .9099 − .5 = .4099.

z	.00	.01	.02	.03	.04	.05	.06	.07	.08	.09
0	.5000	.5040	.5080	.5120	.5160	.5199	.5239	.5279	.5319	.5359
.1	.5398	.5438	.5478	.5517	.5557	.5596	.5636	.5675	.5714	.5753
.2	.5793	.5832	.5871	.5910	.5948	.5987	.6026	.6064	.6103	.6141
.3	.6179	.6217	.6255	.6293	.6331	.6368	.6406	.6443	.6480	.6517
.4	.6554	.6591	.6628	.6664	.6700	.6736	.6772	.6808	.6844	.6879
.5	.6915	.6950	.6985	.7019	.7054	.7088	.7123	.7157	.7190	.7224
.6	.7257	.7291	.7324	.7357	.7389	.7422	.7454	.7486	.7517	.7549
.7	.7580	.7611	.7642	.7673	.7704	.7734	.7764	.7794	.7823	.7852
.8	.7881	.7910	.7939	.7967	.7995	.8023	.8051	.8078	.8106	.8133
.9	.8159	.8186	.8212	.8238	.8264	.8289	.8315	.8340	.8365	.8389
1.0	.8413	.8438	.8461	.8485	.8508	.8531	.8554	.8577	.8599	.8621
1.1	.8643	.8665	.8686	.8708	.8729	.8749	.8770	.8790	.8810	.8880
1.2	.8849	.8869	.8888	.8907	.8925	.8944	.8962	.8980	.8997	.9015
1.3	.9032	.9049	.9066	.9082	.9099	.9115	.9131	.9147	.9162	.9177
1.4	.9192	.9207	.9222	.9236	.9251	.9265	.9276	.9292	.9306	.9319
1.5	.9332	.9345	.9357	.9370	.9382	.9394	.9406	.9418	.9429	.9441
1.6	.9452	.9463	.9474	.9484	.9495	.9505	.9515	.9525	.9535	.9545
1.7	.9554	.9564	.9573	.9582	.9591	.9599	.9608	.9616	.9625	.9633
1.8	.9641	.9649	.9656	.9664	.9671	.9678	.9686	.9693	.9699	.9706
1.9	.9713	.9719	.9726	.9732	.9738	.9744	.9750	.9756	.9761	.9767
2.0	.9772	.9778	.9783	.9788	.9793	.9798	.9803	.9808	.9812	.9817
2.1	.9821	.9826	.9830	.9834	.9838	.9842	.9846	.9850	.9854	.9857
2.2	.9861	.9864	.9868	.9871	.9875	.9878	.9881	.9884	.9887	.9890
2.3	.9893	.9896	.9898	.9901	.9904	.9906	.9909	.9911	.9913	.9916
2.4	.9918	.9920	.9932	.9925	.9927	.9929	.9931	.9932	.9934	.9936
2.5	.9938	.9940	.9941	.9943	.9945	.9946	.9948	.9949	.9951	.9952
2.6	.9953	.9955	.9956	.9957	.9959	.9960	.9961	.9962	.9963	.9964
2.7	.9965	.9966	.9967	.9968	.9969	.9970	.9971	.9972	.9973	.9974
2.8	.9974	.9975	.9976	.9977	.9977	.9978	.9979	.9979	.9980	.9981
2.9	.9981	.9982	.9982	.9983	.9984	.9984	.9985	.9985	.9986	.9986
3.0	.9987	.9987	.9987	.9988	.9988	.9989	.9989	.9989	.9990	.9990
3.1	.9990	.9991	.9991	.9991	.9992	.9992	.9992	.9992	.9993	.9993
3.2	.9993	.9993	.9994	.9994	.9994	.9994	.9994	.9995	.9995	.9995
3.3	.9995	.9995	.9995	.9996	.9996	.9996	.9996	.9996	.9996	.9997
3.4	.9997	.9997	.9997	.9997	.9997	.9997	.9997	.9997	.9997	.9998

Second, to calculate the probability that a project will take longer than any specified time, we must first calculate the probability that it will take less than the specified time. Subtracting that probability from 1 gives us the probability that it will take longer than the specified time.

Finally, Excel®'s NORMDIST function can be used as an alternative to Table 5-7 for calculating the probability that a path finishes by a specified time, D. The syntax of this function is as follows:

$$= \text{NORMDIST}(D, \mu, \sigma_\mu, \text{TRUE})$$

To illustrate, the probability that path **a-b-d-g-h** is completed on or before 50 days can be calculated with Excel® as = NORMDIST (50, 47, 2.719, TRUE).

Selecting Risk and Finding D

Risk

We can also work this problem backwards. Assume that a client is very important, very demanding, and will be very upset if the project is late. The client has asked when the project output will be available. The client insists on a firm date. How sure do you wish to be about being on time? (Don't say 100 percent because that implies a time so long that no one will believe you.) Carefully considering the matter, you decide that you want a 95 percent probability of meeting your promised completion date. When should you tell the client to expect delivery?

This is the same problem solved just above, but now D, the desired date, is the unknown while the probability associated with Z is preset at .95. Referring to Table 5-7 we can see that for a .95 probability, Z will have a value of 1.645. Therefore,

$$Z = (D - \mu)/\sqrt{\sigma_\mu^2}$$
$$1.645 = (D - 47)/2.719$$
$$D = 47 + 1.645(2.719)$$
$$D = 51.5 \text{ days}$$

Say, noon of the 52nd day. Note, this result indicates that there is a 95 percent chance of completing path **a-b-d-g-h** in 51.5 days. Remember that this does not mean that there is a 95 percent chance of completing the entire project in 51.5 days.

We can arrive at the same answer using the Excel® NORMINV function. The syntax of this function is

$$= \text{NORMINV (probability}, \mu, \sigma_\mu)$$

In our example, this function would be used as follows:

$$= \text{NORMINV (.95, 47, 2.719)}$$

The Case of the Unreasonable Boss

What happens if your boss is unreasonable, a "pointy-hair" type who insists that he wants the project we have been discussing delivered in 45 days instead of the later delivery times we have considered thus far? To find the likelihood that you can deliver, we return to Z.

In this case,

$$Z = (45 - 47)/\sqrt{7.39}$$
$$= -2/2.719$$
$$= -.74$$

Reference to Table 5-7 reveals that there are no negative Zs. This merely indicates that D is less than μ. A glance at Figure 5-18 will show this because $-.74$ is to the left of μ. To find the probability associated with a negative Z, we find the probability of Z as if it were a positive number—for Z = .74. Because Table 5-4 is based on a normal distribution which is symmetric, the negative Z will be as far below m as the positive Z is above it. Therefore, for a negative number the probability will be 1 minus the probability for the same positive number, $P(-Z) = 1 - P(Z)$. The probability for Z = .74 is .77 and thus the probability of Z = $-.74$ is $(1 - .77) = .23$. (With Excel®'s NORMDIST and NORMINV functions, this transformation is not required.) As the PM—other things being the same—you have between a 1 in 4 and a 1 in 5 chance of completing the project on time, not very good odds. The weasel words "other things being the same" will be removed in the next chapter when we reconsider the problem of the pointy-haired boss.

The Problem with Mergers

We are not, of course, writing of big businesses joining to get bigger, but of paths in a network that merge. When two or more paths through a network join, even at the end of the network, paths that have little slack or high variance may become critical simply by chance. For example, examine path **a-b-c-f** in Figure 5-14, a path with an expected duration of 44.5 days and a path variance of 6.47 days. What is the chance that this path will be longer than our expected project completion time of 47 days?

As we noted earlier, elementary probability theory (see Appendix A) states that if the probability of event A occurring is P(A) and the probability of event B occurring is P(B), then the probability of *both* events A and B occurring is P(A) × P(B), assuming the events are independent. Tasks **a** and **b** are common to both paths, so we ignore them. Tasks **d**, **g**, and **h** have an expected duration of 24.17 days, and their path has a variance of 5.36. Tasks **c** and **f** have an expected duration of 21.67 days, and that path has a 4.44 variance. Because **d**, **g**, and **h** have an expected completion time of 24.17 days, there is .5 chance these activities will take longer than 24.17 days. Therefore, we can ask: What is the probability that the **c-f** path will exceed 24.17 days? Back to Z.

$$Z = (D - \mu)/\sqrt{\sigma_\mu^2}$$
$$= (24.17 - 21.67)/\sqrt{4.44}$$
$$= 2.5/2.11$$
$$= 1.18$$

An examination of Table 5-7 shows that for Z equal to 1.18 the probability that the path **c-f** will be 24.17 days or less is .88. (Using Excel® we can write = NORMDIST (24.17, 21.67, 2.11, TRUE). The probability that both paths will be 24.17 days or less is .5 × .88 = .44.

It is interesting to remember we began by allowing 50 days for this project and found that the apparent critical path had a .88 probability of being completed in 50 days. What is the likelihood that path **a-b-c-f** will take longer than 50 days? You can do the arithmetic, but it is approximately equal to .015. So if we have 50 days for the project, we need not worry too much about **c-f**.

One more problem: Both **g** and **e** are predecessors of **h**. Task **g** is on the path with the highest expected time, but **e** is not. What is the chance that **e** will force **h** to start late? Because tasks **d** and **e** both start at the same time, assuming they both use their ESs, we can ignore their common predecessor, **b**, in answering this question. If **b** is not included, we simply compare **d-g** with **e**. The path **d-g** has an expected duration of 16.3 days and a variance of 4.00. Task **e** has an expected duration of 14.3 days and a variance of 2.78. The question is: What is the probability of e ≥ 16.3 days? Back to Z once again.

$$Z = (16.3 - 14.3)/\sqrt{2.78}$$
$$= 2/1.67$$
$$= 1.20$$

Table 5-4 indicates that **e** will be equal to or less than 16.3 days 88 percent of the time, which means that it will force **h** to start late only about 12 percent of the time.

The probability that both **e** and **g** will be completed by the LS for **h** (39 1/6 days) is .5 × .88 = .44. The chance that *all three paths* will be completed in 47 days (T_E for the apparent critical path) is now equal to .50 × .86 × .88 = .38 or slightly less than 40 percent. The chance that all three will be completed by Day 50, the boss's original due date, is still well above 80 percent. The reason for introducing some slack for the entire project is now clear. It should also be clear that given a large project with considerable uncertainty and many paths from start to finish, this manner of dealing with risk is lengthy and probably tedious. More important than tedium, at times the assumption of statistical independence of the paths is not met. There is an alternative way to deal with risk, but it is based firmly on the concepts and issues we have just discussed, so they must be understood before tackling the alternative, simulation.

Risk

Uncertainty and risk management are introduced. Optimistic, most likely, and pessimistic estimates of task duration are made and expected activity times are calculated as well as the standard deviation and variance of task time distributions. From this data the mean times for all paths are calculated, and the probability of the paths being completed on or before a predetermined date can be found. In addition, the probability of completion can be set in advance and the path delivery date consistent with that probability can be determined. The problem of merge bias is then investigated.

5.3   SIMULATION

Risk

Best Practice

In this section we can take a different approach to managing risk. Specifically, we build on the probabilistic foundation established in the previous section and use simulation to handle the arithmetic as well as help us to understand the consequences of uncertainty. Simulation analysis can provide insight into the range and distribution of project completion times. To illustrate this, once again we use the project activities listed in Table 5-4 and the corresponding network diagram shown in Figure 5-14.

For the purpose of this example, we will make one simplifying assumption. As in Chapter 4, we will assume that the activity times may be reasonably represented by a beta distribution. The spreadsheet shown in Table 5-8 was created to simulate the project.

Table 5–8   Data from Table 5–4 Entered into a CB Spreadsheet with Assumption and Forecast Cells

	A	B	C	D	E	F	G	H	I	J	K	L	M
1	Activity	Activity	Activity	Activity	Activity	Activity	Activity	Activity	Path	Path	Path	Path	Completion
2	a	b	c	d	e	f	g	h	a-b-c-f	a-b-d-f	a-b-d-g-h	a-b-e-h	Time
3	10	12	12	6	14	10	10	8	44	38	46	44	46
4													
5													
6													
7	Formulae												
8	Cell I3	=A3+B3+C3+F3											
9	Cell J3	=A3+B3+D3+F3											
10	Cell K3	=A3+B3+D3+G3+H3											
11	Cell L3	=A3+B3+E3+H3											
12	Cell M3	= MAX(I3:L3)											
13													

Having opened Excel® and Crystal Ball® (CB), we devoted a column to each activity (i.e., columns A through H) and these will be our assumption variables. We then devoted one column (columns I through L) to each path through the network. Finally, we calculate the network Completion Time in column M by taking the maximum value of columns I–L, and this cell becomes our forecast cell. This gives us a very simple model for a complex problem. The hardest part of constructing this model is to identify all paths through the network. On small networks like our example, this is easy. On large networks it may be quite difficult.* Using an MSP PERT network to identify paths can be very helpful.

Reminding the reader that it is easier to follow our instructions if you have the software running, we can now enter data into what becomes Table 5-8.

1. First enter the proper column labels in the first two rows of the spreadsheet, and then enter the most likely time for activity **a** (from Table 5-4) in cell **A3**—10 days. CB won't let you define an assumption cell for an empty cell.

2. Click on **Define Assumption** in the CB ribbon.

3. Click on BetaPERT in the **Distribution Gallery** and then the OK button.

4. In the **BetaPERT Distribution Minimum** and **Maximum** text boxes enter the pessimistic and optimistic times. Note that when you entered the most likely time in step 1, that time already appeared in the **BetaPERT Distribution Likeliest** text box when it was displayed. Note also that the distribution box assumed pessimistic and optimistic times. Simply click on those boxes and change the times to the ones shown in Table 5-4. When you have done this, click **Enter** and then **OK**.

5. Enter the rest of the activity times. Note that activity time for **d** is a constant. Simply enter "6" in cell **D3** and do not use any distribution for the cell.

6. We trust you found the four paths through the network. Identify each path as shown in Figure 5-14 or 5-15, and enter the path duration formulas that simply sum the activity times for each path. (Caution: Recall that the Excel® copy/paste command will not work, though may appear to do so. Enter the data manually for best results or use the CB copy/paste command.)

7. Now enter the project duration formula in cell **M3**, that is, = MAX(I3:L3). Click on the cell and then on **Define Forecast** in the CB ribbon. Label the forecast text-box "Project Completion Time" or whatever you fancy. The **Units** are "Days." Click **OK**. Save the spreadsheet you have created before proceeding with the next step. We will use this spreadsheet again in Chapter 6.

*If there are too many paths, then only those that appear likely to be close to the critical path due to their completion times and variances need be simulated.

8. If the "Trials" box is not set to 1000, adjust it and then click on the "Start" green arrow. After the run, you will see a statistical distribution similar to Figure 5-19. To view summary statistics, click on the "View" menu option in the **Forecast** dialog box (see Figure 5-19) and the click on "Statistics" to see a table similar to Table 5-9.

Table 5-9 shows that we made 1000 trials and that the mean project completion time was 47.83 days (in the run made for this writing), the shortest completion time was 41.02 days, and the longest was 55.59 days. Recall that the mean completion time with the analytic approach using the beta distribution was 47 days. The different assumptions about the distribution of the activity times may account for some of the difference between the two estimates of completion time, but most of the difference is

Figure 5-19   CB frequency chart for project completion time.

Table 5-9   CB summary Statistics for Project
Completion Time

Forecast Name	Completion Time
Trials	1,000
Mean	47.83
Median	47.74
Mode	---
Standard Deviation	2.64
Variance	6.99
Skewness	0.143
Kurtosis	2.79
Coeff. of Variability	0.0553
Minimum	41.02
Maximum	55.59
Mean Std. Error	0.08

probably due to the inclusion of path mergers in the simulation solution. As usual, you can determine the probability that the actual result of the project will have a duration above or below any given time by entering those times in the plus or minus Infinity boxes of the distribution of times; see Figure 5-19.

Incorporating Costs into the Simulation Analysis

Risk

In the previous chapter we addressed the topic of budgeting. As you can likely imagine, the cost to complete a project is driven in large part by the time required to complete the project. The longer it takes to complete a task the more resources that are required which in turn leads to greater costs. Furthermore, in a similar fashion to activity durations being uncertain, the cost to complete an activity can be uncertain. For example, the cost to complete an activity may depend on which resources as well as how many resources are assigned to it. Therefore, it stands to reason that we can get a better understanding of the uncertainty surrounding the project's budget by incorporating both schedule and cost uncertainty into our analysis. This is perhaps best illustrated with an example.

For the purpose of our discussion, we extend the analysis conducted in the previous example. More specifically, we supplement the information provided in Table 5-4, with the cost information shown in Table 5-10. As shown in Table 5-10, optimistic, most likely, and pessimistic cost rates have been estimated for each activity. These cost rates are multiplied by the activity duration to determine the cost of the activity. For example, activity A's most likely duration is 10 days (see Table 5-4). At a normal cost rate then, we expect activity A to cost $750 (10 days × $75/day).

Based on the cost estimates provided in Table 5-10, the simulation model shown in Table 5-8 can be enhanced to develop a distribution of potential project costs in addition to the distribution of project completion times as shown in Table 5-11. To develop the enhanced model shown in Table 5-11, the same steps discussed earlier were used to define new Assumption Cells and a new Forecast Cell. More specifically, Assumption Cells for the cost rate of each activity were added in row 7. For the purpose of this example, the cost rates were assumed to follow a triangular distribution. Next, formulas to calculate the cost of each activity were added in row 11. Again, the cost of completing an activity was computed by multiplying its duration in row 3 by its cost rate in row 7. Note that in our enhanced model, we have two sources of uncertainty, namely, the activity durations and

Table 5-10 Sample Set of Project Activities with Uncertain Cost Rates

Activity	Cost Rates ($/Day)		
	Optimistic	Most Likely	Pessimistic
a	50	75	100
b	35	40	50
c	20	30	45
d	15	25	30
e	25	30	35
f	40	50	75
g	20	25	35
h	60	70	85

Table 5-11 Simulation Model from Table 5-8 Extended to Analyze Cost of Completing the Project

	A	B	C	D	E	F	G	H	I	J	K	L	M	N
1	Activity	Activity	Activity	Activity	Activity	Activity	Activity	Activity	Path	Path	Path	Path	Completion	
2	a	b	c	d	e	f	g	h	a-b-c-f	a-b-d-f	a-b-d-g-h	a-b-e-h	Time	
3	10	12	12	6	14	10	10	8	44	38	46	44	46	
4														
5	Cost Rate	Cost Rate	Cost Rate	Cost Rate	Cost Rate	Cost Rate	Cost Rate	Cost Rate						
6	a	b	c	d	e	f	g	h						
7	75	40	30	25	30	50	25	70						
8														
9	Activity Cost	Activity Cost	Activity Cost	Activity Cost	Activity Cost	Activity Cost	Activity Cost	Activity Cost	Total					
10	a	b	c	d	e	f	g	h	Cost					
11	$750.00	$480.00	$360.00	$150.00	$420.00	$500.00	$250.00	$560.00	$3,470.00					
12														
13	New Formulae													
14	Cell A11	=A3*A7 copy to B11:H11												
15	Cell I11	=SUM(A11:H11)												

cost rates for the activities (except for Activity D, the duration of which is known with certainty). To complete the simulation model, a formula that calculates the cost of the project was added as the sum of activity costs A through H in Cell I11, and then this cell was specified to be a Forecast Cell.

The distribution of the total cost of the project based on simulating the project 1,000 times is shown in Figure 5-20. Likewise, summary statistics for the total cost of the project are shown in Table 5-12. As can be observed from Table 5-12, the analysis suggests that the project is expected to cost $3,606.76 with a range of $2,646.95 to $4,338.51.

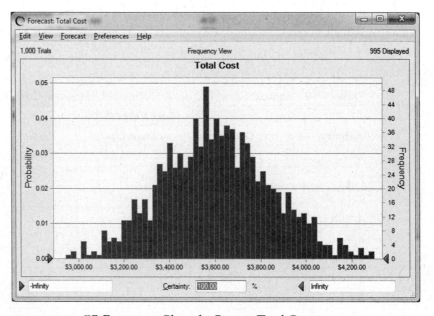

Figure 5-20 CB Frequency Chart for Project Total Cost.

Table 5-12   CB Summary Statistics for the Total Cost of the Project

Forecast: Total Cost	
Edit View Forecast Preferences Help	
1,000 Trials	
Statistic	Forecast values
▶ Trials	1,000
Base Case	$3,470.00
Mean	$3,606.76
Median	$3,600.55
Mode	---
Standard Deviation	$245.54
Variance	$60,291.17
Skewness	0.0736
Kurtosis	3.06
Coeff. of Variability	0.0681
Minimum	$2,646.95
Maximum	$4,338.51
Mean Std. Error	$7.76

Traditional Statistics vs. Simulation

Risk

At many conferences and in the literature of project management, there are sessions devoted to risk management. The participants at one recent conference, all highly experienced PMs from several different industrial sectors, were not of a single mind about the optimum way to handle the problems we have discussed in this chapter. Some favored the traditional statistical approach, some favored simulation, and some favored adding sizable contingency allowances in both the budget and the schedule, and then ignoring uncertainty. A decade ago, the group that ignored uncertainty would have been in the majority, but they were the smallest of the three groups at this discussion. Dealing with risk is no longer the esoteric interest of a few statisticians, but is now an everyday problem for the PM.

The major difficulty is making sure that the risk analyst understands risk analysis. Irrespective of how the arithmetic is performed, by human or machine, the analyst must understand the nature of the calculations, what they mean and what they do not mean. Conducting a risk analysis by examining the many paths through a large network, and finding those that may turn out to be critical or near-critical, can be an overwhelming task. There may be hundreds or thousands of activities and dozens of paths to be examined. Simply identifying the paths is a daunting job.

Some Common Issues   There are a number of issues associated with either the statistical approach or simulation. With an important exception we note just below, both procedures assume that task durations are statistically independent. As we noted above, this might not be the case when resources are shared across the tasks, but the problem can be handled by re-estimating task durations based on the altered resource. Second, with the same exception, both procedures assume that the paths are independent.* Even when paths have tasks in common, the common task durations (and variances)

---

*Calculating the probability of the project being completed by a specific time by multiplying the individual path probabilities is dependent on the assumption that the paths are statistically independent. In the case of simulation, this assumption is automatically met unless the analyst has modeled path dependency as a part of the simulation.

are the same for every path in which they are an element during any given estimate of path duration by whatever procedure. It is as if a constant is being added to each path.

The exception we mention is that simulation has a direct way of circumventing the assumption of statistical independence if the assumption is not realistic. With simulation, one simply includes the activity or path dependencies as a part of the model. The dependencies are modeled by expressing the functional relationship between the activities or paths along with its distribution, mean, and variance so that it may become a variable in the simulation. While this can be done in the statistical approach also, it is much more difficult to handle.

Using the statistical process, the analyst must find the T_E and variance for each path. Using simulation, the computer selects a sample from the distribution of activity times for each activity and then calculates the path duration for each path enumerated.

On the other hand, no matter which method is used, it is rarely necessary to evaluate every path carefully. In a large network, many paths will have both short duration and low variance when compared to high duration paths. Even when it is technically possible for one of the short paths to be critical, it is often very unlikely. For example, consider the path **a-b-d-f** in our example. It shares activities **a**, **b**, and **d** with **a-b-d-g-h**, the path with the longest T_E. Activity **f** has a pessimistic time of 10 days. Activities **g** and **h** have optimistic times of $5 + 4 = 9$ days. What is the probability that **f** will take on its maximum value at the same time that both **g** and **h** take on their minimum values so that **a-b-d-f** will be longer than **a-b-d-g-h**, not to mention simultaneously longer than the remaining two paths? Given that these estimates were made at the $\pm 3\sigma$ limit, the probability of **g** or **h** being at or below their optimistic estimates is $(1 - .9987) = .0013$ for each. It is the same for **f** being at or above its pessimistic estimate. These three things must happen at the same time for **a-b-d-f** to be longer than **a-b-d-g-h**. The probability is $.0013^3 = .000000002$. That probability is not zero, but most PMs will not spend time and effort worrying about it. Even when estimates of the optimistic and pessimistic times, a and b, are made at the 90 percent level, the chance that the activities on these particular paths will simultaneously take on their high or low extreme values is about one in a thousand.

The PM will discover the duration of each activity when, and only when, the activity is completed, which is to say after the fact, regardless of the method used to estimate and calculate project duration. Dealing with activity duration as certain does not make it so. We cannot know which of the paths will take the longest time to complete until the project is actually completed. And because we cannot determine before the start of the project which path will be critical, we cannot determine how much slack the other paths will have. We can, however, often make reasonable estimates. We can put our managerial efforts on the activities and paths most likely to require our efforts.

Simulation   Because of the computational effort required by the statistical method, we recommend simulation as the preferred tool for risk analysis—after, and only after, the analyst understands the underlying theory of the analysis.

Best Practice

Risk

We have included Crystal Ball® with this book because it is user-friendly software that can be used to facilitate and enhance the simulation of the project networks as well as simulate a wide variety of other types of problems. In addition to the uses we have demonstrated, CB can also facilitate the task of selecting the best distributions to be used to model alternative activities if historical data are available for these activities. Likewise, CB can determine the best distribution to use to characterize project completion times and other outputs of the simulation analysis. Furthermore, it has a comprehensive set of probability distributions available and the selection of these distributions is facilitated by graphically showing the analyst the shape of the distribution based on the parameters specified. This capability allows the user to interact with the software when specifying the parameters of a distribution. The analyst can immediately assess the impact that alternative parameter settings have on the shape of the distribution. Another powerful feature of Crystal Ball® is its ability to quickly calculate the probability associated with various outcomes such as the probability that the project can be completed by a specified time. In addition, CB can display the results in a variety of formats including frequency charts, cumulative frequency charts, and reverse cumulative frequency charts. It also provides all relevant descriptive statistics as was illustrated earlier.

Risk

> Using the sample problem, risk analysis is carried out by a simulation using Crystal Ball®. Each step in the process is described. Conclusions similar to those reached in the statistical procedure of Section 5.2 are reached through simulation. The two procedures are compared by examining the assumptions on which they are based as well as the problems encountered in using them. The computational effort and assumptions required by the traditional statistical approach lead us to the conclusion that simulation is the preferred technique for carrying out risk analysis.

5.4   THE GANTT CHART

Henry Gantt, a major figure in the "scientific management" movement of the early twentieth century, developed the Gantt chart around 1917. A Gantt chart displays project activities as bars measured against a horizontal time scale. It is the most popular way of exhibiting sets of related activities in the form of schedules.

The Chart

Figure 5-21 shows a Gantt chart of the sample project in Table 5-4. The expected times are used in this illustration. Clearly, Gantt charts are easy to draw. Because task names are usually descriptive, each task shows its name, WBS number, or ID number in order to identify predecessors. Any activity that has no predecessors starts at the beginning of Day 1 and extends to its duration (as in task **a**). An activity with predecessors begins when its latest predecessor has been completed (as in task **f** or **h**).

Problems in understanding the chart can arise, however, when several tasks begin at the same time and have the same duration. If one such task is on the critical path and the others are not, it may be difficult to find the critical path on a Gantt chart. For instance, had **c** and **d** both been the same duration, it would not have been possible to tell which was predecessor to **f** and which to **g**, just by looking at the chart. This is only a problem when the Gantt chart is prepared manually. Most software, MSP included, will use arrows, bolded bar outlines, colored boxes, or some other visible means of marking the critical path on a Gantt chart as in Figure 5-22.

Even with software aid, the technical dependencies are harder to see on a Gantt chart than on a PERT/CPM network. On the network, technical dependencies are the

WBS	Task	Duration	Predecessors	Month 1	Month 2	Month 3
1	a	10.67 days		a ▭		
2	b	12.17 days	1	b ▭		
3	c	12.33 days	2		c ▭	
4	d	6 days	2		d ▭	
5	e	14.33 days	2		e ▭	
6	f	9.33 days	3, 4			f ▭
7	g	10.33 days	4		g ▭	
8	h	7.83 days	5, 7			h ▭

Figure 5-21   A Gantt chart of a sample project in Table 5-4 (MSP).

WBS	Task	Estimate dur	Start	Finish	Late start	Late finish
1	a	10.67 days	01/14	01/28	01/14	01/28
2	b	12.17 days	01/28	02/15	01/28	02/15
3	c	12.33 days	02/15	03/03	02/18	03/07
4	d	6 days	02/15	02/23	02/15	02/23
5	e	14.33 days	02/15	03/07	02/17	03/09
6	f	9.33 days	03/03	03/16	03/07	03/20
7	g	10.33 days	02/23	03/09	02/23	03/09
8	h	7.83 days	03/09	03/20	03/09	03/20

Timeline columns (February / March): 09, 16, 23, 30, 06, 13, 20, 27, 05, 12, 19. Annotations shown on chart: "2 days", "2.5".

Legend: Critical task ▭ | Task ▭ | Slack ———

Critical path and slack shown

Figure 5-22   A Gantt chart of the sample project in Table 5-4 showing critical path, path connections, slack, ES, LS, EF, and LF (MSP).

focus of the model. As can be seen in Figure 5-22, information can easily be added to the chart to show such things as ES, EF, LS, LF, and slack.

Selecting another example for illustration purposes, it is simple to show resource requirements as in the Day Care project (see Table 5-6). The three-time estimates can be shown in Figure 5-23 as well as in Table 5-6, but Figure 5-23 shows only T_E to save space. Time and resource requirements may also be automatically transferred to the Gantt chart if desired.

It is also easy to show the current status of a project that is partially complete, as in Figure 5-24. This project was started on April 21, and its progress is being measured as of June 6. (The calendar dates shown as column titles above the bars indicate the first

Day Care Service Investigation Project Plan

ID	Task Name	Predecessors	TE Duration	April 04/02 04/16	04/30	May 05/14 05/28	June 06/11 06/25	July 07/09 07/23	August 08/06 08/20
1	Develop employee survey to assess need and desire		2 wks	Proj Mgr					
2	Send survey out to staff	1	0 wks	◇					
3	Develop and campaign to get staff to participate in survey	1	1.67 wks		Marketing				
4	Surveys returned	2, 3	2.33 wks						
5	Analyze results	4	1.27 wks			Proj Mgr			
6	Meet with YMCA to assess and verify proposal service		2.83 wks		HR, Proj Mgr				
7	Identify other centers in the area (usage, fee structure, etc.)		5.83 wks		HR				
8	Cost/Benefit analysis complete	6, 7, 5	1.5 wks			Finance, Proj Mgr			
9	Go/No Go decision	8	1.07 wks				Exec Team		
10	If Go, develop implementation action plan	9	3 wks				HR, Proj Mgr, Marketing		

Critical path, slack, and resources shown   Task ▭   Critical task ▬

Milestone ◇   Slack ——

Project start date: 04/21
Project finish date: 07/20

Figure 5-23   A Gantt chart of a day care project showing expected durations, critical path, milestone, and resource requirements (MSP).

183

Day Care Investigation

ID	Task Name	Actual Dur.	Baseline Dur.	Start	Finish	Baseline Start	Baseline Finish						
								04/02	04/30	05/28	06/25	07/23	
1	Develop employee survey to assess need and desire	2 wks	2 wks	04/21	05/04	04/21	05/04						
2	Send survey out to staff	0 wks	0 wks	05/04	05/04	05/04	05/04						
3	Develop ad campaign to get staff to participate in survey	1.67 wks	1.67 wks	05/05	05/17	05/05	05/17						
4	Surveys returned	2.33 wks	2.33 wks	05/19	06/05	05/17	06/01						
5	Analyze results	0.2 wks	1.27 wks	06/09	06/19	06/02	06/12						
6	Meet with YMCA to assess and verify proposal service	2 wks	2.83 wks	04/21	05/04	04/21	05/11						
7	Identify other centers in the area (usage, fee structure, etc.)	5.83 wks	5.83 wks	04/21	06/01	04/21	06/01						
8	Cost/Benefit analysis	0 wks	1.5 wks	06/19	06/28	06/12	06/21						
9	Go/No Go decision	0 wks	1.07 wks	06/28	07/06	06/21	06/29						
10	If Go, develop implementation action plan	0 wks	3 wks	07/06	07/27	06/29	07/20						

Project start date: 04/21
Project current date: 6/06

Progress shown

Task ▭
Progress ▬

Baseline task ▭
Completed milestone ◇

Milestone ◇

Figure 5-24   A progress report on a day care project showing actual progress vs. baseline (MSP).

day of the period, in this case, 4 one-week periods.) Note that Activity 4 starts 1½ days late. It was scheduled to start at midday on May 17, but did not begin until May 19. Activity 4 finishes a week late. If nothing is done to correct the matter, and if nothing happens to increase the lateness, the project will finish about a week late.

Software such as MSP makes it easy to use a Gantt chart or network to view critical tasks and paths of a project. One can even experiment with adjustments to the project—play "what if" with the project schedule, immediately observing results of the experiments on the screen. At times the PM may question an estimate of task duration, or of the a, m, and b time estimates, submitted by a member of the project team. It is simple to enter alternate time estimates and instantly see the impact on project duration. Of course, this can also easily be done using MSP's PERT network and using simulation.

A great deal of information can be added to Gantt charts without making them difficult to read. A construction firm of our acquaintance added the following symbol to activities that were slowed or stopped because of stormy weather . They used other symbols to indicate late deliveries from vendors, the failure of local government to issue building permits promptly, and other reasons why tasks might be delayed. Milestone symbols—diamonds, ◇, in MSP—are added to the charts, with different shading or color to differentiate between "scheduled" and "completed" milestones. MSP is limited only by the PM's imagination in what can be shown on a network, Gantt chart, or in a project plan.

The major advantage of the Gantt chart is that it is easy to read. Such charts commonly decorate the walls of the project office (or "war room"). They can be updated easily. This is both the strength and the weakness of the Gantt chart. Anyone interested in the project can read a Gantt chart with little or no training—and with little or no technical knowledge of the project. This is the chart's strength. Its weakness is that to interpret beyond a simplistic level what appears on the chart or to alter the project's course may require an intimate knowledge of the project's technology—not necessarily visible on the chart, but available on the network or the project plan. Not uncommonly, the Gantt chart is deceptive in its apparent simplicity.

We should add that one must be cautious about publicly displaying Gantt charts that include activity slack, or LSs and LFs. Some members of the project team may be tempted to procrastinate and tackle the work based on the LS or LF. If done, this makes a critical path out of a noncritical path and becomes an immediate source of headaches for the PM who, among other things, loses the ability to reschedule the resources used by tasks that once had slack. Senior managers have even been known to view activity slack as an invitation to shorten an entire project's due date. We recommend caution and careful education of the boss.

At base, the Gantt chart is an excellent device to aid in monitoring a project and/or in communicating information on its current state to others. Gantt charts, however, are not adequate replacements for networks. They are complementary scheduling and control devices.

The Gantt chart is a useful complement to a project network. It is easily constructed and read. It can contain a considerable amount of information and is an excellent communication device about the state of a project. Its major weakness is that it does not easily expose the project's technology, that is, the technical relationships between a project's many activities. Even with predecessors marked on a Gantt chart, it is difficult to see the project technology and, thus, to use the Gantt chart alone to manage a complex project. PERT/CPM networks are often used as complements to Gantt charts.

5.5   EXTENSIONS TO PERT/CPM

There have been several extensions to both network and chart forms of project scheduling. At times these extensions are quite sophisticated; for example, the application of fuzzy set theory to aid in estimating activity durations in cases where activity durations are difficult to estimate because project activities cannot be well defined (McMahon, 1993). In this section we briefly discuss one significant extension of traditional scheduling methods, precedence diagramming. (Elihu Goldratt's Critical Chain (1997) is also a significant addition to traditional scheduling methods. It uses networks that combine project scheduling with resource allocation. It is discussed in Chapter 6 on resource allocation.)

Precedence Diagramming

One shortcoming of the PERT/CPM network method is that it does not allow for leads and lags between two activities without greatly increasing the number of subactivities to account for this. That is, our regular network methods described earlier assume that an activity can start as soon as its predecessor activities are completed. Sometimes, however, the restrictions are more complex—for example, when a follow-on activity cannot begin until a certain amount of time after (or even before) its predecessor is completed (or sometimes started). For instance, a successor may have to wait for paint to dry or cement to harden. In this case, we might add a fictitious activity after painting or pouring the cement that takes the required time (but no resources) and then let the follow-on begin. For a leading activity, we might break the predecessor activity into two activities *a* followed by *b* and let the follow-on start after *a* is completed and operate in parallel with *b*, the remainder of the predecessor activity. In construction projects, in particular, it is quite common for the following restrictions to occur. (Node designations are shown in Figure 5-25.)

- **Finish to Start** Activity 2 must not start before Activity 1 has been completed. This is the typical arrangement of an activity and its predecessor. Other finish-start arrangements are also possible. If the predecessor information had been written "1 FS + 2 days," Activity 2 would be scheduled to start at least 2 days after the completion of Activity 1, as shown in Figure 5-25. For instance,

Figure 5-25   Precedence diagramming conventions.

if Activity 1 was the pouring of a concrete sidewalk, Activity 2 might be any activity that used the sidewalk.

- **Start to Start** Activity 5 cannot begin until Activity 4 has been underway for at least 2 days. Setting electrical wires in place cannot begin until 2 days after framing has begun.

- **Finish to Finish** Activity 7 must be complete at least 1 day before Activity 8 is completed. If Activity 7 is priming the walls of a house, Activity 8 might be the activities involved in selecting, purchasing, and finally delivering the wallpaper. It is important not to hang the paper until the wall primer has dried for 24 hours.

- **Start to Finish** Activity 11 cannot be completed before 7 days after the start of Activity 10. If Activities 10 and 11 are the two major cruising activities in a prepaid weeklong ocean cruise, the total time cannot be less than the promised week. The S–F relationship is rare because there are usually simpler ways to map the required relationship.

Precedence diagramming is an AON network method that easily allows for these leads and lags within the network. MSP handles leads and lags without problems. Network node times are calculated in a manner similar to PERT/CPM times. Because of the lead and lag restrictions, it is often helpful to lay out a Gantt chart to see what is actually happening. Most current project management software will allow leads, lags, delays, and other constraints in the context of their standard AON network and Gantt chart programs.

Final Thoughts on the Use of These Tools

Three decades ago it was common to hear, "No one uses PERT or CPM." It was not true. One decade ago we heard, "No one uses that probability stuff." It was not true. We even heard, "No one uses _____ computer package," which was also untrue. These statements were not true a decade ago—and they are even less true (if that is semantically possible) today. Current software makes it easy to use networks and Gantt charts. Current software handles three-time estimates of duration and can do all the calculations almost instantly. Current software makes simulation a straightforward procedure.

Excel® and other popular spreadsheets can calculate variances and find expected times. MSP can do some of these calculations, but not others. MSP does not find the standard deviation or variance of three-time duration estimates and cannot find the probability of completing a task or the entire project within a given time limit. Probability calculations are, however, easily handled by simulation. The analyst, of course, must examine the paths, and select those for further analysis. The software can do the arithmetic, but the analyst must enter the appropriate numbers and ask for the appropriate calculations for each path to be analyzed, and then find the probabilities. With large networks, this will probably be a massive and tedious task. On the other hand, it is almost never required to enumerate and evaluate all paths in a simulation— even if simulation could do so rapidly.

As we have noted several times, the same arguments and methods are appropriate for managing uncertainty in resource usage and preparing project budgets. The calculations and simulations are the same as those used with task and project duration.

 When struggling with risk analysis and management, it is well to remember why the PM must engage the struggle. The PM is responsible for keeping the project within its budget and on time. This chapter is devoted to developing the information the PM requires to meet these responsibilities. The PM does not manage the project as

Risk

a totality; rather he or she manages the specific tasks and subtasks that make up the project. The methods introduced above are intended to help the PM understand precisely where management effort is needed.

As we noted briefly above, it is relevant to point out that identifying one or more paths as critical might actually be detrimental to project performance—if the PM is not managing the project team as well as the project. If the PM is not alert to the possibility, activity slack may lead to neglect of noncritical activities. As Parkinson teaches us, work tends to fill the time allowed, and activities lose their slacks. For example, noncritical paths may slip far enough behind schedule that they become critical—simply because the project team perceives them to be of low priority. At the same time, the apparently critical path may finish ahead of schedule because of the extra management attention it receives.

Goldratt (1997, Ch.13) refers to other causes of project delay resulting from "human nature." There is, for instance, the "student syndrome." Given the deadline for a homework assignment, students often plead for more time. Given more time, many simply postpone starting the assignment. Goldratt also reminds us that if a task is finished early, its successor tasks are still started when they were originally scheduled. The result is that delays resulting from tasks finishing late are not offset by the potential gains from those that finish early. There is also the fact that "five plus five equals thirteen." If one team member estimates that one task will require 5 days and a second team member estimates that a successor task will require 5 days, the boss then estimates that the pair will require 13 days—just to be safe. The work, of course, will expand to require at least 13 days.

If the PM becomes entranced with the technology of the project and fails to manage the project team, the team itself can become confused and frustrated as the reality of the project unfolds. Today's path-slack disappears and a new critical path is born—only to change tomorrow when some other path becomes critical. In such cases, and they are common in reality, it is not easy to remind oneself that *recognizing and analyzing uncertainty does not cause uncertainty—nor does it cause uncertainty to disappear.* The PM's job includes teaching project team members enough about risk that they can understand its nature and, thereby, cooperate in developing ways to deal with it.

Risk

At this point, it is helpful to remember that there are problems for which risk analysis, by whatever method, is probably not required. Routine maintenance and routine construction projects are among such cases—unless the projects are quite large or have not been performed recently. In most such projects the routine character of the work means that the variances of task durations are quite small and the cost of carrying out a careful risk analysis is rarely justified.

The section discusses a significant extension of Gantt charts and PERT/CPM. Precedence diagramming, developed as a convenient way to include leads and lags between activities, is explained. Finally, we consider some of the managerial problems often associated with risk analysis.

In the next chapter, we turn our attention to resource allocation and the problems of controlling the use and flow of resources. We also deal with the issue of integrating schedule and budget by examining the nature of time-resource trade-offs.

REVIEW QUESTIONS

1. How would a PM manage critical path tasks differently than noncritical path tasks?

2. How is slack determined?

3. How do you determine the ES for an activity with two predecessors? How do you determine the LF for an activity with two successors?

4. Will all the activities on a noncritical path have the same slack? Why or why not?

5. For the following project,
   (a). List all predecessors of task 5.
   (b). List all predecessors of task 4.
   (c). List all predecessors of the network finish (F).

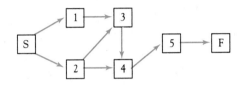

6. What is a "dummy" activity?

7. Consider Figure 5-14. Paths a-b-c and a-b-d converge at activity f, but we ignored this potential merge problem in the text. Why?

8. What is meant by "project slack"?

9. When using AON networks, how does one indicate an event such as a project milestone?

10. A probabilistic network has a critical path of 21 days and a .95 probability of completing this path in 24 days. Therefore, the project has a .95 chance of being finished by the end of the 24th day. True or False? Briefly explain your answer.

11. "Not uncommonly, the Gantt chart is deceptive in its apparent simplicity." Briefly explain.

12. When activity times are known with certainty, the critical path is defined as the set of activities on a path from the project's start event to its finish event that, if delayed, will delay the completion date of the project. Why must this definition be modified in situations where the activity times are not known with certainty? Are there any dangers associated with not modifying the definition?

DISCUSSION QUESTIONS

13. How might you use the network approach to help prepare cost estimates?

14. When would it be accurate to determine the probability of project completion by multiplying the probabilities of all the paths through the network together? When would it not be accurate?

15. Reconsider Question 14. If this approach is *not* accurate, would the probability of completion considering the critical path alone be more accurate? How might you estimate the correct probability without resorting to simulation?

16. Why do you think most PMs use MSP's Gantt chart format (see Figure 5-22) more commonly than the network format?

17. Which of the linkages in precedence diagramming do you think is most commonly used? Why?

18. In the calculation of variance for optimistic and pessimistic activity duration estimates made at the 95 or 90 percent level, the denominator of the fraction that approximates the standard deviation of the time distribution changes from the traditional $(b - a)/6$ to $(b - a)/3.3$ for 95 percent and to $(b - a)/2.6$ for 90 percent. Where did the 3.3 and the 2.6 come from?

19. Given all the estimating done to determine the duration of project activities, what does it mean to say that "only after the fact do we know which path was actually the critical path?"

20. It was noted that "the PM must manage the project team as well as the project." Explain why.

21. Why do you think scheduling has been the major focus of effort throughout the history of project management rather than performance or budgeting?

PROBLEMS

22. Refer to the network in Figure 5-14. What is the probability that path a-b-c-f will interfere with the promised project completion of 50 days? Recall that the critical path, a-b-d-g-h, had a probability of .86 for a 50-day completion. What is the probability that both paths will be complete in 50 days?

23. Refer to Table 5-4 and Figure 5-14. Recalculate the variance for each activity on the assumption that the optimistic and pessimistic estimates were made with a 95 percent probability. Recalculate the probability that the critical path will be completed in 50 days.

24. Refer to Table 5-4 and Figure 5-14. Recalculate the variance for each activity on the assumption that the optimistic and pessimistic estimates were made with a 90 percent probability. Again, recalculate the likelihood that the critical path will be finished in 50 days.

25. Given the information in the following table:

Activity	Duration	Predecessor
a	4	None
b	6	a
c	4	a
d	2	c
e	4	b
f	5	b, d
g	3	c
h	4	f, g
i	2	e, h

a. Construct the network diagram.

b. Find each activity's ES, EF, LS, and LF.

c. Identify all paths. Which path is the critical path?

d. Calculate the slack for each activity.

e. How long will it take to complete the project?

26. Given the information in the following table, draw the AOA network. Using the same information, enter the data into MSP assuming a 7-day workweek. (To change the calendar in MSP from its 5-day week default, click "**Help**," type "calendar change," and follow directions.) Develop the appropriate AON network and Gantt chart. Using any method you wish, find the critical path and critical time for the network. Then find the slack for all activities.

Activity	Predecessor	Duration
a	—	5 days
b	—	7
c	—	4
d	a	6
e	b	9
f	b	6
g	c	4
h	d, e	6
i	d, e	8
j	f, g, h	9
k	i	10
l	j	9

27. In the following table, task durations are given in weeks. The estimates were made at the 95 percent level (see Section 5.2, Calculating Probabilistic Activity Times subsection).

Activity	Predec.	Opt.	Normal	Pess.
a	—	2	4	6
b	—	3	5	9
c	a	4	5	7
d	a	4	6	10
e	b, c	4	5	7
f	d	3	4	8
g	e	3	5	8

a. Find the expected time and variance for each task.

b. Draw the network (either AOA or AON) and find the critical path and time.

c. Find the probability that the critical path will be completed in 23 weeks.

d. Find the probability that the other main paths will be completed in 23 weeks.

e. What is the probability that the entire network will be completed in 23 weeks?

28. Given an auditing project with the following activities:

Activity	Std. Dev.	Critical	Duration (wks)
a. Add	2	Yes	2
b. Balance	1		3
c. Count	0	Yes	4
d. Deduct	3		2
e. Edit	1	Yes	1
f. Finance	2		6
g. Group	2	Yes	4
h. Hold	0	Yes	2

Using the critical path, find:

a. The probability of completing this project in 12 weeks or less, as the client desires.

b. The probability of completing this project in 13 weeks or less.

c. The probability of completing this project in 16 weeks or less, the client's drop-dead date.

d. The number of weeks required to assure a 92.5 percent chance of completion, as guaranteed by the auditing firm.

29. Given the following information regarding a project involving an initial public offering (IPO):

Activity	Duration (weeks)	Preceding Activities
a. Check feasibility	3	—
b. Determine funding	1	—
c. Find possible banks	3	a
d. Select two possibles	4	a
e. Interview two banks	4	b
f. Analyze funding costs	5	b
g. Determine chance of success	2	c, e
h. Sign contract	3	f

a. Draw the network.

b. What is the critical path?

c. When will the offering be available (end of the project)?

d. What is the effect on the project if activity e (approvals) takes an extra week? Two extra weeks? Three extra weeks?

30. Enter the following information into an Excel® spreadsheet. The time estimates were made at the 90 percent level (see Section 5.2, Calculating Probabilistic Activity Times subsection). All activity times are in days.

Activity	Predec.	Opt.	Normal	Pess.
a	—	5	6	9
b	—	4	4	6
c	—	7	9	15
d	a	6	6	6
e	b	4	5	7
f	b	12	16	17
g	c	8	12	20
h	c	7	9	16
i	d, e	10	14	18
j	f, g	6	12	20
k	h	7	9	14

a. Draw the network. (You may use MSP, or draw an AOA or AON network by hand.)

b. Using Excel®, calculate the expected time (T_E) and variance for each activity.

c. Using the expected times, find the critical path and critical time. (Use the analytic method.)

d. Find the probability that the critical path will be completed in 38 days or less.

e. Are there any serious sources of merge bias? What are they? Calculate the probability of finishing the project on or before day 38 when merge bias is included.

f. Assume that the times in the table were made on the 99+ percent level. Recalculate the activity variances with this assumption and find the probability that the critical path will be complete in 38 days. (Note, the altered assumption will change activity variance, but not the expected activity durations.) Briefly explain the difference in probabilities.

g. How many days are required for the critical path to have a .9 probability of completion?

31. Given the project in Problem 27, simulate the completion of the project 1000 times, assuming that the activity times follow a normal distribution and that the time estimates are made at the 95 percent level.

a. Determine the probability of each path becoming the critical path.

b. What is the probability that the project is completed in 23 weeks?

c. How do your answers compare with your answers in Problem 27?

32. The project referred to in Problem 31 has been partially completed. Task **a** required 4 weeks, task **b** 9 weeks, task **c** 4 weeks, and task **d** 5 weeks. Update the simulation model you developed for Problem 31 and calculate the probability that the project will be finished in 23 weeks. Explain why the probability of completing the project in 23 weeks has changed.

33. Given the project in Problem 30, simulate the completion of the project 1000 times, assuming that the activity times are at the 99+ percent level and follow a triangular distribution.

a. Determine the probability of each path becoming the critical path.

b. What is the probability that the project is completed in 32 days? In 34 days? In 38 days?

c. How do your answers compare with your answers in Problem 30?

DISCUSSION PROBLEM

34. The following activities were listed during a brainstorming session on product development. Find the appropriate predecessor-successor relationships and then construct an AON network to reflect the project using the activity duration times given in the information table. Assume a 5-day workweek. Find the critical path and time for the project. Find the slack for all activities.

1. **Organize the sales office:** Hire sales manager. (6 weeks)
2. **Hire sales personnel:** The sales manager will recruit and hire the salespeople needed. (4 weeks)
3. **Train sales personnel:** Train the salespeople hired to sell the product to the distributors. (7 weeks)
4. **Select advertising agency:** The sales manager will select the agency best suited to promote the new product. (2 weeks)
5. **Plan advertising campaign:** The sales office and advertising agency will jointly plan the advertising campaign to introduce the product to the public. (4 weeks)
6. **Conduct advertising campaign:** The advertising agency will conduct a "watch for" campaign for potential customers. (10 weeks)
7. **Design package:** Have packaging engineer design the package most likely to "sell." (2 weeks)
8. **Set up packaging facility:** Prepare to package the products when they are received from the manufacturer. (10 weeks)
9. **Package initial stocks:** Package stocks received from the manufacturer. (6 weeks)
10. **Order and receive stock from the manufacturer:** Order the stock from the manufacturer. The time given includes the time for delivery. (13 weeks)
11. **Select distributors:** The sales manager will select the distributors whom the salespeople will contact to make sales. (9 weeks)
12. **Sell to distributors:** Take orders from the distributors for the new product, with delivery promised for the product-introduction date. If orders exceed stock, assign stock on a quota basis. (6 weeks)
13. **Ship stock to distributors:** Ship the packaged stock to distributors in accord with their orders or quota. (6 weeks)

Question: What managerial problems and opportunities do you see as a result of your work?

INCIDENTS FOR DISCUSSION

Springville Fire Department

The city of Springville is building a new fire station in their city. The city is expanding and is in need of a second fire station closer to the newer areas of the city to ensure shorter response times. The project manager and the project team have been selected for the project. The team is very interested in selecting the scheduling technique that will be used to follow the project through to completion.

The project manager, city manager, and chief of the fire department have set the following criteria for the process of selecting the scheduling technique: easy to use, shows durations of tasks, shows milestones, can see the flow of work, can see the sequence of events, can depict which tasks can be undertaken at the same time, and can tell how far tasks are from completion. The city manager favors the Gantt chart, the chief likes PERT, and the project manager prefers CPM.

Question: If you were the project manager, which method would you use, and why?

Attack of the Killer Worm

Lee Antoinio was the CIO of a large publishing house. Her network administrator, Andy McPester, came to her one sunny September afternoon and informed her that a worm had attacked their network. It had shut down two of their 45 servers and had potential to harm the other servers as well as the 323 personal workstations throughout the enterprise. Andy knew that he could not report this problem to Lee without a recommended project plan for a solution. Andy and Lee had a good, trusting relationship, but Lee insisted that Andy investigate all options and come to her with the most viable solution to any problem.

Andy's project plan outlined that it would take 30 to 45 minutes to touch each PC to protect them from the worm, and longer if they were already infected. It would take almost an hour to check the other servers and repair them. Andy discussed the time estimates with his desktop staff. Andy proposed paying six staff members overtime to work 4 hours after their normal business day for the next week or two to check each personal workstation. He did not want to affect productivity of the company's staff during the day. Andy proposed repairing the servers the same way with two additional staff members in the evenings. Lee felt that the time estimates and costs were too high. She did not think it would take that amount of time for each machine to get repaired. She was concerned that some of Andy's staff may have overestimated the time needed. She also was not sold on the notion that all the work would be done at night, paying staff overtime.

Question: How would you recommend they reach a consensus on the project plan?

C A S E

St. Dismas Assisted Living Facility Program Plan—3

The steering team meeting held August 31 went quite well. Fred felt that his team members had worked well together at determining the steps and the associated costs of the program. The CFO presented the program budget first, and then project team members presented their draft project plans.

The COO presented the following project plan:

ID	Task Name	Duration	Predecessors	Resource Names
55	Operational Implementation Plan			
56	Management/Organization structure	87 days		CFO, Legal, VP Mktg
57	Recruit & hire Executive Director	17.4 wks		Splient
58	Interior design issues decided (furnishings, etc.)	20 days		COO
59	Determine what was provided with lease and what was furnished in some units	2 wks		
60	Determine budget for interior	10 days		
61	Carpet and wall finish determined	2 wks	59	
62	Furniture and room layout	2 wks	59	
63	Facility and equipment needs defined	4 wks		COO
64	Staffing determined	2 wks		COO, Dr. Link
65	Office space for physicians	4 wks		Dr. Link
66	Medical staffing needs determined & Director appointed	4 wks		Dr. Link
67	Food service	45 days		
68	Menus selected	8 wks		
69	Waiting and service staffing needs determined	4 wks		
70	Additional equipment needs	4 wks	68FS—3wks	
71	Telecommunications services	45 days		
72	Investigate phone service options	45 days		Chief Engineer
73	Certification/Accreditation requirements	42 days		
74	Investigate requirements & timing of applicants with Dept. of Health to open facility	0 days		Legal
75	Develop clinical and operational quality monitoring systems	0 days		
76	Develop financial systems (billing, etc.)	6 wks		CFO
77	Human resources	79 days		HR Director
78	Work force management recommendations	6 wks		HR Director
79	Project plan for recruitment developed	2 wks	78	
80	Policies and procedures developed	60 days		
81	Obtain 'samples' of assisted living policies & procedures from other institutions	4 wks		Legal

ID	Task Name	Duration	Predecessors	Resource Names
82	Investigate assisted living laws proposed in other states/federal	12 wks		Legal
83	Technology & information systems	344 days		CIO
84	Develop plan for technology access for residents (TV, Cable, PC's)	3 wks		
85	Investigate software/technology options for residents	12 wks		CIO

The Chief Legal Counsel for the medical center presented his project plan. Fred had asked him to join the team when it became apparent that there were significant compliance and legal issues associated with this project.

ID	Task Name	Duration	Predecessors	Resource Names
36	Legal and Licensing Requirements	154 days		
37	Research licensing requirements for residential care facility	38 days		Legal
38	Uniform accessibility standard compliance (# hndcp accessible beds)	2 wks		
39	Investigate law firm and outline services	4 wks		
40	Prepare project plan for license	2 wks	39	
41	File license—by opening date	0 days	40	
42	Curb-cut approval from county (access to County Rd.)	53 days		Legal
43	Investigate corporate structure for assisted living	115 days		Legal, CFO
44	Determine Board of Trustee membership	3 wks		
45	Appoint Board of Trustees	4 wks	44	
46	Prepare draft Code of Regulation	4 wks	45	
47	Prepare document and filing of governance structure	12 wks	46	
48	Draft service agreement with St. Dismas for services provided	4 wks	47	Legal
49	Lease issues	110 days	48	Legal
50	Research Long Term Care insurance requirements	12 wks		
51	Facility "rules" defined (i.e., smoking, firearms, pets, financial planning)	4 wks	50	
52	Spell out changes for residents in moving from "light" to "heavy" assisted	6 wks		
53	Lease template prepared	6 wks	52, 50, 51	
54	Review all marketing materials for compliance	154 days		Legal

The Vice President of Marketing presented her project plan and stated that she and her staff were responsible for every step in the plan. She was still working with her staff to determine who does what. The Marketing VP made it clear to the team that she needed 5 months for the marketing plan implementation to be able to meet the occupancy requirements at start-up. She restated that her team must have this lead time to the completion of the construction and furnishing phase of the Program.

ID	Task Name	Duration	Predecessors
86	Marketing	270 days	
87	Community mailing about construction project	0 days	
88	Initial informational meetings	16 days	
89	St. Dismas volunteers	1 day	
90	Community groups	4 days	
91	St. Dismas staff (all shifts)	3 days	
92	Presentation prepared for Speaker's Bureau	0 days	88
93	Provide updates to community	0 days	92
94	Inquiry log established	0 days	88
95	Groundbreaking ceremony—during National Hospital Week	0 days	
96	Marketing plan developed and implemented	180 days	
97	PR firm contracted	4 wks	
98	Marketing plan developed	8 wks	97
99	Determine name and signage for facility	0 days	98
100	Hire Marketing Director	4 wks	98
101	Marketing plan ready to implement	0 days	98, 100
102	Implementation of marketing plan—5 months before facility ready, then ongoing	20 wks	101

As Fred was explaining that the next job of the group was to complete a final version of all project plans and firm up the schedule of the Program, the Construction Project Manager stated that it was his turn to present his broad project plan for construction of the facility. He also added that he had a major scheduling issue to bring to the team. The Construction Project Manager presented the following broad project plan for facility construction.

ID	Task Name	Duration	Predecessors
1	Construction & Furnishing	369 days	
2	Facility construction	329 days	
3	Phase 1 - Foundation & excavation (basement/1st floor slab)	95 days	
4	Phase 2 - Structure (steel/framing)	113 days	3FS—60 days
5	Phase 3 - Enclosure (masonry/windows/roof)	134 days	3
6	Phase 4 - Interiors (drywall/ceiling/flooring/case goods)	234 days	3
7	First 45 (light assisted) units ready to prepare for occupancy	0 days	6FS—5 wks
8	First 45 units ready for residents	8 wks	7
9	Remaining 57 units (light & heavy) ready to prepare for occupancy	0 days	6
10	Construction complete	0 days	9
11	Building ready for residents	8 wks	10

The construction PM proceeded to explain that the scheduling constraints that the Board of Trustees gave the team were not feasible. The Board wanted construction to begin immediately after the elections in November and to be ready for occupants by June. The contractor did not want to begin the project at the beginning of winter. The first phases of the project plan detailed work that needed to be completed outside. If the weather was bad, the construction PM knew the schedule would be affected. The construction project manager also pointed out that the schedule created by the contractor was designed around a 40-hour, 5-day workweek. If the building project began in November, the estimated project duration would be increased by 1 to 2 months, during which time some construction crewmen would have to be paid, thereby increasing the building cost.

The PM recommended that construction begin in February or March of the following year, which would give the facility a shorter build time and a lower cost. The budget and project duration submitted were based on a March 1 start date. He stated that the construction phase of the project did not need to hold up the other members of the Program team—they could begin their work on their projects anytime.

QUESTIONS

1. Draw a Gantt chart for the construction phase of the program. What is the completion date if construction starts in March? What is the completion date of the project if construction is started in November?

2. Why is it not possible to meet the scheduling constraints set by the Board? What is your recommendation to handle the scheduling problem?

3. When will the program be completed based on your recommendation?

4. Develop a Gantt Chart of the Marketing Plan and Implementation Phase of the Program. Determine the start date of the Marketing Plan project in order to meet your recommended facility ready for occupancy date.

5. What is the next step the team members must take in order to complete their project plans?

C A S E

NutriStar

NutriStar produces a line of vitamins and nutritional supplements. It recently introduced its Nutri-Sports Energy Bar, which is based on new scientific findings about the proper balance of macronutrients. The energy bar has become extremely popular among elite athletes and other people who follow the diet. One distinguishing feature of the Nutri-Sports Energy Bar is that each bar contains 50 milligrams of eicosapentaenoic acid (EPA), a substance strongly linked to reducing the risk of cancer but found in only a few foods, such as salmon. NutriStar was able to include EPA in its sports bars because it had previously developed and patented a process to refine EPA for its line of fish-oil capsules.

Because of the success of the Nutri-Sports Energy Bar in the United States, NutriStar is considering offering it in Latin America. With its domestic facility currently operating at capacity, the President of NutriStar has decided to investigate the option of adding approximately 10,000 square feet of production space to its facility in Latin America at a cost of $5 million.

The project to expand the Latin American facility involves four major phases: (1) concept development, (2) definition of the plan, (3) design and construction, and (4) start-up and turnover. During the concept development phase, a program manager is chosen to oversee all four phases of the project and the manager is given a budget to develop a plan. The outcome of the

concept development phase is a rough plan, feasibility estimates for the project, and a rough schedule. Also, a justification for the project and a budget for the next phase are developed.

In the plan definition phase, the program manager selects a project manager to oversee the activities associated with this phase. Plan definition consists of four major activities that are completed more or less concurrently: (1) defining the project scope, (2) developing a broad schedule of activities, (3) developing detailed cost estimates, and (4) developing a plan for staffing. The outputs of this phase are combined into a detailed plan and proposal for management specifying how much the project will cost, how long it will take, and what the deliverables are.

If the project gets management's approval and management provides the appropriations, the project progresses to the third phase, design and construction. This phase consists of four major activities: (1) detailed engineering, (2) mobilization of the construction employees, (3) procurement of production equipment, and (4) construction of the facility. Typically, the detailed engineering and the mobilization of the construction employees are done concurrently. Once these activities are completed, construction of the facility and procurement of the production equipment are done concurrently. The outcome of this phase is the physical construction of the facility.

The final phase, start-up and turnover, consists of four major activities: pre-start-up inspection of the facility, recruiting and training the workforce, solving start-up problems, and determining optimal operating parameters (called *centerlining*). Once the pre-start-up inspection is completed, the workforce is recruited and trained at the same time that start-up problems are solved. Centerlining is initiated upon the completion of

these activities. The desired outcome of this phase is a facility operating at design requirements.

The following table provides optimistic, most likely, and pessimistic time estimates for the major activities.

Activity	Optimistic Time (months)	Most Likely Time (months)	Pessimistic Time (months)
A: Concept Development	3	12	24
Plan Definition			
B. Define project scope	1	2	12
C. Develop broad schedule	0.25	0.5	1
D. Detailed cost estimates	0.2	0.3	0.5
E. Develop staffing plan	0.2	0.3	0.6
Design and Construction			
F. Detailed engineering	2	3	6
G. Facility construction	8	12	24
H. Mobilization of employees	0.5	2	4
I. Procurement of equipment	1	3	12
Start-up and Turnover			
J. Pre-start-up inspection	0.25	0.5	1
K. Recruiting and training	0.25	0.5	1
L. Solving start-up problems	0	1	2
M. Centerlining	0	1	4

QUESTIONS

1. Draw a network diagram for this project. Identify all paths through the network diagram.

2. Simulate the completion of this project 1,000 times, assuming that activity times follow a betaPERT distribution. Estimate the mean and standard deviation of the project completion time.

3. Develop a histogram to summarize the results of your simulation.

4. Calculate the probability that the project can be completed within 30 months. What is the probability that the project will take longer than 40 months? What is the probability that the project will take between 30 and 40 months?

C A S E

Launching E-Collar

Pet Technologies Inc. has completed the development of a revolutionary pet collar code named e-collar. E-collar is designed for dogs and allows pet owners to identify the

location of their dog using their smartphones. In addition to purchasing the e-collar, the pet owners must download a free app for their smartphone and pay a small monthly fee that is yet to be determined in order to connect the e-collar to a cellular network.

In the past, Pet Technologies has used the services of Ad Jungle to develop its advertising campaigns. Ad Jungle is located in the same city as Pet Technologies and is a boutique advertising agency with 25 full-time employees and a similar number of people it contracts with on an ad hoc basis. Pet Technologies has reached out to Ad Jungle and has requested an estimate for the cost of developing an advertising campaign for the e-collar.

Ad Jungle begins the process of developing an ad campaign by first meeting with the client to learn about the product to be advertised. Based on what is learned, Ad Jungle works with the client to define the target audience for the advertising campaign. Because the target audience may be different than its current customer base, market research is often required. Historical data suggests that defining the target market typically takes 80 hours (2 weeks). In some cases, determining the target audience is fairly routine and can be done in as little as a day and a half (12 hours in total) while in other cases much less is known about who will use the product and defining the target market can take as long as 4 weeks (160 hours). Also, the number of people working on the task at any one time varies as does their hourly bill rate. Given this, the average amount the customer is billed for the work to determine the target audience typically averages $170 per hour. In some cases, however, the hourly rate was as low as $100 per hour and in other cases as high as $450 per hour.

Once the target audience has been defined, alternative concepts for the advertising campaign are developed. A key aspect of developing the concept is deciding on the tone the campaign will use such as humorous, dramatic, or informative. Concept development is a highly creative process and often requires several iterations between Ad Jungle and its clients. On average, concept development takes 2 weeks (80 hours) but has been completed in as little as 1 week (40 hours) or as long as 5 weeks (200 hours). Only one person from Ad Jungle works on concept development,

and typically these employees are billed out at $125 per hour. However, the least experienced employee is billed out at $75 per hour and the most experienced person is billed out at $200 per hour.

Once the client signs off on the concept, the development of the creative collateral (brochures, print ads, scripts for TV commercials, and so on) and determining the mix of media are done concurrently. The amount of time it takes to develop the creative collateral depends on how many media channels will be used (e.g., print, TV, online), how many people are assigned to work on developing the creative collateral, and how much involvement the client wants to have in the process. Typically, developing the creative collateral requires 3 weeks (120 hours) but has been done in as little as 1 week (40 hours) and on other occasions required 6 weeks (240 hours). Furthermore, the number of people and their bill rates varies from project to project. On average, the hourly bill rate for developing the collateral is $275 but has been as low as $145 and as high as $425.

Determining the mix of media is almost always done by the same person at Ad Jungle. This person is currently billed out at $150 per hour. The amount of time it takes to determine the mix of media that will be used ranges from half a day (4 hours) to 2 days (16 hours), but it typically takes 1 day (8 hours).

Once the collateral has been developed and the mix of media determined, the final step is production where the advertising materials are developed. The production of the advertising materials is outsourced to firms, and Ad Jungle assigns one account manager to oversee the work. The account managers are billed out at an hourly rate of $200. On average, 80 hours of the account manager's time is needed to oversee production. In some cases, as little as 30 hours of the account manager's time was required, while in other cases as many as 160 hours were needed.

QUESTIONS

1. Draw a network diagram for this project. Identify all the paths through the network diagram.

2. Simulate the completion of this project 1,000 times, assuming that activity times and costs follow a triangular distribution. Estimate the mean and standard deviation of the project completion time. Also, estimate the mean and standard deviation of the amount the client would be billed for the project.

3. What is the probability the project can be done for less than $100,000? What is the probability the project will take between 350 and 450 hours?

4. Based on the results of your simulation analysis, how would you respond to Pet Technologies' request for an estimate of the project costs and duration?

BIBLIOGRAPHY

DE MEYER, A., C. H. LOCH, and M. T. PICH. "Managing Project Uncertainty: From Variation to Chaos." *MIT Sloan Management Review*, Winter 2002. (This article provides a useful classification of uncertainty faced in projects and provides specific suggestions for managing each type of uncertainty.)

GOLDRATT, E. M. *Critical Chain*, Great Barrington, MA, North River, 1997.

HULETT, D. T. "Project Schedule Risk: Monte Carlo Simulation or PERT?" *PM Network*, February 2000. (Hulett comes to the same general conclusion that we do. Simulation is superior to the statistical methods of PERT for complex problems. In stating his case, however, he fails to note that for a PM to use simulation effectively, the PM should understand the statistics of simulation.)

KAMBUROWSKI, J. "New Validations of PERT Times." *Omega, International Journal of Management Science*, Vol. 25, No. 3, 1997.

KEEFER, D. L., and W. A. VERDINI. "Better Estimation of PERT Activity Time Parameter." *Management Science*, September 1993.

LAWRENCE, J. A., Jr., and B. A. PASTERNAK. *Applied Management Science*, New York: Wiley, 1998. (This book has solution techniques for finding the critical path and time for a network using Excel's® Solver.)

LEACH, L. "Schedule and Cost Buffer Sizing: How to Account for the Bias between Project Performance and Your Model." *Project Management Journal*, June 2003. (This article identifies a variety of sources of schedule and cost biases and provides recommendations for coping with them.)

LIBERATORE, M. J. "Project Schedule Uncertainty Analysis Using Fuzzy Logic." *Project Management Journal*, December 2002. (Our discussion in this chapter addresses schedule uncertainty from both a probability theory approach and using computer simulation. This article demonstrates the use of fuzzy logic for assessing project schedule uncertainty.)

MCMAHON, C. S. "Using PERT as an Approximation of the Fuzzy-Project Network Analysis." *IEEE Transactions on Engineering Management*, May 1993.

MEREDITH, J. R., and S. J. MANTEL, Jr. *Project Management: A Managerial Approach*, 8th ed., Hoboken, NJ: John Wiley, 2012.

PRITSKER, A. A. B. "Gert Networks." *The Production Engineer*, October 1968.

RUSKIN, A. M. "Using *Unders* to Offset *Overs*." *PM Network*, February 2000.

Allocating Resources to the Project

In this chapter we consider the problem of allocating physical and human resources to projects.* The physical and human resources are granted to and used by the project in order to meet the project's objectives. The amount of resources that can be allocated, of course, depends on the timing of the allocation as well as on the total supply of resources available for allocation. Mainly, resource allocation concerns how we allocate specific, limited resources to specific activities (or projects) when there are competing demands for the same limited resources.

Projects compete with each other for the same resources in two different ways. First, consider a resource that is limited but is not consumed when used, the services of a specific technical specialist for instance. The problem here is which project gets to use the resource first and which must wait. Second, consider a resource that is limited and is consumed when used, a specific chemical reagent for instance. In this case, the second project may have to wait until more of the reagent can be purchased and delivered. In both cases, the project that must wait may suffer a schedule delay that makes it late. Just as projects may compete for resources, different activities of the same project may compete. Two or more concurrent activities might require the same personnel, or equipment, or even work space. One activity will be given priority, and the other(s) must wait.

Trade-Offs

In order to manage resources in such a way as to optimize the use of a limited supply, trade-offs must be made. The interaction of project scheduling and resource scheduling is clear, but we will examine several different solutions to the allocation problem. Those include the Critical Path Method (CPM), Goldratt's "critical chain" (1997), and many different priority rules for allocating scarce resources. The primary cause of concern is resource scarcity. If some resources (including time) were not scarce,

---

*With few exceptions, we will not make a distinction between human and nonhuman resources in this chapter. We need not distinguish between them in order to consider the allocation problem. The tasks of administering the human and nonhuman resources are quite different, of course.

the resource allocation problem would be concerned solely with profit maximization—a relatively easy problem.

In Chapter 5 we evaluated project durations solely in terms of time. A project was either on time or not. Now we must also consider when and for what purposes scarce people, equipment, material, and facilities are used. The PM's performance is judged by the skill with which the trade-offs of time, resources, and scope are managed, so the PM must make constant use of cost/benefit analysis. There are countless questions to be answered. "If we come in late on this project, we face a $1,000 per day penalty. How much project slack do we need and what resources at what costs are required to get it?" "If I hire Cheatem Engineering Associates as design consultants, can I improve project performance by 3 percent without extending the project's due date?" "Adding project slack and hiring a consultant require monetary resources that could be used for other things. Are these the best uses for the dollars?"

At times, the PM is asked to take on a project in which there are the usual time, budget, and scope goals, but which also constrain the trade-offs that the PM may wish to make if required to help the project meet its most important goals. For example, some projects are *time constrained* and must be completed by a fixed time. In such cases, resources (and possibly performance) are variable. Some projects are *resource constrained* and cannot go over budget or use more than a fixed amount of a specific resource. In these cases, time (and possibly performance) is variable. Occasionally, a senior manager suffers from a case of the micromanagement virus and fixes time, cost, and scope, thereby leaving the PM with no flexibility whatsoever. Such projects are certain to fail unless the micromanager has been profligate with the firm's resources, which is highly unlikely for micromanagers. The fault actually lies with the PM who accepts command of such a project. (For those who are thinking that such a PM may find him- or herself without a job following a refusal of an assignment, we would note the senior manager in question is insuring that the PM will fail. Do you want to work for someone who will not allow you to succeed?)

We will start our tour through the wilds of resource allocation by reconsidering the problem of dealing with a pointy-haired boss who insists that a project be completed in much less time than its expected duration.

6.1 EXPEDITING A PROJECT

The unreasonable boss problem in Chapter 5, Section 5.2 could be used as our example here, but a smaller problem will help avoid unnecessary arithmetic. Our problem is set in a deterministic world rather than in a probabilistic one, for the same reason. (Please remember that in reality all projects are carried out under conditions of uncertainty.) Finally, we must also take note of an assumption usually adopted when activities are scheduled, as we did in Chapter 5. That assumption is that all estimates of task duration, whether deterministic or probabilistic, are based on normal or standard resource loadings.

The Critical Path Method

In traditional PERT/CPM, the rules of "standard practice" apply and the *normal* task duration estimate is made with the normal or standard-practice resource usage. Then a second estimate, referred to as the *crash* duration, is made based on the resources required to expedite the task. More resources of the type already used might be added; more workers and shovels if there is a ditch to be dug. On the other hand, the technology used to dig the ditch might be totally altered, utilizing a backhoe or a Ditch

Witch®, for example. When making estimates for crashing, it is important to make sure that the resources required to crash the project are, in fact, available. Using a machine to dig the ditch in three hours instead of the 3 days required for a worker with a shovel is dependent on the fact that the machine is available and can be on site when needed. (Of course, the warning about resource availability applies equally to normal resource requirements as well as to crash requirements.) There are times when the PM may expedite activities that have little or no impact on the network's critical time, such as when the resources used must be made available to another project. It is important to remember that when we change technology, we may also be changing the level of risk in carrying out the activity. Finally, we must remind ourselves that some tasks *cannot* be crashed. One must not assume that because it takes one woman 9 months to carry and bear a child that nine women can accomplish the same result in 1 month.

Risk

Consider the project described in Table 6-1. There is a set of activities, predecessors, normal task duration estimates, crash duration estimates, and estimates for normal cost and crash cost. One crash duration is marked with a single asterisk. For this activity, the task may be carried out in normal time or crashed 1 day at a time. Another activity is marked with a double asterisk. In this case, the duration must be one or the other; it cannot be broken down to 1-day segments. Activities are charged at the "cost per day" (*activity slope*) increments shown in the last column. A given activity may have only two or three technically feasible durations. If an activity cannot be split into 1-day segments, the cost is as indicated. The "slope" information for non-or-partially segmented activities is normally given in the slope chart. Activity slope is computed as follows:

$$\text{slope} = \frac{\text{crash cost} - \text{normal cost}}{\text{crash time} - \text{normal time}}$$

When crashing a project, starting with the normal schedule for all project activities, crash selected activities, one at a time, to decrease project duration at the minimum additional cost. To crash a project, follow two simple principles: First, focus on the critical path(s) when trying to shorten the duration of a project. Crashing a non-critical activity will not influence project duration. Second, when shortening a project's duration, select the least expensive way to do it.

Given these guides, consider the network shown in Figure 6-1(a) that was constructed from the data in Table 6-1. It is easier to illustrate the impact of crashing on an activity-on-arrow (AOA) network than on an activity-on-node (AON) network, so we use that approach here. Also, we use dummy activities in this case not to illustrate precedence but to show time durations and slack on the time axis.

As indicated in Table 6-1, activity **d** can be partially crashed for $30, but it is not on the critical path and will not shorten the project. Activity **e** involves a technological discontinuity and must take either 3 days to complete at $10 or 1 day at

Table 6-1   An Example of a Normal/Crash Project

Activity	Precedence	Duration, Days (norm, crash)	Cost (norm, crash)	Slope ($/day)
a	—	3, 2	$ 40, 80	40/−1 = −40
b	a	2, 1	20, 80	60/−1 = −60
c	a	2, 2	20, 20	—
d*	a	4, 1	30, 120	90/−3 = −30
e**	b	3, 1	10, 80	−70 (2 days)

*Partial crashing allowed
**Partial crashing not allowed

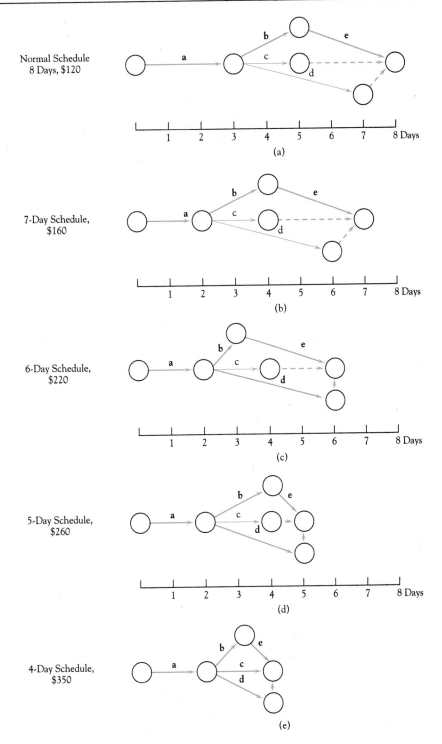

Figure 6-1   A PERT/CPM example of crashing a project, AOA network.

$80. In general, the impact of having such a technological discontinuity is that the best solution for crashing n days might not be part of the best solution for crashing $n + 1$ days. Rather, it may be best to crash the activity with the technological discontinuity at

$n + 1$ days and not crash another activity that could be crashed for n days. This situation is illustrated in the discussion that follows.

The network's critical path is **a-b-e**, the project duration is 8 days, and the normal total cost is $120, as illustrated in the network of Figure 6-1(a). The decision about which activities to crash depends on how much we need to reduce the duration of the project. To reduce the total network duration by 1 day, we must reduce the time required by one of the activities along the critical path. Inspecting Table 6-1 to see which critical activity can be reduced at the least cost, we find it is activity **a**, which adds $40 to the project's current cost of $120. Activity **b** could be crashed at an added cost of $60 or we could even crash **e** 2 days for an additional cost of $70. Of course, crashing **e** would only shorten the project duration by 1 day because when **e** is shortened, the path **a-d-dummy**, 7 days long, becomes the critical path and does not allow the project to be shortened to 6 days. Of the three options, crashing **a** is the lowest cost and therefore preferable, see Figure 6-1(b). Notice that crashing **a** also shortens **a-d-dummy** and **a-c-dummy** by 1 day.

Suppose the project must be crashed by 2 days. What are the options? Reconsidering Table 6-1 and Figure 6-1(a), we see that we could crash activity **e** for 2 days ($70), but path **a-d-dummy** (7-days' duration) must also be crashed at least 1 day. We choose **d** ($30/day) because it is cheaper than **a** ($40). The total cost of crashing is $100, and the total project cost is $120 + $100 = $220. Alternatively, we could crash **a** and **b**, also for a cost of $100 ($40 + $60). Arbitrarily, we choose the latter option [Figure 6-1(c)].

Now suppose we wanted to crash the project by 3 days, from the original 8 days down to 5 days. Clearly **e** must be crashed by 2 days, costing $70, and **a** or **b** by a day. We choose **a**, the cheapest, for an additional $40. This leaves **d** to be crashed by 1 day for another $30, resulting in a total crashing cost of $140 and a project cost of $120 + $140 = $260 [Figure 6-1(d)]. Note that we did not crash **b** this time, as we did for 6 days. This is due to the technological discontinuity in activity **e**.

Last, let us consider crashing the project by 4 days down to a project duration of 4 days. Since we crashed **e**, the technological discontinuity, to reach a 5-day duration, all the remaining activities can be incrementally crashed. Thus, we can simply inspect Figure 6-1(d) to see what else needs incremental crashing to reduce the project by another day. Notice in Figure 6-1(d) that **a-b-e** and **a-d-dummy** are both critical paths. Only **b** and **d** can still be crashed so we crash each by 1 day for an additional cost beyond the 5-day schedule of Figure 6-1(d) of $60 + $30 = $90 for a total project cost of $260 + $90 = $350 [Figure 6-1(e)]. Note that **c** is now critical; therefore, *all* paths are critical. Since the critical paths **a-b-e** and **a-c** are at their full extent of crashing, the project duration cannot be further reduced, even though activity **d** could be crashed another day. Thus, Figure 6-1(e) is *not* the all-crash network, although it equals the all-crash time schedule of 4 days.

Whether all this crashing is worthwhile is another matter. On the cost side, Figure 6-2 shows the time/cost relationship of crashing the project. On the benefit side, some projects have penalty clauses that make the parent organization liable for late delivery—and sometimes bonuses for early delivery. Starting at the right (all-normal) side of Figure 6-2, note that it becomes increasingly costly to squeeze additional time out of the project. Charts such as the one shown in Figure 6-2 are useful to the PM in exercising control over project duration and cost. They are particularly helpful in dealing with senior managers who may argue for early project completion dates with little understanding of the costs involved. Similarly, such data are of great benefit when clients plead for early delivery. If the client is willing to pay the cost of crashing, or if the firm is willing to subsidize the client, the PM can afford to listen with a sympathetic ear. (While we advise the PM to ignore overhead costs over which he or she has no control, it should be noted that indirect costs are often altered when a project is crashed.)

One final note on crashing projects. The same method is used when the task durations are probabilistic, that is, using three time estimates. In this case, optimistic, most likely, and

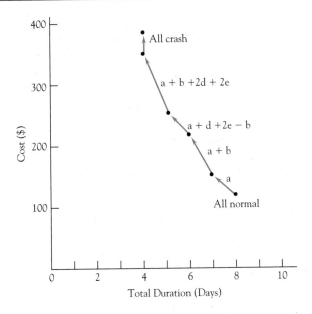

Figure 6-2   CPM crash cost-duration history.

pessimistic activity duration estimates are made for the "normal" resource loading and new optimistic, most likely, and pessimistic duration estimates must be made for crash resource loading. The PM should remember that the variance of both the normal and crash activity times largely depends on the technology used to accomplish the activity in question. Thus the variance of the normal activity time may be quite different from the variance of the crash time. The project budget can be determined in exactly the same way. The solution to project duration and resource cost levels can be reached by using the standard analytical method used in the last chapter, or by simulation, also described in Chapter 5.

Fast-Tracking a Project

In addition to crashing a project in order to expedite it, a project may also be *fast-tracked*. Used primarily in the construction industry, the term refers to an expediting technique in which the design and planning phases of a project are not actually completed before the building phase is started. Usually design and plan are finished before the building is started (referred to as the "waterfall" approach), so letting them overlap reduces project duration—if the fact that design and planning are incomplete does not result in a significant amount of rework and change orders during the building phase.

For many projects in construction, maintenance, and similar areas, a large proportion of the work is routine. In these cases, fast-tracking rarely causes serious problems. The number of change orders in fast-tracked construction projects is not significantly different from that for similar projects that were not fast-tracked (Kurtulus and Narula, 1985).

Project Expediting in Practice

Expediting can occur in three different ways. First, the PM may know ahead of time that this is a time-critical project and will need to take steps to finish the project as early as possible. Second, the PM may get the word during the execution of the project that the due date has had to be moved up. Or finally, something happens during the project to delay some activities so that the due date is going to be missed. In all cases, the sooner the PM knows that the project needs to be expedited, the more opportunities there will be to bring the project in ahead of time, or on time if a delay occurred. Whenever it appears that the project may be later than the stakeholders expected, it is imperative that the stakeholders be informed immediately and kept apprised of the follow-on developments as they occur. We can divide the opportunities for expediting a project into those that occur before the project begins and those that are available once the project is under way.

Opportunities Before the Project Begins First, it is worth noting that most of the time in practice, projects are not planned using the three-time method of estimating (i.e., optimistic, most likely, pessimistic). Instead, PMs simply try to get a reasonably accurate estimate of each activity time from those who will be responsible for the activity or, failing that, estimate the time themselves. Then, after they determine the critical path, they often add a cushion or "buffer" to the critical activities' times in case they turn out to be too optimistic (i.e., short). Next, to account for the possibility that other paths may turn out to be critical instead, a project time contingency, which is noted as such, is added as well.

Also, they may try to identify the "key" activities and deliverables (that is, those that have the biggest effect on the schedule or success) and plan to monitor those especially closely. To be safe, they may even order the long-lead time items early, or arrange for possible airlifting of those items if expediting is later deemed necessary.

Opportunities When the Project Is Underway If the need to expedite occurs once the project is underway, there are many actions PMs may try in order to expedite the project, as follows:

- First, they will focus on the critical path and see if there is any way to shorten it. If they haven't already, they will identify the key activities that would help expedite the project and manage those extremely closely, making sure that they don't use up their activity time cushions/buffers.

- In a similar vein, they may request permission to use some of the contingency time they budgeted for the project.

- They may pull resources from less critical activities, activities with a surplus, or just chronologically later activities, to apply to more critical, earlier activities.

- Similarly, they may move later activity time cushions/buffers up to earlier, more critical activities.

- They may try to shorten, or even skip, certain steps like testing, documentation, or training.

- They may postpone activities that involve non-core team members, or other stakeholders.

- They may move some activities to a post-project phase, such as installation, implementation, or service.

- They may see what activities they can "fast-track" (run in parallel), or even what activities can be done early or ahead of time (e.g., on weekends), which most commonly are those that do not involve the user or other stakeholders.

- They will try various forms of "compression" such as pressuring the team to work harder or faster, or get permission for overtime.

- They may attempt to get additional resources, either money for overtime or additional people to work on the project.

- They may seek permission to reduce the scope of the project, so the critical deliverables can occur on time.

Risk

- Finally, for PMs with lots of experience with projects such as these, they may simply choose to wait and see if something comes up later that allows them to make up the time. (Less-experienced or younger PMs are typically too risk averse and have less self-confidence to try this.)

When task durations are estimated, an assumption is made that task resources are set at "normal" levels. This is the "standard practice" assumption. Traditionally, CPM project duration estimates also include a "crash" estimate together with estimates of the crash time and the resources required to shorten the duration of project activities. By selectively choosing which activities to crash and by how much, we can determine the minimum cost for all possible project completion times.

6.2   RESOURCE LOADING

From the first day on the job, the PM is concerned with *resource loading*. Resource loading refers to the amounts of specific resources that are scheduled for use on specific activities or projects at specific times. It usually takes the form of a list or table. Figure 6-3 is an MSP-generated project plan and Gantt chart of a project aimed at producing a short documentary DVD. Task names, WBS numbers, durations, finish dates, and the resource requirements for each step in the process are shown. (Precedences are not listed, but they are illustrated on the Gantt chart.)

After the project plan was developed, the PM confirmed the availability of each required resource, and obtained schedules for each. MSP allows the PM to create an individual availability calendar for each resource on the project. From these calendars, resource schedules are automatically generated, and Table 6-2 shows the schedules for several of the required resources. (Any resource not shown in Table 6-2 works a 5-day week, 8:00 AM to 5:00 PM with an hour off for lunch, usually 12 PM–1 PM, without exceptions during the period of the project.) Among other things, the PM noted the following:

- The scriptwriter is available to work 6 days per week, and 9 hours per day.
- The editing room has limited availability, 9:30 AM to 3:00 PM each day.
- The client, whose input is required for several activities, will be on vacation between April 13 and April 20.

When the calendars for each resource were entered into MSP's database for the project, the project schedule was recalculated. The revised plan is shown in Figure 6-4. Note that the project completion date has been extended from May 31 to June 11. The client's vacation and the availability of the editing room are major contributors to the extension.

From the project plan, the new schedule, and the list of resources required, a resource-loading table was derived by MSP; see Table 6-3. As we noted earlier, a project's resource loading is a list of the amounts of various specific resources that are scheduled for use on specific activities at specific times during the life of the project. A brief study of the data in Table 6-3 reveals that in the first week of the project [Wednesday through Saturday (March 1–4)] the scriptwriter is overallocated. During the first 6 days of the project this

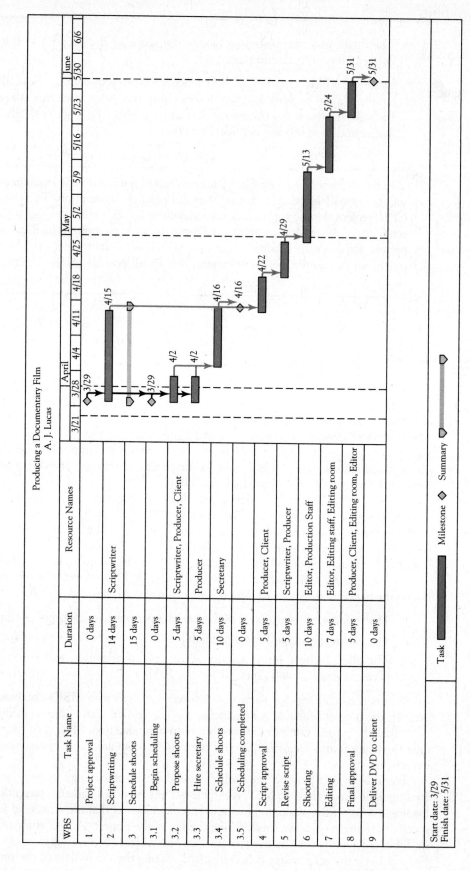

Figure 6-3 Project plan and Gantt chart for production of a short documentary film (MSP).

Table 6-2 Resource Availability Calendars for Selected Resources for Documentary Film Production (MSP)

Project: Producing a DVD	Resource Availability Calendars			
	Name	Standard Rate	Overtime Rate	Work
Scriptwriter		$75.00/hr	$100.00/hr	192 hr
	RESOURCE CALENDAR	(modified Standard)		
	Day	Hours		
	Monday	8:00 AM - 12:00 PM, 1:00 PM - 6:00 PM		
	Tuesday	8:00 AM - 12:00 PM, 1:00 PM - 6:00 PM		
	Wednesday	8:00 AM - 12:00 PM, 1:00 PM - 6:00 PM		
	Thursday	8:00 AM - 12:00 PM, 1:00 PM - 6:00 PM		
	Friday	8:00 AM - 12:00 PM, 1:00 PM - 6:00 PM		
	Saturday	8:00 AM - 12:00 PM, 1:00 PM - 6:00 PM		
	Sunday	Nonworking		
	Exceptions:	None		
Producer		$100.00/hr	$150.00/hr	200 hr
	RESOURCE CALENDAR	(unmodified Standard)		
	Day	Hours		
	Monday	8:00 AM - 12:00 PM, 1:00 PM - 5:00 PM		
	Tuesday	8:00 AM - 12:00 PM, 1:00 PM - 5:00 PM		
	Wednesday	8:00 AM - 12:00 PM, 1:00 PM - 5:00 PM		
	Thursday	8:00 AM - 12:00 PM, 1:00 PM - 5:00 PM		
	Friday	8:00 AM - 12:00 PM, 1:00 PM - 5:00 PM		
	Saturday	Nonworking		
	Sunday	Nonworking		
	Exceptions:	None		
Client		$0.00/hr	$0.00/hr	120 hr
	RESOURCE CALENDAR	(modified Standard)		
	Day	Hours		
	Monday	8:00 AM - 12:00 PM, 1:00 PM - 5:00 PM		
	Tuesday	8:00 AM - 12:00 PM, 1:00 PM - 5:00 PM		
	Wednesday	8:00 AM - 12:00 PM, 1:00 PM - 5:00 PM		
	Thursday	8:00 AM - 12:00 PM, 1:00 PM - 5:00 PM		
	Friday	8:00 AM - 12:00 PM, 1:00 PM - 5:00 PM		
	Saturday	Nonworking		
	Sunday	Nonworking		
	Exceptions:			
	Date	Hours		
	04/13–04/20	Nonworking		
Editing room		$250/use	$0.00/hr	96 hr
	RESOURCE CALENDAR	(modified Standard)		
	Day	Hours		
	Monday	9:30 AM - 3:00 PM		
	Tuesday	9:30 AM - 3:00 PM		
	Wednesday	9:30 AM - 3:00 PM		
	Thursday	9:30 AM - 3:00 PM		
	Friday	9:30 AM - 3:00 PM		
	Saturday	Nonworking		
	Sunday	Nonworking		
	Exceptions:	None		

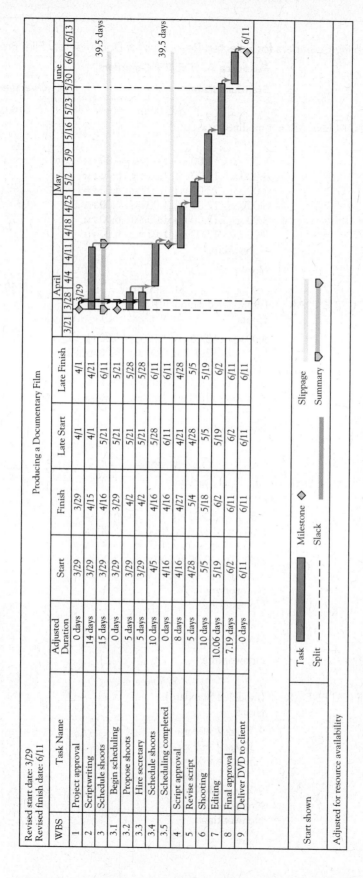

Revised start date: 3/29
Revised finish date: 6/11

Producing a Documentary Film

WBS	Task Name	Adjusted Duration	Start	Finish	Late Start	Late Finish
1	Project approval	0 days	3/29	3/29	4/1	4/1
2	Scriptwriting	14 days	3/29	4/15	4/1	4/21
3	Schedule shoots	15 days	3/29	4/16	5/21	6/11
3.1	Begin scheduling	0 days	3/29	3/29	5/21	5/21
3.2	Propose shoots	5 days	3/29	4/2	5/21	5/28
3.3	Hire secretary	5 days	3/29	4/2	5/21	5/28
3.4	Schedule shoots	10 days	4/5	4/16	5/28	6/11
3.5	Scheduling completed	0 days	4/16	4/16	6/11	6/11
4	Script approval	8 days	4/16	4/27	4/21	4/28
5	Revise script	5 days	4/28	5/4	4/28	5/5
6	Shooting	10 days	5/5	5/18	5/5	5/19
7	Editing	10.06 days	5/19	6/2	5/19	6/2
8	Final approval	7.19 days	6/2	6/11	6/2	6/11
9	Deliver DVD to client	0 days	6/11	6/11	6/11	6/11

Start shown

Task
Split

Milestone ◇
Slack

Slippage
Summary

Adjusted for resource availability

Figure 6-4 Gantt chart for DVD project, adjusted for client availability (MSP).

Table 6-3 Resource Loading Chart for DVD Production (MSP)

Producing a Documentary Film
Resource Loading

ID	Resource Name	Standard Rate	Overtime Rate	Work	Details	April				May					June			
						3/28	4/4	4/11	4/18	4/25	5/2	5/9	5/16	5/23	5/30	6/6	6/13	6/20
	Unassigned	$0.00/hr	$0.00/hr	0 hrs	Work													
	Project approval			0 hrs	Work													
	Begin scheduling			0 hrs	Work													
	Scheduling completed			0 hrs	Work													
	Deliver DVD to client			0 hrs	Work													
1	Scriptwriter	$75.00/hr	$100.00/hr	192 hrs	Work	94 hrs	54 hrs	4 hrs		37 hrs	3 hrs							
	Scriptwriting			112 hrs	Work	54 hrs	54 hrs	4 hrs										
	Propose shoots			40 hrs	Work	40 hrs												
	Revise script			40 hrs	Work					37 hrs	3 hrs							
2	Producer	$100.00/hr	$150.00/hr	200 hrs	Work	80 hrs		16 hrs	24 hrs	24 hrs	16 hrs				21.5 hrs	18.5 hrs		
	Propose shoots			40 hrs	Work	40 hrs												
	Hire secretary			40 hrs	Work	40 hrs												
	Script approval			40 hrs	Work			16 hrs	24 hrs									
	Revise script			40 hrs	Work					24 hrs	16 hrs							
	Final approval			40 hrs	Work										21.5 hrs	18.5 hrs		
3	Client	$0.00/hr	$0.00/hr	120 hrs	Work	40 hrs		0 hrs	24 hrs	16 hrs					21.5 hrs	18.5 hrs		
	Propose shoots			40 hrs	Work	40 hrs												
	Script approval			40 hrs	Work			0 hrs	24 hrs	16 hrs								
	Final approval			40 hrs	Work										21.5 hrs	18.5 hrs		
4	Secretary	$25.00/hr	$40.00/hr	80 hrs	Work		40 hrs	40 hrs										
	Schedule shoots			80 hrs	Work		40 hrs	40 hrs										
5	Editor	$50.00/hr	$85.00/hr	176 hrs	Work						24 hrs	40 hrs	40 hrs	32 hrs	21.5 hrs	18.5 hrs		
	Shooting			80 hrs	Work						24 hrs	40 hrs	16 hrs					
	Editing			56 hrs	Work								24 hrs	32 hrs				
	Final approval			40 hrs	Work										21.5 hrs	18.5 hrs		
6	Production Staff	$40.00/hr	$70.00/hr	80 hrs	Work						24 hrs	40 hrs	16 hrs					
	Shooting			80 hrs	Work						24 hrs	40 hrs	16 hrs					
7	Editing staff	$40.00/hr	$70.00/hr	56 hrs	Work								24 hrs	32 hrs				
	Editing			56 hrs	Work								24 hrs	32 hrs				
8	Editing room	$0.00/hr	$0.00/hr	96 hrs	Work								16.5 hrs	27.5 hrs	27.5 hrs	24.5 hrs		
	Editing			56 hrs	Work								16.5 hrs	27.5 hrs	12 hrs			
	Final approval			40 hrs	Work										15.5 hrs	24.5 hrs		

Overallocated resources bolded

211

person is scheduled to work 94 hours. That seems a bit much, not allowing time for eating, sleeping, and all of life's other activities. The scriptwriter's first full week is overallocated by 40 hours. The producer's first week is also overallocated at 40 hours. Something must be done, and it will be discussed in the next section.

An examination of this table reveals an interesting anomaly in MSP and most other project management software. Unless specified otherwise, MSP assumes that any resource assigned to an activity will work on that activity 100 percent of the time available on the resource calendar. For example, Figure 6-3, WBS 3.2, "Propose shoots" lists the client as a resource (in addition to the producer and scriptwriter). The activity is scheduled to take 5 days. The PM is aware that in all likelihood the client will only be needed to attend one or two meetings (an hour or two each) to approve or amend the shoots proposed by the producer and scriptwriter. Nonetheless, the resource-loading table (Table 6-3) indicates that the client will spend 40 hours (5 days at 8 hours/day) on the activity.

Were this a large project with a large number and variety of resources, it might be necessary to correct this "error." MSP and other software packages have several ways to do this. The PM could allocate a specific percentage of a resource's time for work on the project, or could restrict the availability of the resource on the calendar, for example. In this case, however, because the client has no cost per hour, and because everyone involved in the project, including the client, understands the nature of the client's work, the matter can be ignored.

Quite apart from problems in scheduling the activities, there are other resource-loading issues that may face the PM. For instance, there are cost and management issues that must be considered. It is easy to overutilize resources, particularly human resources; note the hours required of the scriptwriter and producer during the first days of the project. For hourly workers, overtime work is usually quite expensive. In the case of the scriptwriter, overtime hours are not sufficient, and another writer may be needed for the first 1 or 2 weeks. On the other hand, it is common to find middle managers consistently working 45–60 hours per week—if they have a desire for upward mobility. In the software industry or in architecture, to pick two typical examples, individuals often work 60–80 hours per week or more in order to complete specific projects on time. Because we usually overload our best people, they are the ones most apt to quit and go elsewhere—and they rarely tell us why in their exit interviews. For most senior executives, the workloads are often very heavy—consistently 65–70 or more hours per week. These are the people who are overstressed at the very times they must make momentous decisions.

Such resource-loading documents as Table 6-3 are among management's most frequent requests of the PM, precisely so they can monitor such situations. As we will see in the section on resource leveling, managers sometimes make incorrect assumptions about the capacity of work groups, and the PM must take on an educational role.

The Charismatic VP

The Vice-President and Manager of a division of a large chemical company became aware that a number of projects he had assigned to his subordinates were not being completed on time. Some were finished late, and others were simply unfinished. The VP was tireless, spending 60–80 hours per week at work. He was very well liked, and his people tried hard to please him. If he asked a subordinate if a task could be handled, invariably the answer was "Yes."

The VP began to suspect that he was overcommitting his subordinates. He suggested this to his people, but most of them insisted that they could handle the work. Not entirely convinced, the VP installed a project-oriented management system and initiated resource-loading reports for all personnel doing project work. The reports showed clearly that the division had an urgent need for additional staff engineers.

As is typical of such cases, the individuals most overworked were the most experienced and most skilled people. Those engineers with spare time were the least skilled and, for the most part, recent hires. The untrained remained untrained. The Vice-President, however, altered work assignments and ordered that additional engineers be hired. Overscheduling was limited to 125 percent (50 hours per week), and at that level for a limited time only. A policy of partnering new engineers with experienced cohorts was instituted. Within 6 months, division projects were progressing reasonably on time.

> Resource loading is usually displayed as a list of the amounts of specific resources assigned for use on specific project activities at specific times, or as a graph showing the level of a resource's capacity required against the project calendar. To be useful for scheduling, the resource must have a calendar showing the resource's availability. The calendar should include hours—and days—worked each week, any holidays on which the resource will not be available, and any other information affecting the availability of the resource. Resource cost per unit of usage should be included on the calendar, plus any additional cost for overtime or overuse. Overscheduling a resource may cause serious problems for the PM.

6.3   RESOURCE LEVELING

Look once again at Figure 6-4. Tasks 2, 3.2, and 3.3 are all scheduled to start on March 29. The scriptwriter is required for the first two of the three items and the producer for the last two. The scriptwriter's calendar (Table 6-2) indicates that the scriptwriter can work a 54-hour week—6 days per week at 9 hours per day. The producer is available for a standard 40-hour week. The resource-loading table (Table 6-3) shows the above-mentioned tasks assigned to the scriptwriter and producer. Apparently both are expected to do two different jobs at the same time.

The scriptwriter's conflict must be reduced. Figures 6-5 and 6-6 illustrate the problem clearly. Both illustrations are MSP outputs. Figure 6-5 lists all tasks for which the scriptwriter is scheduled. Figure 6-6 indicates that the scriptwriter is overallocated by a factor of 2 during the period from March 29 to April 2.[*]

WBS	Task Name	Duration	Scheduled Start	Scheduled Finish
				Project start date: 3/29 — Project finish date: 6/11 — Resource Overallocated: Scriptwriter
2	Scriptwriting	14 days	3/29	4/12
3	Schedule shoots	15 days	3/29	4/16
3.2	Propose shoots	5.5 days	3/29	4/2
5	Revise script	6.63 days	4/27	5/4

Prior to resource leveling

Task ▬▬▬   Milestone ◇   Slippage
Split ─ ─ ─ ─   Slack ▬▬▬   Summary ▽▬▬▽

Figure 6-5   Resource overallocation report for scriptwriter showing all activities (MSP).

---

[*]If MSP's Gantt chart view is set to show weekly intervals, it indicates resource usage for an entire week even if the resource is actually used for only 1 day during that week. To see resource usage with more precision, set the MSP calendar to show daily or hourly intervals.

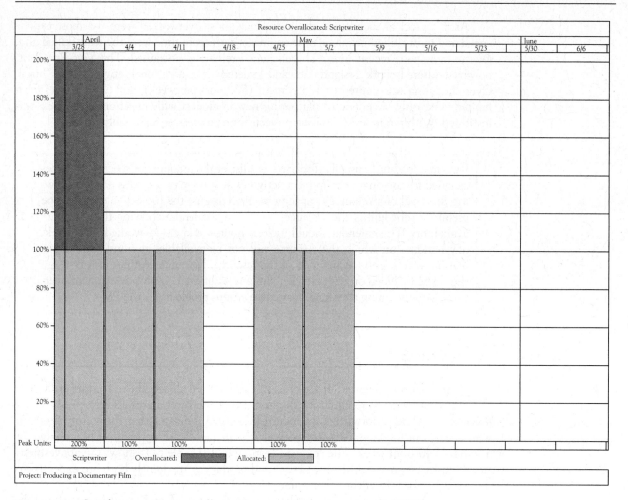

Figure 6-6   Graphic resource overallocation report for scriptwriter (MSP).

Figure 6-5 also shows considerable slack in WBS 3.2. If we ask MSP to level resources, the software will move activities so that resources do not exceed their capacities—and will do so by using available slack first, *where possible*, rather than extending the project duration. (Clearly, the PM could do the same thing manually, but the job becomes complex and time-consuming on all but small projects.) Figures 6-7 and 6-8 show the effect of resource leveling on the scriptwriter's workload. In this case the project duration was not affected because there was sufficient slack in WBS 3.2, and the leveling operation used it. (PMBOK covers the topic of resource leveling in Chapter 6 on Time.)

To understand Figure 6-7 correctly requires an understanding of MSP. The figure appears to report that the scriptwriter is still working overtime on Tasks 2 and 3.2. This would also mean that there was an error in Figure 6-8 that shows no such thing. The scriptwriter's efforts are, in fact, solely devoted to scriptwriting (Task 2), but the producer and the client are working on Task 3.2, so the task is shown as being underway. MSP has split Task 3.2, and the scriptwriter begins work on the task on Monday, April 12 after work on Task 2 has been completed. The second part of Task 3.2 does not begin until all work

Project start date: 3/29
Project finish date: 6/11

Resource Leveled: Scriptwriter

WBS	Task Name	Duration	Scheduled Start	Scheduled Finish
2	Scriptwriting	14 days	3/29	4/12
3	Schedule shoots	25 days	3/29	4/30
3.2	Propose shoots	10 days	3/29	4/16
5	Revise script	6.63 days	4/27	5/4

Gantt chart legend (After resource leveling): Preleveled Task, Preleveled Split, Task, Split, Milestone, Slack, Slippage, Delay, Summary

Task bar labels: Scriptwriter; Scriptwriter, Producer, Client; Scriptwriter, Producer

Figure 6-7 Resource leveled report for scriptwriter showing all activities (MSP).

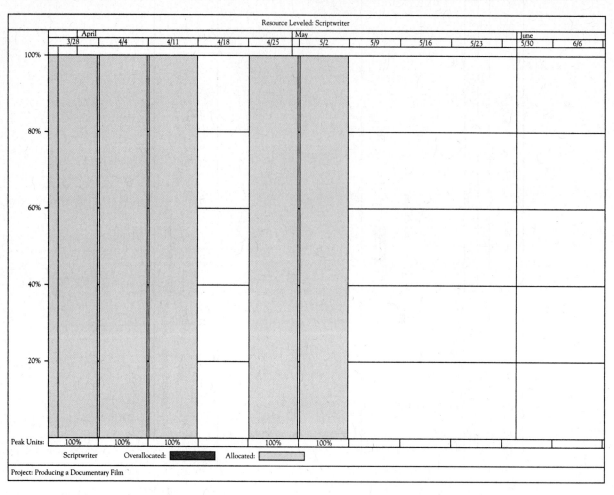

Figure 6-8   Graphic resource leveled report for scriptwriter (MSP).

on Task 2 is complete. It is easy to verify that this has happened. Figure 6-9 shows the resource allocation, after leveling the scriptwriter's workload, using a daily calendar. The scriptwriter is not assigned more than 9 hours per day. On Monday, April 12 work transfers from Task 2 to Task 3.2.

The problem of the still overallocated producer is another matter. This is the same problem we discussed above concerning the client's need to attend some meetings. The fact that the producer is overscheduled is not really a problem. Neither of the conflicting tasks (WBS task 3.2 and 3.3) requires 8 hours per day of work by the producer. The duration of 5 days for Task 3.2 (Propose shoots), for example, indicates that the producer will be spending some time during a 5-day period on the job of proposing locations and settings for filming. Similarly, Task 3.3 (Hire secretary) will require the producer to interview some candidates for the secretarial position during the same 5-day period, but this will not be a full-time job either. The 5-day durations are an indication of when the tasks are expected to be complete. *Task duration is not necessarily dictated by the amount of labor required to complete the task, but by the calendar time required to complete it.* Sometimes, of course, the amount of labor may be the determinant of calendar time, but often it is not.

At this point a short digression is appropriate. As a student of project management reading this book, you probably know little of the reality of the projects used here as

Table 6-4   Daily Resource Loading Chart for DVD Project, Scriptwriter Leveled (MSP)

Producing a Documentary Film
Resource Work Hours
Scriptwriter Leveled

ID	Resource Name	Work	Details	M	T	W	T	F	S	S	M	T	W	T	F	S	S	M	T
	Unassigned																		
	Project approval	0 hrs	Work																
	Begin scheduling	0 hrs	Work																
	Scheduling completed	0 hrs	Work																
	Deliver DVD to client	0 hrs	Work																
1	**Scriptwriter**	192 hrs	Work								9 hrs	9 hrs	9 hrs	9 hrs	9 hrs	9 hrs	9 hrs	9 hrs	9 hrs
	Scriptwriting	112 hrs	Work								9 hrs	9 hrs	9 hrs	9 hrs	9 hrs	9 hrs	9 hrs	4 hrs	9 hrs
	Propose shoots	40 hrs	Work								0 hrs	0 hrs	0 hrs	0 hrs	0 hrs	0 hrs	0 hrs	5 hrs	9 hrs
	Revise script	40 hrs	Work																
2	**Producer**	200 hrs	Work	16 hrs	16 hrs	16 hrs	16 hrs	16 hrs											
	Propose shoots	40 hrs	Work	8 hrs	8 hrs	8 hrs	8 hrs	8 hrs											
	Hire secretary	40 hrs	Work	8 hrs	8 hrs	8 hrs	8 hrs	8 hrs											
	Script approval	40 hrs	Work																
	Revise script	40 hrs	Work																
	Final approval	40 hrs	Work																
3	**Client**	120 hrs	Work	8 hrs	8 hrs	8 hrs	8 hrs	8 hrs											
	Propose shoots	40 hrs	Work	8 hrs	8 hrs	8 hrs	8 hrs	8 hrs											
	Script approval	40 hrs	Work																
	Final approval	40 hrs	Work																
4	**Secretary**	80 hrs	Work																
	Schedule shoots	80 hrs	Work																
5	**Editor**	176 hrs	Work																
	Shooting	80 hrs	Work																
	Editing	56 hrs	Work																
	Final approval	40 hrs	Work																
6	**Production Staff**	80 hrs	Work																
	Shooting	80 hrs	Work																
7	**Editing staff**	56 hrs	Work																
	Editing	56 hrs	Work																
8	**Editing room**	96 hrs	Work																
	Editing	56 hrs	Work																
	Final approval	40 hrs	Work																

Producing a Documentary Film
A. J. Lucas

WBS	Task Name	Resource Names	Duration	Start	Finish
1	Project approval		0 days	3/29	3/29
2	Scriptwriting	Scriptwriter[200%]	7 days	3/29	4/5
3	Schedule shoots		30 days	3/29	5/7
3.1	Begin scheduling		0 days	3/29	3/29
3.2	Propose shoots	Scriptwriter, Producer, Client	10 days	3/29	4/9
3.3	Hire secretary	Producer	5 days	4/5	4/23
3.4	Schedule shoots	Secretary	10 days	4/26	5/7
3.5	Scheduling completed		0 days	5/7	5/7
4	Script approval	Producer, Client	5 days	4/5	4/12
5	Revise script	Scriptwriter, Producer	5.5 days	4/12	4/19
6	Shooting	Editor, Production Staff	10 days	4/19	5/3
7	Editing	Editor, Editing staff, Editing room	10.06 days	5/3	5/17
8	Final approval	Producer, Client, Editing room, Editor	7.19 days	5/17	5/26
9	Deliver DVD to client		0 days	5/26	5/26

Start date: 3/29
Finish date: 5/26

Additional scriptwriter added to activity 2

Task   Milestone ◇   Summary   Split

Figure 6-9   Final DVD project Gantt chart schedule, with two scriptwriters and producer leveled (MSP).

examples of this or that project management problem. As a PM working on a real-world project, you know a great deal more about the reality of your project than could possibly be explained in this book on the subject. The PM of the documentary project knows that there will be no problem raised by the apparent conflict in the allocation of the producer's time. The PM could have used one of the methods we noted in the discussion of resource loading to handle the matter, but elected not to take the time and effort. This, then, is another of the trade-offs the PM must make. Not every facet of a project requires equal managerial care. The PM must decide where to expend his or her managerial efforts—and then take responsibility for the decision.

Trade-Offs

A resource allocation decision may be intended to avoid future problems rather than to cure a present problem. While the scriptwriter is not overallocated, the PM decided to add a second scriptwriter to WBS 2. The PM also leveled the producer's apparent overallocation just to add some slack to the producer's schedule. Both of these additions were made to ensure that the project was not made late by a glitch in the producer's work or in the scriptwriting activity, which is on the project's critical path. (See Section 6.5 for additional information about the advisability of having some excess capacity in projects.) The result of all these moves is seen in Figure 6-9. The project can be finished 2 weeks or 16 days earlier than indicated in Figure 6-4.

When resources are added to a project, the PM may be asked to explain just how the project budget came to be underestimated. To answer such a question, the PM would be well advised to contact the administration of any large city that has recently built a sports stadium.

A more or less steady state demand for human resources is highly desirable—if it is not seriously inconsistent with the technological demands of the project. The cost of adding, laying-off, or permanently releasing human beings is very high for both hourly and salaried personnel. If the parent organization is quite large and is operating many projects that have reasonably high commonality in their demand for certain skills, it is often possible to set up "pools" for such skills as clerical, machine operation, and similar types of workers. When pools are used to supply resources for projects, careful records must be kept to ensure fast determination of skill availability and that the proper charges are made to all projects.

Pools of like resources from which labor can be added temporarily to projects tend to cut costs for the firm as a whole. Pools also cut the cost of managing the project. The PM's job is made easier, and the cash flows of the project are less volatile. The PM will spend far less time trying to find and recruit personnel. Such pools, however, are useful only if the labor is not subdivided into highly specialized subtasks. Secretarial skills are less specialized than, say, the skills required to design, generate, or test computer software. The conclusion is that secretarial pools are feasible, but that software design, generation, and testing should be done by "teams" in which the required specialists are available.

Resource Loading/Leveling and Uncertainty

Figure 6-10 is a resource-loading chart for a software engineering group in a large firm. The chart depicts the total number of hours required of a resource group (all members from one department assigned to the firm's projects) displayed against the group's capacity. (MSP resource-loading information was exported to an Excel® spreadsheet and displayed graphically. The process of producing such displays is not difficult.) There are 21 members of the group. They are scheduled for 40 hours per 5-day week by the firm. Figure 6-10 covers a 34-week period. The graph shows estimated work-hours (28,282) committed by this team for projects that are currently on the company's books. The delivery-date commitments are such that group workloads exceed the group's capacity through much of March and April, for a brief period in the middle of

May, and again in the latter part of June. (The total of these overloads is 1,747 hours, or a bit more than 83 hours per person.)

A rough estimate of group capacity is

$$21 \text{ (people)} \times 40 \text{ (hours per week)} \times 34 \text{ (weeks)} = 28,560 \text{ labour-hours}$$

But a few corrections are in order. There are three national holidays in the period: Memorial Day, the Fourth of July, and Labor Day. The time lost for the holidays is

$$21 \times 3 \text{ (days)} \times 8 \text{ (hours)} = 504 \text{ labour-hours}$$

which lowers capacity to 28,056 labor-hours. Assume further that 11 people take a 2-week vacation during the 34-week period, a conservative assumption given the fact that the period includes May through September. The time for 11 vacations is an additional capacity loss of

$$11 \times 2 \text{ (weeks)} \times 40 = 880 \text{ labor-hours}$$

There are now $28,056 - 880 = 27,176$ labor-hours available, and even if the group's work were evenly distributed across the 34-week period, the team's capacity is about 1,100 less than the scheduled demand for work. The workload is $28,282/27,176 = 1.04$ or 104 percent of capacity.

A 4 percent shortage of capacity does not seem like much. Why not increase the hours worked per week for these salaried software engineers to 41.6 hours per week? The added capacity will (roughly) equal the estimated workload. While such a move might help, it would not begin to solve the problem. For instance, is it likely that no engineers in the group will be ill and absent on any of the 170 workdays? Is it likely . . . no; is it possible that every task the group is scheduled to perform will be ready for the group's work exactly on schedule? Is it possible that all required facilities and equipment will be available when needed? Is it possible that there will be no change orders extending the time required for any phase of the work the group is committed to complete? In reality, the probability that any of the above conditions will be met is, as mathematicians are wont to say, vanishingly small. But even if they were met, what about that large bulge of work required in March and April?

Figure 6-10
Thirty-four-week resource loading chart for a software engineering group (MSP and Excel®).

For many years, the study of Operations Management has included the subject of "line balancing." (See Meredith and Shafer, 2013, pp 55 ff.) The purpose of line balancing is to construct a manufacturing production line such that the individual production units on the line can generate the required amount of product with as little excess capacity as possible. Minimizing excess capacity in the elements of a production line is one test of production line efficiency. This concept, when applied to the resources used by projects—as it often is—is a precursor to disaster. Even in production lines, some excess capacity is required to deal with minor problems and variations that arise during the production process. In projects, the level of uncertainty surrounding the "production process" is so much greater that the amount of excess capacity in the work force needs to be much larger. If this flies in the face of managerial instinct, it is because that instinct is sometimes in error. We will revisit this problem in the following section.

The result of the situation displayed in Figure 6-10 is that all the projects to which this team of engineers is devoted are going to be late and over budget unless some drastic steps are taken to prevent it. The firm in question is known for high-quality work, and it is assumed that the projects will be completed more or less on time with a reasonable percent of the promised specifications in place and working. How this comes about is quite simple. Engineers in this firm are scheduled to work a 40-hour week. They do not, however, work 40-hour weeks. They average between 50 and 60 hours per week. At a 55-hour week, for example, the capacity of the group is approximately 37,500 labor-hours. Given the 28,282 labor-hour workload, the system would operate, on average, at about 75 percent of capacity—which explains the engineering group's ability to meet most of its delivery-date commitments.

> Most project management software will, when asked politely, level out the loads (usage) for individual resources and warn the PM when a resource is scheduled for greater-than-capacity workloads. Whenever possible, the leveling will utilize any available activity slack rather than extend the duration of the project. When a resource is assigned to an activity, it is assigned for 100 percent of its availability unless the PM specifies otherwise.
>
> It is often necessary to have significant excess resource capacity on projects because of the uncertainty that exists in all projects. Dealing with this issue is a major reason for the installation of a competent risk-management system.

Risk

6.4 ALLOCATING SCARCE RESOURCES TO PROJECTS

When we leveled resources in the case of the overworked scriptwriter, MSP simply used the available activity slack to reschedule WBS item 3.2 (see Figure 6-9). The project completion date was not altered because the WBS 3.2's slack was large enough to swallow the added time. Often, that is not possible and the software needs instruction about what priority to use when allocating scarce resources to several tasks—which tasks should get the resources immediately and go first, and which may be delayed. In order to select a suitable method for assigning priorities, we need to understand how the problem is solved.

Most solutions start with the PERT/CPM schedule. Given this initial solution, each activity is examined period by period and resource by resource. If the demand for a resource exceeds its supply, the software considers the tasks one by one and assigns resources to the tasks according to some priority rule chosen by the PM. Tasks that receive resources under this rule proceed as originally scheduled. Tasks that do not get resources are delayed until ongoing tasks are completed and the required resources are freed-up for use. If this increases the project duration, the change will be visible on the project's Gantt chart or network as it was when the videotape project client was not available while on vacation. (See Figures 6-3, 6-4, and 6-9.) No matter what priority rule is used, the project's technology always takes precedence.

Some Comments about Constrained Resources

Every time a project falls behind schedule, the PM is apt to plead for more resources. In spite of the PM's complaints about the scarcity of resources, serious cases of resource scarcity rarely apply to resources in general, but rather to one or two very specific resources. We call such resources "Walts." The term was derived from the name of an individual, Walter A., who is employed by a large insurance company. Walt is a specialist in the rules and laws affecting insurance policies for certain types of casualty losses in the firm's commercial lines of business. He has an excellent analytical mind and many years of experience. His knowledge is required when designing new policies in this area of risk. The firm has only one Walt, and while the firm is training others, such training takes years. Walt is a true scarce resource. Projects requiring Walt's input are scheduled around his availability.

There are many other examples. Military combat missions may be scheduled around the availability of attack aircraft. Construction projects may be scheduled around the availability of a large crane. A Broadway opening may be scheduled around the availability of a star actress. The key problem to be solved is deciding which activities get the scarce resource and in what order.

Some Priority Rules

There are many possible rules for assigning preference to some activities over others when allocating scarce resources. Most popular project management software packages have a limited number of rules that can be automatically applied to level overallocated resources so many of the priority rules for assigning scarce resources to activities may have to be applied manually. Fortunately, as we will see, this is not as difficult as it might seem. Several of the most commonly used rules are as follows:

As soon as possible—This is the standard rule in scheduling. Activities are scheduled to start on their earliest start times (ES), and resources are made available with that in mind.

As late as possible—With this rule, resources are made available so that activities start on their latest start times (LS) whenever possible without increasing the project's duration. This may seem irrational, but it preserves the firm's resources and delays cash outflows as long as possible. This rule is also compatible with Eliyahu Goldratt's contention that the "student syndrome" leads workers to delay starting an activity until the last possible moment (Goldratt, 1997, Ch. 13).

Shortest task duration first—Always consistent with technological precedences, shorter tasks are given priority over longer tasks. This rule maximizes the number of tasks that can be completed by a system in a given time period.

Minimum slack first—Tasks are supplied with resources in inverse order of their slacks. This rule usually minimizes the number of late activities.

Most critical followers—The number of successors on the critical path(s) for each activity is counted. Activities with a higher number of critical successors take precedence. The rationale here is that such activities would cause the greatest damage to the desired project schedule if they are late.

Most successors—The same as the previous rule except that all successors are counted. This rule has the same rationale as the preceding rule.

Most resources first—With this rule, the greater the use of a specific resource on a task, the higher the task's priority for the resource. This rule is based on the assumption that more important activities have a greater demand for scarce resources.

In addition to these rules, there are many others. For example, it may be company policy to put favored customers' projects at the head of the resource line—or to reserve special resources for such clients by withholding them from the available supply. The same type of favoritism is sometimes shown to specific projects of high value to the parent firm. (Some firms show favoritism to specific high-value *activities*, but this rule makes little sense because *all* activities of an individual project must be completed to finish the project.) Application of a value measure for allocating scarce resources across several projects is both rational and common.

There are many other priority rules that might be used, but most project management software packages recognize only a few; however, assigning scarce resources manually is not difficult. From our earlier example, recall Figure 6-5, in which all tasks requiring the scriptwriter were listed alone on a Gantt chart showing the task duration, scheduled start, scheduled finish, activity slack, and other needed information. The scheduled start dates would allow us to apply either the early or late start rules. Information on activity slack allows us to use the minimum slack rule. Task duration is the necessary input to apply the Shortest Task Duration rule. The project network, Gantt chart, and the task list all allow a simple count of followers, critical or not. MSP and most other project management software allow verbal or numeric priorities to be assigned easily. This allows the use of any priority system required.

Considerable research has been done on these rules* and the minimum slack rule is usually best or second best. It rarely performs poorly. If a high-slack task is not given resources in one period, its slack is automatically decreased and in the next period it has a better chance of receiving resources. The resource allocation is repeated periodically (hourly, daily, weekly, or monthly, etc.), depending on the time frame of the project's activities. If a task becomes critical, that is, all the slack is used up before the activity receives resources, the project will be delayed. We will consider borrowing resources from ongoing tasks when we discuss the allocation of scarce resources among several projects.

> When a resource is overallocated, MSP can level resource usage by adopting a variety of priority rules, including available activity slack. If there is insufficient slack, other priority rules may be used to allocate the scarce resource. Most of the priority rules originated as job shop scheduling rules. The minimum slack rule usually works best. Only a few critical resources are actually scarce in the sense that project schedules must be adjusted to resource availability.

6.5 ALLOCATING SCARCE RESOURCES TO SEVERAL PROJECTS

When the problem of allocating scarce resources is extended to the case when several projects are being carried out concurrently, the size and complexity of the problem increase but the nature of the underlying problem remains the same. The projects might be independent or members of one large superproject. In any case, there is a decided advantage if several projects are joined as a set.

---

*Kurtulus and Davis (1982) and Kurtulus and Narula (1985) in two excellent research papers extended the earlier work of Fendley. They tested many more priority rules than can be covered here.

Consider a single project for a moment. It is composed of a set of first-level tasks connected in a technological relationship of predecessors and successors. Each first-level task is composed of a set of second-level tasks, also arranged in technologically determined ways. The second-level tasks are divided into third-level tasks, and so on, much like the fleas in Jonathon Swift's famous verse:

> So, naturalists observe, a flea
> Hath smaller fleas that on him prey;
> And these have smaller still to bite 'em;
> And so proceed *ad infinitum.*

If we take several projects, we can link them together with *pseudoactivities,* here defined as activities that have duration but do not require any resources. The set of projects linked in such a way becomes a sort of superproject and can be "managed" like any other. We can use the pseudoactivities to establish precedences between the projects they connect, and thus we can separate the projects in time. This is simplest to illustrate as an AOA network (see Figure 6-11), but a Gantt chart could be used by displaying the projects with leads and lags. Each node in Figure 6-11 represents a project, and the arrows connecting them are pseudoactivities. The temporal relationships of the projects are altered by varying the duration of the pseudoactivities.

The individual projects are interrelated by specifying predecessor/successor relationships in MSP. Thus they appear (to MSP) to be parts of one project. If the original project calendars are put on the same time base (exactly as we did with individual activities when scarce resources were allocated among several activities in a single project), we can use the single-project resource-allocation methods for several projects at a time. (MSP's ability to handle projects with a very large number of activities on multiple levels is not limited by the software but by the size of the computer's memory.) MSP can also easily link many large projects, treated as separate and independent, but they share the same set of resources. The pseudoactivities may represent technological relationships among the projects—which will often be the case when individual projects are parts of an overall program. Pseudoactivities may separate projects according to planned delivery dates, or the separations may be completely arbitrary.

Putting a set of projects into a format that deals with them as a single project allows us to use MSP's resource loading and leveling charts and tables. Remembering that the calendars of all projects should be adjusted to the same time-base, we can examine

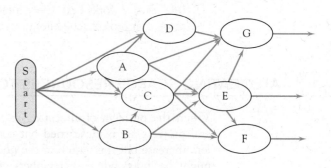

Figure 6-11 Multiple projects connected with pseudoactivities shown on a time line.

Months

the status of resource allocation—or overallocation—for all activities in all projects over any time period. By using the leveling routines, we can also examine the consequences of adopting different resource allocation priority rules. Further, we can examine the implications of adding more resources by comparing the costs of additional resources with the costs that might accrue from late deliveries or delays if the resources are not added. The assignment and handling of various priority rules are, of course, the same as in the single project case. The number of cases to be investigated will be larger in the multiproject case, but few genuine Walts are involved. Extending or contracting the pseudoactivities is the mechanism by which we change the start or finish dates of projects in order to avoid overallocation of Walts.

Criteria of Priority Rules

Whatever the priority rule, the PM faces the problem of choosing between the alternative outcomes that result from different priority rules, as well as different arrangements and durations of the pseudoactivities. There are many measurable criteria available to help us choose a priority rule. The most useful for projects are *schedule slippage, resource utilization,* and *in-process inventory.*

Trade-Offs

Schedule slippage simply measures the amount by which a project, or a set of projects, is delayed by application of a leveling rule (or by extending a pseudoactivity so that a project finishes later because it starts later). As we noted above, the PM (and senior management) must trade off penalty costs or the possible displeasure of clients against the cost of adding resources, if that is possible, or by reducing the overallocation of Walts. Just as serious is the ripple effect that often occurs when a delay in one project causes a delay in others. Indeed, expediting one project typically causes disturbances in the schedules of others.

The shortest-task-first rule for assigning resources minimizes the level of in-process inventory or how much unfinished work is in the system. Clients have little desire to pay for things they have not yet received—though partial prepayment is sometimes arranged by contract—and the organization carrying out projects may have large quantities of human and material resources invested in projects that have little value until they are complete.

Best Practice

The minimum slack rule is probably the best overall priority rule according to research on the subject. It gives the best combination of minimum project slippage, minimum resource idle-time, and minimum in-process inventory (Fendley, 1968). While first-come-first-served may be the client's idea of "fair," it is a poor priority rule when measured against almost any of the others. If the minimum slack rule produces ties among two or more projects (or activities), the shortest task rule seems to be the best tie-breaker.

The Basic Approach

It is now appropriate to stop for a moment and consider a matter. The basic approach taken here to solve project loading and leveling problems is borrowed from a manufacturing model that has widespread application and works equally well for projects. Our problem is that there exists a set of activities belonging to one or more projects all eager for processing by a limited set of facilities or other resources. Not all activities require the same subset of facilities or resources, and some activities are more in need of immediate attention than others. To make matters worse, some activities need more work than others, and some insist (for technological reasons, of course, rather than natural cussedness) on being dealt with before some others.

As if this were not enough, the activities do not have access to the facility or resources at precise, predetermined times so the PM or facility manager does not know—with any great precision—when to expect specific activities to be ready for processing. Finally, even when an activity does arrive, and when the facility is ready to begin, there may still be considerable uncertainty about exactly how much time it requires to do the processing. Remember that we are discussing the unfinished outputs of some projects. They have completed a previous activity and are now waiting for resources to engage in the next activity for which they are scheduled. All of these activities involve the use of a scarce resource (or two) that we must allocate to the waiting activities.

In this setting, a scarce facility (resource) is like a bottleneck. A line or queue of activities waiting to be processed forms in front of the processor. Assume that jobs arriving to join the queue arrive randomly at an average or expected rate of λ jobs per unit of time. Also assume that the time required for the processor to service the activities is random and has an average or expected rate of μ jobs per unit of time. The behavior of queues has been studied for many years and under our assumptions, not unreasonable for the constrained resource, multiproject problem, the average number of jobs in the waiting line is given by $J = (\lambda/\mu)/(1 - \lambda/\mu)$. Note what happens when the arrival rate of tasks approaches the system's capacity, for example λ approaches. μ. J, the number of jobs in the queue, heads toward infinity. This supports our earlier contention that production or servicing systems must have excess capacity unless they are tightly controlled assembly-line type operations—and even these need a small amount of excess capacity to handle the normal, small variations in arrival or service rates.

Resource Allocation and the Project Life Cycle

Whatever the scheduling rule, the scheduling method assigns scarce resources to activities on the basis of the degree to which the activity meets some priority conditions. Once the most urgent cases (as measured by the priority rule) have been given resources, the next most urgent cases receive their resources. The process continues until there are no more activities qualified under the rule.

If all critical activities demanding scarce resources are supplied, but the remaining stock of scarce resources is depleted before all noncritical activities are resource loaded, the less urgent activities go unsupplied. When this happens, the less urgent activities become more urgent as period after period passes until they rise far enough up the priority rank list and receive their resources. But what happens if the stock of scarce resources is depleted before all the critical activities receive resources? For example, when using the minimum slack rule, what happens if we run out of our scarce resource before we run out of critical (zero slack) activities?

When this condition occurs, it is often possible to borrow some resources from another (ongoing) activity that is lower on the priority list, that is, has some slack in the case of the minimum slack rule. Perhaps we could even deschedule such an activity and take all the scarce resource being used, restoring the scarce resource later when the descheduled activity has risen higher on the priority list. The decision about whether to borrow some resources from a high-slack ongoing task or whether to stop the task and use all its resources is made by looking at the implication of either action on the project. Borrowing the scarce resource may only slow down progress on an activity or it may stop the activity altogether. If borrowing does the latter, it would make sense to borrow all other resources at the same time.

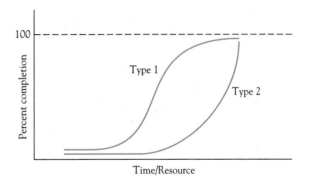

Figure 6-12
Project or task life
cycles.

We can also use our knowledge of the project's life cycle to help make the decision. Figure 6-12 shows both types of project life cycle that were discussed in Chapter 1, Section 1.4. The Type 1 life cycle shows decreasing returns to additional resources toward the end of the project. If we borrow from or deschedule activities late in the life of a Type 1 project, we lose proportionately little from the project. If we borrow from or deschedule activities late in the life of a Type 2 project, we may destroy it completely. On the other hand, if the borrowing or descheduling is done near the middle of the life of the project, our conclusion might be exactly the opposite. We need to understand the general shape of the project's life cycle curve in order to assess the implications of slowing or stopping it.

Allocating scarce resources among multiple projects is more complicated than the single project case, but is not different in its basic logic. The several projects are linked with pseudoactivities and treated as if they were the individual activities of a single project. Schedule slippage, resource utilization, and in-process inventory are measures of the goodness of any priority rule.

Much of the allocation problem results because project facilities/resources have insufficient excess capacity to handle the uncertainties associated with projects. The shape of the project's life cycle helps determine whether or not resources can be borrowed from ongoing activities to supply stalled activities with critical resource needs.

6.6 GOLDRATT'S *CRITICAL CHAIN*

Much research has been done on scheduling with constrained resources, and the findings verify what was expected—projects are completed faster when there are fewer of them struggling for attention from a limited set of facilities (Adler, Mandelbaum, Nguyen, and Schwerer, 1996). More recently, in the book *Critical Chain* (1997) Eliyahu Goldratt applies his Theory of Constraints—so brilliantly developed in his famous book, *The Goal* (Goldratt and Cox, 1992)—to the constrained resource problem. While Goldratt's focus in the *Critical Chain* is on a single project with multiple demands on a scarce resource, the logic extends to the multiproject case without alteration. PMBOK covers the critical chain in Chapter 6 on Project Time Management.

In the following few pages you will note that the exposition focuses mainly on scheduling. But isn't this chapter supposed to be about resource usage? It should be quite clear by now that resource usage and project schedules are inextricably bound together. The technological necessities that force schedules to be ordered in very

PMBOK Guide

specific ways simultaneously force resources to be used in very specific ways. To schedule work is also to schedule resource usage. If technology is the prime force behind scheduling the activities of a project, resource availability constrains all solutions to the scheduling problem.

To begin our discussion of Goldratt's approach, imagine for the moment that you are sitting in a room full of people with extensive experience as both project team members and project managers. Now imagine the responses you would hear if the group were asked the question: "What things bugged you most about the projects you have been involved with?" Typical of the responses that we have gotten to that question are:

- Project due dates are too often unrealistic.

- There are too many changes made in the project's scope.

- Key resources and data are often unavailable when needed.

- The budget is frequently unrealistic and therefore often exceeded.

- It seems like my project is always in competition for resources with other projects.

One interesting observation is that these same issues are raised regardless of the organizational context. Thus we hear strikingly similar complaints regardless of whether the group is referring to a construction project, a software development project, a project to develop an advertising campaign, or an R&D project. Hussain and Wearne (2005) asked more than 1000 project managers to identify the "greatest problem of project management," a subtly different question than we asked, and they found that project "organization," "resource," and "time" issues were paramount. ("Change in scope was ranked 11th in their research.) Based on these findings, it is not farfetched to conclude that the causes of these problems are generic to all types of projects. As we have discussed throughout this book, project management is fundamentally concerned with effectively trading off scope, cost, and time. Referring back to the lists of complaints, it can be seen that each issue (excepting "organization") deals with one or more of the three primary project objectives.

Given our conclusion that the problems encountered when managing projects are strongly related to the need to trade off one project objective for another, a natural question arises about the extent to which the need to make these trade-offs are caused by human decisions and practices. In other words, can more effective project management minimize the occurrence of these problems? To investigate this issue, let's examine the complaint regarding unrealistic due dates in more detail.

One way to investigate this issue is to see if we can identify any generally accepted practices that would tend to cause the shared perception of many project workers that project due dates are often set too optimistically. To make our discussion more concrete, consider the three AOA network diagrams shown in Figure 6-13. The primary difference between the three diagrams is the degree of interdependence across the paths. In scenario 1, there is only a single path. In scenario 2, the path B-C-D-E is preceded by three activities: A1, A2, and A3. Therefore, the completion of path B-C-D-E depends on which of its three preceding tasks takes the longest. In scenario 3 there are two completely independent paths each consisting of five tasks.

Assume that as project manager you are told that all of the tasks in the three network diagrams require 10 days to complete. What completion time would you calculate for each project? If you assume that the activity times are known with certainty, then all three projects would have the same duration of 50 days. If you find this result somewhat unsettling, you are in good company. Thinking about it intuitively, how can a simple project like scenario 1 with a single path and only five activities have the same duration as scenario 2 with three paths and seven activities, or with scenario 3 with two paths and ten activities?

Figure 6-13   Three project scenarios.

(Scenario 1)

(Scenario 2)

(Scenario 3)

Part of the problem is our assumption that the activity times are known with certainty. To investigate this further, let's assume that all activity times are normally distributed with a mean of 10 days and standard deviation of three. The results of simulating the completion of the three projects 200 times each are summarized in Table 6-5.

As you can see from Table 6-5, removing the assumption that the activity times are known with certainty leads to quite different results. Scenario 1's average duration was slightly higher than the 50 we calculated earlier under the assumption of deterministic time estimates. To a large extent with this linear structure and with our assumption of normally distributed activity times, activities that take less than the expected time tend to cancel out the variability of activities that take more than the expected time, resulting in an overall average completion time that is close to the expected completion time for the project. (Remember, in Chapter 5 we discovered that this canceling out rarely happens in the real world, because activities may start late or on time, but rarely start early because resources are usually not available before the activity's earliest start time.) Also observe that the more interdependent scenarios 2 and 3, on average, take even longer than scenario 1 and that their minimum times are significantly longer than scenario 1's minimum time.

Most important, note that while the average completion times of the projects are still close to 50, this is simply the average project completion time after simulating the execution of each project 200 times. That is, approximately 50 percent of the time the projects will be completed in less than 50 days and 50 percent of the time the projects will be completed in more than 50 days under the reasonable assumption that the distribution of project completion times follows a symmetrical distribution. (Note that

Table 6-5   Project Completion Time Statistics Based on Simulating Three Projects 200 Times

	Scenario 1	Scenario 2	Scenario 3
Average	50.4	51.9	53.4
Std. Dev.	7.1	6.3	5.3
Max.	69.4	72.7	69.3
Min.	30.1	36.1	39.3
Median	50.0	51.8	53.1

here we are referring to the distribution of project completion times as being symmetrical, not the project activity times.) In other words, had we determined the project duration based on the assumption that the activity times are known with certainty (when they were actually probabilistic), we would incur a greater than 50 percent chance that the actual project duration would exceed this estimate. How would you like to have responsibility for a project that has less than a 50 percent chance of being completed on time? *This example clearly demonstrates how the commonly made assumption of known activity times in practice can lead to quite unrealistic project deadlines.*

It is important to point out that the results would have been even more dramatic had the activities required some common resources. Similarly, the results would have been more dramatic and realistic had a nonsymmetrical distribution been used to model the activity times. Why, you might ask, would a nonsymmetrical distribution more realistically model the activity times? Suppose you scheduled a status meeting to last 20 minutes. Is there *any* chance the meeting will last 40 minutes longer than expected, or 60 minutes? What about 40 minutes less, or –20 minutes?

Estimating Task Times

Based on the discussion to this point and assuming that project workers have a general desire to be recognized for good performance, what do you imagine project workers do when they are asked to provide time estimates for tasks if they will be held responsible for actual task duration? Do you think they give an estimate that they believe provides them with only a 50 percent chance of being met? Or, more likely, do you imagine they inflate or *pad* their estimate to increase the likelihood of successfully completing the task on time? What would you do?

If you are like most people, you would inflate your time estimate. Unfortunately, inflated time estimates tend to create even more problems. First, inflating the time estimate has no impact on the actual probability distribution of completing the activity. Second, what do you imagine happens in cases when a project team member finishes early? All too often, the team member believes that it is in his or her best interest to remain silent about completing activities in less than the allotted time so that future time estimates are not automatically discounted by management based on a track record of early task completions. Moreover, there are sometimes penalties or additional costs associated with early completion, such as the need to store partially finished materials because the resources required for the next activity are not yet available. Third, just as things tend to fill available closet and storage space in your home, work tends to fill available time. Thus, the work done on the task may be expanded to fill the available time, as Parkinson's Law dictates.

Perhaps even more dangerous than the inflated estimate becoming a self-fulfilling prophecy is that, after receiving approval for a task based on an inflated time estimate, workers may perceive that they now have plenty of time to complete the task and therefore *delay starting the task*. As we noted in Chapter 5, Goldratt (1997) refers to this as the *student syndrome*, likening it to the way students often delay writing a term paper until the last minute. The problem of delaying the start of a task is that obstacles are frequently not discovered until the task has been underway for some time. By delaying the start of the task, the opportunity to cope with these obstacles and complete the task on time is greatly diminished.

In summary, we observe that the common practice of simply adding up task durations often leads to unrealistic project due dates. This is primarily the result of assuming the task times are known with certainty, and that we ignore path mergers and assume that the paths are independent. A natural consequence of this is that project team members will tend to inflate their time estimates. Inflated time estimates further compound the problem, particularly in cases where the student syndrome comes into play. In other words, this system tends to cause unethical behavior.

In our discussion we used computer simulation to investigate the impact that increasing interdependencies in a project network has on the distribution of project completion times. Crystal Ball® can also be used to investigate a variety of issues related to resource allocation. To illustrate this, let's investigate the impact of not reporting early completion times.

The Effect of Not Reporting Early Activity Completion

Once again, refer to Table 5-8 and consider the project described, solved, and then simulated in Chapter 5. When simulating this problem, we suggested that you should save the spreadsheet you created because we intended to use this problem in Chapter 6. We used BetaPERT distributions to reflect the uncertainty in activity duration times. The same distributions can be used, but in order to reflect Goldratt's contention (and ours) that early completion times go unreported (and even if they were reported, the appropriate resources would probably not be available because managers avoid gathering resources until the last moment), we can truncate the distributions so that the lower bound is equal to the most likely time estimate. In effect, this means that no time below the most likely time can be reported. The required changes are easily made.

1. Call up the spreadsheet for the simulation you performed for the project shown in Table 5-8.

2. Click on cell **A3**. Then click on **Define Assumption** in the CB ribbon.

3. The BetaPERT distribution you used for the prior simulation will appear. In the box above the **Minimum** box, type in the most likely time for the activity—10 days for activity **a** as shown in Figure 6-14. Then click on **OK**.

4. Proceed to alter each of the activities **b-h** (excepting **d**, which is a constant) similarly.

5. Simulate the project 1,000 times.

Figure 6-15 shows the statistical results of the simulation. A comparison of this figure with Table 5-19 clearly shows the impact of a failure to report early activity finishes. The mean completion time is increased by approximately 2.5 percent. The time for completion with a 95 percent probability ($Z = 1.645$) increases by 4.6 percent.

The main lesson to be learned is that single point estimates of activity duration are not adequate for planning real-world projects. For a number of reasons discussed above, the earlys and lates do not cancel out. The most likely time is, therefore, not a satisfactory substitute for a three-time estimate of activity duration.

Multitasking

Up to this point, our perspective has been a single project. We now investigate another problem created by conventional practice—the practice of assigning people concurrently to multiple projects.

Figure 6-14 Truncated BetaPERT distribution for activity **a** reflecting the assumption that early completion times are not reported.

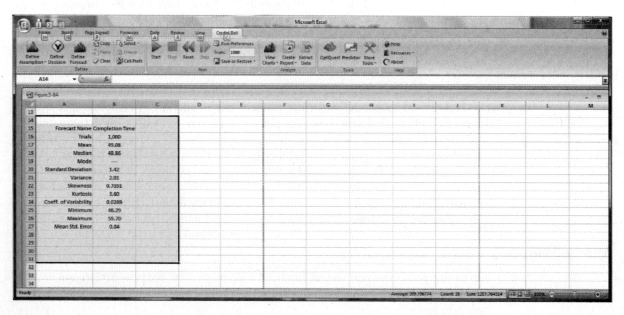

Figure 6-15 Summary statistics for project completion times when early activity completion times are not reported.

Figure 6-16 Two small projects.

☐ You   ☐ Other resources

When project team members are assigned to multiple projects, they have to allocate their time across these projects or *multitask*. Multitasking involves switching from a task associated with one project to another task associated with a different project. To illustrate this, consider the two small projects shown in Figure 6-16. The completion of each of the projects' three tasks requires you and one additional resource. Further, the completion of each task requires 5 days.

In Figures 6-17(a) and 6-17(b), Gantt charts have been developed for two alternative ways of completing the tasks. In Gantt chart 6-17(a), you switch between projects after each task is completed, while in Gantt chart 6-17(b) you complete all of your assigned tasks for Project A before beginning any work on Project B. In both of these cases the two projects are finished in 25 days; therefore, aren't both sequences equally desirable? The answer is absolutely not. First, while it is true that in both cases Project B is finished by time 25, in the first sequence Project A finishes in 20 days, while in the second sequence Project A finishes 5 days earlier. Therefore, the sequence shown in the second Gantt chart is preferable because it results in Project A finishing 5 days earlier with no penalty to Project B.

Even more important, our analysis overlooks another significant factor. Specifically, there is typically a penalty or cost associated with switching from working on one project to another. In your own experience as a student, is it more efficient to complete the assignment for one course and then move on to another course or is it more efficient to complete one project management homework problem, then move on to an accounting problem, then on to a statistics problem, then back to a project management problem, and so on? Obviously each time you switch to a different course you have to retrieve the appropriate textbook, find the right page, recall where you left off, and (perhaps most significantly) get into the proper frame of mind. As this example demonstrates, switching attention from project to project is likely to extend activity times. Eliminating such switching costs further increases the benefits associated with the Gantt chart shown in Figure 6-17(b).

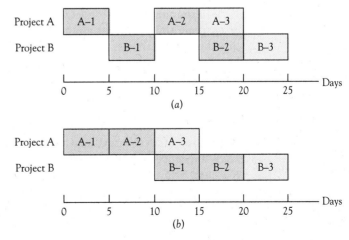

Figure 6-17 Alternative Gantt charts for projects A and B.

Common Chain of Events

According to Goldratt, the activities discussed above lead to the following chain of events:

1. Assuming that activity times are known and that the paths are independent leads to underestimating the actual amount of time needed to complete the project.

2. Because the time needed to complete the project is underestimated, project team members tend to inflate their time estimates.

3. Inflated time estimates lead to work filling available time, workers not reporting that a task has been completed early, and the ever-present student syndrome.

4. An important caveat then becomes that safety time is usually visible to project workers and is often misused.

5. Misused safety time results in missed deadlines and milestones.

6. Hidden safety time further complicates the task of prioritizing project activities.

7. The lack of clear priorities likely results in poor multitasking.

8. Task durations increase as a result of poor multitasking.

9. Uneven demand on resources—some overloaded and others underloaded—may also occur as a result of poor multitasking.

10. In an effort to utilize all resources fully, more projects will be undertaken to make sure that no resources are underutilized. (Recall the impact of this policy from our discussion of waiting lines in Section 6.5.)

11. Adding more projects further increases poor multitasking.

According to Goldratt, this chain of events leads to a vicious cycle. Specifically, as work continues to pile up, team members are pressured to do more poor multitasking. Increasing the amount of poor multitasking leads to longer activity times. Longer activity times lead to longer project completion times, which ultimately lead to more projects in the waiting line.

It might have occurred to you that one way to reverse this cycle would be to add more resources. According to Goldratt, however, the appropriate response is to reduce the number of projects assigned to each person in an effort to reduce the amount of bad multitasking. Incidentally, a simple way to measure the amount of bad multitasking is to calculate the difference between the time required to do the work for a task and the elapsed time actually required to complete the task.

Determining when to release projects into the system is the primary mechanism for ensuring that the right amount of work is assigned to each person. If projects are started too early, they simply add to the chaos and contribute to poor multitasking. On the other hand, if projects are started too late, key resources may go underutilized and projects will be inevitably delayed.

Trade-Offs

Consistent with his Theory of Constraints, Goldratt suggests that the key to resolving this trade-off is to schedule the start of new projects based on the availability of bottleneck resources or Walts. Goldratt further suggests that time buffers be created between resources that feed bottleneck resources and the bottleneck resources.

While properly scheduling the start of new projects does much to address the problems associated with poor multitasking, it does little to address the problem of setting unrealistic project deadlines and the accompanying response of inflated time estimates. Relying on elementary statistics, it can be easily shown that the amount of safety time needed to protect a particular path is less than the sum of the safety times required to protect the individual activities making up the path. The same approach is commonly used in inventory management where it can be shown that less safety stock is needed at a central warehouse to provide a certain service level than the amount of safety stock that would be required to provide this same service level if carried at multiple distributed locations.

Based on this intuition, Goldratt suggests reducing the amount of safety time added to individual tasks and then adding some fraction of the safety time reduced back into the system as safety buffer for the entire project, called the *project buffer*. The amount of time each task is reduced depends on how much of a reduction is needed to get project team members to change their behavior. For example, the allotted time for tasks should be reduced to the point that the student syndrome is eliminated. Indeed, Goldratt suggests using activity durations where in fact there is a high probability that the task will not be finished on time.

The Critical Chain

Another limitation associated with traditional approaches to project management is that the dependency between resources and tasks is often ignored. To illustrate this, consider the network diagram shown in Figure 6-18. According to the figure, the activities emanating from node 1 require resource **A**, while the activities emanating from nodes 2 and 3 require resources **C** and **B**, respectively. Using traditional approaches to project management, two paths would be identified: **A1-C1** with a duration of 17 days and **A2-B1** with a duration of 11 days. Taking this approach a step further we would conclude that path **A1-C1** is the critical path.

The problem with this logic is that activities **A1** and **A2** are not truly independent as the diagram would seem to indicate since their completion requires the same resource. Based on this new insight, we see that if resource **A** completes activity **A1** first, thereby delaying the start of **A2** for 7 days, then path **A1-C1**'s duration remains 17 days while path **A2-B1**'s duration increases from 11 to 18 days. Likewise, if resource **A** completes activity **A2** first, then path **A1-C1**'s duration increases from 17 to 22 days while path **A2-B1**'s duration remains 11 days. (This is precisely what was considered when we examined the process of resource leveling.)

To address the need to consider both precedence relationships and resource dependencies, Goldratt proposes thinking in terms of the longest chain of consecutively dependent tasks where such dependencies can arise from a variety of sources including precedence relationships among the tasks and resource dependencies. Goldratt coined the term *critical chain* to refer to the longest chain of consecutively dependent activities.

Based on this definition of the critical chain, there are two potential sources that can delay the completion of a project. One source of delay is in the tasks that make up the critical chain. The project buffer discussed earlier is used to protect against these delays (see Figure 6-19). The second source of delay is in the tasks external to the critical chain. These tasks can also delay the completion of the project if delays in these "feeder" paths end up delaying one or more of the tasks on the critical chain. As shown in Figure 6-19, safety time can be added to these paths as well to ensure that they do not delay tasks on the critical chain. The safety time added to chains other than the critical chain is called a *feeding buffer* since these paths often feed into or merge with the critical chain. Thus, the objective of feeding buffers is to ensure that noncritical chains are completed so that they do not delay tasks on the critical chain.

Figure 6-18
Sample network
diagram.

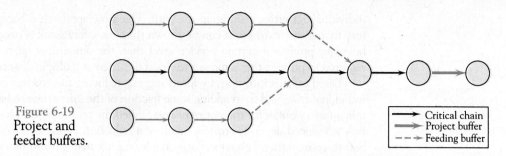

Figure 6-19
Project and
feeder buffers.

Critical chain
Project buffer
Feeding buffer

Clearly, activities on the critical chain should be given the highest priority. Likewise, to ensure that resources are available when needed, they should be contracted at the start of the project. It is also wise to keep these resources updated on the status of the project and to remind them periodically of when their input will be needed. Goldratt suggests reminding these resources 2 weeks before the start of their work, then 3 days prior to their start, and finally the day before they start. Since any delay of an activity on the critical chain can cause a delay of the entire project, it is important that a resource immediately switch to the task on the critical chain when needed.

> The critical chain concept identifies the facts that activity times are unknown and independent, that workers will inflate their time estimates to protect themselves, early completion tasks will not be reported, the work will expand to fill the time, tasks will not be started until the last minute, multitasking will be misapplied, resource demands will be uneven and result in task delays, and more projects and tasks will be undertaken to increase resource utilization. All these contribute to project delays and inefficiencies. To correct these problems, feeder time buffers are cut severely to change behavior, a project buffer is added at the end of a project, the release of projects and tasks is based on the availability of bottleneck resources, and time buffers are added to resources that feed bottleneck resources.

The last three chapters on budgeting, scheduling, and allocating resources are the outcome of the planning process we described in Chapter 3. These subjects, taken together, are a description of what to do. Now we turn to two allied subjects: how to report what is going on and how to control it.

REVIEW QUESTIONS

1. Given the fact that a project's resource requirements are clearly spelled out in the project plan, why are PMs so concerned with resource allocation?

2. Explain the difference between a project that has a fixed delivery day and one that has a fixed limit on resource usage. Why might a PM be interested in this difference?

3. What does it mean to "fast-track" a project?

4. List as many things as you can think of that should be entered into a specific resource's calendar.

5. Explain why project-oriented firms require excess resource capacity.

6. The arrival and departure times of commercial aircraft are carefully scheduled. Why, then, is it so important to have excess capacity in the airport control tower?

7. Explain the difference in the problems faced by a PM who is short of secretarial resources and one who is short of a "Walt."

8. When allocating scarce resources to several different projects at the same time, why is it important to make sure that all resource calendars are on the same time base (i.e., hourly, daily, weekly . . .)?

9. List and describe the three most common criteria by which to evaluate different resource allocation priority rules.

10. Why is the problem of allocating scarce resources to a set of projects similar to the problem of scheduling a job shop?

11. What is meant by the term "student syndrome"?

DISCUSSION QUESTIONS

12. Describe the fundamental trade-offs made when deciding whether or not to crash a project. If the decision is made to crash, what additional trade-offs must be made?

13. Discuss the advantages of "labor pools" in a project-oriented company. Are there any potential disadvantages with the use of pools?

14. What purpose(s) might be served by using each of the following priority rules for allocating scarce resources?
    a. As late as possible
    b. Shortest task duration time first
    c. Minimum slack first

15. Linking a group of projects together with pseudoactivities creates a sort of superproject. What does this mean, and why would anyone want to do it?

16. Describe in your own words what is meant by Goldratt's critical chain. How does it work?

17. Projects A and B are both nearing completion. You are managing a super important project C that requires an immediate input of a resource being used by both projects A and B, but is otherwise unavailable. Project A has a Type 1 life cycle. Project B's life cycle is Type 2. From which (or both or neither) do you borrow the resource? Why?

18. Goldratt suggested that to avoid the "student syndrome," it is a good idea to set activity durations so short that there is a high probability that the task will not be finished on time. On the other hand, it has long been known that setting people up for failure is strongly demotivating. What should the PM do?

19. Describe as many types of resource allocation problems as you can, based on the situations described in the chapter.

PROBLEMS

20. Given the following project to landscape a new building site:

Activity	Immediate Predecessor	Activity Duration (days)	Resource Used
A	—	2	X, Y
B	A	2	X
C	A	3	X
D	B, C	4	X, Y
E	D	3	W, X
F	D	1	W, X, Y
G	E, F	2	X, Y

(a) Draw a Gantt chart using MSP.

(b) Assuming a 5-day week, find the critical path and project duration in days.

(c) Given that each resource is assigned 100 percent to each task, identify the resource constraints.

(d) Using the MSP default, level the resources and determine the new project duration and critical path.

(e) Identify what alternative solutions can be used to shorten the project duration without overallocating the resources.

21. Given the following project (all times are in days):

Activity	Predecessor	Normal Time	Normal Cost	Crash Time	Crash Cost
a	—	5	$50	3	$150
b	—	4	40	2	200
c	b	7	70	6	160
d	a, c	2	20	1	50
e	a, c	3	30	—	—
f	b	8	80	5	290
g	d	5	50	4	100
h	e, f	6	60	3	180

(a) Draw the network (AOA or AON) and find the critical path, time, and cost for an all-normal level of project activity.

(b) Calculate the crash cost-per-day (all activities may be partially crashed).

(c) Find the optimal way of getting an 18-day delivery time. What is the project cost?

(d) Find the optimal way of getting a 16-day delivery time. What is the project cost?

(e) Calculate the shortest delivery time for the project. What is the cost?

22. Given the following AOA network, determine the first activity to be given extra resources by the following priority rules:

(a) Shortest task first

(b) Minimum slack first

(c) Most critical followers

(d) Most successors

23. Given the project shown in Figure 5-10 of Chapter 5, assume that a facility used by activities **c** and **d** is scarce. To which activity would you assign the facility first, given the following rules:

(a) Minimum slack rule

(b) Most followers

(c) Most critical followers

(d) Shortest task first

(e) As late as possible

24. Consider the following activity information and the constraint that the project must be completed in 16 weeks.

Activity	Duration (weeks)	Preceding Activity
A	3	—
B	6	—
C	8	—
D	7	A
E	5	B
F	10	C
G	4	C
H	5	D, E, F
I	6	G

In addition, activity **C** may be crashed to 7 weeks at a cost of $40, activity **F** may be crashed to 6 weeks at a cost of $20/week, activity **H** may be crashed to 2 weeks at a cost of $10/week, and activity **I** may be crashed to 3 weeks at a cost of $30/week. Find the best schedule and cost.

25. Consider the project network below. Suppose the duration of both activities **A** and **D** can be reduced to 1 day, at a cost of $15 per day of reduction. Also, activities **E, G,** and **H** can be reduced in duration by 1 day, at a cost of $25 per day of reduction. What is the least-cost approach to crash the project by 2 days? What is the shortest "crashed" duration, the new critical path, and the cost of crashing?

INCIDENTS FOR DISCUSSION

Lab Results, Inc.

Sam G. Farshe runs a medical laboratory in Pittsburgh. He has contracts with several doctors' offices to conduct their lab work. He runs the lab tests and reports the results on their patients. Lab Results, Inc. has a reputation of always delivering quality results within the time specifications of each contract. Sam is pleased with his company's results. His crew of technicians works hard. He prides himself on the fact that there is no excess capac-

ity in his operation. He pays overtime to his technicians weekly, but always includes those costs in his contracts.

Sam has been asked to bid on a contract to do the lab work for an area hospital whose lab is being renovated. The hospital needs to outsource their lab services temporarily. They estimate construction will take 2–3 months, and they want a free-standing lab service to cover their needs for 4 months; then the hospital will resume the service. Sam is treating this as a project and intends to estimate the work hours needed based on the number of tests the hospital estimates. He will then be able to determine his bid price for the job. Sam wants this contract. He has heard rumors that some of the other hospitals in the city are considering outsourcing their lab work permanently as a cost saving measure. Sam thinks that he can submit the low bid if he just has his current staff 'buckle-down' for the 4-month time period and pick up this additional work. The hospital is estimating a significant amount of work, but Sam believes if he just adds additional overtime to his bid, he can cover the increase in work load and win the contract.

Questions:

1. Do you think Sam's plan is going to work? Why or why not? How would you handle the bid on the new project?

2. Would Crystal Ball® be useful in assessing Sam's plan and changing it, if necessary?

Southern Kentucky University Bookstore

Southern Kentucky University (SKU) bookstore is beginning a major project of automating their inventory system. The bookstore is organized into four business units: Textbooks, General Merchandise—insignia merchandise (sweatshirts, coffee mugs, etc.), General Books, and Convenience (candy, soft drinks, etc.). Lisa O'Brien, the Bookstore Manager, has decided to name each business unit supervisor as the PM of his or her area's automation project. Each department has its own information systems person assigned, so Lisa feels that each area can work independently and then all meet her deadline of completion. The project is scheduled for completion right before school starts in the fall, with staggered "Go Live" dates for each of the business units. Each unit will do its own data entry and then work with the others on testing and implementation.

Missy Motz is the supervisor of the Textbook division of the bookstore. Missy is concerned that her department will not have enough resources to complete the automation project. The Textbook department is always swamped with book orders from professors right before school starts. Missy thinks she has enough staff to handle the data entry, but is concerned about supplying personnel at the times and quantities required as the implementation is phased in over each of the business units.

Missy knows a little bit about resource allocation techniques. She remembers that one of the most effective allocation techniques is to work first on the activity with minimum slack, so she instructed her staff to approach any tasks they are assigned as members of the project team on that basis.

Questions:

1. Is the minimum slack rule a reasonable way to schedule resources of the Textbook division? Why or why not?

2. What complication is added by making this project four separate projects?

C A S E

St. Dismas Assisted Living Facility Resource Usage—4

The team for the Assisted Living Facility (ALF) program was working to prepare in-depth plans, complete with the resource requirements for their projects' tasks.

Marc Alison, MD, the Medical Director of Rehabilitation Services for St. Dismas Medical Center was responsible for developing a project plan with the objective of identifying the scope and associated costs of health services to offer residents. The Medical Director included in the plan the development of an assessment tool that would be used to determine the required level and cost of care for prospective residents. This tool would also be used to ensure that the appropriate population was housed at the facility. It was important to have a way to distinguish a person who was too sick and needed a more intense level of care than that offered by the Assisted Living Facility. Once the assessment of a potential resident was completed, the facility staff could determine if the person assessed was a good candidate for the facility. This phase of the project plan was critical to the success of the project.

Dr. Alison's approach was to develop the assessment tool and test it on individuals that matched the marketing department's target population of the assisted living facility. He felt he had a great opportunity to find his test population by using some of the current St. Dismas patients who were almost ready for discharge from the hospital. He could also use some of the older volunteers who currently worked at the hospital. Dr. Alison felt strongly that a physician should assess potential residents but he also knew that it might be cost prohibitive to have such an expensive resource conducting pre-admission assessments. He thought that if a physician developed and tested the tool first, then additional testing could be conducted using less costly health care professionals to conduct the evaluations.

Dr. Alison knew he would have to work with Dr. Zen Link, Head of Geriatric Medicine, on developing the tool. Dr. Link was familiar with the elderly population that the marketers were targeting and could offer valuable insights on how to assess the health status of potential residents. Dr. Link also had an extensive practice at St. Dismas and would have some patients who might agree to help test the assessment tool. Dr. Alison would also need the services of the CFO and his staff to determine the cost of the health services the residents would need. Dr. Alison prepared and presented the following plan to the project steering team:

ID	Task Name	Duration	Predecessors	Resource Names
1	Medical/Health services determined	48.25 days		
2	Physical health assessment tool for residents developed	25.75 days		Alison, Link
3	Develop tool	2 wks		Alison, Link
4	Test of assessment tool conducted by physicians (12 patients)	6 hrs	3	Alison, Link
5	Revise tool as necessary	1 wk	4	
6	Test of tool conducted by other health professionals (i.e., phys. asst., RN, therapist)	2 wks	5	
7	Admission & discharge criteria finalized	1.5 wks	6	Alison, Splient
8	Investigate copyrighting assessment tool	3 wks	4	Legal
9	Assessment tool finalized	0 days	7	
10	Copyright tool	0 days	8, 9	
11	Financial impact of health services determined	15 days		
12	Costs determined	1 wk	9	Alison, CFO
13	Scope of health services determined to include in base rate	2 wks	12	Proj. Steering Team
14	Scope of services to provide on a fee for service basis	2 wks	12	Proj. Steering Team
15	Finalize services and programs to be offered	0 days	13, 14	

The ALF team was impressed with the thought that went into Dr. Alison's project plan. They were delighted with the prospect of copyrighting an admission and discharge assessment tool, but they raised some questions about Dr. Alison's resource assignments. The COO asked how Drs. Alison and Link were going to assess a sufficient sample of people in 6 hours' time given their busy clinical schedules. Dr. Alison replied that he and Dr. Link would be doing all of the other steps in the plan during their normal 8 AM to 5 PM workday. The step to test the tool on real patients, however, would take some scheduling. Dr. Alison added that his colleague intended to conduct evaluations of current patients, with their permission, during their regular office visits. Dr. Alison admitted he had not figured out how he was going to see his share of the test group. He knew he could see some inpatients ready for discharge from the hospital during the time he did his rounds. He also wanted to test the tool on at least a dozen people from the volunteer staff who matched the prospective resident population. He informed the team that his secretary had agreed to phone the volunteers and see if any of them were interested. She said she could do this during her normal workday, so he had not included her time in the plan.

Dr. Alison sat silently thinking about how long this step in his plan would take, given his current workload. He knew that he would only be available to do the assessments during the time that he allocated for administrative hospital work, Wednesday from 8:00 AM to noon. He did not want to give up any of his clinical time, because his patients had been scheduled months in advance. Dr. Alison wanted to personally test the tool on at least 12 people. He estimated each assessment would take no more than a half hour (that is why he said that step would take six hours to complete).

Dr. Alison was not sure what to do next. He told the project team he would get back to them.

QUESTIONS

1. Prepare a Gantt chart with resources for the project plan Dr. Alison submitted. Begin this project on January 3. Prepare a resource calendar for Dr. Alison.

2. How would you handle Dr. Alison's resource problem?

3. Given Dr. Alison's availability, how long will it take to complete testing of the assessment tool?

4. Prepare a Gantt chart for Dr. Alison's plan incorporating any changes you recommend.

C A S E

Charter Financial Bank

Charter Financial Bank operates three branches in a southeastern city. Ray Copper, Vice-President of Information Technology at the bank, has recently been charged by the bank's president to develop a mobile app that can be used on smartphones and tablet computers to promote bank services, to provide access to customer account information, and to allow individuals to apply online for loans and credit cards.

Ray decided to assign this project to Rachel Smith, one of two directors in the information technology group. Since this would be Charter Financial's first mobile app, Ray and Rachel agreed that an appropriate starting point for the project would be for the project team to benchmark existing apps in order to gain a better understanding of the state-of-the-art in this area. At the conclusion of their first meeting, Ray asked Rachel to prepare a rough estimate of how long this project would take and how much it would cost if it were pursued at a normal pace. Noting that the president appeared particularly anxious to develop the app, Ray also requested that Rachel prepare a time and budget estimate related to developing the app as quickly as possible.

During the first project team meeting, the team identified seven major tasks associated with the project. The first task was to benchmark existing apps. The team estimated that completing this task at normal pace would likely require 10 days at a cost of $15,000. However, the team estimated that this task could be completed in as few as 7 days at a cost of $18,750 if the maximum allowable amount of overtime was used.

Once the benchmark study was completed, a project plan and project definition document would need to be prepared for top management approval. The team estimated that this task could be completed in 5 days at a cost of $3,750 working at a normal pace or in 3 days at a cost of $4,500.

After the project received the approval of top management, the app design could begin. The team estimated that app design would require 15 days at a cost of $45,000 using no overtime or 10 days at a cost of $58,500 using all allowable overtime.

After the app design was complete, three tasks could be carried out simultaneously: (1) developing the server code to support the app, (2) developing and coding the actual app, and (3) developing and coding the app's user interface. The team estimated that developing the server code would require 10 days and cost $9,000 using no overtime, but could be completed in 7 days at a cost of $11,250 using overtime. Likewise, the team estimated that developing and coding the app would require 10 days and cost $15,000 using no overtime or could be reduced by 2 days at a total cost of $19,500. Developing the user interface was to be subcontracted out and would take 7 days at a cost of $8,400. The organization that was to be used to create the user interface does not provide an option for paying more for rush jobs.

Finally, once the code for the server, the code for the app, and the user interface were completed, the entire app would need to be tested and debugged. The team estimated that this would require 3 days at a cost of $4,500. Using overtime, the team estimated that the testing and debugging task could be reduced by a day at a total cost of $6,750.

QUESTIONS

1. What is the cost of completing this project if no overtime is used? How long will it take to complete the project?

2. What is the shortest amount of time in which the project can be completed? What is the cost of completing the project in the shortest amount of time?

3. Suppose that the benchmarking study actually required 13 days as opposed to the 10 days originally estimated. What actions would you take to keep the project on a normal schedule?

4. Suppose the President wanted the app developed in 35 days. What actions would you take to meet this deadline? How much extra would it cost to complete the project in 35 days?

C A S E

Rand Contractors

Brothers Anthony and Bruce Rand own and operate a house renovation business. Recently they signed a contract with a homeowner for a fairly extensive addition to the house. In particular, the home addition involves knocking out the back wall of the kitchen and the corresponding wall in the basement and expanding the space on both levels. Also, the roof of the new addition will serve as a terrace for the master bedroom located on the second floor, so a door leading to the terrace will also have to be installed in the master bedroom. While a cost estimate for the project has been approved by the homeowner, the Rand Brothers need an estimate of how long the project will take so they can provide a start date to the customer of their next project.

The first task in the renovation project is to knock out the walls in the basement, kitchen, and master bedroom. The brothers work together on this task. Based on their experience, their best estimate of the time it will take to knock out the walls is 3 days. However, they feel if the task goes particularly well, they may be able to knock out all the walls in 2.5 days. On the other hand, if they encounter unforeseen problems, they estimate that knocking out the walls could take as long as 5 days.

Once the walls have been knocked out, the framing for the new addition can be started. Only Anthony has the skills to do the framing. His best guess is that the framing will take 9 days, but he believes there is a chance he might be able to complete it in 8 days. By the same token, if he encounters some difficulties, he estimates that framing the addition could take as long as 12 days.

Once the framing has been complete, either the plumbing or electrical work can be started which are both done by Bruce. Bruce estimates that the plumbing will take 3 days, but might be done in as few as 2 days or as long as 6 days. Likewise, he estimates that the electrical work will take him 3 days, but that he might be able to finish it in 2 days or require as many as 5 days.

After both the plumbing and electrical work are completed, the drywall and trim work can be started. Anthony does the drywall and trim work. He estimates this will take 6 days, could possibly be done in 5 days, and might take as long as 9 days.

Finally, after the drywall is finished, the new addition can be painted, which is done by both brothers. Based on past projects, the brothers estimate that painting will take 3 days. If the job goes well, they could possibly get the task done in 2 days, while if it goes slower than expected it could take up to 4 days. Also, note that the exterior brickwork is being subcontracted out to another contractor and can commence as soon as the framing is complete.

QUESTIONS

1. Assuming the activity times follow a beta distribution, simulate the home renovation project 10,000 times ignoring for the moment which brother performs a given task? What is the expected project completion time? What are the shortest and longest amounts of time you estimate it will take to complete the project?

2. What is the probability the project can be finished in 25 days or less? What is the probability the project will require 27 days or more to complete? What is the probability the project can be completed in 24 to 26 days?

3. Revise your simulation model so that in addition to considering the precedence relationships, it also considers who will be doing the tasks. Now what is the expected project completion time? What is the shortest and longest amount of time you estimate it will now take to complete the project?

4. Based on the revised simulation model, what is the probability the project can be finished in 25 days or less? What is the probability the project will require 27 days or more to complete? What is the probability the project can be completed in 24 to 26 days?

5. How do the results compare between the two simulation models? What are the implications of these differences for a project manager?

6. Based on your simulation results, how would you respond to the next customer regarding when their remodeling project will start?

BIBLIOGRAPHY

ADLER, P. S., A. MANDELBAUM, V. NGUYEN, and E. SCHWERER. "Getting the Most Out of Your Product Development Process." *Harvard Business Review*, March–April 1996.

FENDLEY, L. G. "Towards the Development of a Complete Multiproject Scheduling System." *Journal of Industrial Engineering*, October 1968.

GOLDRATT, ELIYAHU M. *Project Management the TOC Way* (uncorrected proofs). The North River Press: Great Barrington, MA, 1998.

GOLDRATT, E. M. *Critical Chain*. Great Barrington, MA: North River, 1997.

GOLDRATT, E. M., and J. COX. *The Goal*. 2nd rev. ed., Great Barrington, MA: North River, 1992.

HUSSAIN, R., and S. WEARNE, "Problems and Needs of Project Management in the Process and Other Industries." *Transactions of the Institution of Chemical Engineers*, Part A, April 2005.

IBBS, C. W., S. A. LEE, and J. I. Li. "Fast-Tracking's Impact on Project Change." *Project Management Journal*, December 1998.

KURTULUS, I., and E. W. DAVIS. "Multi-Project Schedul-ing Categorization of Heuristic Rules Performance."*Management Science*, February 1982.

KURTULUS, I., and S. C. NARULA. "Multi-Project Scheduling: Analysis of Project Performance." IEEE Transactions on Engineering Management, March 1985.

MEREDITH, J. R. and S. M. SHAFER. Operations Management for MBAs, 5th ed. New York: John Wiley, 2013.

7

Monitoring and Controlling the Project

PMBOK Guide

Project monitoring and control are, in some ways, simply the opposite sides of project selection and planning. The bases for selection as described in Chapter 1 dictate what to monitor and the details of planning identify the elements to be controlled. PMBOK covers these topics in Chapter 3 on Processes, but more explicitly covers the topic of controlling in Chapter 8 on Quality. *Monitoring* is the collection, recording, and reporting of project information that is of importance to the project manager and other relevant stakeholders. *Control* uses the monitored data and information to bring actual performance into agreement with the plan. Clearly, the need to exert proper control mandates the need to monitor the proper activities and elements of the project. Frequently, the distinction between monitoring and control is blurred, and their interaction often makes us think we are working on a single task, but they are quite distinct.

Although the data gathered from monitoring often serve many objectives—auditing, keeping management informed, learning from mistakes—these are all secondary compared to the purpose of control. The purpose of monitoring is to ensure that all interested parties have available, when needed, the information required to exercise control over the project through the use of tools such as the project portfolio process of Section 1.6. Thus, the key issue in designing an effective monitoring and control system is to create an information system that gives the project manager and others the information they need to make informed, timely decisions that will keep project scope as close as possible to the plan.

7.1   THE PLAN-MONITOR-CONTROL CYCLE

Managing a project involves continually planning what to do, checking on progress, comparing progress to plan, taking corrective action to bring progress into agreement with the plan if it is not, and replanning when needed. As noted previously, the fundamental items to be planned, monitored, and controlled are time, cost, and scope so that the project stays on schedule, does not exceed its budget, and meets its specifications.

This plan-monitor-control cycle constitutes a "closed-loop" process that continues until the project is completed. Figure 7-1,* illustrates the information and authority flows for such a cycle in an engineering project. Note that the information flows up the organization and the authority flows down.

Unfortunately, it is often the case that when particularly complex, challenging, or uncertain projects are initiated, the planning-monitoring-controlling effort is minimized so that "the real work" can be done. It is a great temptation to focus on doing something, anything, rather than to spend time on planning, monitoring, and controlling, especially if the stakes are high and the project is a difficult one. It is precisely such projects, however, that most desperately need a mature project manager, particularly one who realizes the importance of creating an effective planning-monitoring-controlling process. Only this will ensure that the project and its output are in full compliance with the law, as well as with the expectations of both senior management and the client.

We are familiar with many firms that incurred tremendous expense and large losses because the planning process was inadequate for the project tasks undertaken. For example, a retailer won a bid to supply a regional office of a national firm with a computer, terminals, and software. Due to insufficient planning, the installation was completed far beyond the due date with very inadequate performance. The project failure disqualified the retailer from bidding on an additional 20 installations planned by the national firm. Another firm in the construction industry ran 63 percent over budget and 48 percent over schedule on a

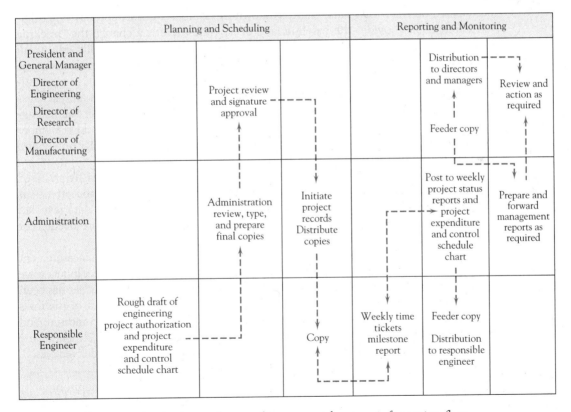

Figure 7-1 Project authorization and expenditure control system information flow.
Source: Dean, 1968.

---

*Dean (1968) was a classic work in the infant field of project management that proposed several major innovations in the field.

major project because the PM had managed similar projects several times before and "knew what to do without going into all that detail that no one looks at anyway."

Designing the Monitoring System

The key to setting up a monitoring system is to identify the special characteristics of scope, cost, and time that need to be controlled in order to achieve the project goals as stated in the project plan. The exact boundaries within which these characteristics should be controlled must be determined, as well as the specified performance characteristics for each level of detail in the project activities. In order to manage for overall project success, control must be exercised at the detailed work level for each aspect of project performance or there is no guarantee that the desired changes will result.

The project plan identifies what is being done, when, and the planned level of resource usage for each task and subtask in the project, so real-time data must be identified to measure achievement against the plan. Mechanisms to gather and store such data must be designed. In addition to collection systems for hard data, the monitoring system should include telephone logs, change tracking/control systems, documentation processes for both formal (e.g., meetings) and informal communications, and other such softer data collection systems. Once again, monitoring is the direct connection between project planning and control.

One way of linking planning and control is to monitor project progress at each milestone or phase of the project. Alternatively, progress can be monitored continuously based on the MSP Gantt chart, as shown in Figure 5-24 of Chapter 5. The original Gantt chart provides the baseline, and every time there is a change the "tracking Gantt" chart is updated to reflect the change. The software automatically adjusts all information to reflect the change. Another way illustrated later in this chapter is to use an "earned value" chart with its preestablished baseline. A fourth method is to monitor the critical chain buffers described in Chapter 6. Critical chain software packages such as ProChain® include buffer reports in their output which can direct the managers to problem areas where attention needs to be focused. The PM should remember to number and save each version of all monitoring documents to ensure a timely and accurate record for the project history that is discussed in Chapter 8.

It is temptingly easy to focus monitoring activities on data that are easily gathered rather than those that are important for control purposes. For example, too often it is the hard, "objective" measures that are monitored when soft, "subjective" data revealed in phone calls and water-cooler or happy-hour conversations are what are needed for proper control.

Too often, intensity of activity is measured instead of results. Because the measurement of project performance may be difficult, there is a strong tendency to let project inputs serve as surrogate measures of output, such as assuming that if 50 percent of the budget has been spent, and/or 50 percent of the scheduled time has passed, then 50 percent of the tasks must be completed. Far, far too often we measure cost (because it is easy to measure and both executives and accountants are used to dealing with cost), and completely ignore any consideration of the actual state of the task or project in terms of developing deliverables.

> It is essential to spend time up front designing the planning-monitoring-controlling process, especially for more challenging projects. The project plan is the primary document to guide the design of the monitoring system in terms of the detailed tasks and resources that need to be controlled in order for the project to achieve its time, cost, and output goals. Common errors in setting up monitoring systems are monitoring easy measures instead of relevant measures, monitoring activity in place of results, monitoring inputs as surrogates for outputs, and monitoring measures that don't change from one period to the next.

DATA COLLECTION AND REPORTING

Once we have decided on the type of data we want to monitor, the next question is how to collect these data and turn them into information useful for controlling the project. This is the activity of data collection and reporting. In this section we cover the physical collection of data and the analysis of that data, if necessary, to transform them into information. Once transformed, however, there are many ways to present the information and these are covered under the topic of *reporting*, including a discussion of the three main types of reports. A very special means of both collecting and disseminating data, and even sometimes information, is the proverbial "meeting," and we offer some advice for this often painful phenomenon—both in-person and virtual meetings are included. The use of electronic means for distributing information or reports is briefly examined.

At some point we have to decide what data we need to collect, when we need to collect them, and precisely how we should go about collecting them. A number of questions are raised. Should we design and use special forms? Should data be collected just before or after an important milestone or phase of the project? Should time and cost data always be collected at the same time each month? There are many such issues that arise when considering the data collection process and most of them can only be answered in the context of a specific project. There are a few generalizations that can be made concerning the information needed to control projects; these are described in the next section.

Data Collecting

The majority of data to be collected will eventually exist in one of the following five formats.

1. **Frequency counts** A simple tally of the occurrence of an event is common—for example, days without an accident. Often a count of events per time period or as a fraction of some standard number is used, such as complaints per month, defects per thousand products, and fraction of luggage lost.

2. **Raw numbers** Actual amounts are used, usually in comparison to some expected or planned amount, such as dollars spent, hours required, and pounds consumed. The comparison to plan may take the form of variances, that is, differences between planned and actual, or ratios of one to the other. The ratio format is particularly appealing for reporting on a control chart with predetermined limits, as is described later in the chapter. When collecting raw amounts it is important that the basis, time period, and collection process always be the same.

3. **Subjective numeric ratings** These are usually subjective estimates of some quality offered by specialists in the topic, such as ordinal "rankings" of performance. They can be reported in the same ways as raw numbers, but they often cannot be mathematically processed in the same ways raw numbers can.

4. **Indicators and surrogates** When it is especially difficult to find a direct measure of a variable, indicators or surrogates are frequently used instead. If this approach is taken, it is important that the indicator or surrogate be as directly related to the variable as possible. For example, body temperature is an indicator of infection and years of experience can be a surrogate for expertise. The number of salespersons, however, would be a poor, and clearly indirect, measure for level of customer service.

5. **Verbal characterizations** Other variables that are difficult to measure, such as team spirit or client–supplier cooperation, may take the form of verbal characterizations. These forms of data are acceptable and useful as long as the terminology is limited and is uniformly understood by all parties.

Figure 7-2 Number of bugs per unit of test time during test of Datamix software program.

Data Analysis

Following the collection of the data through the monitoring system, it is frequently necessary to analyze or process the data in some manner before reporting it for control purposes. This may take the form of simple aggregation of the data, such as averaging the values, or something as complex as fitting statistical distribution functions to the data to ascertain relationships, effects, and trends. Crystal Ball® can do this with ease. Some of the quality management techniques for the presentation and analysis of data are often useful here (e.g., see Meredith and Shafer, 2013). As an example, a common graph used in quality management shows the range of sample values taken on a periodic basis, such as daily. If the samples' range—the largest minus the smallest value—appears to be increasing over time, this may indicate that a machine is wearing out or needs maintenance.

Figures 7-2 and 7-3 illustrate curve fitting where charts are updated on a regular basis and curves are fit to the data in order to help the PM estimate the cost and time required to achieve the performance goals for the project. Figure 7-4 shows the trend in the ratio of actual material cost to planned cost so the PM can step in should the values indicate a likely problem.

In general, significant differences from plan should be highlighted or "flagged" in some way so the PM or other person exercising control cannot overlook the potential problem. The many techniques of statistical quality control (see Meredith and Shafer, 2013, Ch.3) are helpful for determining what size variances are "significant," and may even help in determining causes and effects. These formal approaches, however, are often "after the fact" techniques for correcting (controlling) problems—variances occur, are reported, investigated, and then some action is taken. The astute PM, however, is much more interested in *preventing* fires rather than putting them out, thus the value of timely data collection and reporting.

Figure 7-3 Percent of specified performance met during successive repeated trials.

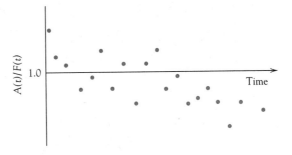

Figure 7-4 Ratio of actual material cost to estimated material cost for aircraft parts company.

Risk

Last, it should be noted that data analysis is sometimes used for the assignment of blame. The PM will not find this a helpful endeavor in managing the project. The goal is to achieve the project objectives through correcting deviations from plan, not to find scapegoats or assign guilt. The PM needs all team members performing at the top of their capabilities. Frequent blame placing strongly encourages team members to avoid taking the risks necessary to achieve a project's goals, or from mentioning problems when discovered.

Reporting and Report Types

PMBOK Guide

After the data have been collected and analyzed, they need to be reported in some form. For example, PMBOK suggests in Chapter 10 that routine performance reports include status reports, progress reports, and forecasts. There are also many other possible report formats, such as time/cost reports, variance reports, update presentations, and similar documents. All tables, charts (such as PERT/CPM and Gantt), and especially project plans should be updated to reflect current reality. In addition to alerting team members to potential problems, such updates help maintain team morale. Where known, some form of "comparables" should also be reported such as distributions of previous data, perhaps from earlier but similar projects, so that the PM and others can better interpret the data. As we have noted before, any time project reports, plans, or other documents are updated, great care should be taken to preserve all documents from earlier stages of the project's life. These materials will be invaluable when the project is completed and a project final report (project history) is written.

Although everyone concerned with the project should be tied into the reporting system in some fashion, not everyone needs to receive the same information. In addition to, say, aggregating the data for senior managers with many other such projects under their authority, reports may vary in terms of the frequency of distribution and detail as well as the particular measures being reported. The client may wish to have reports on cost and schedule while functional management may wish to see reports on technical accomplishments, for example. Project team members may need information at the task or subtask level on a frequent, perhaps daily, basis.

In general, it is a good idea to avoid *periodic* reports except in those cases in which the flow of data is periodic, for example, accounting data. Let the project's milestones, scope changes, problems, and the project team's needs for information dictate the timing of reports. It is our feeling that reports issued routinely every day, week, month, or quarter do not get read. An exception to this rule against periodic reporting is made for reports mandated by senior management who must examine the status of many projects and may need to compare the performance of many projects against the same time frame.

The explosion of electronic media for both collecting and disseminating data and information, including project management software such as MSP, makes it possible to customize a wide range of information for different audiences. This means that more data are available for collection, and more frequent updating is possible. Clearly, this can lead to an overload of reporting that is just as dangerous as underreporting. Important events, problems, and trends tend to be hidden in a mountain of detail. Thus, it is crucial that the reporting system be well designed to make use of such modern technological marvels without abusing the recipient of their capabilities. More is said about this later in this section.

The reports delivered to those engaged in carrying out or managing the project should be timed to allow control to be exercised before completion of the task in question. The project plan, again, identifies the level of tasks and responsibilities according to the level of management, and this provides guidance for both the level of detail and the timing of reports. For example, drug efficacy tests require a long time to conduct, so frequent reports would not be appropriate. In contrast, performance verification tests on new silicone chips can result in hundreds of discrepancies within a matter of hours, so daily or even more frequent reports are necessary.

In addition to WBS-determined data and information, individual managers may wish to see specific types of information in their reports, and these should be included as well. Moreover, they may even have preferences on the timing of reports, which should also be followed when they are within reason. The PM, however, must make sure that the relevant (for their level) information about project progress is included in their reports, and in such a way that it cannot be overlooked. Similarly, it is of no value reporting information or data to those who cannot use it for purposes of control, such as reporting overhead costs to the project chemist.

For projects, there are primarily three distinct types of reports: *routine* (which we have been describing), *exception*, and *special analysis*.

- Exception reports are primarily intended for special decisions or unexpected situations in which affected team members and outside managers need to be made aware of a change, and the change itself needs to be documented.

- Special analysis reports are prepared to disseminate the results of a special study in a project concerning a particular opportunity or problem for the project. They may be distributed to top management, other project managers who would benefit from the knowledge, functional managers, or anyone who might be affected or interested. Typical subjects might include studies of new materials, capabilities of new software, and descriptions of the impact of new government regulations.

In addition to the benefits of reports for the purposes of control, they offer these benefits.

- They provide the mutual understanding between stakeholders in a project regarding the goals, progress, difficulties, successes, and other ongoing events of importance to the project.

- They help communicate the need for coordination among those working on the tasks and subtasks of the project.

- They establish and maintain a communication network for global projects.

- There are often changes to the goals and functioning of projects. Reports can communicate this information in a timely and appropriate fashion, thus minimizing the confusion often encountered during such changes.

- They help maintain the visibility of the project, and the project team, to top management, functional managers, colleagues, and clients.

- Finally, unless the project is a disaster, status reports help keep the project team motivated.

It is not by chance that the PMI has labeled these collections of project reports, plans, charters, change orders, project histories, and other such documents as organizational "assets."

A special problem often encountered in designing project monitoring and reporting systems is the relationship between the project's information system and the overall organization's information system. The PM is, understandably, not free to define costs and other measures in ways that differ from the organization's definition of such measures as documented in the overall information system. Thus, the PM is advised to use the regular information system as the definitional prototype for project monitoring and reporting, making adjustments and additions as necessary for the special circumstances and measures needed for the project at hand. The PM should be aware, however, of another danger—modules of the parent organization's information system may not fit the needs of project monitoring and reporting. For example, an accounting module to track costs for an assembly line will not be adequate for tracking project costs.

Software packages such as MSP offer extensive and varied reporting mechanisms. Gantt charts show the current status of a project (see Chapter 5, Figure 5-24), and reports show the availability of various resources (see Chapter 6, Table 6-2) or the demands for work from individuals or groups (see Table 6-3 or Figure 6-5), just to name a few. MSP not only allows the PM to distribute the information anywhere that has electronic communication capability, but also allows easy customization of the reports limited only by the PM's imagination. A PM can highlight tasks that are running late (or running early if such exist), and add large red Xs to mark cost overages. The level of detail reported on Gantt charts is also completely controllable, so the PM can send only first-level tasks to senior management, and the highest level of detail to project team members.

Meetings

For many project workers and managers, meetings are about as welcome as Herpes diseases or a call from the IRS. So far in our discussion, we have talked about reports as if they were going to be delivered by hand, snail mail, or email. Often, however, they (or their substance) are delivered through face-to-face meetings. These meetings can range from regular, highly formalized and structured presentation/question/answer sessions to informal, off-the-cuff get-togethers. Project review meetings, regardless of the format, are always important.

Although such meetings are usually dreaded because of their length, lack of actionable conclusions, and general waste of time, this need not be the case. The following guidelines should help avoid the problems with such meetings.

- Some meetings, such as the Weekly Progress Report (also known as "show and tell"), should rarely be held at all. Although not always possible, try to hold meetings only for making group decisions or generating input among meeting members for dealing with important problems or opportunities. That is, hold meetings to take advantage of face-to-face interaction when no other approach or technology is an adequate substitute.

- Distribute a written agenda in advance of the meetings. The lead time for distributing the agenda should be sufficient to allow attendees to prepare to deal with agenda items. In addition to a list of the issues that will come before the group, the agenda should announce the meeting's pre-set starting and stopping times. Stick with both. Don't wander off the agenda, don't let the meeting run into overtime, and especially do not penalize those who show up on time by making them wait for those who are late. Obviously, in the case of meetings called to deal with emergencies, feel free to disregard the advice in this section.

- If a crisis arises and a meeting is deemed necessary to deal with it, make sure the meeting is restricted to that issue. If a stopping time cannot be predetermined, an acceptable alternative is "when the crisis is resolved."

- If homework needs to be done before the meeting by the attendees, check to be sure they will be prepared, and above all make sure you are prepared.

- If you chair the meeting, you should take your own minutes. The minutes should contain a final set of action items including what is to be done, by whom, and by when. The minutes are a critically important piece of documentation for a project, documenting important decisions and responsibilities. Do not delegate this responsibility. Microsoft Word® has a template for creating an agenda and for taking minutes that focus on action items.

- Avoid attributing remarks to individuals in the minutes. Remarks are meant to foster group process, not to be documented for eternity and for all to see. (Obviously this doesn't apply to designated or volunteered responsibilities.) As well, do not record and report votes taken in the meeting. It seems inappropriate to report that the motion to send a get-well card to the boss was passed—four yea and three nay. When the group has made a decision, by whatever means, that decision becomes the unanimous position of the group. Disagreement and debate are appropriate during the meeting, not after the decision is made.

- Although courtesy is always in order, excessive formality at project meetings is not. Robert's Rules of Order can safely be left at the door.

Virtual Meetings, Reports, and Project Management

Virtual meetings are now commonplace. Microsoft Livemeeting® is one of several packages that allows any number of people to meet, hear, view, and discuss presentations or training sessions on conference call telephone lines and computers. Multiway voice and data communication allows questions and answers, either live (interrupting the meeting) or submitted via the computer. Multiperson conversations are quite possible.

In this chapter on monitoring, reporting, and control, it is important to note that PMs can and do effectively utilize what has come to be called the "information revolution." Using the Internet to communicate and report about the project's status is now easily accomplished whether project team members are in the next cubicle or across the world. One large high technology company uses secure Web pages on the Internet to collect, store, and disseminate information on various projects. They have several Web pages that are specifically designed to communicate project information to and from clients. Others are designed for the sole use of members of the project team. Still others are created to communicate with the firm's senior management.

A senior project manager in the software firm mentioned above offered the following comments on project communication:

> In today's entrepreneurial corporate environment, it is necessary to communicate project information at varying levels of detail. Users run the gamut from software engineers to Business Unit (BU) general managers. Many of these users may not know or need to know how to use the project manager's planning tools. In addition, management may not want users from other BUs to have the same level of access as users doing and managing most of the work. It is important to have tools capable of limiting the detail if the user is not interested in it or is not permitted to see it, and providing detail where and when the user needs it. There are third-party software tools that claim to do at least some of this.

Web pages can hold any information that the project manager wants to share, such as progress-to-date on a project, resources assigned to a task, status of a particular task, and expenses to date. The amount of information that can be shared is limited only by the planning and monitoring processes that are put into place and the project manager's imagination.

Software programs such as Microsoft Project Server let you utilize the organization's local area network or intranet, as well as the Internet, to help with project communication and monitoring. A project manager can electronically check the status of a task or any resource used on the project and have updated information automatically entered into a project plan. Electronic work groups can be set up to monitor task completion, resource usage, and to provide reports to a group of individuals who have an interest in the project's status. For example, milestone reports can be sent to a senior management work group, and up-to-date personnel usage reports can be sent to the Human Resources department.

Using Microsoft Project, the converse is also true. With MSP and an appropriate computer network, anyone with authorized access can update his or her section of a project plan and submit it back to the PM for inclusion. Project teams and management at any site across the world will greatly benefit from these features. Using this network capability, users do not need access to a "resident" copy of the software. Valuable real-time reports can be prepared without lengthy phone conversations, or costly on-site meetings. The technological progress of the current "turn of the century" only means more effective and timely use of project information for planning, monitoring, and communicating. Utilizing video conferencing, virtual presentations, Web posting, email, etc. greatly enhance the PM's ability to manage a project.

Thus *virtual project teams* are created, perhaps spread across continents, with members contributing their own pieces of the project and being monitored and controlled by the PM at another location (Adams and Adams, 1997). In addition to its use for helping with the planning, monitoring, and control of projects, the Internet can also be a rich source of information. The project team can find building codes, technical aid, databases, patent information, expert contacts, and almost anything else on the Internet.

For the monitoring system, data in various forms have to be collected, analyzed, and reported. Data also need to be aggregated, manipulated in various ways, and compared with planned values in order to allow effective control. The monitoring system helps PMs prevent problems instead of having to solve them. Project reports vary in content and frequency, depending on who the reports are targeted to and what controls they will exert. A special consideration is the relationship between the organization's information system and the project's system. In addition to printed reports, reports may also have to be given orally at meetings, but steps can be taken to maximize the effectiveness of such meetings. The Internet and the organization's local area network or intranet have enhanced project communication and meetings as well as facilitated the management of geographically dispersed virtual projects.

7.3 EARNED VALUE

So far, we have discussed monitoring segments of a project—tasks, subtasks, and such. Of primary importance, however, is deriving some measure of overall project progress in terms of performance, budget, and schedule. Such a measure is "earned value."

The common problem with comparing actual expenditures against plan (a.k.a. baseline or budget) for any given time period is that the comparison fails to consider the actual progress made on the project. Thus, if expenditures are lower than expected for a given period, it may be either good or bad, depending on whether progress is in line with that amount of expenditure. Similarly, if expenditures are higher than expected, this may be acceptable if progress is sufficiently greater than planned for that period. *The performance of a task or project cannot be evaluated by considering cost factors alone.*

The *earned value* (EV) of a task (or a project) is the budgeted cost of the work actually performed. It is calculated by multiplying the budgeted cost of the task by the percentage of completion of the task and summing over all tasks for the project. This process is more difficult than it might sound. The budgeted cost of a task is clear, but the percentage of completion is not. In particular, the percent of a task's budget actually spent is not, in general, a particularly good indicator of the percent of that activity's completion. For example, the major cost for a task might be for obtaining the machinery to do the task, a cost that will be incurred before any progress is made on that task. Or perhaps the major cost will not be charged until completion of the task. *To the best of our knowledge, there is no satisfactory way to measure accurately the percent of completion of most tasks, let alone to measure accurately the percent of completion of an entire project.*

As a result, three conventions have been adopted for estimating progress on tasks, but they must not be confused with reality. The most popular is 50–50: the task is listed as 50 percent complete when work on it is initiated, and the other 50 percent is added when the task is completed. This approach avoids the difficult problem of trying to estimate progress while the task is being executed. Clearly, this overstates the EV of tasks that have recently begun, but understates the EV of tasks nearing completion. In a large project, of course, with multiple on-going tasks starting and stopping at different times, the overstating and understating may tend to even out resulting in a relatively accurate portrayal of project progress. Another convention is 100 percent when the task is complete and zero percent before that. This is a very conservative approach that will only show project progress that is definitely achieved. Projects, however, will always appear to be "behind schedule," and upper management will be in a constant state of worry about the project's progress (not to mention the project manager's competence). The last approach is the common, intuitive one of trying to estimate percentage completion by using the ratio of cost expended to the total cost budgeted for a task, the ratio of the actual time elapsed relative to the total scheduled task time, or some combination of both. There is no strong evidence that either the time or cost ratio is an accurate estimator of percent completion.

These conventions are meant for application only to individual tasks on a project, not to the project as a whole. (At the end of this section, we show how aggregating the task EVs can be used to estimate the progress of the project as a whole.) In fact, applying these conventions to the project as a whole may result in a seriously misleading number because none of the conventions noted has much semblance of reality. If one must estimate the percent complete for an activity—and as we shall see, one must—the best guess of a knowledgeable person is probably the most that can be expected for most tasks.

Best Practice

As the earned value of a project is calculated, a graph such as that shown in Figure 7-5 can be constructed. Given the limitations of the input data, such a figure provides a basis for evaluating cost, schedule, and performance to date. The earned value completed to date tells the manager whether progress is up to expectation, the "baseline" planned for this point in time. Any difference is called the "schedule variance," which shows how much the project is ahead of or behind schedule. As seen in the figure, the value completed to date is less than the baseline estimate for this point in the project's life and rep-

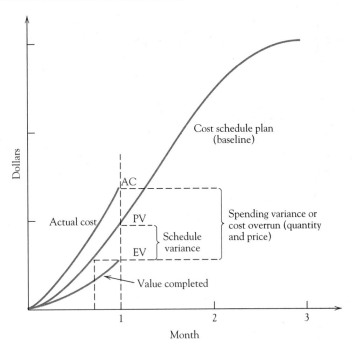

Figure 7-5   Earned value chart.

resents about a 10-day delay, resulting in a negative schedule variance (delay is negative). The actual cost, however, is considerably above the amount of value completed, resulting again in a negative (bad) "spending variance," and even exceeds the baseline cost for this point. Thus, this figure represents a difficult situation—a project significantly behind schedule and considerably over budget at this time in the project's life.

The variances on the earned value chart are calculated based on two simple rules:* (1) A negative variance is "bad," and a positive variance is "good"; and (2) the spending and schedule variances are calculated as the earned value minus some other measure. Specifically, the cost or spending variance is the *earned value* (EV) less the *actual cost* (AC) of the work performed. The schedule variance is the EV less the *planned cost* (PV) of the work budgeted and scheduled to have been performed to date as determined from the baseline plan. All measures are made as of the same date. For a variety of examples of different possible scenarios, see Figures 7-6(a), (b), and (c).

Although the above method of calculating variances is relatively standard, another way of handling the data is more useful for making comparisons at different points in time, or across different projects, or among different project managers. This procedure is simply to take the ratios of the measures rather than their differences. Thus, the spending or cost variance becomes the *Cost Performance Index* (CPI) = EV/AC, and the schedule variance becomes the *Schedule Performance Index* (SPI) = EV/PV. Values less than 1.0 are undesirable.

We illustrate the above with a simple example. Suppose that work on a project task was expected to cost $1,500 to complete the task and the workers were originally scheduled to have finished today. As of today, however, the workers have actually

Best Practice

PMBOK Guide

Figure 7-6(a)
Positive schedule
variance, negative
spending variance.

Figure 7-6(b)
Negative schedule
variance, negative
spending variance.

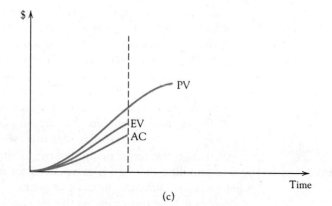

Figure 7-6(c)
Negative schedule
variance, positive
spending variance.

expended $1,350, and our best estimate is that they are about 2/3 finished. Our calculations follow:

$$
\begin{aligned}
\text{Cost/spending variance} &= EV - AC = 1{,}500(2/3) - 1{,}350 = -350 \\
\text{Schedule variance} &= EV - PV = 1{,}500(2/3) - 1{,}500 = -500 \\
CPI &= EV/AC = 1{,}500(2/3)/1{,}350 = .74 \\
SPI &= EV/PV = 1{,}500(2/3)/1{,}500 = .67
\end{aligned}
$$

Thus, we are spending more than the baseline plan indicates and, given what we have spent, we have not made as much progress as we should have.

We can use these calculations to determine some additional items of interest as well, such as the *estimated (remaining cost) to completion* (ETC) and the projected (*total cost) estimated at completion* (EAC) if nothing is done to correct the problem. Given that the *budget at completion* (BAC) is 1,500 and the EV is 1,500(2/3) = 1,000,

$$ETC = (BAC - EV)/CPI = (1,500 - 1,000)/.74 = 676$$

Note that this assumes that the work will be completed at the same level of efficiency or inefficiency as conducted thus far. The total cost to complete the task is

$$EAC = ETC + AC = 676 + 1350 = 2,026$$

That is, the projected additional cost to complete this task is $676 which, when added to the cost accrued to date of $1,350 gives a total task cost to completion of $2,026 rather than the original estimate of $1,500. (See Barr, 1996, and Flemming and Koppleman, 1996.)

Tables 7-1 and 7-2 illustrate the application of some of these variance calculations for a project to produce a documentary film. Tables 7-1 and 7-2 were generated by MSP. Table 7-1 depicts a status report for the documentary film project outlined in Chapter 6.

Table 7-1 is an overview of the actual information on the project steps compared to the baselines for duration, start dates, finish dates, cost, and hours worked. The project began 3/29 and is scheduled to be completed by 5/26. The project baseline or budgeted task and cost information is compared to what actually happened.

At any point during the project the project plan can easily be updated. MSP uses earned value analysis as a tool to compare the actual to the baseline plan. Table 7-1 shows the project updated as of 5/2. Task 2.0 has a baseline (budgeted) duration of 7 days. It actually took 12 days to complete. Task 3.3 took only 3 days instead of the baseline of 5 days. Since we hired the secretary earlier, we could start task 3.4 for scheduling the shoots earlier than expected. Because task 2.0 took longer, however, task 4.0 was delayed in starting. (MSP makes these adjustments automatically once actual information is entered.) All other tasks were on schedule. Step 6 is underway and not yet completed. Steps 7 to 9 have not yet begun.

Table 7-2 is the earned value table prepared by MSP once the project information is updated. Note that only completed stand-alone tasks or subtasks have final cost variances calculated for them. Summary tasks show the roll-up variances for their subtasks. The columns titled EAC, BAC, and VAC show "estimate at completion," "budget at completion," and "variance at completion (VAC = BAC − EAC)," respectively. MSP does not automatically adjust the estimate to complete by the CPI of the project to date as we did above.

PMBOK Guide

As noted above, some older versions of MSP do not calculate earned value variances recommended by the PMI. The MSP earned value numbers in Table 7.2 have been corrected to reflect the PMI Project Management Body of Knowledge (PMBOK, Chapter 11) definitions. (In some older versions, MSP calculation methods even differ from the MSP "help" file definitions.) The calculations used in this book are those recommended by the PMI. Our detailed calculations above were for a particular project task, but the approach can sensibly be extended to an entire project to give a *reasonable* estimate of the percent completion of the project. The conventional 0/100, 50/50, or percent of budget (time) expended are too ham-handed to apply to the project as a whole. An alternative is to aggregate the calculations made for individual tasks, as shown in Table 7-2. Using the overall task data for the project to date, one can estimate the project CPI and SPI, and thus the cost and schedule at completion for the project.

Table 7-1   MSP Project Status Report for DVD Project, 5/2

Producing a Documentary Film

Project Status as of: 5/2

WBS	Task Name	Act. Start	Baseline Start	Act. Finish	Baseline Finish	Actual Duration	Baseline Duration	Act. Cost	Baseline Cost	Act. Work	Baseline Work
1	Project approval	3/29	3/29	3/29	3/29	0 days	0 days	$0.00	$0.00	0 hrs	0 hrs
2	Scriptwriting	3/29	3/29	4/9	4/5	12 days	7 days	$14,400.00	$8,400.00	192 hrs	112 hrs
3	**Schedule shoots**	**3/29**	**3/29**	**4/21**	**5/7**	**18 days**	**30 days**	**$11,400.00**	**$13,000.00**	**224 hrs**	**240 hrs**
3.1	Begin scheduling	3/29	3/29	3/29	3/29	0 days	0 days	$0.00	$0.00	0 hrs	0 hrs
3.2	Propose shoots	3/29	3/29	4/9	4/9	10 days	10 days	$7,000.00	$7,000.00	120 hrs	120 hrs
3.3	Hire secretary	4/5	4/5	4/7	4/23	3 days	5 days	$2,400.00	$4,000.00	24 hrs	40 hrs
3.4	Schedule shoots	4/8	4/26	4/21	5/7	10 days	10 days	$2,000.00	$2,000.00	80 hrs	80 hrs
3.5	Scheduling completed	4/21	5/7	4/21	5/7	0 days	0 days	$0.00	$0.00	0 hrs	0 hrs
4	Script approval	4/9	4/5	4/16	4/12	5 days	5 days	$4,000.00	$4,000.00	50 hrs	80 hrs
5	Revise script	4/19	4/12	4/23	4/19	5.5 days	5.5 days	$7,000.00	$7,000.00	80 hrs	80 hrs
6	Shooting	4/26	4/19	NA	5/3	5 days	10 days	$3,600.00	$7,200.00	80 hrs	160 hrs
7	Editing	NA	5/3	NA	5/17	0 days	10.06 days	$0.00	$5,290.00	0 hrs	168 hrs
8	Final approval	NA	5/17	NA	5/26	0 days	7.19 days	$0.00	$6,250.00	0 hrs	160 hrs
9	Deliver DVD to client	NA	5/26	NA	5/26	0 days	0 days	$0.00	$0.00	0 hrs	0 hrs

Table 7-2 MSP Earned Value Report for DVD Project, 5/2

Project Status as of: 5/2   ***Producing a Documentary Film***

Earned Value Chart

WBS	Task Name	PV	EV	AC	SV	CV	EAC	BAC	VAC
1	Project approval	$0.00	$0.00	$0.00	$0.00	$0.00	$0.00	$0.00	$0.00
2	Scriptwriting	$8,400.00	$8,400.00	$14,400.00	$0.00	($6,000.00)	$14,400.00	$8,400.00	($6,000.00)
3	**Schedule shoots**	**$12,000.00**	**$13,000.00**	**$11,400.00**	**$1,000.00**	**$1,600.00**	**$11,400.00**	**$13,000.00**	**$1,600.00**
3.1	Begin scheduling	$0.00	$0.00	$0.00	$0.00	$0.00	$0.00	$0.00	$0.00
3.2	Propose shoots	$7,000.00	$7,000.00	$7,000.00	$0.00	$0.00	$7,000.00	$7,000.00	$0.00
3.3	Hire secretary	$4,000.00	$4,000.00	$2,400.00	$0.00	$1,600.00	$2,400.00	$4,000.00	$1,600.00
3.4	Schedule shoots	$1,000.00	$2,000.00	$2,000.00	$1,000.00	$0.00	$2,000.00	$2,000.00	$0.00
3.5	Scheduling completed	$0.00	$0.00	$0.00	$0.00	$0.00	$0.00	$0.00	$0.00
4	Script approval	$4,000.00	$4,000.00	$4,000.00	$0.00	$0.00	$4,000.00	$4,000.00	$0.00
5	Revise script	$7,000.00	$7,000.00	$7,000.00	$0.00	$0.00	$7,000.00	$7,000.00	$0.00
6	Shooting	$7,020.00	$3,600.00	$3,600.00	($3,420.00)	$0.00	$7,200.00	$7,200.00	$0.00
7	Editing	$0.00	$0.00	$0.00	$0.00	$0.00	$5,290.00	$5,290.00	$0.00
8	Final approval	$0.00	$0.00	$0.00	$0.00	$0.00	$6,250.00	$6,250.00	$0.00
9	Deliver DVD to client	$0.00	$0.00	$0.00	$0.00	$0.00	$0.00	$0.00	$0.00
	Totals	$38,420.00	$36,000.00	$40,400.00	($2,420.00)	($4,400.00)	$55,540.00	$51,140.00	($4,400.00)

If the earned value calculations indicate a cost or schedule deficiency, the PM must still figure out what to do (control) to get the project back on budget or schedule. Options include borrowing resources from other tasks, holding a brainstorming meeting with the project team, requesting extra resources from senior management, or informing the client and/or senior management of the projected deficiency. Unfortunately, research on 700 military projects indicated that the chances of correcting a poorly performing project more than 15–20 percent complete were effectively nil (Christensen, 1994).

An interesting exception to this situation is that of ViewStar Corporation, under contract to design an Accounts Receivable imaging system for Texas Instruments. As the project progressed, although costs were under control, earned value progress fell behind. To catch up, ViewStar directed the project team to meet only *key* project requirements at the least cost and time (Ingram, 1995). Earned value thereafter rapidly increased back to the planned schedule.

> Earned value represents a way to capture both in-process performance and cost on a certain date as measured against budget or schedule. Including the planned costs and actual costs allows the calculation of spending and schedule variances, where negative values are undesirable. Using these figures, a projection can be made of costs to completion and total cost for the task or project under consideration. Although percentage completion makes limited sense for individual tasks and work elements, it has little meaning for the project as a whole. Nonetheless, one can aggregate the individual task earned values and variances to make reasonable estimates of project completion costs.

7.4   PROJECT CONTROL

Control, the act of reducing differences between plan and actuality, is the final element in the planning-monitoring-controlling cycle. Monitoring and comparing activities with plan, and reporting these findings is to no avail if actions are not taken when reality deviates significantly from what was planned. In fact, the simple act of noting and reporting discrepancies may motivate the actions required to correct the deviations. When it does not, however, active control is needed to bring performance, schedule, cost, or perhaps all three, back in line with plan. Control has the primary purpose of ensuring that the project is in compliance with its objectives. Particularly in large projects with a wealth of detail and constant hubbub, it is all too easy to lose sight of these three fundamental targets. Large projects develop their own momentum and tend slowly to move out of hand, going their own way regardless of the wishes of the PM, top management, and even the client. In large projects early control is crucial!

Control is one of the PM's most difficult tasks, invariably involving both mechanistic and human elements. Sometimes humans, through action or inaction, set in motion a chain of events that eventually results in a discrepancy between actuality and plan. Sometimes events occur that affect people in a negative way, leading to undesirable discrepancies. Anger, frustration, irritation, helplessness, apathy, despair, and many other emotions arise during the course of a normal project and affect the activities of the project team members who experience them. It is over this welter of confusion, emotion, inertia, fallibility, and general cussedness that the PM tries to intervene and exert control.

Control is difficult for a number of reasons, perhaps the most important of which is that it involves human behavior. The problem that the human element poses for control by the PM is that it invariably involves the project team—a "we" group rather than a "they" group—a group we perceive as our friends. Yet it is difficult to criticize friends, which is exactly what control does. Control means interceding in an activity that someone has been doing and "correcting" it, thereby implying that someone was at fault and doing something wrong.

Another reason that control is difficult is that problems are rarely clear cut, so the need for change and redirection is also fuzzy. In fact, most discrepancies uncovered by a monitoring system turn out to be "messes," in the terminology of Russell Ackoff*. A "mess" is a general condition of a system that, when viewed by a manager, leads to a statement that begins "%#@*&+#!!!" and goes downhill from there. The discovery of a mess leads the PM to suspect that there is a problem(s) affecting the project; and in situations as complex as a project, identification of the real problems is difficult. Determining what to control raises further difficulties. Indeed, it is rarely clear if someone took an incorrect action, and thus needs to be corrected, or if the discrepancy (mess) was simply the work of an unkind Mother Nature.

Purposes of Control

There are two primary purposes of control: the stewardship of organizational assets and the regulation of results through the alteration of activities. So far in this chapter we have primarily discussed the latter in terms of the plan-monitor-control cycle, and we will spend the majority of the rest of the chapter on this purpose also. Thus, we take a moment to discuss the first purpose, conserving the organization's three primary assets: physical, human, and financial.

Physical asset control is concerned with the maintenance and use of the project's physical assets. This includes the timing as well as quality of maintenance being conducted on the assets. For example, it is important to conduct preventive maintenance prior to that last stage of the project life cycle known as the *Last Minute Panic* (LMP), even though the precise timing of the LMP is usually unknown. And, of course, physical inventory must be received, inspected, certified for payment to suppliers, and perhaps stored prior to use. All project assets, even the project coffeepot, project team's couch, and project library, must be controlled. Most important, however, is the set of physical equipment that was charged to the client that must be delivered to the client at the end of the project.

The stewardship of human resources primarily involves controlling and maintaining the growth and development of the project team. Fortunately, projects provide a particularly fertile environment for cultivating humans, given that each project typically offers a unique professional experience over a short duration. These experiences, more than performance appraisals and reports, foster growth and development of project team members.

Last, financial control involves stewardship of the organization's expenditures on the project, including both conservation of financial resources and regulation of resource use. Most accounting tools used for projects are excellent in this area of control: current asset controls, project budgets, capital investment controls, audits, and even representation on the project team through the project accountant. We cannot overemphasize the importance of proper conformance to both the organization's and the client's financial control and record-keeping standards. Recall that all project records, plans, budgets, evaluations, etc. are an organization's "assets" and are subject to the most rigorous control and preservation.

---

*The term "mess" originated in a provoking but delightful after-lunch speech to a large, mixed business/academic audience at a meeting of the American Institute of Decision Sciences (renamed the D.S.I. following the AIDS epidemic in Africa) in Boston, MA on November 16, 1973. In his speech Ackoff draws a useful distinction between detecting and describing a "mess" (the task of managers), and translating the mess into a set of "structured problems" (the task of the analyst/academic).

Nevertheless, the PM is invariably more inclined toward the *use* of project assets than to their conservation. Although most PMs view the conservationist mindset as that of the fabled librarian who is happiest when all the library's books have been collected from readers and are neatly sorted in their proper places on the bookshelves, PMs must realize the dual, albeit conflicting, roles they have assumed. These antithetical attitudes must, however, be merged and compromised in the PM as best they can.

An example of the use of extensive controls to help produce a successful project was the Metro Turnback project for San Francisco (Wu and Harwell, 1998). This massive, high-risk, 11-year underground construction project was conducted in the high-traffic, downtown region of the city. To keep the project on schedule and within budget, an extensive and complex Management Plan and Control System was devised. To illustrate the depth of this monitoring and control system, its subsystems are listed here: Project Code of Accounts, Cost Code of Accounts, Control Budget, Trend Program, Scope Change Log, Monthly Contract Cash Flow Schedule, Contractual Milestone Summary Schedule, Construction Schedule, 3-Week Rolling Construction Schedule, Quality Control and Quality Assurance Program, Contractor's Nonconformance Report, and Corrective Action Report.

For an example of what happens when control is inadequate, we turn to Cincinnati, Ohio, to quote from *The Cincinnati Enquirer* of January 21, 2000:

> Guesswork, management neglect and possible criminal conduct allowed city engineers to report as completed $15 million in street repairs that were never done, a city audit says.
>
> . . . . In annual reports between 1991 and 1997, the city's Engineering Division reported that a total of 818 lane miles [of street repairs] has been completed at a cost of about $65 million.
>
> The internal audit found that only 460 lane miles have been completed, costing $50.5 million. (*Cincinnati Enquirer*, January 21, 2000, p. 1)

The issue has been assigned to limbo, still in a "blame someone else" state. It displayed certain aspects of low comedy with the city's Engineering Division, City Council, and City Manager all involved in the matter. There is little doubt that inadequate and unaudited reporting coupled with incompetent control by managers on several levels over 7 years all contributed to the fiasco.

> Project control, the final activity in the planning-monitoring-control cycle, involves taking action when reality deviates from plan. It includes both mechanistic and human elements, and because it is closely concerned with human behavior, is one of the most difficult tasks of the PM. It includes two seemingly antithetical purposes: (1) stewardship of the organization's and the client's physical, human, and financial assets; and (2) the use of these assets to bring project actuality into conformance with the plan. Somehow, the PM must meld these two purposes into a uniform focus of activity.

7.5 DESIGNING THE CONTROL SYSTEM

When designing the control system, there are certain helpful guidelines to keep in mind. For instance, the primary purpose of the control system is to correct error, not to identify and punish the guilty. Managers must realize that the past cannot be changed, no matter how loudly they yell. Moreover, investment in the control system is subject to sharply diminishing returns. The cost of control increases faster and faster while the degree of control—and its value—increases more and more slowly.

We could, if we wished, control the quality of "hardware store" type wooden yardsticks, so that they were accurate to 1/10,000th of an inch. But who cares? Moreover, who would be willing to invest the increased cost in a product that is usually given away as a gift? Thus, there is some optimum amount of resources worth investing in the control process. The control system should exert control only to the degree required to achieve its objectives; additional control will not help and may be cost-inefficient.

In the same vein, as the degree of control increases beyond some difficult-to-define point, innovation and creativity are discouraged until they are finally shut off completely. In general, the control system should employ the lowest degree of hassle consistent with accomplishing its goals. It is best to avoid annoying those people whose cooperation is needed to reach project goals. To summarize, the control system should be cost-effective and should operate with the minimum force required to achieve the desired end results.

Best Practice

There are three primary mechanisms by which the PM exerts control: *process reviews*, *personnel assignment*, and *resource allocation*. The process review is directed to an analysis of the process of reaching the project objectives rather than on the results, per se. Because results are largely dependent on the process used to achieve them, the process can be subjected to control even if the results cannot. On R&D projects, for example, project team members usually cannot be held responsible for research or technological outcomes, but they can certainly be held responsible for adherence to the proposal, the budget, and the schedule. Care must be taken, however, not to overstress methods as opposed to results; although methods are controllable, it is still the results that count.

As an example of the effective use of process controls, Australia's 7-year Parliament House construction project matched the inherent construction complexity with an equally sophisticated set of schedule, cost, and time controls. The time controls, for instance, included four levels of increasing detail that could be accessed during progress review and coordination meetings (Nixon, 1987).

Control can also be exercised through personnel assignments based on past project productivity. Although it is relatively easy to separate workers in the top and bottom quartiles by measuring performance or productivity, separating the middle two quartiles is much more difficult, so this approach should be used carefully. Moreover, reassignment can have drawbacks in terms of creating elite groups of top producers but demotivating everyone else in the system.

Controlling resource allocation can be a powerful motivator—and demotivator. Resources are usually allocated to the more productive or important tasks and this can significantly influence the attainment of project results. (Remember that all tasks in a project must be completed to complete the project.) As in the use of other control techniques, the PM needs to exercise care when making decisions about which tasks need the resources in the future, regardless of past efficiencies.

There are some common mistakes PMs and other organizational managers make when trying to control projects. For example, when controlling processes, there is the danger of emphasizing short-run results at the expense of long-run objectives. Excessive control directed to specific objectives can result in sacrificing other project objectives. Across-the-board cuts in resource allocations tend to reward those who have already overspent or overhired while penalizing the frugal and efficient. Finally, focusing on certain items for control can distract the attention of team members from other, equally important items: "What isn't counted, doesn't count." There is hardly a community in the United States that has not adopted a set of standardized tests to measure the learning of school children. The salaries of teachers are affected by these test results. It should, therefore, hardly come as a shock to the public that teachers spend considerable time and effort "teaching to the test."

Types of Control Systems

The process of controlling a project, or any other system, is more complex than might be expected. Decisions must be made concerning where in the project we will try to exert control, what is to be controlled, how it will be measured, and how much deviation from plan will be tolerated before we intercede. It is helpful in making these decisions first to understand thoroughly the primary types of control systems used by project managers: *go/no-go controls* and *post-control*.

Before discussing the nature and use of these control systems, it is important to note that every control system must contain certain elements if it is to be useful. Any project (or production system) can be described in terms of its inputs, the process by which it works on the inputs, and the outputs that result. To control a project (or any production system) requires the following components:

1. Each control must have a *sensor*, the duty of which is to measure any aspect of the project's output that one wishes to control. For instance, it must be able to measure the length of the yardstick we mentioned earlier.

2. The control system must have a *standard* for each thing measured. For the yardstick, the standard is 36 inches.

3. Next, the control system needs a *comparator*, a mechanism that compares the output of the sensor with the standard.

4. Given the results of the comparison, the control system needs a *decision maker* to decide if the difference between what the sensor measured and the standard is large enough to warrant attention. For the yardstick, a group of 23 engineers attending a project management seminar did not expect (or require) accuracy greater than plus or minus ¼ inch. For more precise measurement they would insist on a steel tape measure.

5. The final piece required in a control system is an *effector*. If the decision maker decides that some action is required to reduce the difference between what the sensor measures and the standard requires, the effector must take some action. It may operate on the input or the process (or both) to fix the problem.

Some control systems use all five of these elements automatically; for example, the mechanisms that control the ph (level of acidity) of the blood, the temperature of a home, the speed of an automobile operating on cruise control, or the speed with which a sheet of steel moves through a rolling mill. Such systems are called "cybernetic control systems" (kybernet is Greek for helmsman or steersman) or "negative feedback loops" or "steering controls." All of the parts listed above must be present and operative to control any process. It is the PM's responsibility to ensure that such control elements are available and operating in project control. The process will not be automatic during project control. It must be operated by the PM or the PM's deputy.

The go/no-go control takes the form of tests (sensors) to determine if some specific precondition (standard and comparator) has been met before permission is granted to continue (decision maker and effector). This type of control can be used on almost every aspect of a project. The project plan, budget, schedule, earned value charts, and other such information can all operate as control documents. In addition, the PM has pre-specified project milestones as control checkpoints. The PM can intercede at any level of the project tasks and subtasks for which detail is available in these control documents.

The "phase-gate" method of monitoring and control (also known as "quality gate," "toll gate," and other names) often makes use of the natural milestones in a project as phase gates, though some may be ignored or other phases added. The preconditions to pass each gate are specified beforehand so upper management will not be tempted to let a project slip by without a thorough evaluation, the result of which could be approval to proceed, an order for additional resources, a change in direction, or the termination of the project.

It is worth repeating that a primary aim of the PM is to intercept problems before they arise—at least before they get serious—so it is worthwhile for the PM to include an early warning system with the control system. In this way, potential problems can be exposed and dealt with before they turn into full-blown disasters. Because any project early warning system will include people, it is important for the PM to make it known that the messenger who brings bad news will not be shot, but anyone who sweeps bad news or problems under the rug will be!

An example of a status report used by the agricultural products division of a large chemical company for go/no-go control is illustrated in Figure 7-7. As can be seen, some of the tasks are completed, some are in progress, and some have not yet started. Details from the PM or additional reports about those tasks completed and in progress are used to make the go/no-go decisions.

Post-controls, also known as postperformance reviews, are applied after the project has been completed. Although it might appear that this is the legendary situation of locking the barn door after the horse has been stolen, it is not. The purpose here is not to control the already completed project, but to allow future projects to learn and profit from past project experience. Such lessons might include information about certain suppliers, cost-estimating procedures, or even ways of improving the process of managing projects. Certain managerial methods, organizational procedures, or processes might be altered for future projects, resulting in greater predictability and control and, one hopes, better performance, cost, or schedule results.

The earlier the PM can intercede in a problem, the more likely the project team will be able to correct its activities, but humans respond to these controls in different ways. Response to go/no-go controls tends to be neutral. Because there is no gradation between excellent and barely acceptable, or between terrible and just unacceptable, the fine line of acceptability thus becomes a very sharp knife, subject to complaint and irritation. In a project, however, criticism tends to be leveled toward the team instead of the individual so the response is often less severe than it might have been otherwise.

	Project		
Task	#1	#2	#3
Priorities set	C	C	C
PM selected	C	C	C
Key members briefed on RFP	C	C	C
Proposal sent	C	C	C
Proposal accepted as negotiated	C	C	C
Preliminary design developed	C	W/10	C
Design accepted	C	W/12	C
Software developed	C	NS/NR	N/A
Product test design	C	W/30	W/15
Manufacturing scheduled	C	NS/NR	W/8
Tools, jigs, fixtures designed	W/1	NS/NR	W/2
Tools, jigs, fixtures designed	W/2	NS/NR	W/8
Production complete	NS/HR	NS/HR	NS/HR
Product test complete	NS/HR	NS/HR	NS/HR
Marketing sign-off on product	NS/HR	NS/HR	NS/HR

Notes:

Figure 7-7 Sample project milestone status report.

N/A—Not applicable	W—Work in progress (number refers to months required)	NS—Not started
C—Completed		NR—Need resources
		HR—Have resources

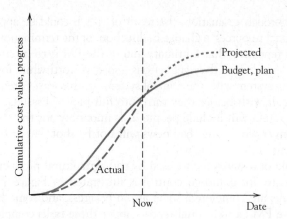

Figure 7-8 Trend projection.

Tools for Control

We have already described some of the tools that can help the PM in designing and applying the control system: variance analysis, trend projections, and earned value analysis. With trend projection, for instance, the PM can plot a budget, plan, or growth curve as shown in Figure 7-8 and then, as actual values come in with project progress, plot these as a dashed line on the same chart. Using the dashed line, the PM can forecast on a continuing basis what the projected completion will be. Based on the projection, the PM can decide if there is a problem, what alternatives exist for control, what they will cost and require, and what they will achieve.

Another useful tool for a PM is the *critical ratio*. A critical ratio indicates to a manager when a task or process is becoming unacceptable, typically when the ratio drops below 1. By tracking the ratio, the manager can anticipate when a problem may be brewing. The calculation of the critical ratio for project tasks is the product of a *schedule ratio* and a *cost ratio*. The schedule ratio is actual progress divided by scheduled progress, as measured by some common standard such as earned value: EV/PV. Clearly, ratios greater than one are desirable. The cost ratio is budgeted cost divided by actual cost, or if earned value data are available, EV/AC. Again, values greater than one are most desirable. Taking the product of these two ratios thus gives us an overall measure that includes performance, cost, and schedule.

$$CR = (actual\ progress/scheduled\ progress) \times (budgeted\ cost/actual\ cost)$$

Note that the two ratios are equally important in the calculation of the critical ratio. If one ratio is bad, it can be offset by the other ratio if it is equally good. For example, if the actual progress is 2 and the scheduled progress is 3, resulting in a schedule ratio of 2/3, and the budgeted cost is 6 and the actual cost is 4, resulting in a cost ratio of 3/2, their product, $2/3 \times 3/2 = 1$. Thus, although the project is behind schedule, the cost is correspondingly below budget so everything is fine if lateness is no problem for this activity. This may not really be acceptable to the PM, so a wise PM will evaluate the components of a critical ratio as well as the overall value. Remember that the measurement of progress is subject to the same warnings we noted in the discussion of earned value.

Similar calculations are given in Table 7-3 where the above example is an illustration of Task Number 1. Task 2 is on budget but progress is lacking, so too much money was spent than should have been spent; when the project is completed, it will probably go over budget. Similarly, Task 3 is on schedule but is over budget, creating another probable cost overrun. The critical ratios for Tasks 4 and 5 both

Table 7-3 Critical Ratio (CR) = (actual progress/scheduled progress) × (budgeted cost/actual cost)

Task Number	Actual Progress		Scheduled Progress		Budgeted Cost		Actual Cost		Critical Ratio
1	(2	/	3)	×	(6	/	4)	=	1.0
2	(2	/	3)	×	(6	/	6)	=	.67
3	(3	/	3)	×	(4	/	6)	=	.67
4	(3	/	2)	×	(6	/	6)	=	1.5
5	(3	/	3)	×	(6	/	4)	=	1.5

Table 7-4 Monitoring the Critical Ratio

Day	Actual Project Progress		Scheduled Project Progress		Budgeted Project Cost		Actual Project Cost		Critical Ratio
July 17	(13	/	14)	×	(28	/	26)	=	1.00
18	(18	/	17)	×	(34	/	26)	=	1.15
:		:			:		:		

exceed 1.0, and none of the subratios is a problem. Task 4 is ahead of schedule and on budget, and Task 5 is on schedule and below budget. The PM may want to look further into these happy events to see what is going on, or if the monitoring system is reporting accurately.

Beyond evaluating each of the activities of a project, a critical ratio for the project as a whole can be calculated as well, as illustrated in Table 7-4. Here, the project is assumed to consist of the five tasks in Table 7-3 and the values of each element of the critical ratio are summed on a daily basis with the critical ratio calculated for each day. This ratio can then be itself tracked in a table (see Table 7-4 where the first day is from Table 7-3) and plotted on a *control chart*. The PM can also set some "control limits" for the critical ratio so that if they are exceeded on the upside or downside, an investigation is in order, as shown in Figure 7-9. Different tasks, of course, may warrant different control limits. Further, the upside limits may be different, probably larger, than the downside (problem) limits.

Dealing with such differences is the purpose of another tool, the *control chart*. Any measure—the volume of raw material being used, the cost of contract labor in the project, the hours of computer time—can be plotted and tracked on a control chart such as that shown in Figure 7-10. As illustrated, control limits for intervention can be set by the PM and shown on the chart, so that when a measure exceeds one of these limits, action is instigated.

Another recent development, *benchmarking*, can be a useful tool for a PM when designing a monitoring and control system (Christensen, 1994; Gupta and Graham, 1997; Ibbs and Kwak, 1998; Thamhain, 1996; Toney, 1997). The process here is to make comparisons to "best in class" practices across organizations, or divisions, or even departments within an organization. An example is a benchmarking study (Ibbs and Kwak, 1998) to generate data for a Project Management Maturity Model. The model measures project processes, tools, techniques, and practices across a range of industries, the various life-cycle phases, and the ten knowledge areas of PMBOK.

PMBOK Guide

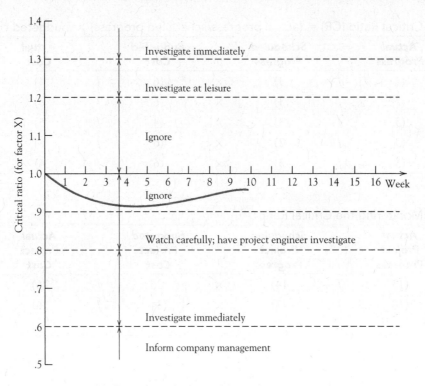

Figure 7-9 Critical ratios with control limits.

Figure 7-10 Cost control chart.

An example of an internal benchmarking study was Johnson Control's benchmarking of the project management procedures of their own highly successful product development project managers, to be used by less-successful project managers. They identified four common sets of procedures these successful PMs all used. These procedures are now used to train new employees, standardize practices, create a common language, tie together company functions, and create a positive project management culture (Reith and Kandt, 1991). Benchmarking and the control chart are tools commonly used in quality management, a subject discussed in more detail in Chapter 8 of PMBOK. (See also Meredith and Shafer, 2013.)

PMBOK Guide

> Designing the project control system entails many issues, but the major guiding objective should be to create a balanced system where the benefits obtained exceed the cost of control. The primary means to active control by the PM are process reviews, personnel reassignment, and resource allocation. Two types of control systems are useful for projects: go/no-go controls and post-controls. Tools to aid the PM in control are variance analysis, trend projections, earned value analysis, critical ratios, control charts, and benchmarking.

7.6 SCOPE CREEP AND CHANGE CONTROL

If midcourse changes in the project specifications are not controlled, the following are typical results: a newspaper front-page headline reading "**Stadium costs soaring;**" an article on an inner page stating that "Change orders . . . are one of the most common sources of waste and fraud during projects, experts say;" and a quote from a County Commissioner, "The project is in trouble, but it's absolutely recoverable. . . . We can work out responsibility for those payments at a later time. Now is not the time to start pointing fingers." An auditor appointed to look into the matter "found that there is not sufficient oversight to properly monitor the change orders, check if they were necessary and determine who is responsible" (see *Cincinnati Enquirer*, February 15, 2000, pp. A-1 and A-4).

As we noted in Chapter 6, input from over 500 project managers regarding things that "bugged" PMs the most indicated that coping with changes is at the top of their list. The most common source of changes is the natural tendency of the client, as well as the project team members, to try to improve the project's output as the project progresses—a phenomenon so frequently encountered, a name for it has been coined: "scope creep." The most common result of scope creep is an upset client who was not (or claims not to have been) told how long the change would delay the project and how much it would raise the project's cost. The general subject of scope management is described in more detail in Chapter 5 of PMBOK.

PMBOK Guide

New technologies and materials become available, new requirements and needs become apparent, and these lead to changed projects. The later these changes are made in the project, the more difficult and costly they become. The one absolutely certain thing about a project—even though virtually nothing in a project is ever certain—is that there will be concerted attempts to change it. PMs must expect these attempts and be prepared to deal with them. Fighting change is not appropriate. The best approach is for the PM to set up a well-controlled, formal process whereby such changes can be introduced and accomplished with as little distress as possible.

This process is known as the *change control system*. The purpose of this system is to:

- review all requested changes (either content or procedural changes)
- identify all impacts the change may have on other project tasks
- translate these impacts into alterations of project scope, schedule, and cost
- evaluate the benefits and disadvantages of the requested changes
- identify and evaluate alternative changes that might accomplish the same ends with greater benefits and/or fewer disadvantages
- install a process so that individuals with appropriate authority may accept or reject the proposed changes
- communicate accepted changes to all concerned parties
- ensure that the changes are implemented properly
- prepare reports that summarize all changes to date and their impacts

Best Practice

Avoiding scope creep is not possible. Controlling it, and thereby reducing some of the pain, is possible—if the PM follows a few rules.

1. Every project plan must include a *change control system* by which requests for changes in the project's plan, processes, budget, schedule, or deliverables are evaluated.
2. Every project change must be introduced by a *change order* that includes a description of the agreed-upon change together with any resulting changes in the plan, processes, budget, schedule, or deliverables.
3. Changes must be approved in writing by the client's agent as well as by a representative of senior management of the firm conducting the project.
4. The project manager must be consulted on all proposed changes prior to the preparation and approval of the change order. (The PM's approval is not required.)
5. Once the change order has been approved, the project plan be amended to reflect the change and the change order becomes a part of that plan.

The process of controlling change is not complicated. For large projects, a change control board consisting of all interested parties is recommended for handling change requests. For smaller projects, a smaller group may be designated. The main source of trouble with requested changes is typically that the PM, in an attempt to avoid bureaucracy, adopts an informal process of handling requests for change. Such a process leads to misunderstanding on the part of the party requesting the change, and before the PM can undo the damage, the organization is committed to extending the scope of the project but without the additional resources and time to do it.

Risk

In March 2003, the United Kingdom's Child Support Agency (CSA) started using their new $860 million software system for receiving and disbursing child support payments (PMI, January 2005). By the end of 2004, however, only about 12 percent of all applications had received payments, and even those took about three times longer to process than expected. CSA is now threatening to scrap the entire system and is withholding $2 million/month in service payments to the software vendor. The problem seems to be due to control both scope management problems and the lack of a risk management strategy. The vendor claims that the project was disrupted constantly by CSA's 2,500 change requests, while CSA maintains that there were only 50 requests, but the contract did not include a scope management plan to help define what constituted a scope change request. The lack of a risk management strategy resulted in no contingency or fallback plan in case of trouble, so when project delays surfaced and inadequate training became apparent, there was no way to recover.

> Scope creep arises quite naturally from both the client as well as the project team as new capabilities and needs surface during the course of the project. Rather than trying to ignore or handle change requests on an informal basis, the PM must anticipate that they will inevitably arise and institute a formal *change control system* to handle them. The purpose of the system is to evaluate each change formally to determine its benefits as well as its costs and other impacts on the project, and to make arrangements for obtaining the resources and altering the project specifications as needed to implement the change, if it is eventually approved.

REVIEW QUESTIONS

1. Why can't the PM use the organization's current information system for project monitoring and reporting?

2. What does it mean to say that project monitoring and control are on the opposite sides of project selection and planning?

3. The monitoring system is the direct connection between project planning and control. Why is this true?

4. Why is it probably a good idea to avoid periodic reports, except in specific cases such as reports tied to the organization's accounting system?

5. Aside from the obvious benefits for project control, what other benefits might result from a good project reporting system?

6. If the calendar should not dictate reporting frequency, what should?

7. Using earned value analysis, explain how the total cost of a partially completed project can be estimated.

DISCUSSION QUESTIONS

8. When making an estimate for the time and cost to execute a project, should the time and cost required to develop the planning, monitoring, and controlling systems be included as well? Should the actions required to monitor and control a project be included in the project's action plan or WBS?

9. The chapter included an example of a firm where the PM dispensed with all the planning formality because no one ever looked at it anyway. What did the PM think the purpose of such planning was in this firm? What should the firm do in the future to correct this problem?

10. In fields such as psychology and sociology, verbal characterizations are frequently used to show the amount of some factor. How might one set up such a measure for a project management characteristic such as the "energy" of the project team?

11. How might one measure team morale?

12. How can the PM circumvent the problem that the monitoring system can only report on activities that have passed, thus telling the PM what has already gone wrong but not what will go wrong in the future?

13. How might using electronic media to report project information lead to problems with control?

14. Explain how the earned value chart captures all three objectives of a project: performance, cost, and schedule.

15. Why isn't there an earned value reporting convention that allows progress on a task to be credited when the task is half completed? Wouldn't this be more accurate than giving credit only when the task is finally completed?

16. When would spending and schedule variances be more informative than ratios? When would ratios be better?

17. How should a PM reconcile the dual purposes of control: conserving resources and regulating results through the use of resources?

18. Identify situations where each of the following control tools might be useful: earned value charts, benchmarking, critical ratios, control charts, variance analysis, trend projections.

19. How might the existence of a change control system affect the behavior of a client, or a project team member, who desires to make a change in the project?

20. "In order to manage for overall project success, control must be exercised at the detailed work level for each aspect of project performance or no significant change will occur." Does this mean that the PM should micromanage the project? If not, what does it mean?

21. Select a hypothetical project (e.g., designing and building a Web site, installing a new machine in an assembly line, or conducting a major inspection and repair of a passenger aircraft), and briefly describe an example of how each of the following types of control data might be used for project control: (a) Frequency counts (b) Raw numbers (c) Subjective numeric ratings (d) Indicator and surrogate measures.

22. Of all the rules for conducting meetings, the most difficult to enforce is the injunction against the weekly (or daily) standard project progress report (the "show and tell" meeting). Why is this, and under what circumstances do you think that such meetings are justified?

23. If your project management software calculates earned value, or any other standard item to be reported, differently than the Project Management Institute suggests, should you deal with this matter in management reports? If so, how?

24. Logically, when using earned value data in the critical ratio formula, should the "budgeted cost" be the planned value or the earned value? What problems occur with each choice?

PROBLEMS

25. A project in its 26th week has an actual cost of $270,000. It was scheduled to have spent $261,000. For the work performed to date, the budgeted value is $272,000. What are the cost and schedule variances for the project? What are the SPI and CPI?

26. A project has just completed the 87th item in its plan. It was scheduled to have spent $168,000 at this point in the plan, but has actually spent only $156,000. The foreman estimates that the value of the work actually finished is about $162,000. What are the spending and schedule variances for the project? What are the SPI and CPI?

27. The following project is at the end of its sixth week. Find the cost and schedule variances. Also find the CPI and SPI. Then find the critical ratio of the project using earned value calculations. Finally, calculate the ETC and EAC for the project.

Activity	Predecessors	Duration (wks)	Budget ($)	Actual Cost ($)	% Complete
a	—	2	300	400	100
b	—	3	200	180	100
c	a	2	250	300	100
d	a	5	600	400	20
e	b, c	4	400	200	20

28. Repeat Problem 27 using MSP (omit calculation of CPI and SPI).

29. Given an activity in a smartphone design project whose planned cost was $13,000 but actual cost to date is $12,000 so far, and whose value completed is only 80%, calculate the cost and schedule variances. Will the client be pleased or angry?

30. Resolve Problem 27 using the 50-50 rule for planned value and earned value.

31. Given the following information about a website design, which activities are on time, which are early, and which are behind schedule?

Activity	Budgeted Cost	Actual Cost	Critical Ratio
A	$300	$200	1.0
B	125	250	0.5
C	225	150	1.5
D	100	100	1.5
E	250	250	0.67

32. Design and plot a critical ratio chart for an advertising project that had planned constant, linear progress from 0 to an earned value of 400 over a 100-day duration. In fact, progress for the first 20 days has actually been: 4, 6,8,12,14,18,24,28,30,34,40,42,42,44,48,52,54,58,62, 66. What can you conclude about this project?

INCIDENTS FOR DISCUSSION

St. Margaret's Hospital

Mary Lynn DeCold is the Quality Improvement Director at St. Margaret's Hospital, a large acute care facility. She is responsible for monitoring all of the performance improvement projects that take place in the hospital. At any given time numerous projects can be underway, some departmental and some enterprise-wide efforts.

The Joint Commission on Accreditation of Healthcare Organizations is scheduled to conduct a survey of St. Margaret's in 9 months. It is a requirement of the accrediting agency that three performance improvement projects be spotlighted during the survey. Mary Lynn wants to be sure that she picks three projects that will be finished within the next month or 2 so that they have at least 6 months' worth of data to show that the project improved performance.

Mary Lynn is having trouble getting information on the status of the three projects she chose. Communication between the project managers and the Quality Improvement Department is not always timely. She wants to be sure that all three are completed in plenty of time before the survey is scheduled. Mary Lynn also wants to be able to tell where the projects are in relation to each other, as they all need to be completed by a certain date. She wonders how she can tell if they are behind or ahead of schedule.

Question: What would you recommend Mary Lynn do?

Stoneworth Paving Company

Stoneworth Paving Company specializes in highway paving jobs for the State of Virginia. When the state first awarded Stoneworth the contract, they stipulated a 1 percent penalty for each week Stoneworth was late on a completion date. Preston Flintrock, the project coordinator for Stoneworth, began to notice that the last two jobs were 3 weeks late, and the paving job that was due to be completed in the next 2 weeks was behind schedule. When Preston went in the field to investigate, he found the job to be understaffed, supplier delays, and a high work rejection rate/repaving needed. As a result, Preston decided to establish a better system of project control and present it to his boss.

Question: If you were Preston, what characteristics would you be looking for in a new control system? Will a new control system be adequate for the problem? Explain.

Happy Customers

J. Z. Smith is a small consulting firm specializing in implementing new information systems installation projects for service agencies. J. Z. Smith has a standard project action plan for the implementation projects they work on. They feel very confident in the project plan they use; all steps are included and the costs are estimated well.

The project teams are very entrepreneurial and have great relationships with their small client base. The company works with their clients informally following the standard action plan. They provide weekly progress reports for the client and for Jeremy Smith, the president of J. Z. Smith. Jeremy has noticed that they have problems with meeting budgets and due dates. He thinks his teams allow their clients to add steps to the projects. A current client, the local welfare department, has asked J. Z. Smith to help them implement a newly purchased Dead-Beat-Parent tracking system. Jeremy is nervous and wants to be sure that they meet the specifications of this new project. He is not sure if the standard action plan needs changing or if there is something else he should do.

Question: What should Jeremy Smith do?

Cable Tech, Inc.

Cable Tech is a contract cable wiring company. It provides support to local cable companies in seven states in the midwest. Cable Tech has one operation in each state, and they vary in size from 60 to 250 employees. A disturbing trend has been developing for the last couple of years that Cable Tech management wishes to stop. Incidences of tardiness and absenteeism are on the increase. Both are extremely disruptive in a contract wiring operation. Cable Tech is nonunion in all seven locations, and since management wants to keep this situation, it wants a careful, low-key approach to the problem. Assistant Personnel Manager Jean Alister has been appointed project manager to recommend a solution. All seven operations managers have been assigned to work with her on this problem.

Jean has had no problem interfacing with the operations managers. They quickly agreed that three steps must be taken to solve the problem:

1. Institute a uniform daily attendance report that is summarized weekly and forwarded to the main office. (Current practice varies from location to location, but comments on attendance are normally included in monthly operations reports.)

2. Institute a uniform disciplinary policy, enforced in a uniform manner.

3. Initiate an intensive employee education program to emphasize the importance of good attendance.

In addition, the team decided that the three-point program should be tested before a final recommendation is presented. They thought it would be best to test the program at one location for 2 months. Jean wants to control and evaluate the test by having a daily attendance report transmitted to her directly at headquarters, from which she will make the final decision on whether or not to present the program in its current format.

Question: Does this monitoring and control method seem adequate? What are the potential problems?

C A S E

St. Dismas Assisted Living Facility Case—5

It is now just 4 months until the Assisted Living Facility program is scheduled to be completed. The team is excited because they can watch the construction of the facility and feel they are moving toward the end of this program.

Every week since construction began, the construction project manager, Kyle Nanno, has been holding a meeting of his project team. At the meetings he invites representatives of the construction company, the facilities manager from St. Dismas, the Director of Security, and other key people as he deems necessary. The meetings are scheduled every Friday at 1:00 PM and last not more than 1 hour. No matter who is or is not there, Kyle starts the meetings exactly at 1:00 PM. Kyle developed the following standing agenda:

1. Review schedule and budget as of today's date
2. Review schedule and budget for next 2 weeks
3. Issues impacting schedule or budget
4. Next steps and action items to be completed

The construction project update presented at the April 11, 2001 meeting is shown on the next page.

After each meeting the construction project manager emails the minutes of the meeting and the action item list generated to each member of the Construction Project team. He also sends the information to Fred Splient, the president of St. Dismas, as well as to each member of the ALF Project Steering Team.

Following the update is the most recent copy of the action items generated at the 4/11/01 construction project meeting.

Upon reading the minutes and action items from the week's meeting, Fred got quite angry. Fred read the minutes every week and would immediately phone Kyle to ask why certain decisions still had not been made. This week he wanted to know why the location of the security panel had not been picked out yet, and what the hair salon issue was about. Kyle decided that these matters would be better discussed face to face. He went to Fred's office.

Kyle proceeded to explain to Fred that the Director of Security, Frank Geagy, had not attended the construction project update meeting in weeks. Kyle said that Frank informed him that in light of the cost cutting going on in the hospital, he is short staffed and cannot hire a new security guard. Frank states that he personally has to cover shifts during the time when the update meetings take place. Kyle told Fred that he was not comfortable making the security panel decision without the head of security's input, and that Frank has not returned his phone calls or answered his emails. Fred Splient proceeded to tell Kyle in a very loud and angry voice, "That guy is not short staffed and is not busy covering anyone's shift. Who does he think he is?" Fred instructed Kyle to tell Frank to answer the contractor's questions immediately or the decisions would be made for him.

Kyle said he would do so and then changed the subject. He told Fred that they were still waiting for the city officials to approve the parking lot construction permit. St. Dismas's legal officer estimated that it would take 8–10 weeks to hear back on approval. Kyle allocated that amount of time in the schedule.

Kyle received notice from Fred to proceed with the parking lot construction on January 11, 2001. On February 9, he submitted the application for a permit, complete with appropriate plans and descriptions of the proposed lot, and allocated 10 weeks to wait for the county to notify him. He expected approval on or before April 19 and scheduled construction to begin April 20. Privately, he doubted he would hear from the county by his target date.

The lot would take 3 weeks to build, 2 weeks to install the lighting and add landscaping, and 1 week to pave and stripe. The plot had to be completed by the end of June so that parking spaces would be available when Marketing wanted to begin showing the facility to potential residents. This was a tight schedule, but the marketing people insisted that residents had to begin preparing for this kind of move at least a month before they took residence. Potential residents needed to see the facility, get familiar with apartment layouts, and they needed a place to park. Also, Marketing insisted on having some occupancy by the opening date.

Kyle told Fred that Legal was calling the county weekly to follow up. Fred wanted to know why the parking lot construction was not outlined on the project plan for facility construction. Fred asked Kyle to add it to the Gantt chart and to do a what-if analysis on the assumption that the county did not respond until May 1. Fred also wanted to know the latest date that they could be notified and still meet a June 15 deadline for completion of the lot.

As Kyle was leaving Fred's office, Fred asked him about the hair salon. Kyle explained that the COO and VP of Marketing had come up with an idea to build and operate a hair salon in the facility for the residents. They thought this might be a great selling point that could generate revenue. They came to Kyle just 2 months ago and asked him to include a hair salon on the first floor of the facility. Kyle explained that he did not have enough information to be able to determine the impact this would have on the construction schedule or the cost of this addition. Fred listened and then wondered if the members of his team had done any analysis to determine if this was a good idea or not. Fred told Kyle he would get back to him on that one. He then made a phone call to the COO and VP of Marketing.

**Assisted Living Facility
Construction Project Update
as of 4/11/01**

ID	Task Name	Baseline Start	Actual Start	Baseline Finish	Actual Finish	Baseline Duration	Actual Duration	Remaining Variance	Dur. Variance	Finish Variance
1	Construction & furnishings	03/01/00	03/01/00	07/30/01	NA	369 days	278.76 days	104.24 days	14 days	14 days
2	Facility construction	03/01/00	03/01/00	06/04/01	NA	329 days	285.12 days	57.88 days	14 days	14 days
3	Phase 1 - Foundation & Excavation	03/01/00	03/01/00	07/11/00	08/01/00	95 days	110 days	0 days	15 days	15 days
4	Phase 2 - Structure	04/19/00	05/24/00	09/22/00	10/09/00	113 days	99 days	0 days	–14 days	11 days
5	Phase 3 - Enclosure	07/12/00	08/01/00	01/15/01	01/15/01	134 days	120 days	0 days	–14 days	0 days
6	Phase 4 - Interiors	07/12/00	08/01/00	06/04/01	NA	234 days	139 days	95 days	0 days	14 days
7	First 45 (light-assisted) units ready to prepare for occupancy	05/01/01	NA	05/01/01	NA	0 days	0 days	0 days	0 days	14 days
8	First 45 units ready for residents	05/01/01	NA	06/25/01	NA	8 wks	0 wks	8 wks	0 wks	14 days
9	Remaining 57 units (light & heavy) ready to prepare for occupancy	06/04/01	NA	06/04/01	NA	0 days	0 days	0 days	0 days	14 days
10	Construction complete	06/04/01	NA	06/04/01	NA	0 days	0 days	0 days	0 days	14 days
11	Building ready for residents	06/05/01	NA	07/30/01	NA	8 wks	0 wks	8 wks	0 wks	14 days

Project Manager: K. Nanno

St. Dismas—Assisted Living Facility
Construction coordination meeting 4/11/01
ACTION ITEM LIST

Item	Date Initiated	Date Required	Date Resolved	Required From	Comments
Provide notice to proceed on parking lots	01/10/2001	ASAP	02/11/2001	St. Dismas	Proposal to St. Dismas 1/18/00
Provide P.S. # for designer to purchase accessories	11/9/2000	12/1/2000	02/8/2001	St. Dismas	
What are the security requirements? There are fire doors, and they do not have locks. We have rough-in for card readers, but no electric hardware.	11/9/2000	12/1/2000		St. Dismas Security	Cost proposal to St. Dismas 1/13/00
Lighting review—will exterior lighting in addition to the building mounted lights be required?	12/14/2000	03/15/2001	03/15/2001	St. Dismas lighting consultant & electrician	
Location of security panel	09/28/2000	ASAP		St. Dismas security	
Room number style and placement	01/18/2000	01/27/2001	02/11/2001	St. Dismas designer	Part of signage discussion
Parking lot permit	02/9/2001	ASAP		Contractor	Permit application 2/9/2001, waiting for City to approve
Fire alarm connection to hospital panel	02/11/2001	ASAP		St. Dismas electrician	Conduit required
Hair salon decision	02/11/2001	ASAP		St. Dismas	
Updated fire alarm drawings	02/7/2001	07/1/01		Contractor & electrician	

QUESTIONS

1. What do you think the construction project manager should have done when the Director of Security stopped attending the project meetings?

2. Do you think it is an effective communications tool to send the construction project meeting minutes to the ALF steering team and the President? Support your answer.

3. How much time has to be made up for the original, baseline schedule to be met?

4. Develop a plan and draw a Gantt chart for the Parking Lot phase of the project as originally planned by Kyle. Answer Fred's questions.

5. What information does Fred need to make a decision about building a hair salon?

C A S E

Palmstar Enterprises, Inc.

Palmstar Enterprises, a leading manufacturer of tablet computers, is currently in the process of developing its next generation device, the model 2000HD. A key feature of the 2000HD is its high definition display. According to the original project schedule, the 2000HD is to be released 1 month from now.

Because the amount of time required to convert the existing software to capitalize on the high definition display was significantly underestimated, the project has fallen behind schedule. The project manager estimates that without additional resources, the development project will be 3 months late. He has also estimated that increasing the project's budget of $3 million by 30 percent

would permit the project to be completed on schedule. The added budget would be used primarily to staff the project with additional software engineers.

If released on schedule, first quarter demand for the 2000HD is forecast to be 200,000 units at an initial price of $450. Demand data for similar products suggest that unit sales will increase 5 percent per quarter over the product's 3-year life. Despite pricing pressures in the market, accounting data indicate that Palmstar is able to maintain a 20 percent contribution margin to profit and overhead through continuous process improvements and efficiencies accruing from producing in larger volumes.

QUESTIONS

1. What has a larger impact on Palmstar's profits: delaying the 2000HD's introduction by 3 months or increasing the project's budget by 30 percent?

2. Are there other factors you would consider in addition to profit?

3. What should Palmstar do? Why?

4. How generalizable do you think the results of your analysis in this particular case are to other situations?

C A S E

Peak Lighting, Inc.

Peak Lighting, Inc. develops stages, lighting systems, and special effects for the concert tours of major musical acts. Recently, they were approached by Bullwhip, a popular band, to develop the stage, lighting, and special effects for its upcoming tour.

The project to develop the stage, lighting, and special effects for a concert tour progresses through four major phases. In the first phase, which lasts about a week, Peak develops a sound track for the concert based on the song list the band provides it for the tour. Using the sound track, Peak employees develop a synchronized lighting and special effects show on a computer that allows them to view an animated stage with the lighting and special effects as the sound track is being played.

In the second phase, the materials needed for the stage, lighting, and special effects are ordered from outside suppliers. The lead time for receiving these mate-

rials is 4 weeks, and during this period the project team members are assigned to other projects.

Once all the materials arrive, the third phase involves constructing the stage with the lighting and special effects. Also, writing the computer code to control the lighting and special effects is done in the third phase. This phase takes 3 weeks.

In the final phase, which takes a week, the lighting and special effects are tested and enhanced. The total cost of the Bullwhip project is estimated to be $600,000 of which $400,000 is for the stage, lighting equipment, and special effects, and $200,000 is for labor costs.

Eric Page was recently hired as Peak's VP of Operations. All the project managers that oversee the stage and lighting projects report to Eric. Prior to joining Peak Lighting, Eric served as a project manager for a leading management consulting firm for 10 years. Based on his extensive project management experience, one of the first things Eric did in his new role as VP was implement a formal project reporting system that would help him monitor the progress of the projects under way.

The Bullwhip project had been underway for 5 weeks, and all the materials had arrived. The project team was now ready to start the third phase of the project and construct the stage with the designed lighting and special effects.

In reviewing the most recent progress report for the Bullwhip project and based on his project management experience, Eric became gravely concerned. According to the report, the project had an earned value of $120,000 based on the project manager Jimmy Rush's estimate that 20 percent of the project had been completed. In further studying the report, Eric observed that the planned value and actual costs incurred were both $440,000.

Based on his concern, Eric decided to walk down the hall to Jimmy's cubicle and discuss his concerns related to the progress on the project.

Eric began:

I just reviewed the progress report for the Bullwhip project, and I am very concerned that the project is falling way behind schedule. Based on my review, it appears there are very significant cost and schedule variances. As you know, we have a hard deadline for completing the project as the Bullwhip needs everything fully operational 2 weeks prior to the start of their tour so they can rehearse with it.

Jimmy responded:

To be perfectly honest, I don't know much about schedule and cost variances but I do have a great deal of experience managing these projects. Again, I don't know how you calculated the variances you mentioned, but in my view we are exactly where we should be.

To this Eric replied:

I don't see how you can possibly think the project is on track when it has an earned value of only $120,000 and the planned value by this point in the project is $440,000? And I am equally disturbed you don't understand basic project management concepts such as earned value.

Later that day, Jimmy shared his frustration about his new boss with one of the project team members. "Eric really chewed me out today. He questioned my ability to manage a project. I wonder if he even understands the nature of these projects. Does he even get it that two thirds of the project costs are for materials and that these costs are incurred in the early part of the project?"

QUESTIONS

1. Calculate the schedule variance and cost variance for the Bullwhip project.

2. Does Jimmy's point about the material costs have merit? If so, does this have any implications for the way the earned valued is calculated at Peak?

3. Who is right about the status of the project? Eric or Jimmy?

4. What advice, if any, would you offer Eric related to his new role of VP of Operations?

BIBLIOGRAPHY

ACKOFF, R. L. "Beyond Problem Solving." *Decision Sciences*, April 1974.

ADAMS, J. R., and L. L. ADAMS. "The Virtual Project: Managing Tomorrow's Team Today." *PM Network*, January 1997. (An excellent brief discussion that covers the nature of virtual projects and some of the communication methods allowing their proliferation.)

BARR, Z. "Earned Value Analysis: A Case Study." *PM Network*, December 1996.

BYRNE, J. "Project Management: How Much Is Enough?" *PM Network*, February 1999.

CHRISTENSEN, D. S. "A Review of Cost/Schedule Control Systems Criterion Literature." *Project Management Journal*, September 1994. (This study of military projects notes that after a project is 15–20 percent complete, its total CPI changes by less than 10 percent and overruns worsen. This article is briefly noted in Flemming and Koppleman, 1996.)

DEAN, B. V. *Evaluating, Selecting, and Controlling R&D Projects*. New York: American Management Association Research Study 89, 1968.

FLEMMING, Q. W., and J. M. KOPPLEMAN. "Forecasting the Final Cost and Schedule Results." *PM Network*, January 1996. (This is one of five excellent, instructional articles on earned value by these authors. They appeared in *PM Network* between January 1994 and May 1996.)

GUPTA, V. K., and D. J. GRAHAM. "A Customer Driven Quality Improvement and Management Project at Diamond Offshore Drilling." *Project Management Journal*, September 1997.

IBBS, C. W., and Y.-H. Kwak. "Benchmarking Project Management Organizations." *PM Network*, February 1998. (This article discusses the development of a tool for finding and assessing the "best" managerial tools for project management.)

INGRAM, T. "Client/Server, Imaging and Earned Value: A Success Story." *PM Network*, December 1995.

MEREDITH, J. R., and S. M. SHAFER. *Operations Management for MBAs*, 5th ed. New York: John Wiley, 2013.

NIXON, T. R. "Project Management at the New Parliament House, Canberra." *Project Management Journal*, September 1987.

PMI, "Lack of Support," *PM Network*, January 2005.

PMI Standards Committee. *A Guide to the Project Management Body of Knowledge* 5th ed. Newton Square, PA: Project Management Institute, 2013.

REITH, W. D., and D. B. KANDT. "Project Management at a Major Automotive Seating Supplier." *Project Management Journal*, September 1991.

THAMHAIN, H. J. "Best Practices for Controlling Technology-Based Projects." *Project Management Journal*, December 1996. (A fine analytical study of finding and assessing the "best practices" for controlling high-technology projects. It not only finds the "best" control practices, but also generates a "benchmark" to which any firm can compare its practices.)

TONEY, F. "What the Fortune 500 Know about PM Best Practices." *PM Network*, February 1997.

WU, C., and G. HARWELL. "The MUNI Metro Turnback Project." *PM Network*, May 1998.

8

Evaluating and Terminating the Project

As the Beagle 2 Mars probe designed jointly by the European Space Agency and British National Space Center headed to the surface of Mars in December 2003, contact was lost and the probe never heard from again (PMI, October 2004). In retrospect, it appears that excessive pressure on time, cost, and weight compromised the mission right from the start. With insufficient public funding, the design team had to spend much of their time raising private funds instead of addressing difficult technical issues. Further, late changes forced the team to reduce the Beagle's weight from 238 pounds to 132 pounds. The three airbags developed to soften the probe's landing impact failed during tests, and a parachute design was installed, but lack of time prevented sufficient testing of it. A review commission recommended that in the future:

Risk

- Requisite financing be available at the outset of a project.
- Formal project reviews be conducted on a regular basis.
- Milestones be established where all stakeholders reconsider the project.
- Expectations of potential failure be included in the funding consideration.
- Robust safety margins be included and funded for uncertainties.

We now come to the final stage in any project—evaluating the result and shutting down the project. As we will see, there are many ways to do both, some relatively formal, some quick and dirty, and some rather casual. We discuss evaluation first, in the generic sense, and then discuss a very specific and often formal type of evaluation known as the project audit. Following this we discuss termination of the project.

8.1   EVALUATION

The term "evaluate" means to set the value of or appraise. A *project evaluation* appraises the progress and performance relative to the project's initial or revised plan. The evaluation also appraises the project against the goals and objectives set for it during the selection process—amended, of course, by any changes in the goals and objectives made during the project's life. In addition, evaluations are sometimes made relative to other similar projects.

The project evaluation, however, should not be limited simply to an after-the-fact analysis. Rather, it is useful to conduct an evaluation at a number of crucial points during the project life cycle. Because the primary purpose of a project evaluation is to give feedback to senior management for decision and control purposes, it is important for the evaluation to have credibility in the eyes of both senior management and the project team. The control purpose of evaluation is meant to improve the process of carrying out projects. The decision purpose is intended to improve the selection process. Thus an evaluation should be as carefully planned and executed as the project itself.

PMBOK Guide

The use of postproject evaluation is to help the organization improve its project-management skills on future projects. PMBOK refers to this as "lessons learned," a topic PMBOK covers in Chapter 8 on Quality. This means that considerable attention must be given to managing the process of project management. This is best accomplished and most effective if there is already a project-management guide or manual detailing standardized project-management practices for the organization. Such manuals commonly cover best practices for planning, monitoring, and controlling projects and may include advice on both selecting and terminating projects. An example of such a manual was that developed by Johnson Controls, described in Chapter 7, where internal benchmarking of their most successful project managers identified four sets of detailed project management procedures. These procedures are updated with each new project experience so that the learning that has occurred is captured and made available for future projects.

Evaluation Criteria

There are many different measures that may be applied in a project evaluation. As indicated, senior management may have particular areas they want evaluated for future planning and decisions, and these should be indicated in the charge to the evaluation committee. Beyond that, the original criteria for selecting and funding the project should be considered—for example, profitability, acquiring new competencies for the organization, or getting a foothold in a new market segment. Any special reasons for selection should also play a role. Was this project someone's sacred cow? Did a scoring model identify particularly important quantitative or qualitative reasons to select this project? Was the project a competitive necessity? How the project is progressing on such criteria should be an important part of the evaluation as well.

Certainly, one of the major evaluation criteria would be the project's apparent "success" to date. One study (Shenhar, Levy, and Dvir, 1997) identified four important dimensions of project success. The first dimension is simply the project's *efficiency* in meeting the budget and schedule. Of course, efficiency does not necessarily translate into performance, or effectiveness, so the second (and most complex) dimension is *customer impact/satisfaction*. This dimension includes not only meeting the formal technical and operational specifications of the project but also the less tangible aspects of fulfilling the customer's needs, whether the customer actually uses the project results—that perennial challenge of customer "satisfaction."

The third dimension is *business/direct success* meaning, for external projects, factors such as the level of commercial success and market share and for internal projects, the achievement of the project's goals such as improved yields or reduced throughput time. The final dimension, more difficult to assess, is *future potential* which includes establishing a presence in a new market, developing a new technology, and such.

Table 8-1   Items to Consider for Project Evaluation Report Recommendations

Risk

- Communication with the client and senior management.
- Locating opportunities for technological advances.
- Reduction of indirect costs and direct costs.
- Improving the project-management process.
- Identification of risks in the organization's use of projects.
- Utilization of the skills resulting from project members' work on projects.
- Employment of general management experience gained by project managers.
- Improving the organization's use of projects.
- Increasing the speed of obtaining results in projects.

The criteria noted above are usually sufficient for purely routine projects, e.g., maintenance projects. For nonroutine projects, however, two other criteria should also be considered: the project's contribution to the organization's unstated goals and objectives, and the project's contributions to the objectives of project team members. To recognize the project's contributions, all facets of the project must be considered in order to identify and understand the project's strengths and weaknesses. The evaluation report should include the findings regarding these two criteria, as well as some recommendations concerning the items in Table 8-1.

Measurement

Measuring the project's performance against a planned budget and schedule is relatively straightforward, and it is not too difficult to determine if individual milestones have been reached. As we have noted several times, there are complications regarding measurement of actual expenditures and earned values, as well as with reporting on difficult technical issues that may have been deferred while progress was being made along other fronts.

If the project selection process focuses on profits, the evaluation usually includes determination of profits and costs and often assigns these among the several groups working on the project. Conflict typically results. Each group wants credit for revenues. Each group wants costs assigned elsewhere. Although there are no "theoretically correct" solutions to this problem, there are politically acceptable solutions. As with budget and schedule, these are most easily addressed if they have been anticipated and decided when the project was initiated rather than at the end. If allocations are made by a predetermined formula, major conflicts tend to be avoided—or at least lessened.

When a multivariate model (e.g., a scoring model, such as Table D in the scoring model example in Chapter 1) has been used for project selection, measurements may raise more difficult problems. Some measures may be objective and easily measured. Others, however, are typically subjective and may require careful, standardized measurement techniques to attain reliable and valid evaluation results. Interview and questionnaire methods for gathering data must be carefully constructed and executed if their results are to be taken seriously.

A project evaluation is an appraisal for use by top management. Its criteria should include the needs of management; the organization's stated and unstated goals; the original selection basis for the project; and its success to date in terms of its efficiency, customer impact/satisfaction, business success, and future potential. Measuring the project's success on budget, schedule, and scope is easier than measuring revenues or qualitative, subjective factors. Establishing the measures at project formation is helpful, as well as using carefully standardized measurement techniques for the subjective factors.

8.2   PROJECT AUDITING

A very special type of evaluation is the formal audit. The project audit is a thorough examination of the management of a project, its methodology and procedures, its records, properties, inventories, budgets, expenditures, progress, and so on. *The project audit is not a financial audit*, but is far broader in scope and may deal with the whole or any part of the project. For a comparison of the two, refer to Table 8-2. It can also be very flexible, and can focus on any issues of interest to senior management. The project audit is also broader than the traditional management audit that focuses its attention on the organization's management systems and operation. Next we discuss the audit process itself and its result, the audit report.

The Audit Process

Best Practice

The timing of the audit depends on the purpose of the audit, as shown in Table 8-3. Because early problem identification leads to easier solutions, it is often helpful to have an audit early in the project's life. Such audits are usually focused on technical issues. Later audits tend to focus more on budget and schedule because most of the technical issues are resolved by this time. Thus, these later audits are typically of less value to the project team and of more interest to general management. An obvious case here is the *postproject audit*, often contractually required by the customer as well as a common ingredient in the Final Project Report.

While audits can be performed at any level of depth, three levels are common. The first is the *general audit*, usually constrained by time and cost and limited to a brief investigation of project essentials. The second is the *detailed audit*, often initiated if the general audit finds something that needs further investigation. The third is the *technical audit*, usually performed by a person or team with special technical skills.

Table 8-2   Comparison of Financial Audits with Project Audits

	Financial Audits	*Project Audits*
Status	Confirms status of business in relation to accepted standard	Must create basis for, and confirm, status on each project
Predictions	Company's state of economic well-being	Future status of project
Measurement	Mostly in financial terms	Financial terms plus schedule, progress, resource usage, status of ancillary goals
Record-keeping system	Format dictated by legal regulations and professional standards	No standard system, uses any system desired by individual organization or dictated by contract
Existence of information system	Minimal records needed to start audit	No records exist, data bank must be designed and used to start audit
Recommendations	Usually few or none, often restricted to management of accounting system	Often required, and may cover any aspect of the project or its management
Qualifications	Customary to qualify statements if conditions dictate, but strong managerial pressure not to do so	Qualifications focus on shortcomings of audit process (e.g., lack of technical expertise, lack of funds or time)

Table 8-3   Timing and Value of Project Audits

Project State	Value
Initiation	Very useful, significant value of audit takes place early—prior to 25 percent completion of initial planning stage
Feasibility study	Very useful, particularly the technical audit
Preliminary plan/ schedule budget	Very useful, particularly for setting measurement standards to ensure conformance with standards
Master schedule	Less useful, plan frozen, flexibility of team limited
Evaluation of data by project team	Marginally useful, team defensive about findings
Implementation	More or less useful depending on importance of project methodology to successful implementation
Post-project	More or less useful depending on applicability of findings to future projects

Typical steps in a project audit are:

1. Familiarize the audit team with the requirements of the project, including its basis for selection and any special charges by upper management.

2. Audit the project on-site.

3. Write up the audit report in the required format (discussed in the next subsection).

4. Distribute the report.

Collection of the necessary data can be expedited by developing forms and procedures ahead of time to gather the required data, such as that inducted by Figure 8-1. To be effective, the audit team must have free access to all information relevant to the project. Most of the information will come from the project team's records or from various departments such as accounting, human resources, and purchasing. Other valuable information will come from documents that predate the project such as the *Request for Proposal* (RFP), minutes of the project selection committee, and minutes of senior management committees that initiated the project.

Special attention needs to be given to the behavioral aspects of the audit. While the audit team must have free access to anyone with knowledge of the project, except the customer, the audit team's primary source of information should be the project team—but project team members rarely trust auditors. Even if the auditor is a member of the project team, his or her motives will be distrusted and thus the information the auditor requires will be difficult to obtain. Worry about the outcome of the audit produces self-protective activity, which also distracts the project team from activity devoted to the project. Audits are always distracting and uncomfortable to those being audited, much like having a police car in one's rear view mirror while trying to drive.

Trust-building is a slow and delicate process that can be easily stymied. The audit team needs to understand the politics of the project team, the interpersonal relationships of the team members, and must deal with this confidential knowledge respectfully. Regardless, the audit team will undoubtedly encounter political opposition during its work, either to rebuff the team's investigation or to co-opt them. As much as possible, the audit team should attempt to remain neutral and not become involved. If information is given to the audit team in confidence, discreet attempts should be made to confirm such information through nonconfidential sources. *If it cannot be so confirmed, it should not be used.* The audit team must beware of becoming a conduit for unverifiable sources of criticism of the project. As in all matters pertaining to projects, the project team and audit team must be honest.

```
┌──────────────────────────────────────────────────────────────┐
│                    DATA COLLECTION FORM                        │
│                                                                │
│  Date: _____        Auditor: _____    │
│  MANAGERIAL DATA:                                              │
│                                                                │
│  Project: _____   │
│  Project manager: _____     │
│  Start date: _____                             │
│  Due date: _____                               │
│    •                                                           │
│    •                                                           │
│    •                                                           │
│  FINANCIAL DATA:                                               │
│  Allocated budget, $: _____               │
│  Spent to date, $: _____                  │
│    •                                                           │
│    •                                                           │
│    •                                                           │
│  SCHEDULE DATA:                                                │
│  Scheduled time for work performed: _____       │
│  Actual time for the work performed: _____      │
│    •                                                           │
│    •                                                           │
│    •                                                           │
│  TECHNICAL DATA:                                               │
│  % User involvement in design: _____                   │
│  User training, hours:                                         │
│       -Planned: _____                                  │
│       -Completed to date: _____                        │
│  Software complexity                                           │
│       -Lines of code: _____                            │
│       -# Modules: _____                                │
│  Organizational complexity                                     │
│       -# Department involved: _____                    │
│    •                                                           │
│    •                                                           │
│    •                                                           │
└──────────────────────────────────────────────────────────────┘
```

Figure 8-1 **Form to audit a software installation project.**

There are other rules the audit team should follow as well. First, project personnel should always be made aware of the in-progress audit. Care must be taken to avoid misunderstandings between the audit team members and project personnel. Critical comments should always be avoided. This is especially true of on-the-spot, offhand opinions and remarks. No judgmental comment should be made in any circumstance that does not represent the consensus opinion of the audit team, and even consensus judgments should be avoided except in official hearings or reports.

The Audit Report

If the audit is to be taken seriously, all the information must be credibly presented. The data should be carefully checked, and all calculations verified. Deciding what to include and what to exclude is also important. The audit report should be written with a "constructive" tone or project morale may suffer to the point of endangering the project. Bear in mind, however, that constructive criticism never feels that constructive to the criticizee. An example audit report is shown in Figure 8-2.

AUDIT REPORT

Auditor: <u>Fred Williams</u>
Audit Team: <u>Sarah Smith, Mustafa Tudesco</u>
Date of Audit: <u>March 5-12, 2001</u>
Project Audited: <u>Software Installation Project</u>
Project Manager: <u>Craig Stoutheart</u>
•
•
•

INTRODUCTION

The aim of this project was to install a limited-version ERP system in out corporate office, Greenville production plant, and our southeastern field offices. This included testing of functionality, training of user personnel, and hand-off to the users.

CURRENT STATUS

Direct charges on the project are slightly in excess of the planned budget, as shown in the attached Gantt charts (*not included here*). The planned milestones have been achieved to date but task 451, Interface to Warehouse Inventory System, is experiencing difficulty and is both behind schedule and over budget, as seen in the earned value charts (*not included*). . . .

FUTURE PROJECT STATUS

At this time, it would appear that the project is progressing satisfactorily. Attention is currently being given to task 451 but it appears that a new approach is needed for interfacing the vendor's system with our current system. However, this appears to be a normal and temporary dilemma; progress is expected to catch up to plan within 6–7 weeks, and the budget may also. At this time, no recommendations for changes in schedule, scope, or budget appear to be necessary. . . .

CRITICAL MANAGEMENT ISSUES

Interfacing with our existing systems seems to be more difficult than we anticipated. Although the vendor's software is reputed to be one of the easiest to tie in with a firm's existing systems, the difficulties were greater than expected. It is recommended that all upcoming interfacing tasks be examined in greater detail in advance so that these kinds of difficulties do not take us by surprise again. . . .

RISK ANALYSIS AND RISK MANAGEMENT

There does not seem to be any reason at this point to expect either project failure at this stage of the program or serious monetary loss. (The next stage, Implementation, is a separate and higher risk project, however.) As noted above, the major risks in the project do not seem to be equipment compatibility, as we had assumed, but rather software interfacing. If more serious interface issues arise, this could delay the project and/or substantially increase the cost of the project. As noted, it is recommended that future projects with significant software interfaces be examined much more carefully before decisions are made. . . .

FINAL COMMENTS

This report has assumed that the software interface issue will in fact be resolved without significant further delay or cost. If this assumption proves to be incorrect, it could have a major effect on the success of the project, and future projects, not only with this software system but other systems as well. . . .

Figure 8-2   Software installation audit report.

The report information should be arranged so as to facilitate the comparison between planned and actual results. Significant deviations should be highlighted and explained in a set of footnotes or comments. This eases the reader's work and tends to keep questions focused on important issues rather than trivia. Negative comments about individuals or groups associated with the project should be avoided. The report should be written in a clear, professional, unemotional style and its content restricted to information and issues relevant to the project.

At a minimum, the following information should be contained in the report.

1. *Introduction*: A brief description of the project that includes the project's direct goals and objectives.

2. *Current status*: This compares the work actually completed to the project plan along several measures of performance. The actual *direct* charges made to the project should be compared to the planned budget. If *total* costs must be reported, including allocated overhead charges, total costs should be presented in addition to the direct charges, not in place of them. The completed portions of the project, especially planned events and milestones, should be clearly noted. The percent completion of unfinished tasks should also be noted if estimates are available. A comparison of work completed with resources expended should be offered—for example, using MSP earned value reports. The need here is for information that can help pinpoint specific problems. Based on this information, projections can be made concerning the timing and amounts of remaining expenditures required for success. Finally, if there are detailed quality specifications for the project, a full review of quality control procedures and the results of quality tests conducted to date must be reported.

3. *Future project status*: The auditor's conclusions regarding project progress and recommendations for changes in technical approach, schedule, or budget should be made in this section. It is not appropriate, however, to try to rewrite the project proposal. The audit report should consider only work that has already been completed or is well under way; no assumptions should be made about technical problems under investigation at the time of the audit.

4. *Critical management issues*: Any issues that the auditor feels senior management should monitor should be identified here. The relationship between these issues and the project objectives should be briefly described.

5. *Risk analysis and risk management*: This section addresses the potential for project failure or monetary loss. The major risks associated with the project and their projected impact on project schedule/cost/performance should be identified. If alternative courses of action exist that may significantly change future risks, they should be noted at this point.

Risk

6. *Final comments*: This section contains caveats, assumptions, limitations, and information applicable to other projects. Any assumptions or limitations that affect the data, accuracy, or validity of the audit report should be noted here. In addition, lessons learned from this audit that may apply to other projects in the organization should also be reported.

Risk

> The project audit is a thorough examination of the entire project at any level of depth. Early audits tend to focus on more technical aspects of the project while later audits focus on schedule and cost. The audit team must have full access to project data and staff familiar with the project, including the project team. Working with the project team is a delicate behavioral process. The final audit report should be written with a professional and constructive tone and should include the following sections: introduction, current status, future status, critical management issues, risk analysis and risk management, plus final comments.

8.3   PROJECT TERMINATION

PMBOK Guide

Eventually the project is terminated, either quickly or slowly, but the manner in which it is closed out will have a major impact on the quality of life in the organization. PMBOK refers to this as "project closure" which is covered in PMBOK's Chapter 4 on Integration. Occasionally, the way project termination is managed can have an impact on the success of the project. Invariably, however, it has a major effect on the residual attitudes toward the project held by senior management, the client, the project team, and even others in the organization. It also has a major effect on the organization's successful use of projects in the future.

In some project-organized industries (e.g., construction or software development), project termination is a less serious problem because the teams often remain relatively intact, moving on to the next project. In other industries, however, the termination of a project, particularly a long and difficult one, is akin to the breakup of a family and may well be stressful, even to the point of grieving. Therefore, the skill and management of the termination process—a project in itself—can have a major impact on the working environment of the larger organization.

When to Terminate a Project

If one adopts the position that sunk costs are irrelevant to current investment decisions, a primary criterion for project continuance or termination should be whether or not the organization is willing to invest the time and cost required to complete the project, given its current status and expected outcome. Although this criterion can be applied to any project, not everyone agrees that sunk costs are irrelevant, nor does everyone agree that this is a primary criterion. The criteria commonly applied for deciding whether to terminate a project fall into two general cat egories: (1) the degree to which the project has met its goals and objectives, and (2) the degree to which the project qualifies against a set of factors generally associated with success or failure. Table 8-4 identifies the most important factors in terminating R&D projects at 36 different companies.

Table 8-4   Rank-Ordered Factors Considered in Terminating R&D Projects

Factors	No. of Companies Reporting the Factor as Being Important
Technical	
Low probability of achieving technical objectives or commercializing results	34
Technical or manufacturing problems cannot be solved with available R&D skills	11
Higher priority of other projects requiring R&D labor or funds	10
Economic	
Low profitability or return on investment	23
Too costly to develop as individual product	18
Market	
Low market potential	16
Change in competitive factors or market needs	10
Others	
Too long a time required to achieve commercial results	6
Negative effects on other projects or products	3
Patent problems	1

Source: Dean, 1968.

In terms of the first category, if a project has met its goals, the time has come to shut it down. The most important reason for the early termination of a project is the likelihood it will be a technical or commercial failure (Baker *et al.*, 1983). The factors associated with project failure, however, vary for different industries, different project types (e.g., R&D versus construction), and different definitions of failure (Pinto and Mantel, 1990).

As we have already noted, there appear to be four generic factors associated with project success (Shenhar, Levy, and Dvir, 1997): efficiency of project execution, customer satisfaction and use, impact on the firm conducting the project, and contribution to the project firm's future. Success on these dimensions appears to be directly related to the effectiveness of the project's management (Ingram, 1994). There also appear to be four fundamental reasons for project failure: (1) a project was not required for this task in the first place; (2) insufficient support from senior management (especially for unanticipated resources); (3) naming the wrong project manager (often a person with excellent technical skills but weak managerial skills); and (4) poor up-front planning.

Risk

Wheatley (2009) takes a broader view of the termination problem. To decide which projects should be continued and which should be dropped, he suggests that the decision makers answer five questions: (1) Which projects have a legal or strategic imperative? (2) Which projects are luxuries? (3) Which projects are likely to drive future revenues and growth? (4) Which projects best match our skill sets and strengths, allowing us to deliver successfully? and, (5) What are the potential risks to the business if we do not service the demands for the project's deliverables? He also suggests taking any pressing current requirements into consideration. For example, if lowering costs to reduce cash flows has suddenly become more important than some longer-run strategic goals, other projects may now take priority over more strategically focused projects.

Types of Project Termination

There are several fundamentally different ways to close out a project: extinction, addition, integration, and starvation. *Project extinction* occurs when the project activity suddenly stops, although there is still property, equipment, materials, and personnel to disburse or reassign. The project was terminated either because it was successfully completed or because the expectation of failure was high. Successful projects are completed and delivered to the client. Failures occur when the project no longer meets cost/benefit criteria, or when its goals have been achieved by another project, often in another firm. An example of the former cause of failure is the cancellation of the *superconducting super collider* (SSC). The SSC project's tremendous costs relative to the lack of clear benefits doomed the project, and it was cancelled during President Clinton's term in office. Other examples of projects facing extinction are when a project's process yield may have been too low, or a drug failed its efficacy tests, or other firms have discovered better alternatives.

One special type of termination that should be noted is termination by "murder," characterized by its unexpected suddenness, and initiated by events such as the forced retirement of the project's champion or the merger of the firm conducting the project with another firm.

Termination-by-addition occurs when an "in-house" project is successfully completed, and institutionalized as a new, formal part of the organization. This may take the form of an added department, division, subsidiary, or other such organizational entity, depending on the magnitude and importance of the project. 3M Corporation often uses this technique to reward successful innovation projects, such as the invention of Post-It Notes®, and Nucor uses its own construction management teams to staff new steel minimills.

Sometimes, project team members become the managers of the new entity, though some team members may request a transfer to new projects within the organization—project life is exciting. Although the new entity will often have a "protected species" status for the first year or so of its life, it eventually has to learn to live with the same burden of overhead charges, policies, procedures, and bureaucracy that the rest of the organization enjoys. Exceptional project status does not carry over to permanent entities. This shift may be a difficult one for the project team to make.

Termination-by-integration With termination-by-addition, the project property often is simply transferred to an existing or newly created organizational entity. With *termination-by-integration*, the output of the project becomes a standard part of the operating systems of the sponsoring firm, or the client. The new software becomes the standard, and the new machine becomes a normal part of the production line. Project property, equipment, material, personnel, and even functions are distributed among the existing elements of the parent or client organization. Whether the personnel return to their functional homes in the organization or become a part of the integrated system, all the following functions of the project need consideration in the transition from project to integrated operations: human resources, manufacturing, accounting/finance, engineering, information systems/software, marketing, purchasing, distribution, legal, and so on.

Termination-by-starvation often occurs when it is impolitic to terminate a project but its budget can be squeezed, as budgets always are, until it is a project in name only. The project may have been suggested by a special client, or a senior executive (e.g., a sacred cow), or perhaps terminating the project would be an embarrassing acknowledgment of managerial failure. Occasionally a few project personnel members remain assigned to such a project along with a clerk whose duty it is to issue a "no-progress" report once each quarter. It is considered bad manners for anyone to inquire about such projects.

The Termination Process

As usual, the following process and advice may be ignored in the case of small, routine projects. For all major and nonroutine projects, however, it is best for a broadly based committee of reasonably senior executives to make the termination decision in order to diffuse and withstand the political pressures that often accompany such decisions. In general, projects do not take kindly to being shut down. To the extent possible, it is best to detail the criteria used and explain the rationale for the committee's decision, but do not expect sweet reason to quell opposition or to stifle the cries of pain. Again, the PM will need the power of persuasion. In any case, shutting down an ongoing project is not a mechanistic process and should not be treated as such. There are times when hunches and beliefs about the project's ultimate outcomes should be followed. The termination committee that treats the decision as mechanistic is sure to make some costly errors.

The activities required to ensure a smooth and successful project termination will have, we hope, been included in the initial project plan. The termination process will have much better results for all concerned if it is planned and managed with care—even treating it as a project in itself, as illustrated in Figure 8-3. Usually, the project manager is asked to close out the project but this can raise a variety of problems because the PM is not a disinterested bystander in the project. We believe it is better to appoint a specialist in the process, a *termination manager* (project undertaker), to complete the long and involved process of shutting down (interring) a project, preferably someone with some experience in terminating projects. The primary duties of the termination manager are given in Table 8-5.

Many of these tasks will be handled, or at least initiated, by the project manager. Some will have been provided for in the project proposal or contract. One of the more difficult jobs is the reassignment of project personnel. In a functional organization, it usually entails a simple transfer back to duty in the individual's parent department; but at those times when a large project is shut down, many team members may be laid off. In a pure project organization there may be more projects to which project personnel

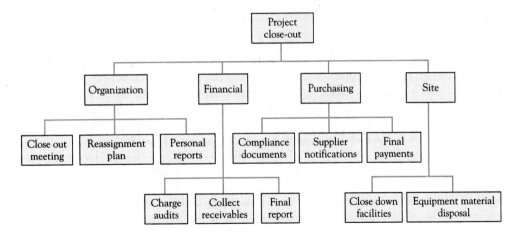

Figure 8-3
A termination
project.

can be transferred but no "holding area" such as a home functional department. As a result, layoffs are more common. The matrix organization, having both aspects, may be the least problematic in terms of personnel reassignments.

The prevalence of corporate mergers in recent years has exacerbated personnel displacement problems. It is expected that the termination manager and the organization's Human Resources department will aid loyal project workers in finding new employment. This is not merely an act of charity. It may prevent the tendency of some team members to seek employment on their own and leave a project early, which can compromise the successful completion of the project. If such people are unsuccessful in finding new jobs, they may drag out the final tasks to give themselves more time—also detrimental to the project. The PM needs to make it clear that midproject resignations as well as tenure-for-life are both unacceptable. Facing the termination decision in a timely and straightforward manner will pay dividends to the PM, as well as the termination manager, in a smooth project transition.

Clearly, the termination process can be handled well or poorly. An example of the former is Nucor's termination-by-addition strategy where the termination of its Crawfordsville, Indiana, steel plant construction project was planned in detail months ahead of time (Kimball, 1988). An example of poor termination is that which resulted when Atlantic States Chemical Laboratories suddenly saw its contract with Ortec canceled, throwing the project, and its close-out, into disarray (Meredith, undated).

Table 8-5   Main Duties of the Termination Manager

- Ensure completion of the work, including that of subcontractors.
- Notify the client of project completion and ensure that delivery and installation are accomplished. Acceptance of the project must be acknowledged by the client.
- Ensure that documentation is complete, including the project final report.
- Clear all accounts and documentation for final billings and client invoicing.
- Redistribute personnel, materials, equipment, and other project resources to appropriate places, including the return of client-provided resources.
- Clear the project with legal counsel, including filings for patents and recording and archiving all nondisclosure documents.
- Determine what records to keep and deliver them to safe and responsible people, such as the organization's archivist, or store them in the organization's archives.
- Ascertain any product support requirements (e.g., spares, service manuals) and ensure that such support will be delivered.
- Oversee the closing of the project's books.

The Project Final Report

The project final report is not another evaluation, though the audits and evaluations have a role in it. With the exception of routine projects where a simple "We did it. No problems" is sufficient, the project final report is a history of the project. It is a chronicle, typically written by the PM, of what went right and what went wrong, who served the project in what capacity, what was done, how it was managed, and the lessons learned. The report should also indicate where the source materials can be found—the project plan and all of its many parts; charter, budget, schedule, earned value charts, audit reports, scope-change documents, resource allocations, all updates of any of the above documents, and so on. It is all too easy to ignore these left-overs from yesterday's project, but it is most important not to do so. The PMI refers to these as the organization's assets, and the Project Report is a critical part of them. We think of them as the experiences all managers should learn by—but so often do not.

How the report is written, and in what style, is a matter of taste and preference. In any case, the following items should be addressed.

- *Project performance*—perhaps the most important information is what the project attempted to achieve, what it did achieve, and the reasons for the resulting performance. Since this is not a formal evaluation of the project, these items can be the PM's personal opinion on the matter. The lessons learned in the project should also be included here.

- *Administrative performance*—administrative practices that worked particularly well, or poorly, should be identified and the reasons given. If some modification to administrative practices would help future projects, this should be noted and explained.

- *Organizational structure*—projects may have different structures, and the way the project is organized may either aid or hinder the project. Modifications that would help future projects should be identified.

- *Project teamwork*—a confidential section of the final report should identify team members who worked particularly well, and *possibly* those who worked poorly with others. The PM may also recommend that individuals or groups who were particularly effective when operating as a team be kept together on future assignments.

Risk

- *Project management techniques*—project success is so dependent on the skill and techniques for forecasting, planning, budgeting, scheduling, resource allocation, control, risk management, and so on that procedures that worked well or badly should be noted and commented upon. Recommendations for improvements in future projects should be made and explained.

The fundamental purpose of the final report is to improve future projects. Thus, recommendations for improvements are especially appropriate and valued by the organization. Of course, none of the recommendations for improvement of future projects will be of any help whatsoever if the recommendations are not circulated among other project managers as well as the appropriate senior managers. The PM should follow up on any recommendations made to make sure that they are accepted and installed, or rejected for cause.

Since most of the information and recollections come from the PM, it is suggested that the PM keep a project "diary." This is not an official project document but an informal collection of thoughts, reflections, and commentaries on project happenings. Not only will the diary help the PM construct the final report, but also it can be a superior source of wisdom for new, aspiring project managers. Above all, it keeps good ideas from getting lost amid the welter of project activities and crises.

Projects are usually terminated either based on (1) the degree to which they are meeting their goals or (2) the degree to which they qualify on factors shown to be linked to success or failure in other projects. The most common reason for early termination is the probability of a technical or commercial failure. The four types of project termination are extinction, addition, integration, and starvation. The termination decision should be decided by a management committee, run by a termination manager, and executed as a project in itself. Placing the project team members in new assignments is a particularly important aspect of termination. The PM should prepare a project final report that makes recommendations for improving the organization's future project-management practices.

REVIEW QUESTIONS

1. If the actual termination of a project is a project in itself, how is it different from other projects?

2. What are some reasons that a failing project might still not be terminated?

3. What might make a project unsuccessful during the termination process?

4. Who would make the best auditors: outside unbiased auditors or inside auditors who are more familiar with the organization, its procedures, and the project? Why?

5. Under what circumstances would you change your answer to the previous question?

6. Would frequent brief evaluations be best, or would less frequent major evaluations be preferred?

7. Should the results of an evaluation or audit be shared with the project team?

8. What are the major purposes served by an after-the-fact project evaluation?

9. Under what circumstances is a detailed audit apt to be useful?

DISCUSSION QUESTIONS

10. How should an audit team handle an audit where it is explicitly restricted from accessing certain materials and/or personnel?

11. What might be some characteristics of a good termination manager?

12. How should a committee decide which termination method to use?

13. What steps might be taken to reduce the anxiety of project team members facing an audit?

14. What are the dangers in evaluating a project based on the reason(s) it was selected (such as its being a competitive necessity), rather than the goals and objectives in the project proposal or contract?

15. It is frequently suggested that items that will become potential problems later in the project life be decided up front, such as how to allocate revenues or dispose of project assets. How can this wisdom be used for project problems that cannot be foreseen?

16. Can you think of any acceptable ways of assigning credit for profits (or responsibility for costs) resulting from a project on which several departments worked?

17. How might an audit team deal with an attempt to co-opt the team?

18. In Section 8.2, subsection *The Audit Report*, six elements are listed that should be included in every audit report. For each element, explain why its inclusion is important.

19. Referring to the "Evaluation Criteria" subsection of Section 8.1, how do you reconcile the difference between the goals and objectives of the project as given to the project manager in Chapter 1 and these criteria by which she or he is now judged?

INCIDENTS FOR DISCUSSION

General Construction Company

General Construction Company has a contract to build three lower-income apartment buildings for the city of Santa Fe, New Mexico. During construction of the first building, the Project Manager formed an auditing team to audit the construction process for each building. He asked the team to develop a list of minimum requirements for the projects and use this as a baseline in the audit. While reviewing the contract documents, one of the audit team members found a discrepancy between the contract minimum requirements and the City's minimum requirements. Based on his findings, he has told the project manager that he has decided to contact the city administrator and discuss the problem.

Question: If you were the project manager, how would you handle this situation? How can a customer be assured of satisfactory project completion?

Lexi Electronics

Lexi Electronics is nearing completion of a 2-year project to develop and produce a new digital phone. The phone is no bigger than a Popsicle stick but has all the features of a standard digital cellular phone. The assembly line and all the production facilities will be completed in 5 months. The first units will be produced in 8 months. The plant manager believes it is time to begin winding down the project. He has three methods in mind for terminating the project: extinction, addition, and integration. He is not sure which method is best.

Question: Which of the three methods would you recommend, and why?

The Shocking Machine

Lithotropic Corporation is the manufacturer of machinery for pulverizing kidney stones with shock waves. They have just completed a new machine. The new machine performs at a medically acceptable level, but it does not precisely meet the specific performance standards that were set for the project. The hospital that contracted for the purchase of the machinery is threatening to sue for failure to deliver to the project specifications. The hospital has contacted Tom Lament, the corporate attorney for Lithotropic.

Question: What do you suggest Mr. Lament do, if anything, to begin his preparation for defending or settling this potential lawsuit?

C A S E

St. Dismas Assisted Living Facility Case—6

It was a beautiful day in mid-May 2001. The St. Dismas hospital Assisted Living Facility project was nearing completion. As usual, the construction project manager, Kyle Nanno, was thinking about the construction project's schedule. It seemed to him that work on finishing the interior of the building was slowing down a bit. He knew that the final weeks of a project always seemed to take forever, but he also knew that the project was running almost 2 weeks late as a result of a problem encountered during the excavation phase of the construction project.

During March and April, it appeared that they were catching up. Kyle had discussed with the construction contractor that St. Dismas would pay overtime to catch up, but the speed-up was temporary, and the job continued to be late. Kyle was not quite sure why. Progress just seemed to be in slow motion. He decided to meet with Fred Splient, the President and CEO of St. Dismas, to discuss the problems.

Fred suggested that Kyle call in someone to audit the project, in particular to examine the project schedule carefully. Fred also wanted the auditor to look at the project expenses to date. Fred had just received a crude spreadsheet from the CFO, and it did not reflect the progress he thought should have been made as this project was coming to an end.

ALF Program Expenses as of 5/24/01

	Budgeted	Actual as of 5/24/01	Remaining $
Construction Costs:			
Building	$6,743,000.00	$6,743,000.00	$0.00
Contingency	674,300.00	453,277.00	221,023.00
Land	600,000.00	600,000.00	0.00
Program development & equipment costs	405,000.00	354,332.00	50,668.00
Furniture	400,000.00	249,679.00	150,321.00
A&E fees			
Financing costs	202,000.00	202,000.00	0.00
Capitalized interest	135,000.00	135,000.00	0.00
Site improvements	125,000.00	147,655.00	−22,655.00
Phone & IS system	30,000.00	22,438.00	7,562.00
Kitchen equipment	30,000.00	23,776.00	6,224.00
Subtotal	$9,691,300.00	$9,278,157.00	$413,143.00
Organizational Costs:			
Legal and accounting	$25,000.00	$0.00	$25,000.00
Initial marketing	250,000.00	0.00	250,000.00
Project consultant	80,000.00	0.00	80,000.00
Follow-up market survey	20,000.00	0.00	20,000.00
Subtotal	$375,000.0	$0.00	$375,000.00
Total	$10,066,300.00	$9,278,157.00	$788,143.00

Fred asked Kyle to find out if anyone in the hospital's accounting department had experience with projects and project-management software. Kyle knew instantly who to call. Caroline Stevens had once helped him on other hospital projects. Kyle trusted her to act impartially and to be able to figure out what was happening.

Caroline agreed to function as the Project Auditor. She began by examining the most recent project schedule from the construction company. She then created a progress-to-date report with MSP. She also did a complete analysis of the CFO's report. The expense report she reviewed and updated is found below.

Using MSP, Caroline created a graphical progress report on the project as of May 24. She marked the actual progress of each unfinished activity by placing a diamond embedded in a circle on the project's Gantt chart. If the symbol was to the left of the May 24 line, that activity was late; the amount of lateness was indicated by the distance of the symbol to the May 24 line. The symbol for on-time activities rested on the May 24 line. If there had been early activities, their symbols would have been to the right of the May 24 line. Caroline's chart is shown above.

Caroline then scheduled a meeting with Kyle and Fred Splient. She reported that she did see a work slowdown. She conducted interviews with the construction team, and it appeared that they were concerned about their next work assignment. They told her that in the past as projects were coming to a close they were told of their next scheduled job. They had not heard anything yet, and they were worried. She also reported that the interior designer had added seven extra days to complete the interiors (Task #6 of the project) because the carpet and wall coverings might arrive a week late from the manufacturer. They actually arrived on schedule. The estimated remaining duration for the interiors to be completed was 34.6 days. The designer did tell her that the furniture had not all arrived, so they were withholding about 30 percent of the payment until it all arrived.

Caroline also reported to Fred that it appeared that the expenses that were allocated to pay back St. Dismas for such things as preliminary marketing efforts, legal support, etc. had not yet been expensed to the project budget. The only thing that was expensed was the original project construction budget. That budget seemed to be right on track. Kyle reported that he intended to spend the rest of the contingency budget for overtime work by the construction crews. He also intended to use the rest of the IS budget to purchase computers for the common areas of the facility and to wire those areas for access to the Internet. In addition, he was waiting

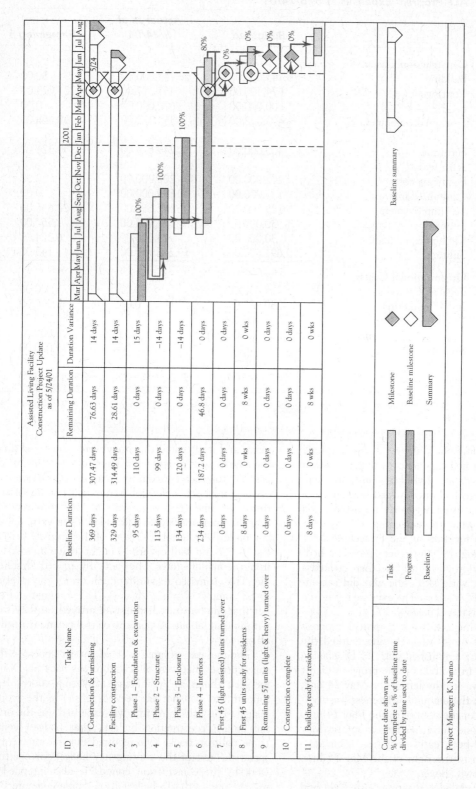

Assisted Living Facility
Construction Project Update
as of 5/24/01

ID	Task Name	Baseline Duration		Remaining Duration	Duration Variance
1	Construction & furnishing	369 days	307.47 days	76.63 days	14 days
2	Facility construction	329 days	314.49 days	28.61 days	14 days
3	Phase 1 – Foundation & excavation	95 days	110 days	0 days	15 days
4	Phase 2 – Structure	113 days	99 days	0 days	–14 days
5	Phase 3 – Enclosure	134 days	120 days	0 days	–14 days
6	Phase 4 – Interiors	234 days	187.2 days	46.8 days	0 days
7	First 45 (light assisted) units turned over	0 days	0 days	0 days	0 days
8	First 45 units ready for residents	8 days	0 wks	8 wks	0 wks
9	Remaining 57 units (light & heavy) turned over	0 days	0 days	0 days	0 days
10	Construction complete	0 days	0 days	0 days	0 days
11	Building ready for residents	8 days	0 wks	8 wks	0 wks

Task
Progress
Baseline

Milestone
Baseline milestone
Summary

Baseline summary

Current date shown as:
% Complete is % of baseline time
divided by time used to date

Project Manager: K. Nanno

*Please note MSP calculates the duration variance for each step of the action plan by subtracting the actual from the baseline. The summary task baseline and actual duration are then rolled up to the summary tasks' baseline and actual duration figures. The summary tasks' duration variance is then calculated by adding the summary task actual duration plus the remaining duration and then subtracting that sum from the baseline duration.

for bills from some of the companies that supplied the required medical equipment. He was planning to spend all that was allocated for that budgeted item. He was over budget on the site improvements and under budget for the kitchen equipment.

Caroline and Fred praised Kyle for his management of the Construction budget.

As soon as Caroline and Kyle left Fred's office, Fred called his CFO to find out why the other items were still not reflected in the project budget.

QUESTIONS

1. Estimate the final construction budget.
2. What should they do about the work slowdown?
3. Create a Gantt chart with the revisions to the duration of the interiors step. When will the project be completed?

4. What is the importance of the fact that the Hospital staff expenses were not reported under the project budget?

C A S E

Datatech

Steve Bawnson joined Datatech's engineering department upon obtaining his B.S. in Electrical Engineering almost 6 years ago. He soon established himself as an expert in analog signal processing and was promoted to Senior Design Engineer just 2 years after joining the firm. After serving as a Senior Design Engineer for 2 years, he was promoted to Project Manager and asked to oversee a product development project involving a relatively minor product line extension.

As Steve was clearing his desk to make room for a cup of coffee, his computer dinged indicating the arrival of yet another email message. Steve usually paid little attention to the arrival of new email messages, but for some reason this message caught his attention. Swiveling in his chair to face the computer on the credenza behind his desk, he read the subject line of the message: Notebook Computer Development Project Audit Report. Steve then noticed that the message was addressed to the Vice-President of Product Development and was cc: to him. He immediately opened and read the message.

Datatech had recently adopted a policy requiring that all ongoing projects be periodically audited. Last week this policy was implemented and Steve was informed that his project would be the first one audited by a team consisting of internal and external experts.

Datatech Inc. is a full-line producer of desktop and notebook computers that are distributed through a network of value-added resellers. After completing the desktop product line extension project about 9 months ago,

Steve was asked to serve as the project manager for a project to develop a new line of notebook computers.

In asking Steve to serve as the project manager for the notebook computer development project, the Vice-President of Product Development conveyed to Steve the importance of completing the project within a year. To emphasize this point, the Vice-President noted that he personally made the decision to go forward with this project and had not taken the project through the normal project selection and approval process in order to save time. Steve had successfully completed the desktop project in a similar timeframe, and told the Vice-President that this target was quite reasonable. Steve added that he was confident that the project would be completed on time and on budget.

Steve wasted no time in planning the project. Based on the success of the desktop project, he decided to modify the work breakdown structure he had developed for the desktop project and apply it to this new project. He recalled the weeks of planning that went into developing the work breakdown structure for the desktop project. The entire project team had been involved, and that was a relatively straightforward product line extension. The current project was more complicated, and there simply was not sufficient time to involve all team members. What was the point of wasting valuable time and resources to re-invent the wheel?

After modifying the work breakdown structure, Steve scheduled a meeting with the Vice-President of Product Development to discuss staffing the project. As was typical of other product development projects at Datatech,

Steve and the Vice-President agreed that the project should be housed within the engineering division. In his capacity as project manager, Steve would serve as liaison to other functional areas such as marketing, purchasing, finance, and production.

As the project progressed, it continued to slip behind schedule. Steve found it necessary to schedule a meeting each week to address how unanticipated activities would be completed. For example, last week the team realized that no one had been assigned to design the hinge system for attaching the screen to the base.

Indeed, Steve found himself increasingly in crisis mode. For example, this morning the manufacturing group sent a heated email to Steve. The manufacturing group noted that they just learned of the notebook computer project and based on the design presented to them, they would not be able to manufacture the printed circuit boards because of the extensive amount of surface mount components required. Steve responded to this message by noting that the engineering group was doing its job and had designed a state-of-the-art notebook computer. He added that it was the manufacturing group's problem to decide how to produce it.

Just as troubling was the crisis that had occurred earlier in the week. The Vice-President of Product Development had requested that the notebook computer incorporate a new type of interface that would allow the notebook computer to synchronize information with a tablet computer Datatech was about to introduce. Steve explained that incorporating the interface into the notebook computer would require changes to about 40 percent of the computer and would delay the introduction by a minimum of several months. Nevertheless, the Vice-President was adamant that the changes be made.

As Steve laid down the audit report, he reflected on its conclusion that the project be terminated immediately. In the judgment of the auditing team, the project had slipped so far behind schedule that the costs to complete it were not justified.

QUESTIONS

1. To what extent were the problems facing the notebook computer development project avoidable? What could have been done to avoid these problems?

2. Would it make sense to apply a project selection model such as the weighted scoring model to this project to determine if it should be terminated?

3. In your opinion, are the types of problems that arose in this situation typical of other organizations? If so, what can organizations in general do to avoid these types of problems?

C A S E

Ivory Tower Systems

Ivory Tower Systems (ITS) was founded by two former computer science professors to develop mobile apps for the consumer market that leverage state-of-the-art research in the computer science field. Typically, the company looks for opportunities to apply sophisticated algorithms to practical problems with mass appeal. Its first app used a sophisticated optimization algorithm to create weekly meal plans based on data the users supplied about their food likes and dislikes, and their weekly food budget.

Currently an app is under development code named Tour Guide. While there are many mapping apps currently available that provide directions from one location to another, Tour Guide allows the users to enter their starting location and multiple destinations. Then, based on a proprietary heuristic algorithm, the app would provide the optimal sequence to travel to all destinations and ultimately end at the starting location. It was envisioned that the app would be used by people to plan weekend errands as well as people on vacation to plan sight-seeing days.

The project was originally planned to take 18 months. The project is now in its 16th month, and technical challenges that should have been resolved months ago remain. As a result, the ITS founders decided to hire an external expert in software development projects to audit the project. The audit report is provided in Figure A.

AUDIT REPORT

Auditor: <u>George Johnson</u>
Date of Audit: <u>January 11</u>
Project Audited: <u>Tour Guide App Development</u>
Project Manager: <u>Roger Gilbert</u>

INTRODUCTION

The purpose of this project is to develop a proprietary heuristic algorithm and then embed the algorithm in a mobile app that people can use to plan trips involving multiple destinations. The app would provide directions to each destination and would end at the starting location.

CURRENT STATUS

The project is significantly behind schedule. The deadline for the project is 2 months from the date of this audit, and several significant technical challenges related to developing the algorithm remain to be resolved. Furthermore, it is likely that numerous other significant challenges will arise as the project team attempts to integrate the algorithm with the mapping database.

FUTURE PROJECT STATUS

Given the known technical challenges and likely challenges to arise, there is virtually no chance the project will meet its original due date. Furthermore, the longer the project is delayed, the more it will go over budget. Given the nature of the current and likely future technical challenges, it is not possible to estimate what changes should be made to the project's schedule or budget.

CRITICAL MANAGEMENT ISSUES

The project has been mismanaged from the start. While Mr. Gilbert has a solid technical background in computer science, he has no prior background or experience in leading a project. One team member confidentially communicated to me that because of his background, Mr. Gilbert spends almost all of his time trying to solve the technical problems related to developing the algorithm and spends little time actually managing the project. I personally found Mr. Gilbert to be very abrasive and unwilling to share key project documents. After meeting with Mr. Gilbert, I believe there is a good chance that his reluctance to share project-related documents stems from the fact that they simply do not exist.

FINAL COMMENTS

There is virtually no chance that the project will finish on schedule and on budget. I recommend that a new project manager be immediately appointed and Mr. Gilbert reassigned as a project team member. Alternatively, senior management may decide to terminate the project.

Figure A

QUESTIONS

1. Do you have any concerns about the audit process at ITS? If so, what are they and what changes to their auditing process would you recommend for the future?

2. Critique the audit report. What are its strengths and weaknesses?

3. What are the pros and cons of using an external auditor in this situation? Which type of auditor would you recommend for this project?

BIBLIOGRAPHY

BAKER, N. R., S. G. GREEN, A. S. BEAN, W. BLANK, and S. K. TADISINA. "Sources of First Suggestion and Project Success/Failure in Industrial Research." *Proceedings: Conference on the Management of Technological Innovation.* Washington, D.C., 1983. (A groundbreaking, early empirical paper on predictions of project success and failure.)

DEAN, B. V. *Evaluating, Selecting, and Controlling R&D Projects.* New York: American Management Association, 1968.

INGRAM, T. "Managing Client/Server and Open Systems Projects: A 10-Year Study of 62 Mission-Critical Projects." *Project Management Journal,* June 1994.

KIMBALL, R. "Nucor's Strategic Project." *Project Management Journal,* September 1988.

MEREDITH, J. R. Private consulting project.

PINTO, J. K., and S. J. MANTEL, Jr. "The Causes of Project Failure." *IEEE Transactions on Engineering Management,* November 1990.

PMI, "Mars or Bust," *PM Network,* October 2004.

SHENHAR, A. J., O. LEVY, and D. DVIR. "Mapping the Dimensions of Project Success." *Project Management Journal,* June 1997.

Wheatley, M. "Making the Cut." *PM Network,* June 2009.

APPENDIX

Probability and Statistics

This appendix is intended to serve as a brief review of the probability and statistics concepts used in this text. Students who require more review than is available in this appendix should consult one of the texts listed in the bibliography.

A.1 PROBABILITY

Uncertainty in project management is a fact of life. The duration of project activities, the costs of various resources, and the timing of a technological change all exemplify the types of uncertainties encountered when managing projects. Each of these *random variables* is more or less uncertain. Further, we do not know when or if a given activity will be successfully completed, a senior official will approve a project, or a piece of software will run without problems. Each *event* is more or less uncertain. We do not know the values that each variable and event will assume.

In common terminology we reflect our uncertainty with such phrases as "not very likely," "not a chance," "for sure." While these descriptive terms communicate one's feeling regarding the chances of a particular event's occurrence, they simply are not precise enough to allow analysis of chances and odds.

Simply put, *probability* is a number on a scale used to measure uncertainty. The range of the probability scale is from 0 to 1, with a 0 probability indicating that an event has no chance of occurring and a probability of 1 indicating that an event is absolutely certain to occur. The more likely an event is to occur, the closer its probability is to 1. This probability definition, which is general, needs to be further augmented to illustrate the various types of probability that decision makers can assess. There are three types of probability that the project manager should be aware of.

- Subjective probability
- Logical probability
- Experimental probability

Subjective Probability

Subjective probability is based on individual information and belief. Different individuals will assess the chances of a particular event in different ways, and the same individual may assess different probabilities for the same event at different points in time. For example, one need only watch the blackjack players in Las Vegas to see that different people assess probabilities in different ways. Also, daily trading in the stock market is the result of different probability assessments by those trading. The sellers sell because it is their belief that the probability of appreciation is low, and the buyers buy because they believe that the probability of appreciation is high. Clearly, these different probability assessments are about the same events.

Logical Probability

Logical probability is based on physical phenomena and on symmetry of events. For example, the probability of drawing a three of hearts from a standard 52-card playing deck is 1/52. Each card has an equal likelihood of being drawn. In flipping a coin, the chance of "heads" is 0.50. That is, since there are only two possible outcomes from one flip of a coin, each event has one-half the total probability, or 0.50. A final example is the roll of a single die. Since all six sides are identical, the chance of any one event occurring (i.e., a 6, a 3) is 1/6.

Experimental Probability

Experimental probability is based on frequency of occurrence of events in trial situations. For example, in estimating the duration for a particular activity, we might record the time required to complete the activity on similar projects. If we collect data on 10 projects and the duration was 20 days on 3 of the 10, the probability of the duration equaling 20 days is said to be 0.30 (i.e., 3/10).

$$\text{probability of event} = \frac{\text{number of times event occurred}}{\text{total number of trials}}$$

Both logical and experimental probability are referred to as *objective* probability in contrast to the individually assessed *subjective* probability. Each of these is based on, and directly *computed* from, facts.

A.2   EVENT RELATIONSHIPS AND PROBABILITY LAWS

Events are classified in a number of ways that allow us to state rules for probability computations. Some of these classifications and definitions follow.

1. *Independent events:* events are independent if the occurrence of one *does not* affect the probability of occurrence of the others.
2. *Dependent events:* events are termed dependent if the occurrence of one *does* affect the probability of occurrence of others.
3. *Mutually exclusive events:* Two events are termed mutually exclusive if the occurrence of one precludes the occurrence of the other. For example, in the birth of a child, the events "It's a boy!" and "It's a girl!" are mutually exclusive.

4. *Collectively exhaustive events:* A set of events is termed collectively exhaustive if on any one trial at least one of them must occur. For example, in rolling a die, one of the events 1, 2, 3, 4, 5, or 6 must occur; therefore, these six events are collectively exhaustive.

We can also define the union and intersection of two events. Consider two events A and B. The *union of A and B* includes all outcomes in A or B or in both A and B. For example, in a card game you will win if you draw a diamond or a jack. The union of these two events includes all diamonds (including the jack of diamonds) and the remaining three jacks (hearts, clubs, spades). The *or* in the union is the *inclusive or*. That is, in our example you will win with a jack or a diamond or a jack of diamonds (i.e., both events).

The *intersection* of two events includes all outcomes that are members of *both* events. Thus, in our previous example of jacks and diamonds, the jack of diamonds is the only outcome contained in both events and is therefore the only member of the intersection of the two events.

Let us now consider the relevant probability laws based on our understanding of the above definitions and concepts. For ease of exposition let us define the following notation.

$$P(A) = \text{probability that event } A \text{ will occur}$$

$$P(B) = \text{probability that event } B \text{ will occur}$$

If two events are mutually exclusive, then their joint occurrence is impossible. Hence, $P(A \text{ and } B) = 0$ for mutually exclusive events. If the events are not mutually exclusive, $P(A \text{ and } B)$ can be computed (as we will see in the next section); this probability is termed the *joint* probability of A and B. Also, if A and B are not mutually exclusive, then we can also define the *conditional* probability of A *given that* B has already occurred or the conditional probability of B given that A has already occurred. These probabilities are written as $P(A \mid B)$ and $P(B \mid A)$, respectively.

The Multiplication Rule

The joint probability of two events that are not mutually exclusive is found by using the multiplication rule. If the events are not mutually exclusive, the joint probability is given by

$$P(A \text{ and } B) = P(A) \times P(B \mid A) \text{ or } P(B) \times P(A \mid B)$$

If the events are independent, then $P(B \mid A)$ and $P(A \mid B)$ are equal to $P(B)$ and $P(A)$, respectively, and therefore the joint probability is given by

$$P(A \text{ and } B) = P(A) \times P(B)$$

From these two relationships, we can find the conditional probability for two dependent events from

$$P(A \mid B) = \frac{P(A \text{ and } B)}{P(B)}$$

and

$$P(B \mid A) = \frac{P(A \text{ and } B)}{P(A)}$$

Also, the $P(A)$ and $P(B)$ can be computed if the events are independent, as

$$P(A) = \frac{P(A \text{ and } B)}{P(B)}$$

and

$$P(B) = \frac{P(A \text{ and } B)}{P(A)}$$

The Addition Rule

The addition rule is used to compute the probability of the union of two events. If two events are mutually exclusive, then $P(A \text{ and } B) = 0$, as we indicated previously. Therefore, the probability of either A or B or both is simply the probability of A or B. This is given by

$$P(A \text{ or } B) = P(A) + P(B)$$

But, if the events are not mutually exclusive, then the probability of A or B is given by

$$P(A \text{ or } B) = P(A) + P(B) - P(A \text{ and } B)$$

We can denote the reasonableness of this expression by looking at the following Venn diagram.

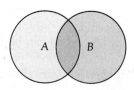

The two circles represent the probabilities of the events A and B, respectively. The shaded area represents the overlap in the events; that is, the intersection of A and B. If we add the area of A and the area of B, we have included the shaded area twice. Therefore, to get the total area of A or B, we must subtract one of the areas of the intersection that we have added.

If the two circles in the Venn diagram do not overlap, A and B are said to be *mutually exclusive* and $P(A \text{ and } B) = 0$. In this case

$$P(A \text{ or } B) = P(A) + P(B)$$

If two events are collectively exhaustive, then the probability of $(A \text{ or } B)$ is equal to 1. That is, for two collectively exhaustive events, one or the other or both must occur, and therefore, $P(A \text{ or } B)$ must be 1.

A.3 STATISTICS

Because events are uncertain, we must employ special analyses in organizations to ensure that our decisions recognize the chance nature of outcomes. We employ statistics and statistical analysis to

1. Concisely express the tendency and the relative uncertainty of a particular situation.
2. Develop inferences or an understanding about a situation.

"Statistics" is an elusive and often misused term. Batting averages, birth weights, student grade points are all statistics. They are *descriptive* statistics. That is, they are quantitative measures of some entity and, for our purposes, can be considered as data about the entity. The second use of the term "statistics" is in relation to the body of theory and methodology used to analyze available evidence (typically quantitative) and to develop inferences from the evidence.

Two descriptive statistics that are often used in presenting information about a population of items (and consequently in inferring some conclusions about the population) are the *mean* and the *variance*. The mean in a population (denoted as μ and pronounced "mu") can be computed in two ways, each of which gives identical results.

$$\mu = \sum_{j=1}^{k} X_j P(X_j)$$

where

     k = the number of discrete values that the random variable X_j may assume

     X_j = a value of the random variable

     $P(X_j)$ = the probability (or relative frequency) of X_j in the population

     Also, the mean can be computed as

$$\mu = \sum_{i=1}^{k} X_i / N$$

where

     N = the size of the population (the number of different items in the population)

     X_i = the value of the ith item in the population

The mean is also termed the *expected value* of the population and is written as $E(X)$. The variance of the items in the population measures the dispersion of the items about their mean (denoted σ^2 and pronounced "sigma squared"). It is computed in one of the following two ways:

$$\sigma^2 = \sum_{j=1}^{k} (X_j - \mu)^2 P(X_j)$$

or

$$\sigma^2 = \sum_{j=1}^{N} \frac{(X_j - \mu)^2}{N}$$

The standard deviation, another measure of dispersion, is simply the square root of the variance (denoted σ)

$$\sigma = \sqrt{\sigma^2}$$

Descriptive versus Inferential Statistics

Organizations are typically faced with decisions for which a large portion of the relevant information is uncertain. In hiring graduates of your university, the "best" prospective employee is unknown to the organization. Also, in introducing a new product, proposing a tax law change to boost employment, drilling an oil well, and so on, the outcomes are always uncertain.

Statistics can often aid management in helping to understand this uncertainty. This is accomplished through the use of one or the other, or both, of the purposes of statistics. That is, statistics is divided according to its two major purposes: *describing* the major characteristics of a large mass of data and *inferring* something about a large mass of data from a smaller sample drawn from the mass. One methodology summarizes all the data; the other reasons from a small set of the data to the larger total.

Descriptive statistics uses such measures as the mean, median, mode, range, variance, standard deviation, and such graphical devices as the bar chart and the histogram. When an entire population (a complete set of objects or entities with a common characteristic of interest) of data is summarized by computing such measures as the mean and the variance of a single characteristic, the measure is referred to as a *parameter* of that population. For example, if the population of interest is all female freshmen at a university and all their ages were used to compute an arithmetic average of 19.2 years, this measure is called a *parameter* of that population.

Inferential statistics also uses means and variance, but in a different manner. The objective of inferential statistics is to infer the value of a population parameter through the study of a small sample (a portion of a population) from that population. For example, a random sample of 30 freshmen females could produce the information that there is 90 percent certainty that the average age of all freshmen women is between 18.9 and 19.3 years. We do not have as much information as if we had used the entire population, but then we did not have to spend the time to find and determine the age of each member of the population either.

Before considering the logic behind inferential statistics, let us define the primary measures of central tendency and dispersion used in both descriptive and inferential statistics.

Measures of Central Tendency

The central tendency of a group of data represents the average, middle, or "normal" value of the data. The most frequently used measures of central tendency are the *mean*, the *median*, and the *mode*.

The mean of a population of values was given earlier as

$$\mu = \sum_{i=1}^{N} \frac{X_i}{N}$$

where

μ = the mean

X_i = the value of the *i*th data item in the population

N = the number of data items in the population

The mean of a *sample* of items from a population is given by

$$\overline{X} = \sum_{i=1}^{N} \frac{X_i}{N}$$

where

$\overline{X}$ = the sample mean (pronounced "X bar")

X_i = the value of the ith data item in the sample

N = the number of data items selected in the sample

The *median* is the middle value of a population of data (or sample) where the data are ordered by value. That is, in the following data set

$$3, 2, 9, 6, 1, 5, 7, 3, 4$$

4 is the median since (as you can see when we order the data)

$$1, 2, 3, 3, 4, 5, 6, 7, 9$$

50 percent of the data values are above 4 and 50 percent below 4. If there are an even number of data items, then the mean of the middle two is the median. For example, if there had also been an 8 in the above data set, the median would be 4.5 = (4 + 5)/2.

The *mode* of a population (or sample) of data items is the value that most frequently occurs. In the above data set, 3 is the mode of the set. A distribution can have more than one mode if there are two or more values that appear with equal frequency.

Measures of Dispersion

Dispersion refers to the scatter around the mean of a distribution of values. Three measures of dispersion are the range, the variance, and the standard deviation.

The *range* is the difference between the highest and the lowest value of the data set, that is,

$$X_{high} - X_{low}$$

The *variance of a population* of items is given by

$$\sigma^2 = \sum_{i=1}^{N} \frac{(X_i - \mu)^2}{N}$$

where

σ^2 = the population variance

The *variance of a sample* of items is given by

$$S^2 = \sum_{i=1}^{n} \frac{(X_i - \overline{X})^2}{n - 1}$$

where

S^2 = the sample variance

The *standard deviation* is simply the square root of the variance. That is,

$$\sigma = \sqrt{\sum_{i=1}^{n} \frac{(X_i - \mu)^2}{N}}$$

and

$$S = \sqrt{\sum_{i=1}^{n} \frac{(X_i - \overline{X})^2}{n - 1}}$$

σ and S are the population and sample standard deviations, respectively.

Inferential Statistics

A basis of inferential statistics is the *interval estimate*. Whenever we infer from partial data to an entire population, we are doing so with some uncertainty in our inference. Specifying an interval estimate (e.g., average weight is between 10 and 12 pounds) rather than a *point estimate* (e.g., the average weight is 11.3 pounds) simply helps to relate that uncertainty. The interval estimate is not as *precise* as the point estimate.

Inferential statistics uses probability samples where the chance of selection of each item is known. A random sample is one in which each item in the population has an equal chance of selection.

The procedure used to estimate a population mean from a sample is to

1. Select a sample of size n from the population.
2. Compute $\overline{X}$ the mean and S the standard deviation.
3. Compute the precision of the estimate (i.e., the limits around $\overline{X}$ within which the mean μ is believed to exist).

Steps 1 and 2 are straightforward, relying on the equations we have presented in earlier sections. Step 3 deserves elaboration.

The precision of an estimate for a population parameter depends on two things: the standard deviation of the *sampling distribution*, and the confidence you desire to have in the final estimate. Two statistical laws provide the logic behind Step 3.

First, the law of large numbers states that as the size of a sample increases toward infinity, the difference between the estimate of the mean and the true population mean tends toward zero. For practical purposes, a sample of size 30 is assumed to be "large enough" for the sample estimate to be a good estimate of the population mean.

Second, the Central Limit theorem states that if all possible samples of size n were taken from a population with any distribution, the distribution of the means of those samples would be normally distributed with a mean equal to the population mean and a standard deviation equal to the standard deviation of the population divided by the square root of the sample size. That is, if we took all of the samples of size 100 from the population shown in Figure A-1, the sampling distribution would be as shown in Figure A-2. The logic behind Step 3 is that

1. Any sample of size n from the population can be considered one observation from the sampling distribution with the mean $\mu_{\overline{x}} = \mu$ and the standard deviation

$$\sigma_{\overline{x}} = \frac{\sigma}{\sqrt{n}}$$

2. From our knowledge of the normal distribution, we know that there is a number (see normal probability table directly following the index) associated with each probability value of a normal distribution (e.g., the probability that an item will be within ± 2 standard deviations of the mean of a normal distribution is 94.45 percent, $Z = 2$ in this case).

3. The value of the number Z is simply the number of standard deviations away from the mean where a given point lies. That is,

$$Z = \frac{(\overline{X} - \mu)}{\sigma}$$

or in the case of Step 3

$$Z = \frac{(\overline{X} - \mu_{\bar{x}})}{\sigma_{\bar{x}}}$$

4. The precision of a sample estimate is given by $Z\sigma_{\bar{x}}$.

5. The interval estimate is given by the point estimate $\overline{X}$ plus or minus the precision, or

$$\overline{X} \pm Z\sigma_{\bar{x}}$$

In the previous example shown in Figures A-1 and A-2, suppose that a sample estimate $\overline{X}$ based on a sample size of 100 was 56 and the population standard deviation σ was 20. Also, suppose that the desired confidence was 90 percent. Since the associated Z value for 90 percent is 1.645, the interval estimate for μ is

$$56 \pm 1.645\left(\frac{20}{\sqrt{100}}\right)$$

or

$$56 \pm 3.29 \text{ or } 52.71 \text{ to } 59.29$$

This interval estimate of the population mean states that the estimator is 90 percent confident that the true mean is between 52.71 and 59.29. There are numerous other sampling methods and other parameters that can be estimated; the student is referred to one of the references in the bibliography for further discussion.

Figure A-1 Population distribution

Figure A-2 Sampling distribution of $\overline{X}$

Standard Probability Distributions

The normal distribution, discussed and shown in Figure A-2, is probably the most common probability distribution in statistics. Some other common distributions are the Poisson, a discrete distribution, and the negative exponential, a continuous distribution. In project management, the beta distribution plays an important role; a continuous distribution, it is generally skewed, as in Figure A-1. Two positive parameters, alpha and beta, determine the distribution's shape. Its mean, μ, and variance, σ^2, are given by

$$\mu = \frac{\alpha}{\alpha + \beta}$$

$$\sigma^2 = \frac{\alpha\beta}{(\alpha + \beta)^2 (\alpha + \beta + 2)}$$

These are often approximated by

$$\mu = (a + 4m + b)/6$$

and the standard deviation approximated by

$$\sigma = (b - a)/6$$

where

    a is the optimistic value that might occur once in a hundred times,

    m is the most likely (modal) value, and

    b is the pessimistic value that might occur once in a hundred times.

Recent research (Keefer and Verdini, 1993) has indicated that a much better approximation is given by

$$\mu = 0.630d + 0.185(c + e)$$
$$\sigma^2 = 0.630(d - \mu)^2 + 0.185[(c - \mu)^2 + (e - \mu)^2]$$

where

    c is an optimistic value at 1 in 20 times,

    d is the median, and

    e is a pessimistic value at 1 in 20 times.

See Chapter 5 for another method for approximating μ and σ^2.

BIBLIOGRAPHY

ANDERSON, D., D. SWEENEY, T. WILLIAMS, J. CAMM, and J. COCHRAN. *Statistics for Business and Economics*. 12th ed. Mason, OH: South-Western, 2014.

BHATTACHARYYA, G., and R. A. JOHNSON. *Mathematical Statistics*. Paramus, NJ: Prentice-Hall, 1999.

KEEFER, D. L., and W. A. VERDINI. "Better Estimation of PERT Activity Time Parameters." *Management Science*, September 1993.

NETER, J., W. WASSERMAN, and G. A. WHITMORE. *Applied Statistics*, 4th ed. Boston: Allyn and Bacon, 1992.

WACKERLY, D., W. MENDENHALL, and R. L. SCHAEFFER. *Mathematical Statistics with Applications*, 7th ed. Belmont, CA: Thompson, 2008.

INDEX

---

*Oracle's Crystal Ball® is referenced frequently throughout the book, and page entries will not be cited except for discussions of the use of the software.

---

*Microsoft Excel® is referenced frequently throughout the book, so page entries will not be cited except for discussions of the use of the software.

The Cumulative (Single Tail) Probabilities of the Normal Probability Distribution (Areas under the Normal Curve from $-\infty$ to Z)

Example: the area to the left of Z = 1.34 is found by following the left Z column down to 1.3 and moving right to the .04 column. At the intersection read .9099. The area to the right of Z = 1.34 is $1 - .9099 = .0901$. The area between the mean (dashed line) and Z = 1.34 is $.9099 - .5 = .4099$.

z	00	.01	.02	.03	.04	.05	.06	.07	.08	.09
0	5000	.5040	.5080	.5120	.5160	.5199	.5239	.5279	.5319	.5359
.1	.5398	.5438	.5478	.5517	.5557	.5596	.5636	.5675	.5714	.5753
.2	.5793	.5832	.5871	.5910	.5948	.5987	.6026	.6064	.6103	.6141
.3	.6179	.6217	.6255	.6293	.6331	.6368	.6406	.6443	.6480	.6517
.4	.6554	.6591	.6628	.6664	.6700	.6736	.6772	.6808	.6844	.6879
.5	.6915	.6950	.6985	.7019	.7054	.7088	.7123	.7157	.7190	.7224
.6	.7257	.7291	.7324	.7357	.7389	.7422	.7454	.7486	.7517	.7549
.7	.7580	.7611	.7642	.7673	.7704	.7734	.7764	.7794	.7823	.7852
.8	.7881	.7910	.7939	.7967	.7995	.8023	.8051	.8078	.8106	.8133
.9	.8159	.8186	.8212	.8238	.8264	.8289	.8315	.8340	.8365	.8389
1.0	.8413	.8438	.8461	.8485	.8508	.8531	.8554	.8577	.8599	.8621
1.1	.8643	.8665	.8686	.8708	.8729	.8749	.8770	.8790	.8810	.8880
1.2	.8849	.8869	.8888	.8907	.8925	.8944	.8962	.8980	.8997	.9015
1.3	.9032	.9049	.9066	.9082	.9099	.9115	.9131	.9147	.9162	.9177
1.4	.9192	.9207	.9222	.9236	.9251	.9265	.9276	.9292	.9306	.9319
1.5	.9332	.9345	.9357	.9370	.9382	.9394	.9406	.9418	.9429	.9441
1.6	.9452	.9463	.9474	.9484	.9495	.9505	.9515	.9525	.9535	.9545
1.7	.9554	.9564	.9573	.9582	.9591	.9599	.9608	.9616	.9625	.9633
1.8	.9641	.9649	.9656	.9664	.9671	.9678	.9686	.9693	.9699	.9706
1.9	.9713	.9719	.9726	.9732	.9738	.9744	.9750	.9756	.9761	.9767
2.0	.9772	.9778	.9783	.9788	.9793	.9798	.9803	.9808	.9812	.9817
2.1	.9821	.9826	.9830	.9834	.9838	.9842	.9846	.9850	.9854	.9857
2.2	.9861	.9864	.9868	.9871	.9875	.9878	.9881	.9884	.9887	.9890
2.3	.9893	.9896	.9898	.9901	.9904	.9906	.9909	.9911	.9913	.9916
2.4	.9918	.9920	.9932	.9925	.9927	.9929	.9931	.9932	.9934	.9936
2.5	.9938	.9940	.9941	.9943	.9945	.9946	.9948	.9949	.9951	.9952
2.6	.9953	.9955	.9956	.9957	.9959	.9960	.9961	.9962	.9963	.9964
2.7	.9965	.9966	.9967	.9968	.9969	.9970	.9971	.9972	.9973	.9974
2.8	.9974	.9975	.9976	.9977	.9977	.9978	.9979	.9979	.9980	.9981
2.9	.9981	.9982	.9982	.9983	.9984	.9984	.9985	.9985	.9986	.9986
3.0	.9987	.9987	.9987	.9988	.9988	.9989	.9989	.9989	.9990	.9990
3.1	.9990	.9991	.9991	.9991	.9992	.9992	.9992	.9992	.9993	.9993
3.2	.9993	.9993	.9994	.9994	.9994	.9994	.9994	.9995	.9995	.9995
3.3	.9995	.9995	.9995	.9996	.9996	.9996	.9996	.9996	.9996	.9997
3.4	.9997	.9997	.9997	.9997	.9997	.9997	.9997	.9997	.9997	.9998